RIN! 1

Satoru Kannagi
Yukine Honami

Translation   WASABI MEDIA

Lettering   GEOFF PORTER

Graphic Design   WENDY LEE

Editing   DARYL KUXHOUSE

Editor in Chief   FRED LUI

Publisher   HIKARU SASAHARA

English Edition Published by
DIGITAL MANGA PUBLISHING
A division of DIGITAL MANGA, Inc.
1487 W 178th Street, Suite 300
Gardena, CA 90248

www.dmpbooks.com

First Edition: October 2006
ISBN-10: 1-56970-920-3
ISBN-13: 978-1-56970-920-7

1 3 5 7 9 10 8 6 4 2

Printed in China

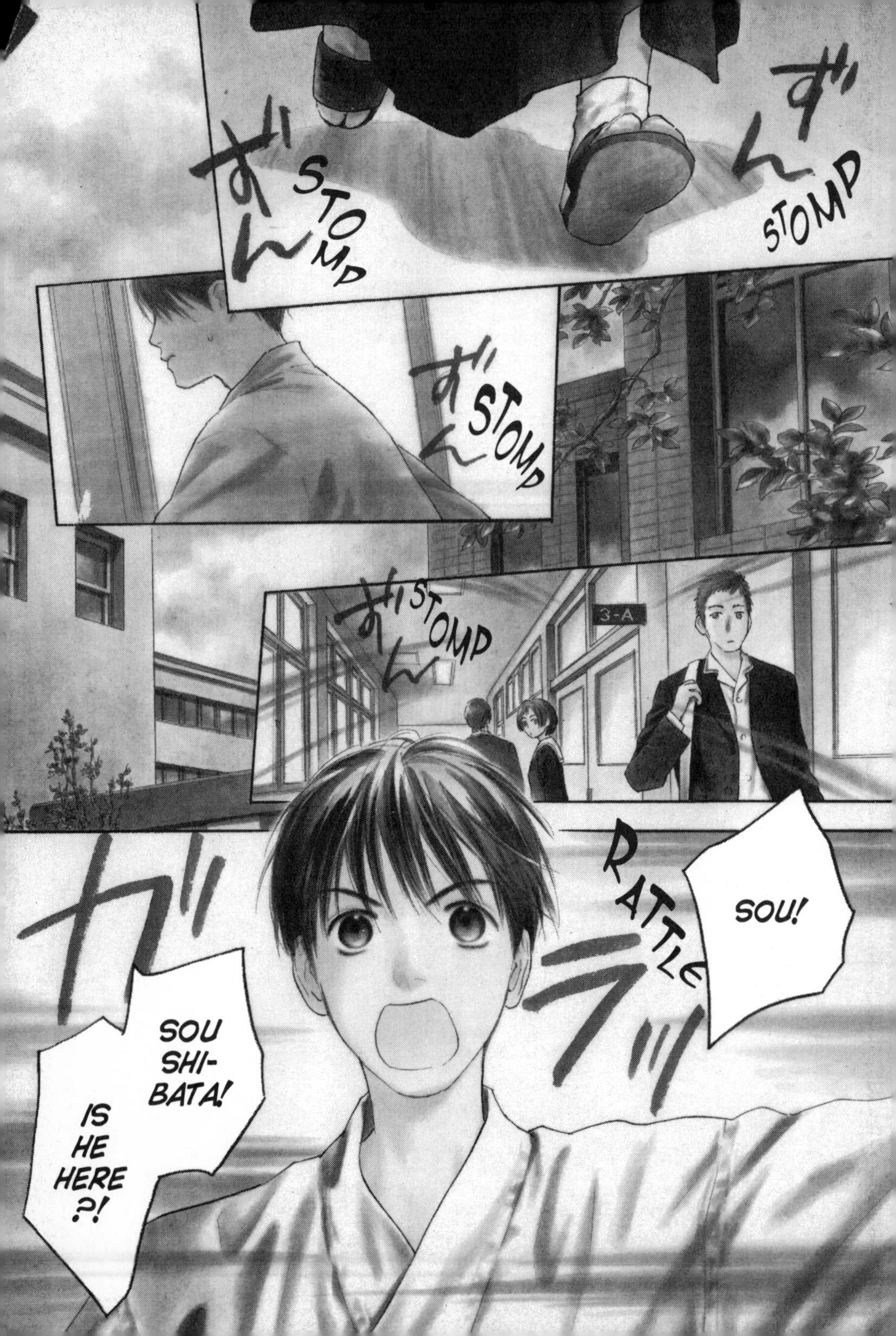
ずん
STOMP
ずん
STOMP
ずん
STOMP
3-A
ずん
STOMP
ガラッ
RATTLE
SOU!
SOU SHI-BATA!
IS HE HERE?!

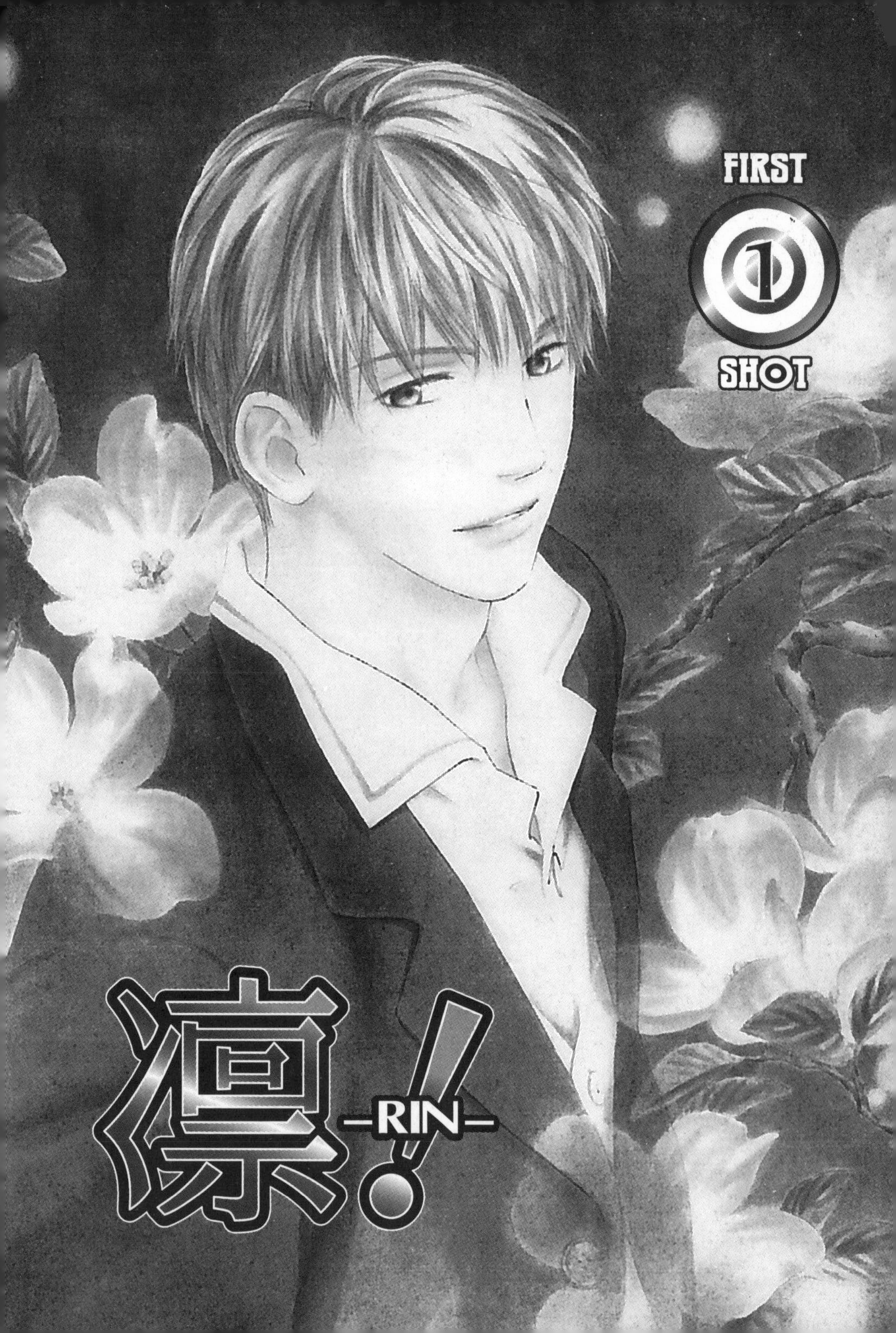
FIRST
1
SHOT
凛!
-RIN-

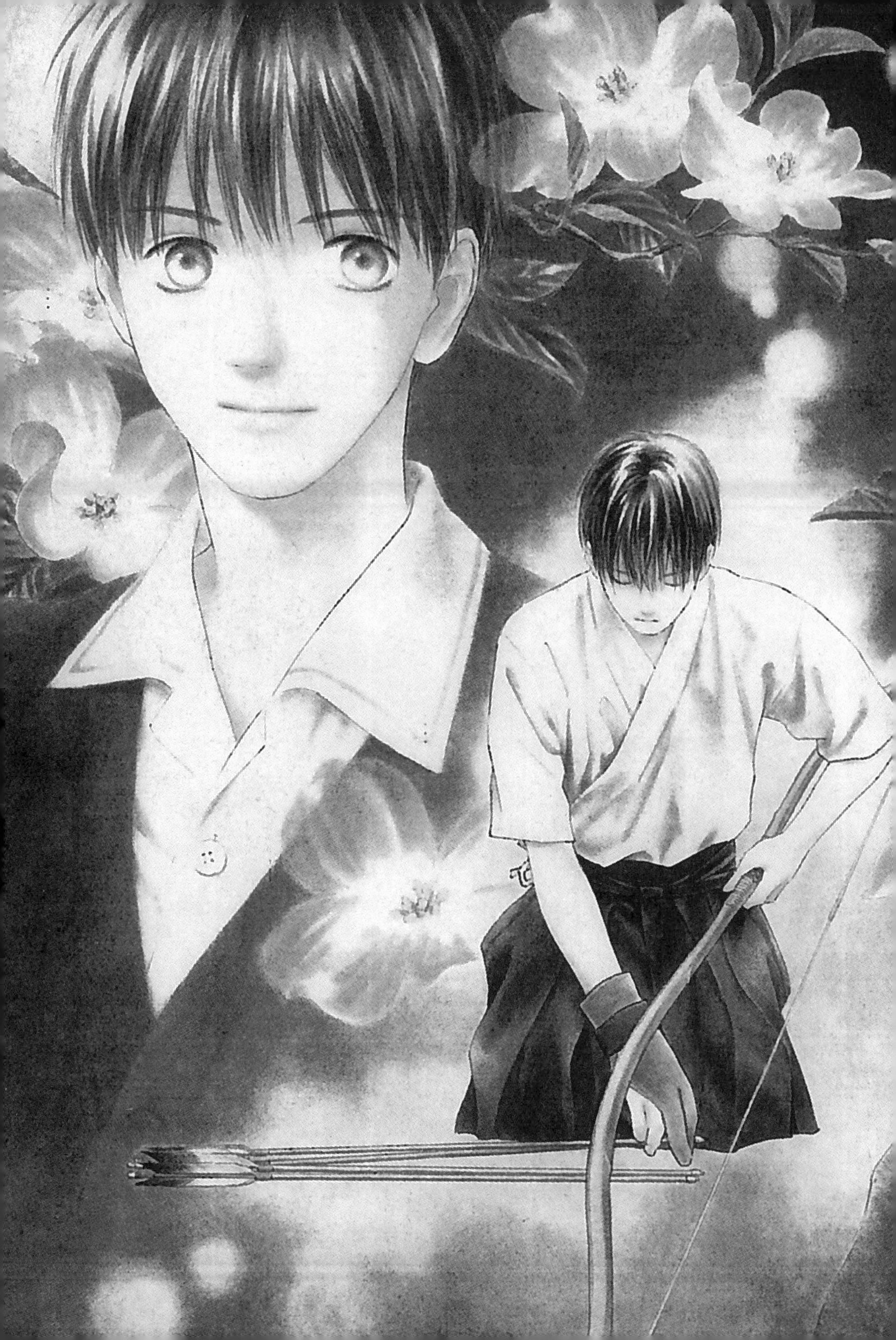

THE BEGINNING OF KATSURA'S JUNIOR YEAR.

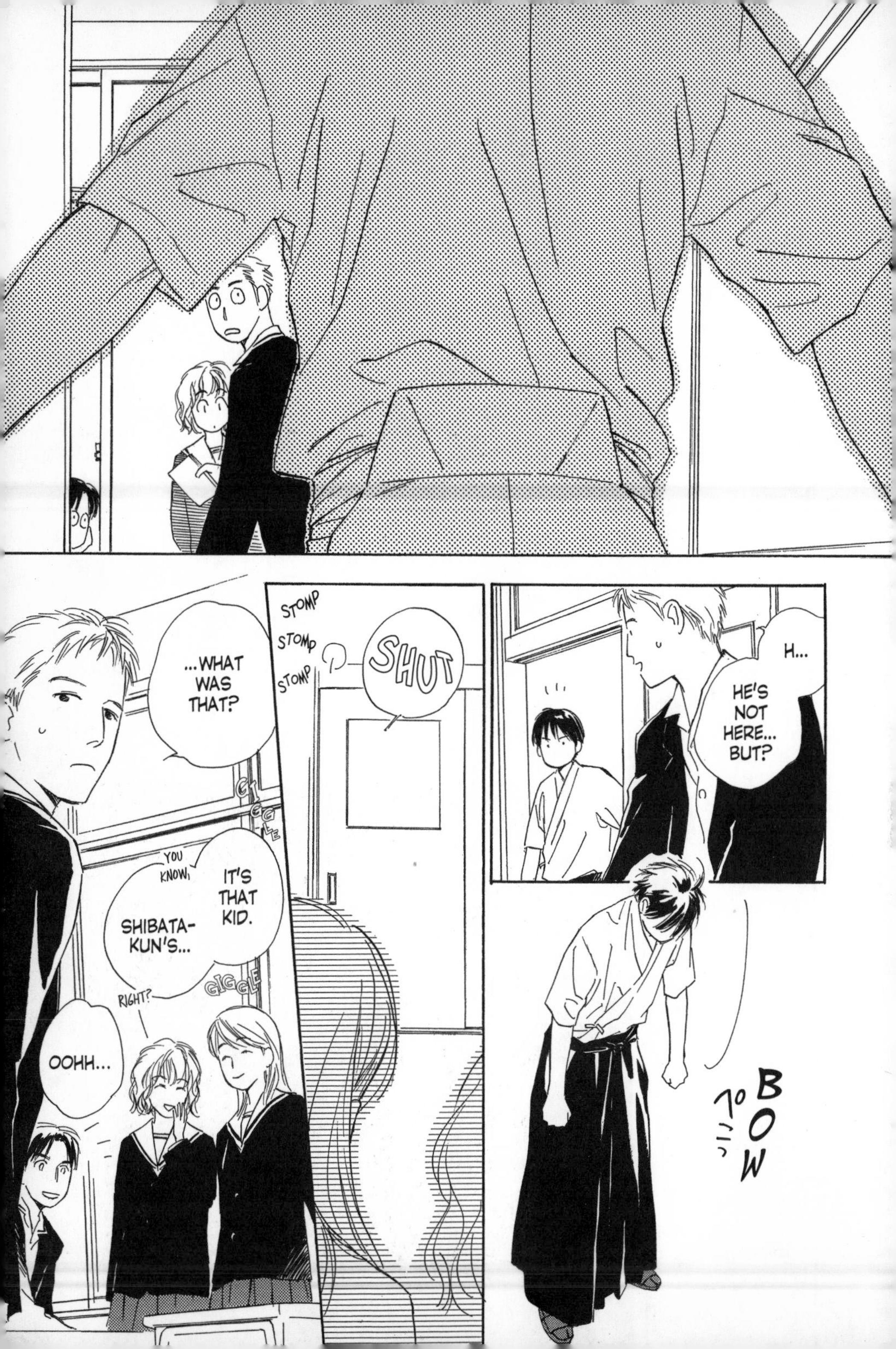
H...
HE'S NOT HERE... BUT?
BOW
STOMP
STOMP
STOMP
SHUT
...WHAT WAS THAT?
GIGGLE
IT'S THAT KID.
YOU KNOW, SHIBATA-KUN'S... RIGHT?
GIGGLE
OOHH...

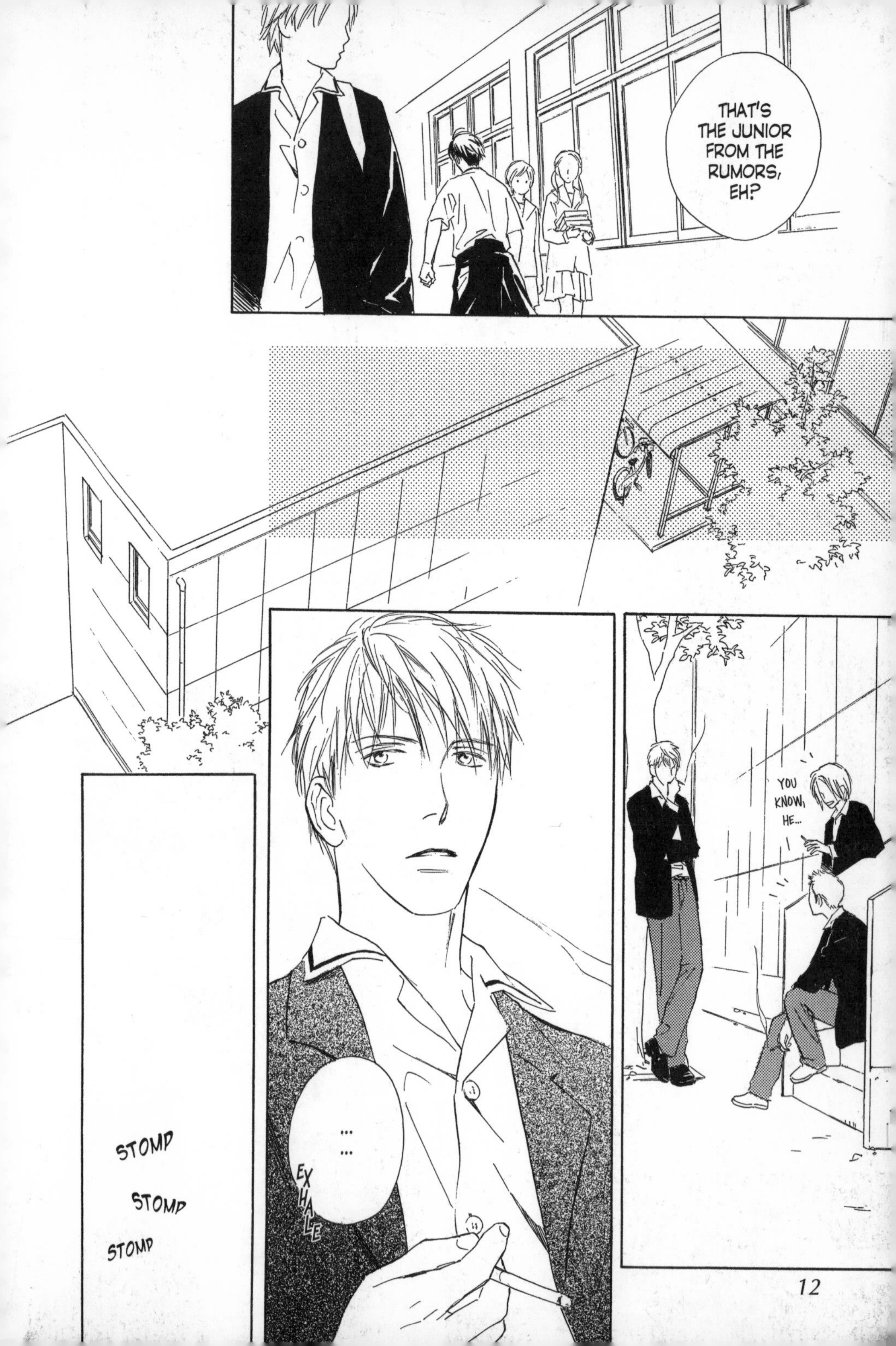
THAT'S THE JUNIOR FROM THE RUMORS, EH?
YOU KNOW, HE...
... ...
EXHALE
STOMP
STOMP
STOMP

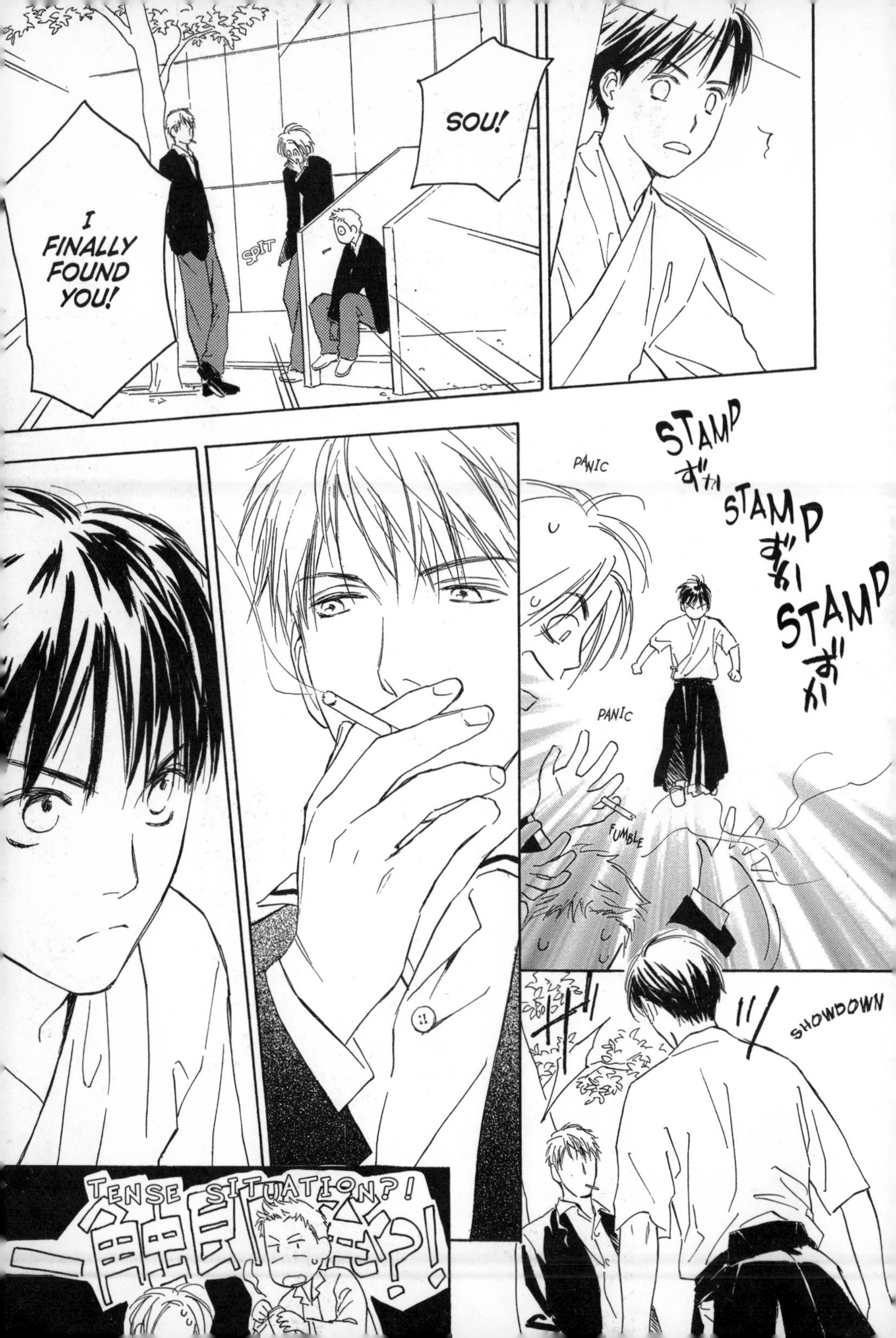
SOU!
SPIT
I FINALLY FOUND YOU!
STAMP
STAMP
STAMP
PANIC
PANIC
FUMBLE
SHOWDOWN
TENSE SITUATION?!

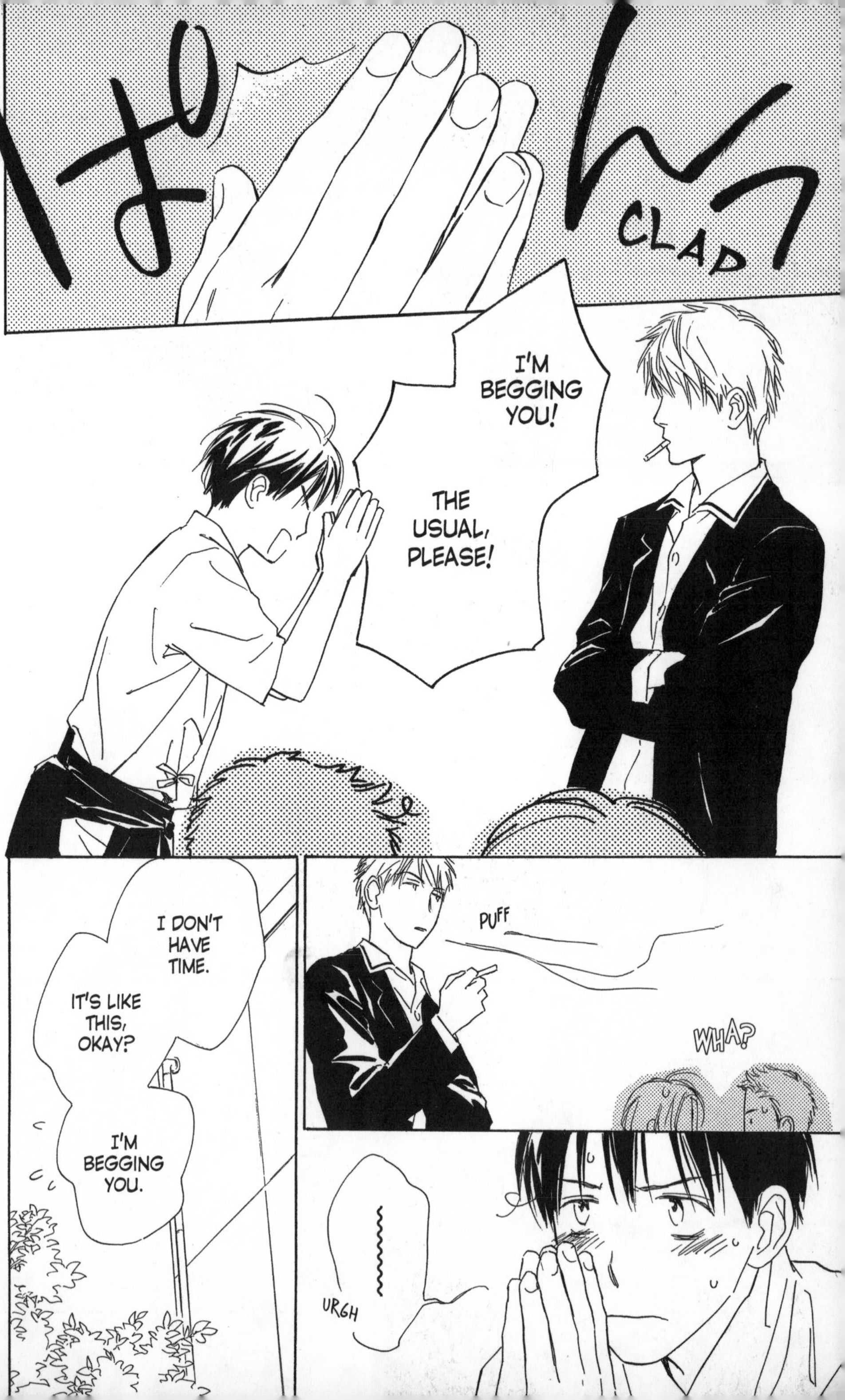
ぱんっ
CLAD
I'M BEGGING YOU!
THE USUAL, PLEASE!
PUFF
WHA?
....
URGH
I DON'T HAVE TIME.
IT'S LIKE THIS, OKAY?
I'M BEGGING YOU.

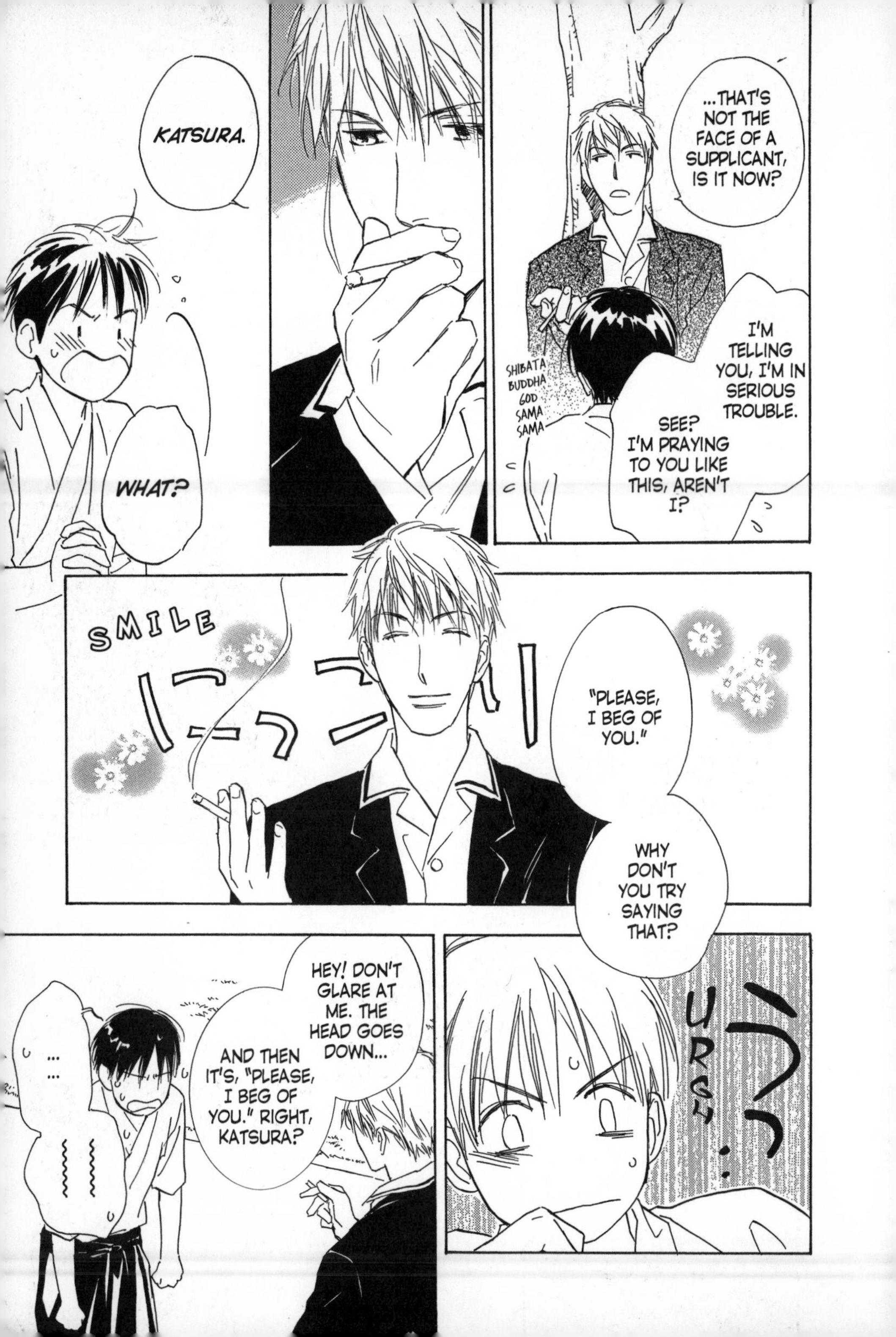
...THAT'S NOT THE FACE OF A SUPPLICANT, IS IT NOW?
I'M TELLING YOU, I'M IN SERIOUS TROUBLE.
SHIBATA BUDDHA GOD SAMA SAMA
SEE? I'M PRAYING TO YOU LIKE THIS, AREN'T I?
KATSURA.
WHAT?
SMILE
"PLEASE, I BEG OF YOU."
WHY DON'T YOU TRY SAYING THAT?
URGH...
HEY! DON'T GLARE AT ME. THE HEAD GOES DOWN...
AND THEN IT'S, "PLEASE, I BEG OF YOU." RIGHT, KATSURA?
... ...

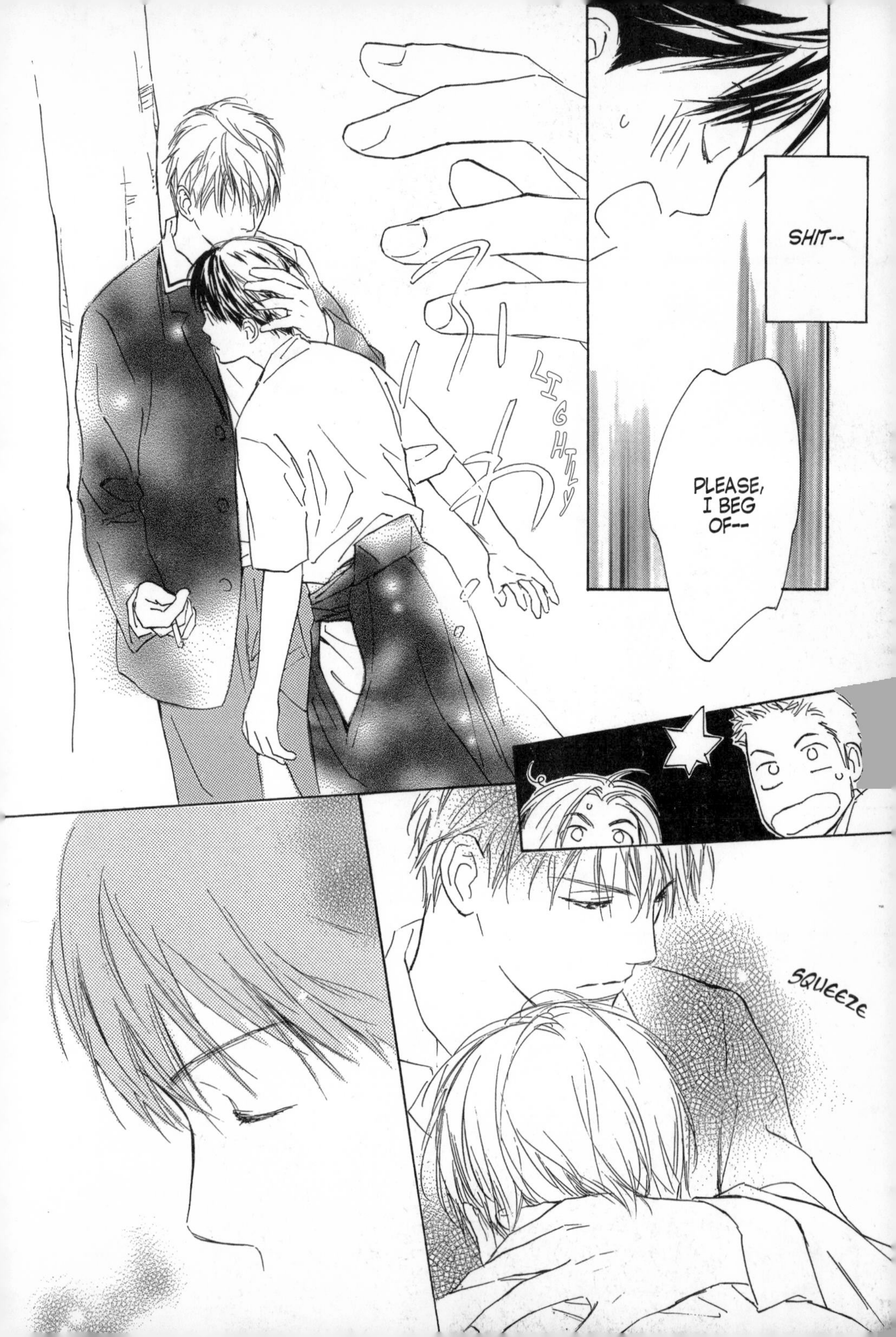
SHIT--
PLEASE, I BEG OF--
LIGHTLY
SQUEEZE

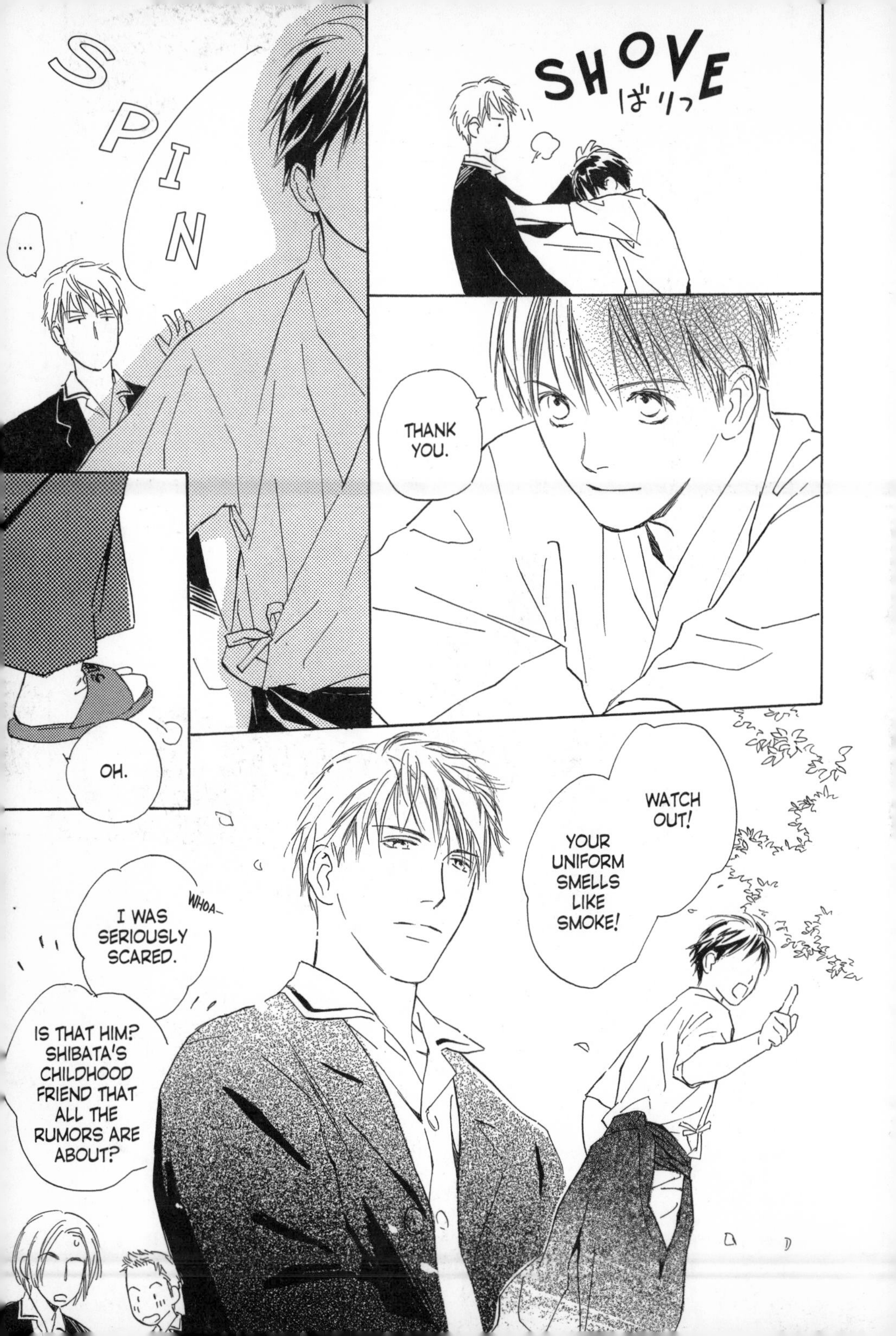
SHOVE
ばりっ
THANK YOU.
SPIN
...
OH.
WATCH OUT!
YOUR UNIFORM SMELLS LIKE SMOKE!
WHOA-
I WAS SERIOUSLY SCARED.
IS THAT HIM? SHIBATA'S CHILDHOOD FRIEND THAT ALL THE RUMORS ARE ABOUT?

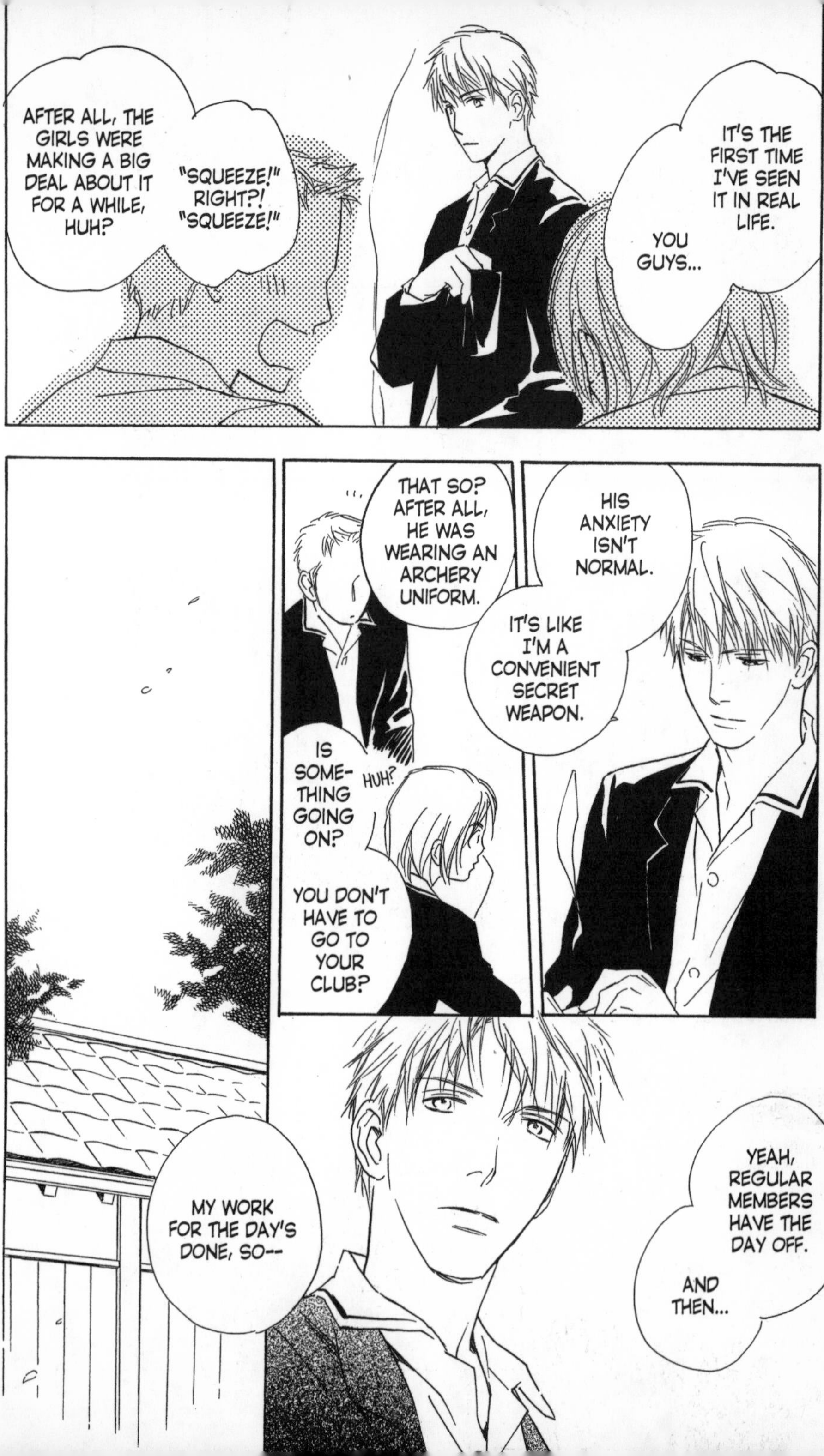
IT'S THE FIRST TIME I'VE SEEN IT IN REAL LIFE.
YOU GUYS...
"SQUEEZE!" RIGHT?! "SQUEEZE!"
AFTER ALL, THE GIRLS WERE MAKING A BIG DEAL ABOUT IT FOR A WHILE, HUH?
HIS ANXIETY ISN'T NORMAL.
IT'S LIKE I'M A CONVENIENT SECRET WEAPON.
THAT SO? AFTER ALL, HE WAS WEARING AN ARCHERY UNIFORM.
HUH?
IS SOME-THING GOING ON?
YOU DON'T HAVE TO GO TO YOUR CLUB?
YEAH, REGULAR MEMBERS HAVE THE DAY OFF.
AND THEN...
MY WORK FOR THE DAY'S DONE, SO--

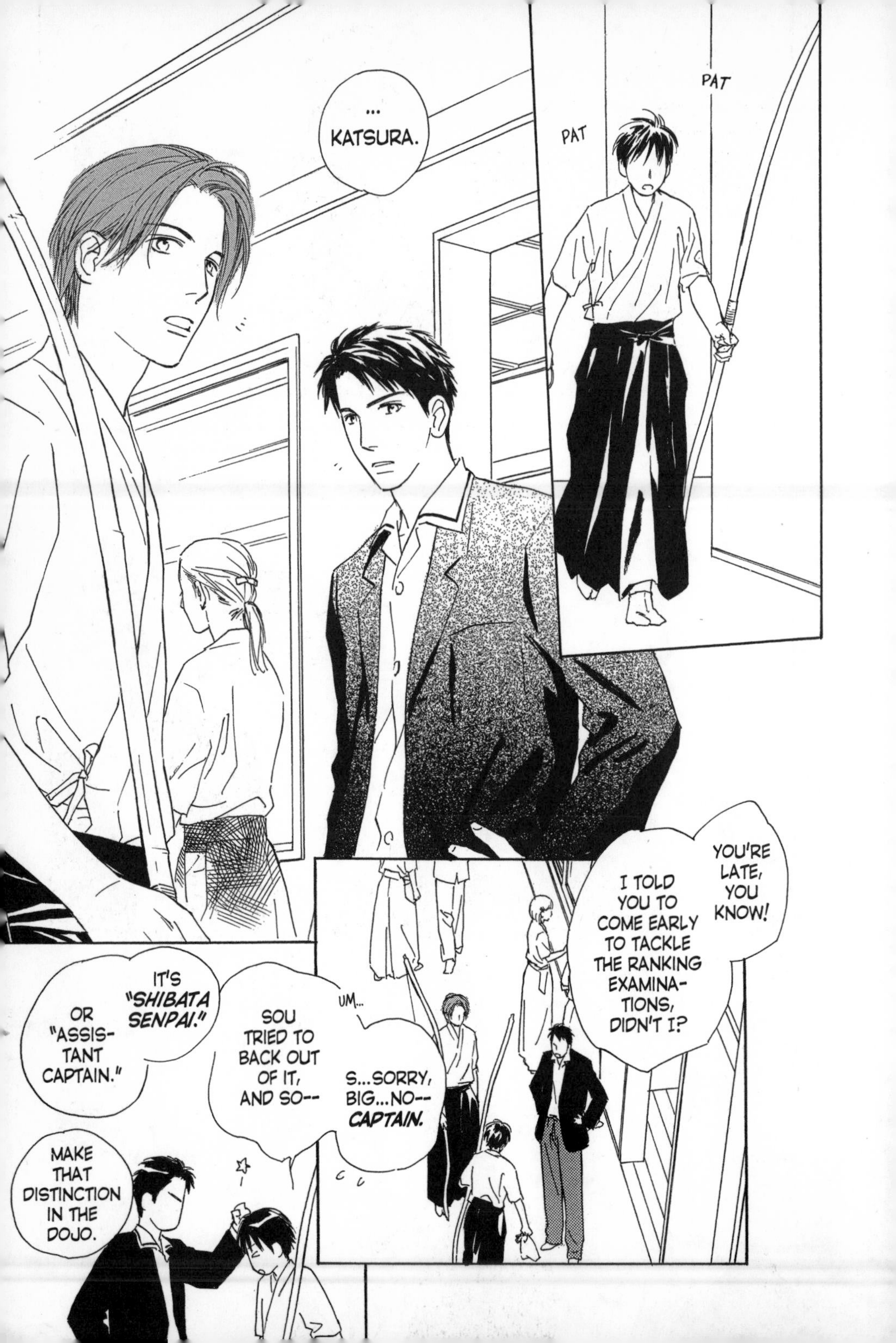
PAT
PAT
... KATSURA.
YOU'RE LATE, YOU KNOW!
I TOLD YOU TO COME EARLY TO TACKLE THE RANKING EXAMINA-TIONS, DIDN'T I?
UM...
S...SORRY, BIG...NO-- *CAPTAIN.*
SOU TRIED TO BACK OUT OF IT, AND SO--
IT'S *"SHIBATA SENPAI."*
OR "ASSIS-TANT CAPTAIN."
MAKE THAT DISTINCTION IN THE DOJO.

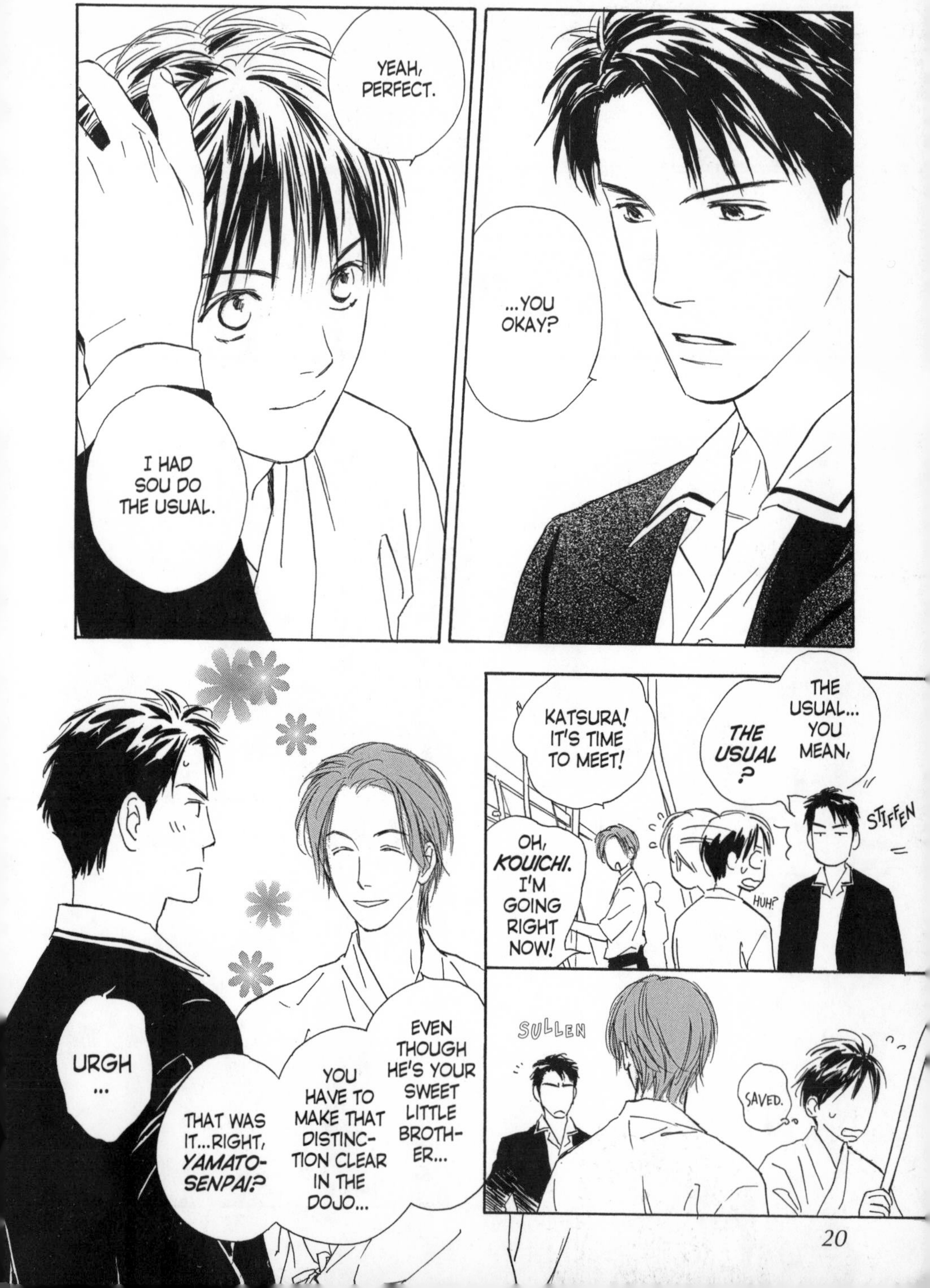
...YOU OKAY?
YEAH, PERFECT.
I HAD SOU DO THE USUAL.
THE USUAL... YOU MEAN,
***THE USUAL*?**
STIFFEN
HUH?
KATSURA! IT'S TIME TO MEET!
OH, ***KOUICHI.*** I'M GOING RIGHT NOW!
SAVED.
SULLEN
EVEN THOUGH HE'S YOUR SWEET LITTLE BROTHER...
YOU HAVE TO MAKE THAT DISTINCTION CLEAR IN THE DOJO...
THAT WAS IT...RIGHT, ***YAMATO-SENPAI?***
URGH...

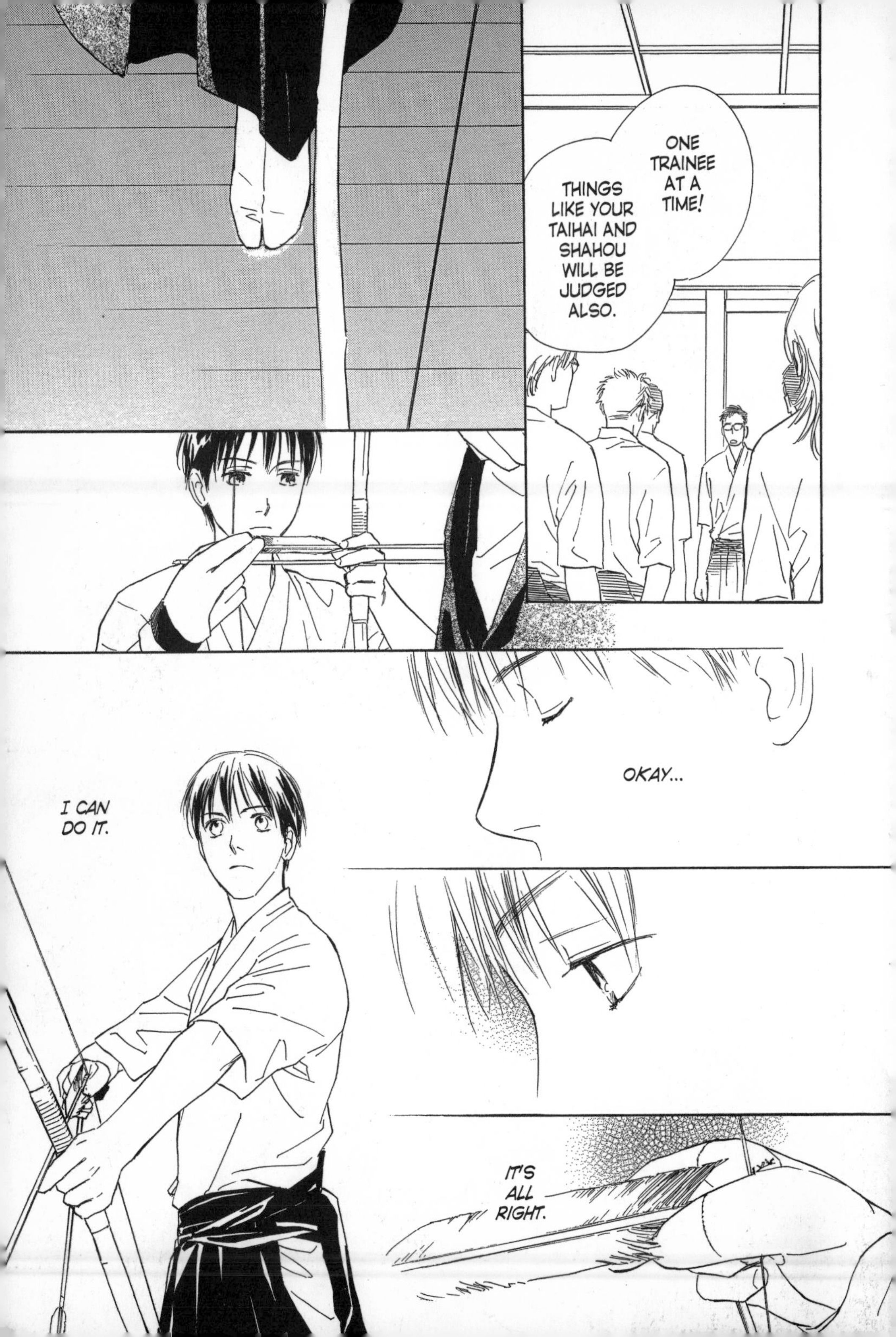
ONE TRAINEE AT A TIME! THINGS LIKE YOUR TAIHAI AND SHAHOU WILL BE JUDGED ALSO.
OKAY...
IT'S ALL RIGHT.
I CAN DO IT.

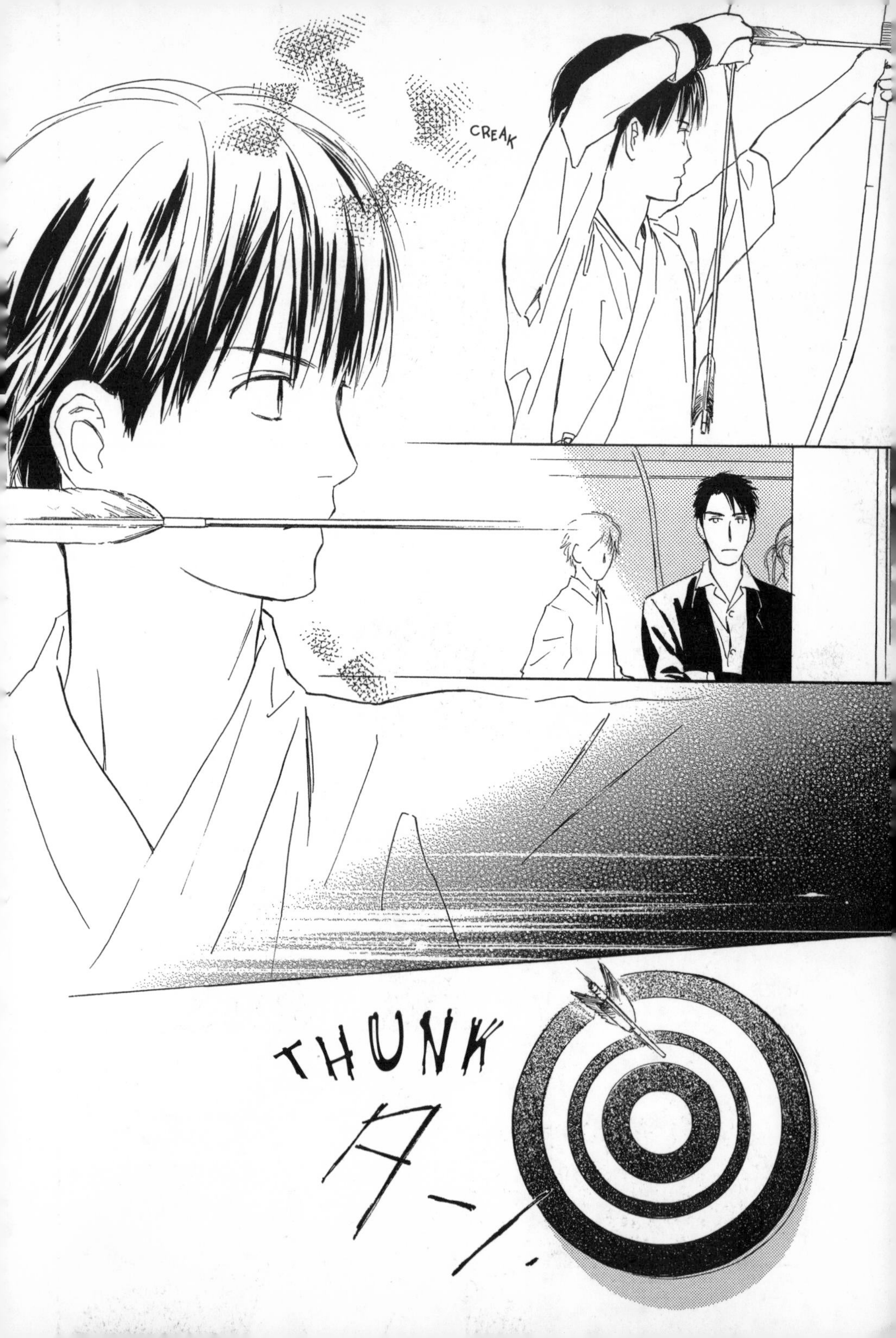
CREAK
THUNK

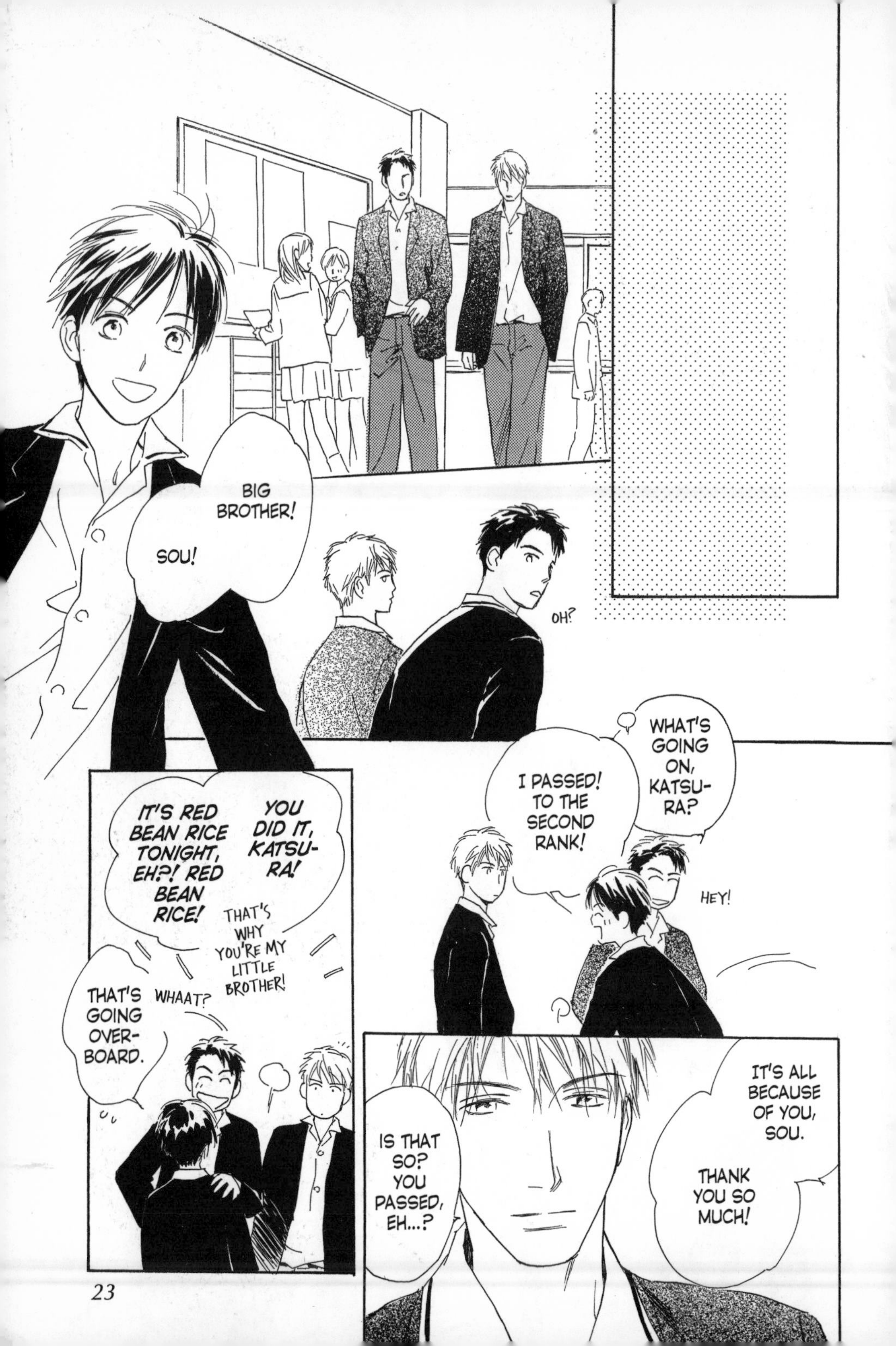
BIG BROTHER!
SOU!
OH?
WHAT'S GOING ON, KATSURA?
I PASSED! TO THE SECOND RANK!
HEY!
IT'S ALL BECAUSE OF YOU, SOU.
THANK YOU SO MUCH!
IS THAT SO? YOU PASSED, EH...?
YOU DID IT, KATSURA!
IT'S RED BEAN RICE TONIGHT, EH?! RED BEAN RICE!
THAT'S WHY YOU'RE MY LITTLE BROTHER!
WHAAT?
THAT'S GOING OVER-BOARD.

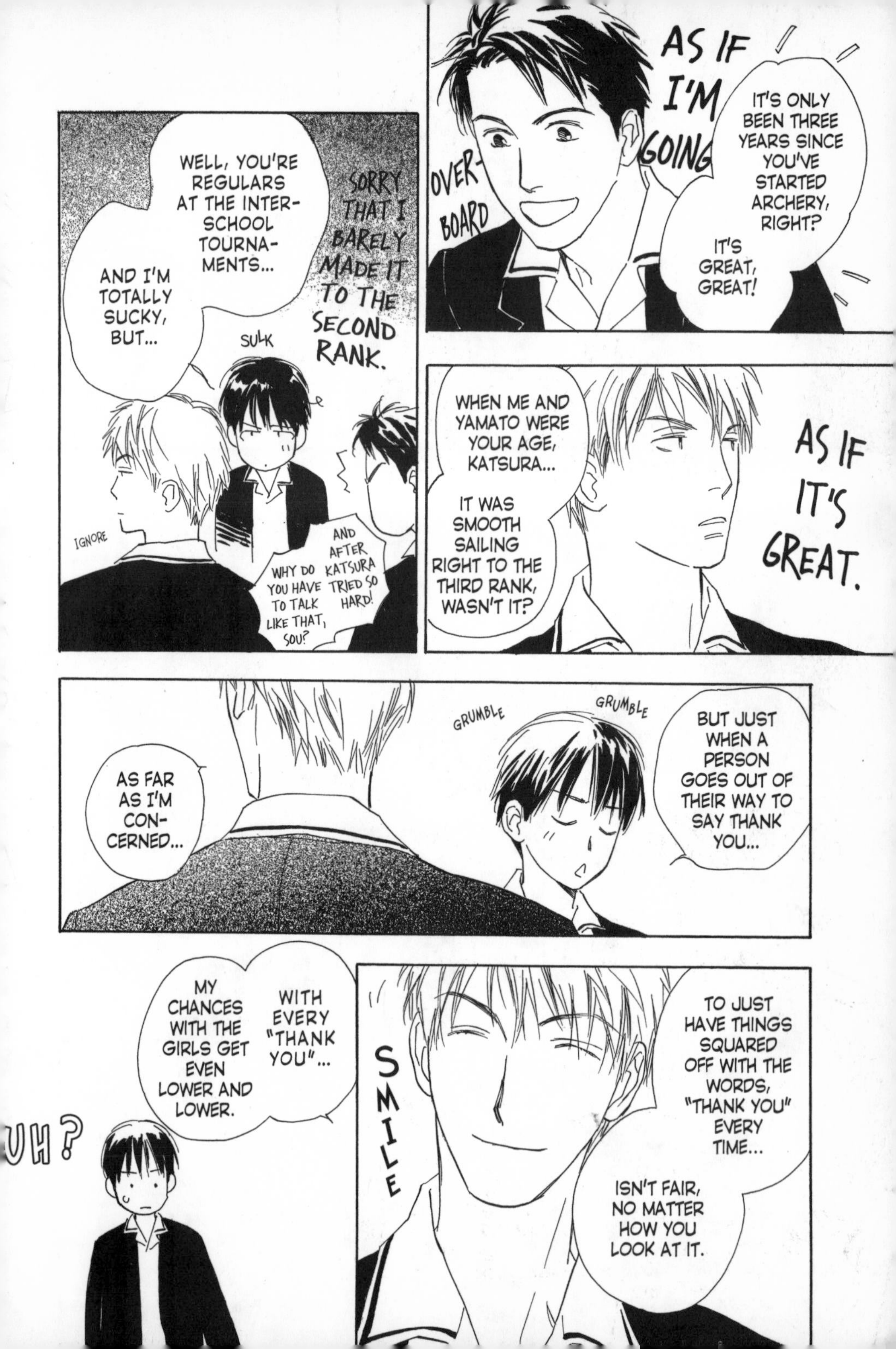

IT'S ONLY BEEN THREE YEARS SINCE YOU'VE STARTED ARCHERY, RIGHT?
IT'S GREAT, GREAT!
AS IF I'M GOING OVER-BOARD
WHEN ME AND YAMATO WERE YOUR AGE, KATSURA...
IT WAS SMOOTH SAILING RIGHT TO THE THIRD RANK, WASN'T IT?
AS IF IT'S GREAT.
SORRY THAT I BARELY MADE IT TO THE SECOND RANK.
WELL, YOU'RE REGULARS AT THE INTER-SCHOOL TOURNA-MENTS...
AND I'M TOTALLY SUCKY, BUT...
SULK
AND AFTER KATSURA TRIED SO HARD!
WHY DO YOU HAVE TO TALK LIKE THAT, SOU?
IGNORE
BUT JUST WHEN A PERSON GOES OUT OF THEIR WAY TO SAY THANK YOU...
GRUMBLE
GRUMBLE
AS FAR AS I'M CON-CERNED...
TO JUST HAVE THINGS SQUARED OFF WITH THE WORDS, "THANK YOU" EVERY TIME...
ISN'T FAIR, NO MATTER HOW YOU LOOK AT IT.
SMILE
WITH EVERY "THANK YOU"...
MY CHANCES WITH THE GIRLS GET EVEN LOWER AND LOWER.
UH?

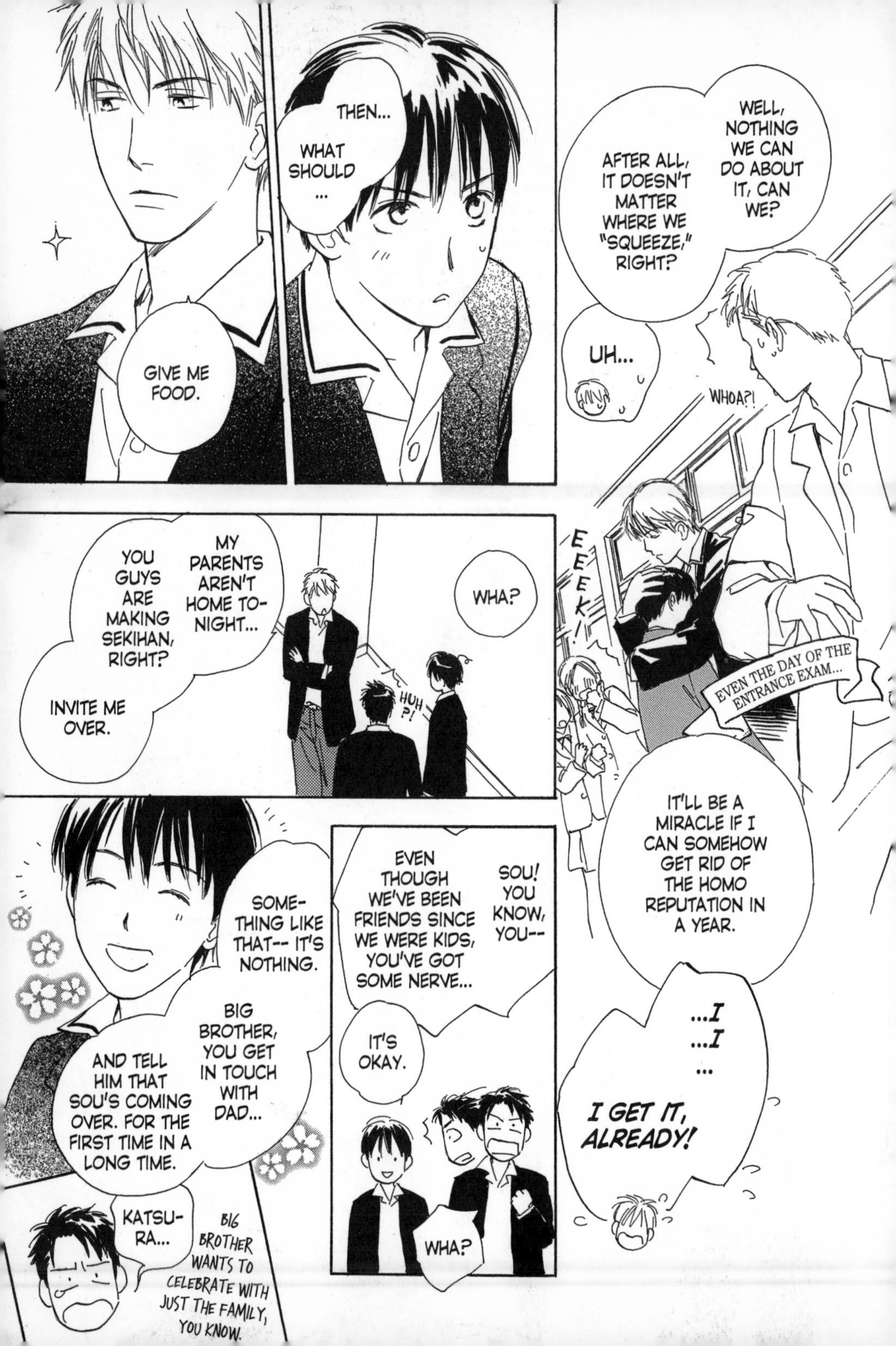
WELL, NOTHING WE CAN DO ABOUT IT, CAN WE?
AFTER ALL, IT DOESN'T MATTER WHERE WE "SQUEEZE," RIGHT?
UH...
WHOA?!
EEEK!
EVEN THE DAY OF THE ENTRANCE EXAM...
IT'LL BE A MIRACLE IF I CAN SOMEHOW GET RID OF THE HOMO REPUTATION IN A YEAR.
...I
...I
...
I GET IT, ALREADY!
THEN...
WHAT SHOULD ...
GIVE ME FOOD.
WHA?
MY PARENTS AREN'T HOME TO-NIGHT...
YOU GUYS ARE MAKING SEKIHAN, RIGHT?
INVITE ME OVER.
HUH ?!
SOU! YOU KNOW, YOU--
EVEN THOUGH WE'VE BEEN FRIENDS SINCE WE WERE KIDS, YOU'VE GOT SOME NERVE...
IT'S OKAY.
WHA?
SOME-THING LIKE THAT-- IT'S NOTHING.
BIG BROTHER, YOU GET IN TOUCH WITH DAD...
AND TELL HIM THAT SOU'S COMING OVER. FOR THE FIRST TIME IN A LONG TIME.
KATSU-RA...
BIG BROTHER WANTS TO CELEBRATE WITH JUST THE FAMILY, YOU KNOW.

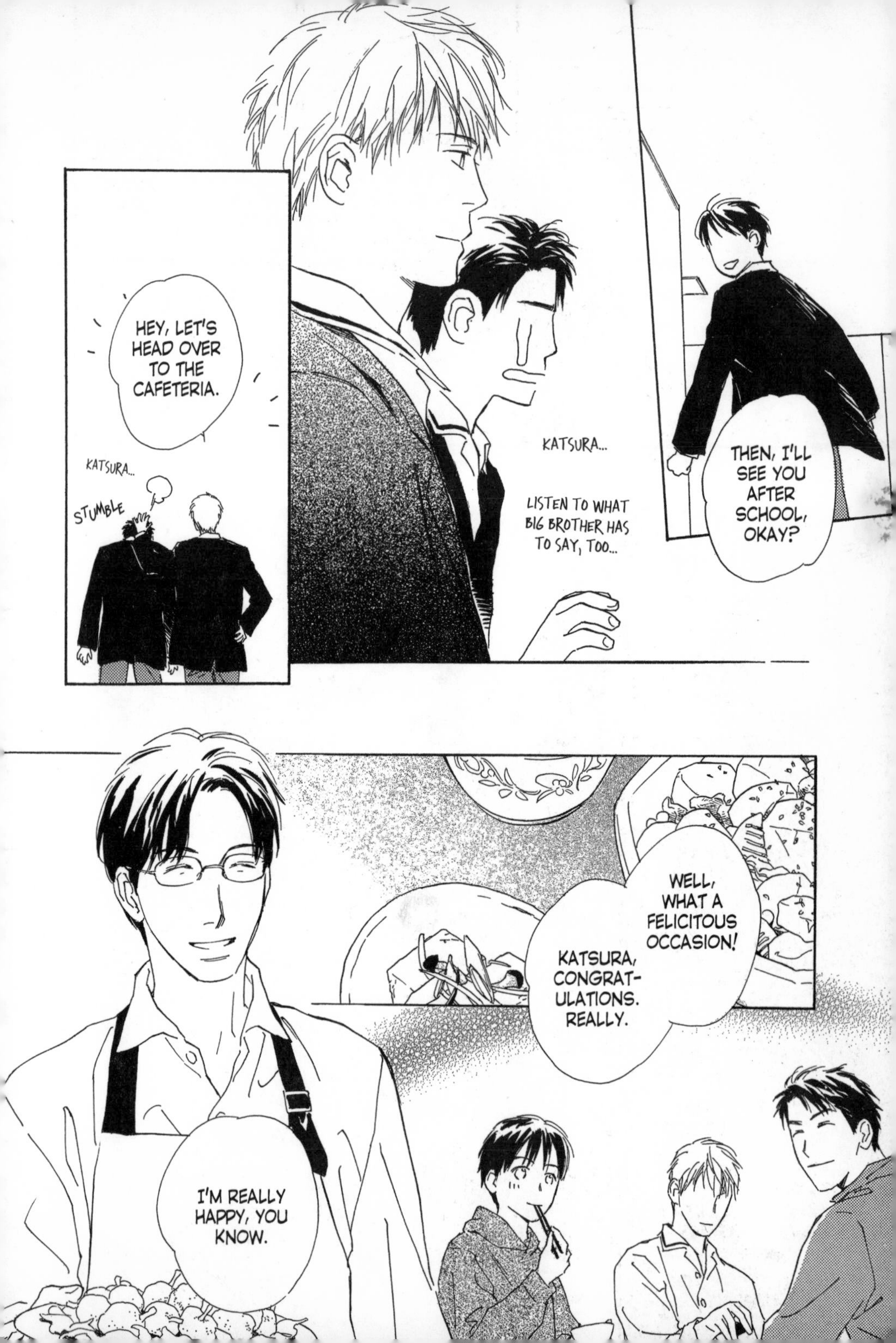
THEN, I'LL SEE YOU AFTER SCHOOL, OKAY?
KATSURA...
LISTEN TO WHAT BIG BROTHER HAS TO SAY, TOO...
HEY, LET'S HEAD OVER TO THE CAFETERIA.
KATSURA...
STUMBLE
WELL, WHAT A FELICITOUS OCCASION!
KATSURA, CONGRATULATIONS. REALLY.
I'M REALLY HAPPY, YOU KNOW.

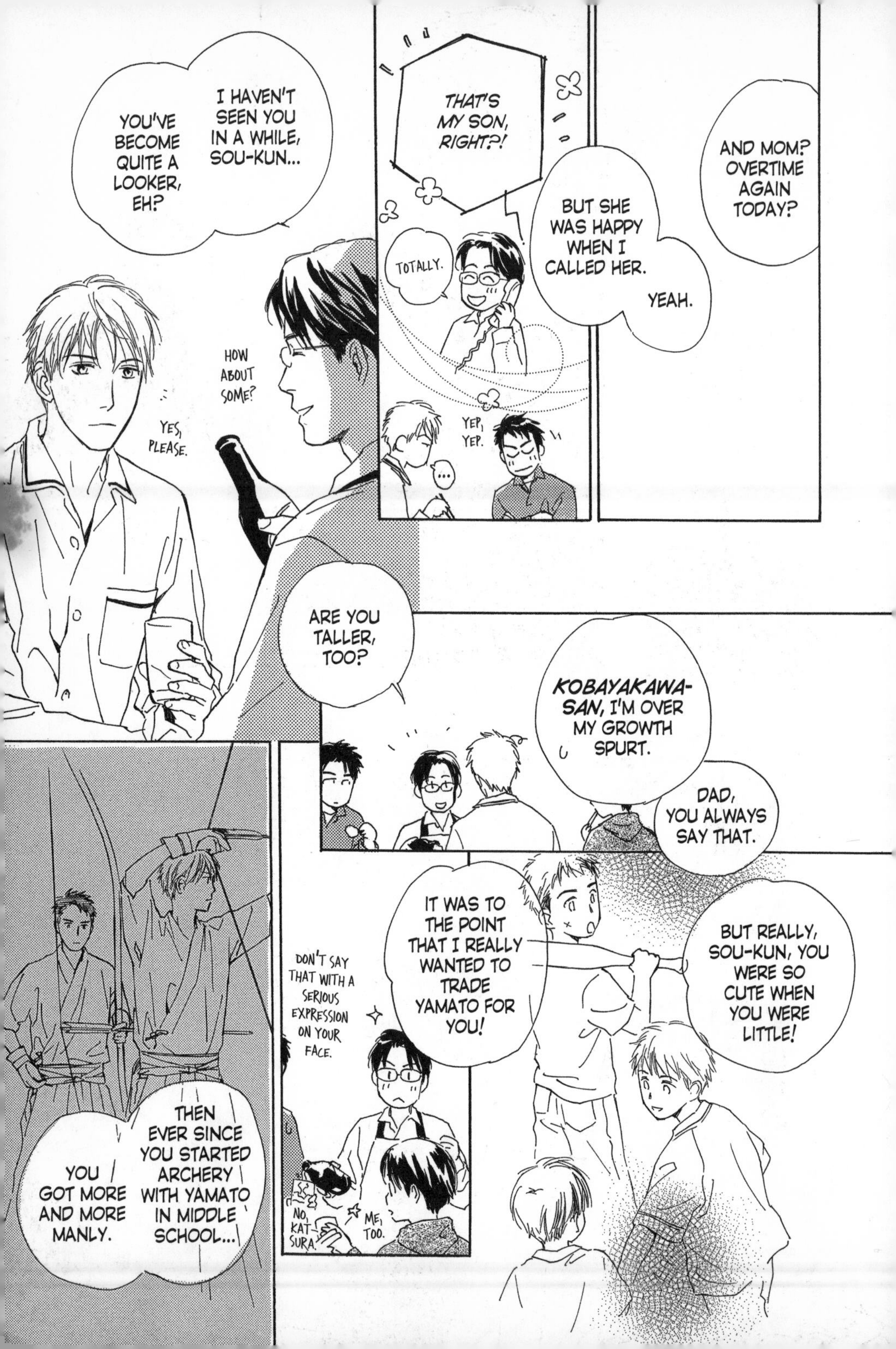
AND MOM? OVERTIME AGAIN TODAY?
BUT SHE WAS HAPPY WHEN I CALLED HER.
YEAH.
THAT'S MY SON, RIGHT?!
TOTALLY.
YEP, YEP.
...
I HAVEN'T SEEN YOU IN A WHILE, SOU-KUN...
YOU'VE BECOME QUITE A LOOKER, EH?
HOW ABOUT SOME?
YES, PLEASE.
ARE YOU TALLER, TOO?
KOBAYAKAWA-SAN, I'M OVER MY GROWTH SPURT.
DAD, YOU ALWAYS SAY THAT.
BUT REALLY, SOU-KUN, YOU WERE SO CUTE WHEN YOU WERE LITTLE!
IT WAS TO THE POINT THAT I REALLY WANTED TO TRADE YAMATO FOR YOU!
DON'T SAY THAT WITH A SERIOUS EXPRESSION ON YOUR FACE.
ME, TOO.
NO, KATSURA.
THEN EVER SINCE YOU STARTED ARCHERY WITH YAMATO IN MIDDLE SCHOOL...
YOU GOT MORE AND MORE MANLY.

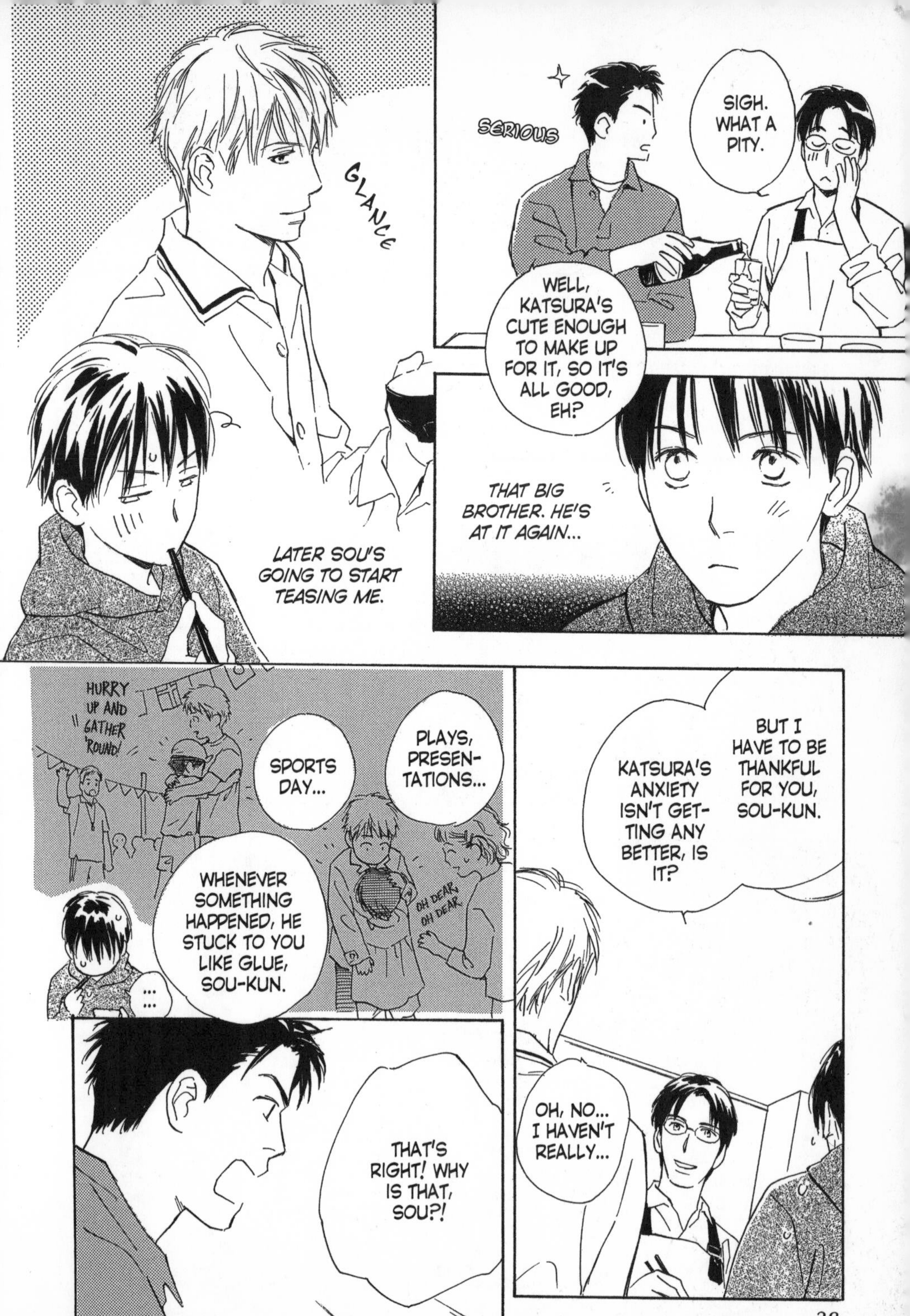
SERIOUS
SIGH. WHAT A PITY.
WELL, KATSURA'S CUTE ENOUGH TO MAKE UP FOR IT, SO IT'S ALL GOOD, EH?
THAT BIG BROTHER. HE'S AT IT AGAIN...
GLANCE
LATER SOU'S GOING TO START TEASING ME.
BUT I HAVE TO BE THANKFUL FOR YOU, SOU-KUN.
KATSURA'S ANXIETY ISN'T GETTING ANY BETTER, IS IT?
OH, NO... I HAVEN'T REALLY...
PLAYS, PRESENTATIONS...
SPORTS DAY...
HURRY UP AND GATHER 'ROUND!
WHENEVER SOMETHING HAPPENED, HE STUCK TO YOU LIKE GLUE, SOU-KUN.
OH DEAR OH DEAR
... ...
THAT'S RIGHT! WHY IS THAT, SOU?!

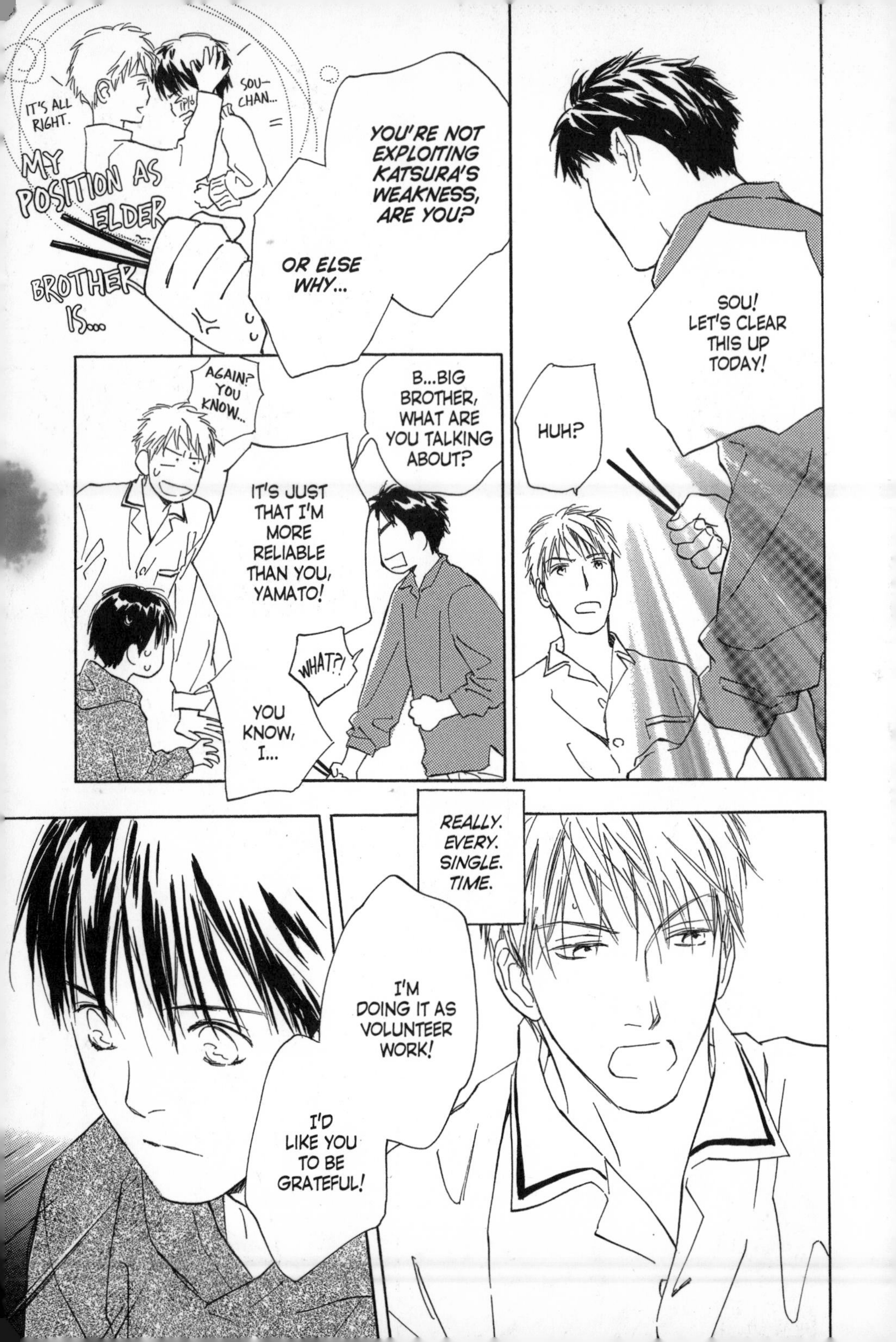
SOU! LET'S CLEAR THIS UP TODAY!
HUH?
YOU'RE NOT EXPLOITING KATSURA'S WEAKNESS, ARE YOU?
OR ELSE WHY...
SOU-CHAN...
IT'S ALL RIGHT.
MY POSITION AS ELDER BROTHER IS...
B...BIG BROTHER, WHAT ARE YOU TALKING ABOUT?
AGAIN? YOU KNOW...
IT'S JUST THAT I'M MORE RELIABLE THAN YOU, YAMATO!
WHAT?!
YOU KNOW, I...
REALLY. EVERY. SINGLE. TIME.
I'M DOING IT AS VOLUNTEER WORK!
I'D LIKE YOU TO BE GRATEFUL!

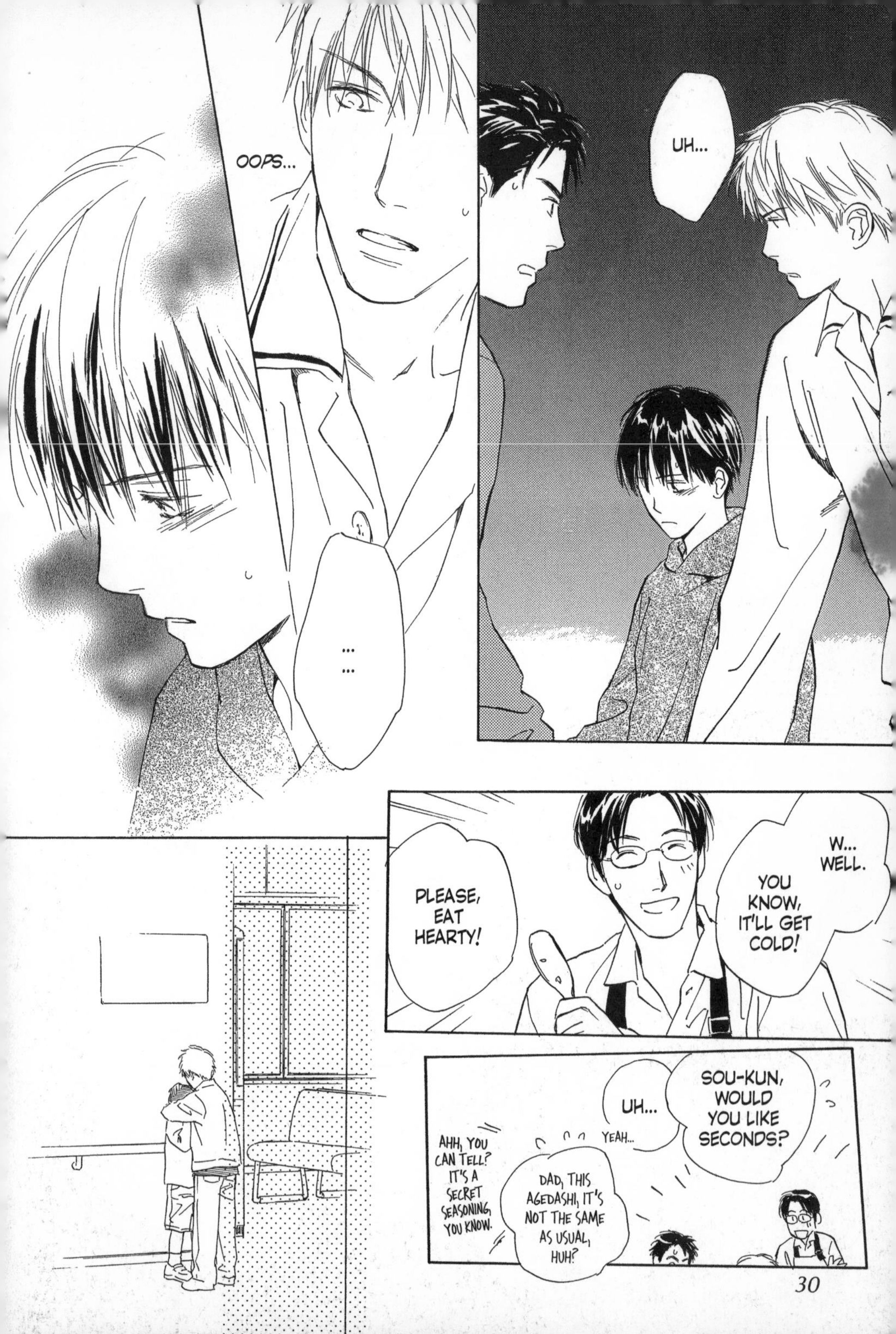
UH...
OOPS...
... ...
W... WELL.
YOU KNOW, IT'LL GET COLD!
PLEASE, EAT HEARTY!
SOU-KUN, WOULD YOU LIKE SECONDS?
UH...
YEAH...
DAD, THIS AGEDASHI, IT'S NOT THE SAME AS USUAL, HUH?
AHH, YOU CAN TELL? IT'S A SECRET SEASONING, YOU KNOW.

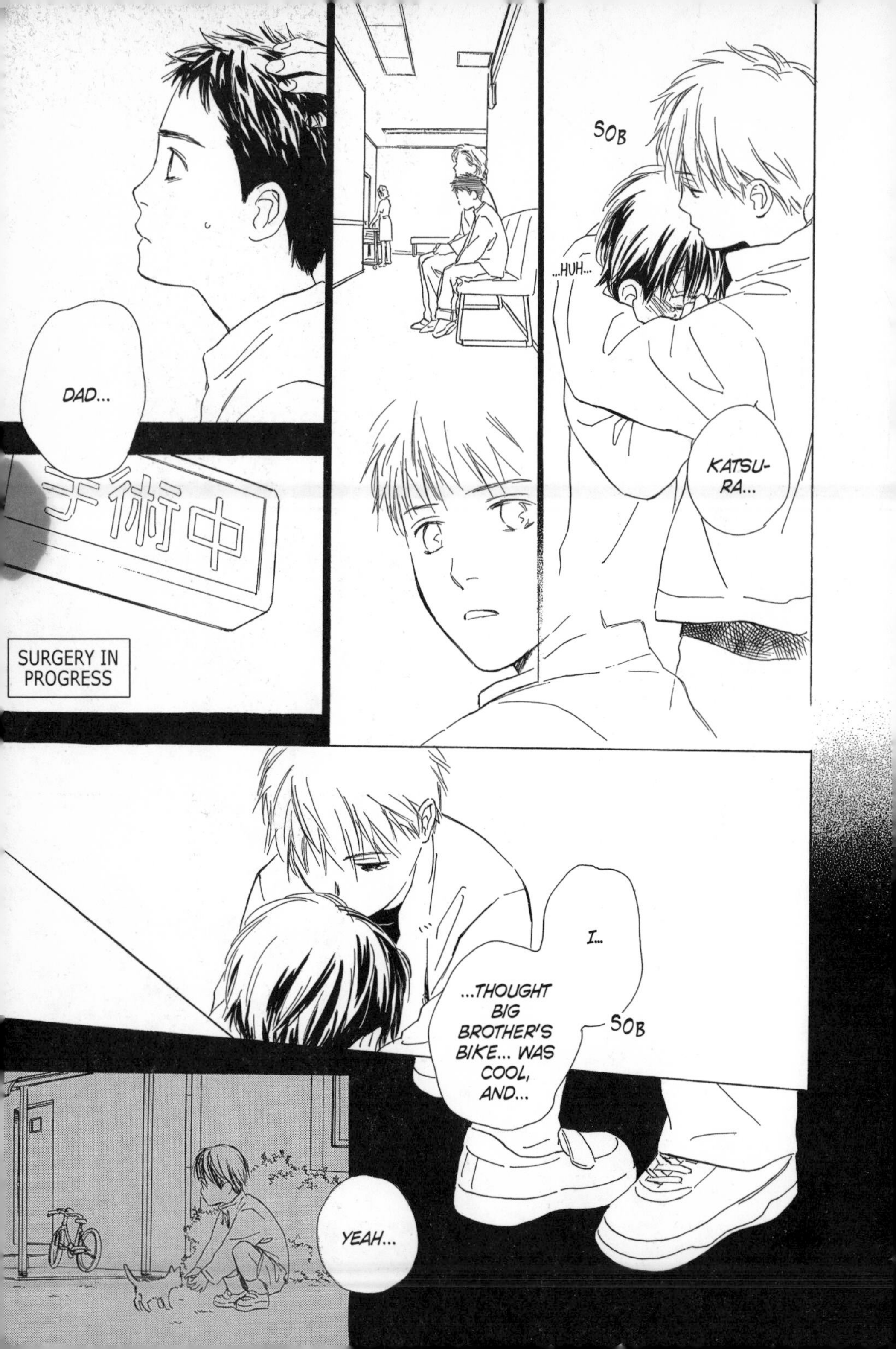
SOB
...HUH...
KATSU-RA...
DAD...
手術中
SURGERY IN PROGRESS
I...
...THOUGHT BIG BROTHER'S BIKE... WAS COOL, AND...
SOB
YEAH...

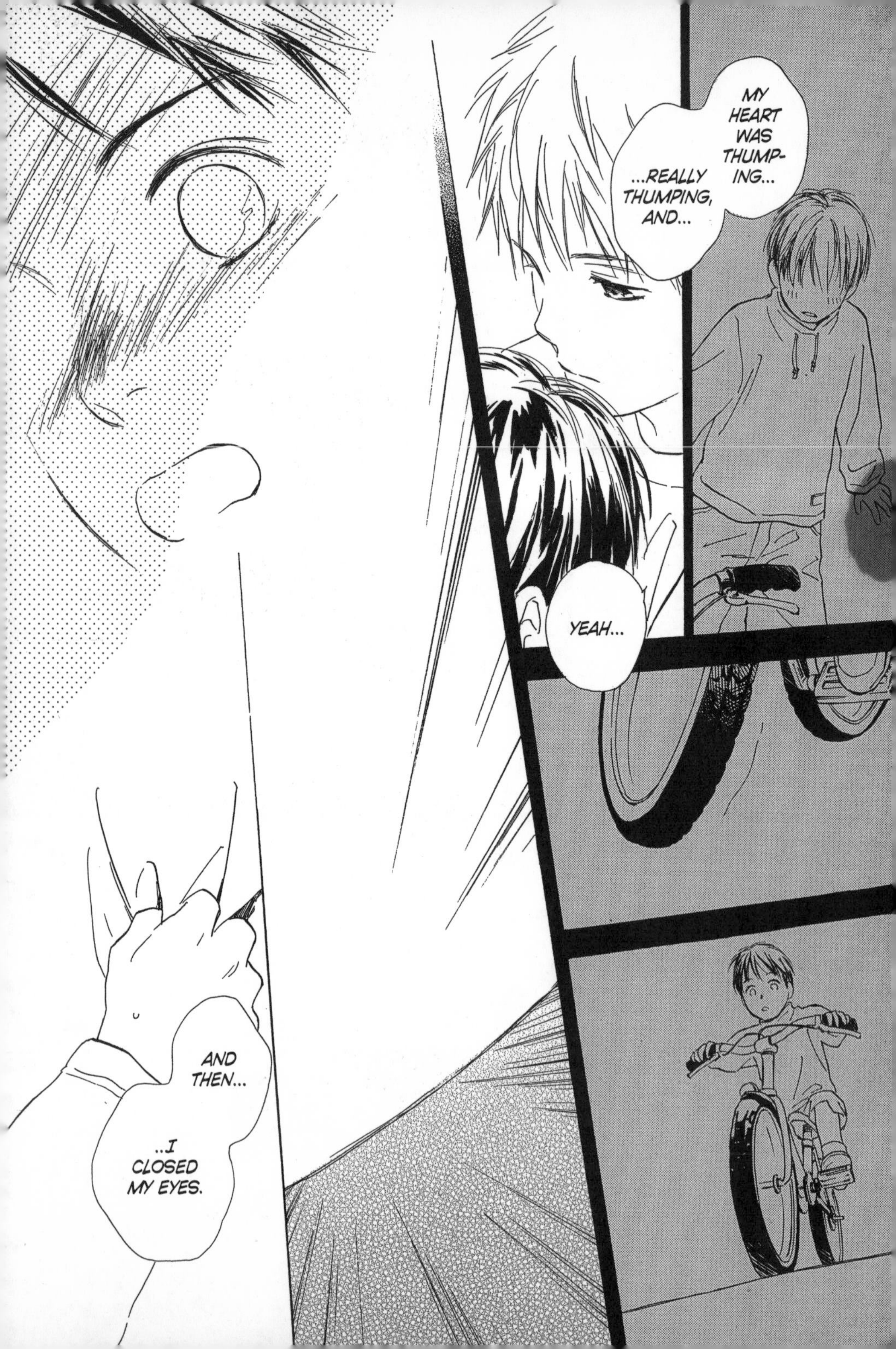
MY HEART WAS THUMPING...
...REALLY THUMPING, AND...
YEAH...
AND THEN...
...I CLOSED MY EYES.

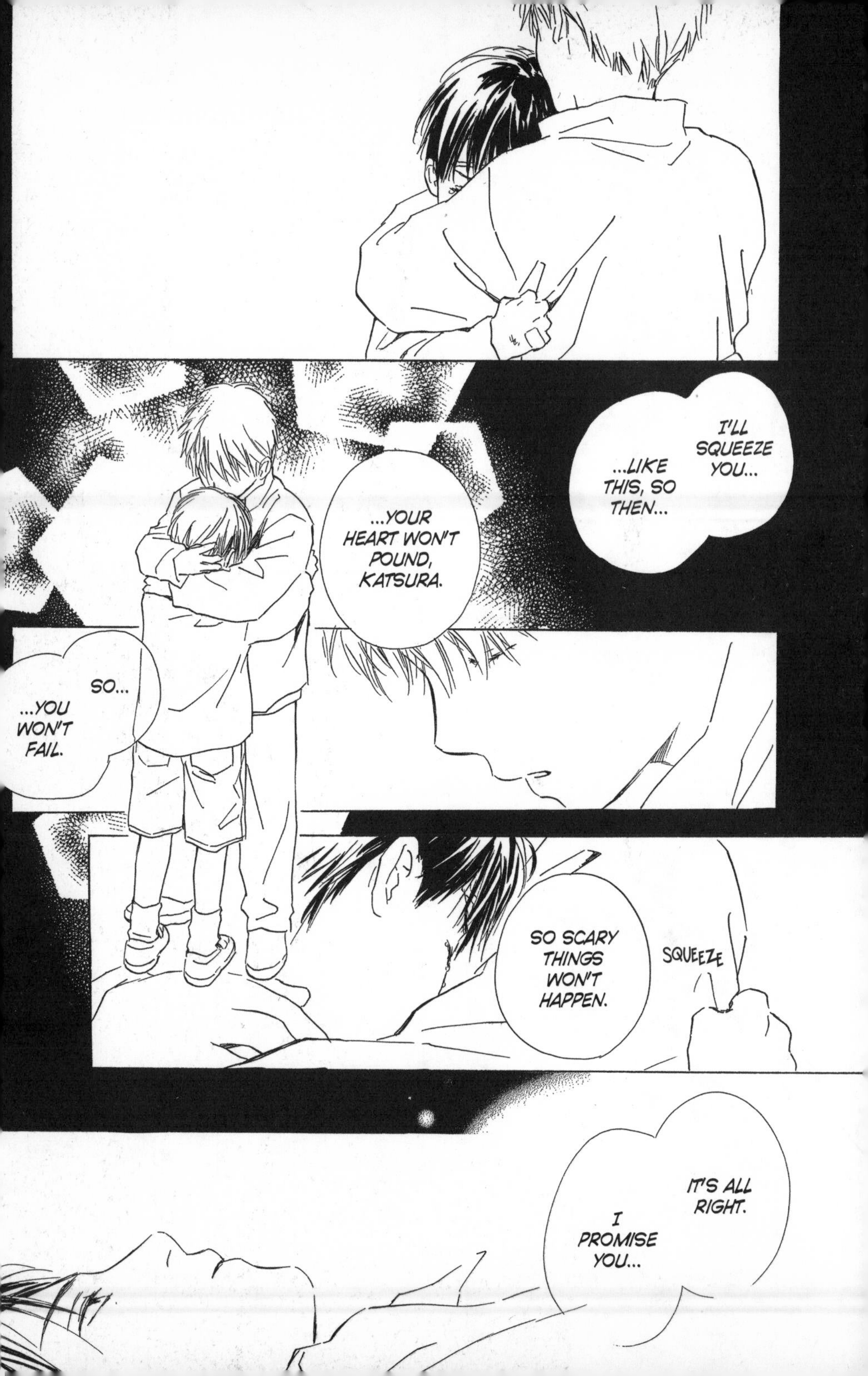
I'LL SQUEEZE YOU...
...LIKE THIS, SO THEN...
...YOUR HEART WON'T POUND, KATSURA.
SO...
...YOU WON'T FAIL.
SQUEEZE
SO SCARY THINGS WON'T HAPPEN.
IT'S ALL RIGHT.
I PROMISE YOU...

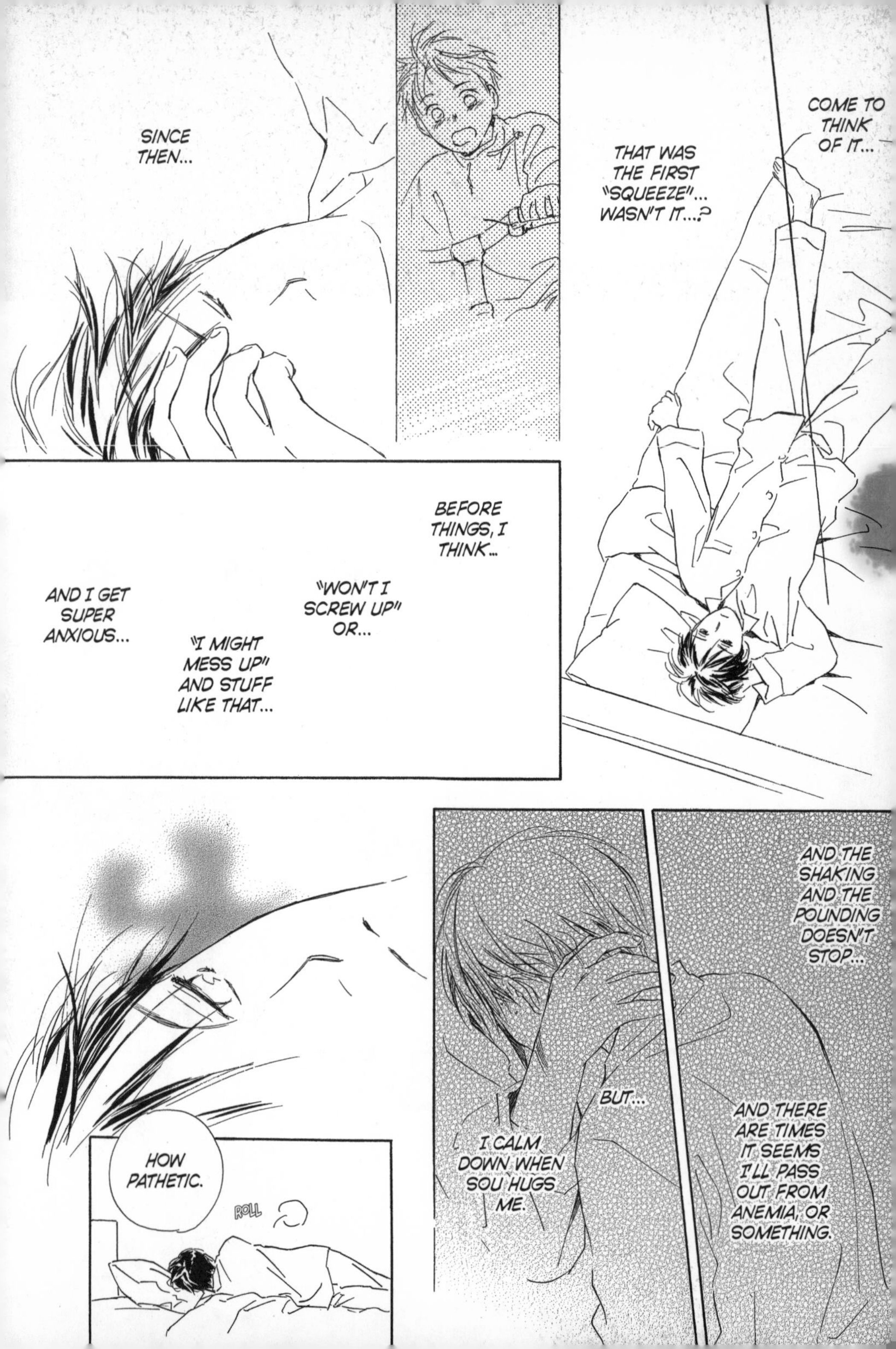

COME TO THINK OF IT...
THAT WAS THE FIRST "SQUEEZE"... WASN'T IT...?
SINCE THEN...
BEFORE THINGS, I THINK...
"WON'T I SCREW UP" OR...
"I MIGHT MESS UP" AND STUFF LIKE THAT...
AND I GET SUPER ANXIOUS...
AND THE SHAKING AND THE POUNDING DOESN'T STOP...
AND THERE ARE TIMES IT SEEMS I'LL PASS OUT FROM ANEMIA, OR SOMETHING.
BUT...
I CALM DOWN WHEN SOU HUGS ME.
HOW PATHETIC.
ROLL

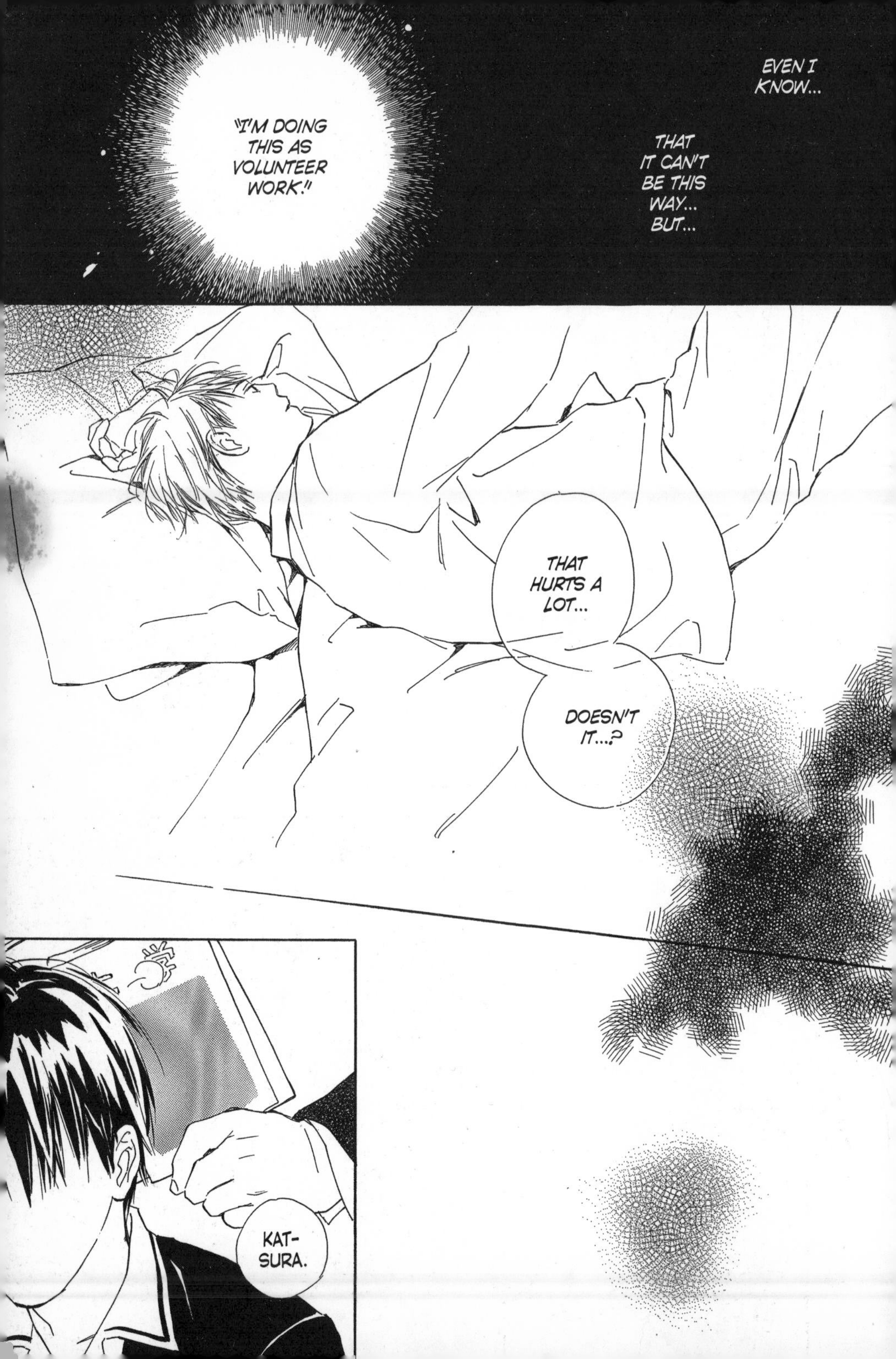
EVEN I KNOW...
THAT IT CAN'T BE THIS WAY... BUT...
"I'M DOING THIS AS VOLUNTEER WORK."
THAT HURTS A LOT...
DOESN'T IT...?
KAT-SURA.

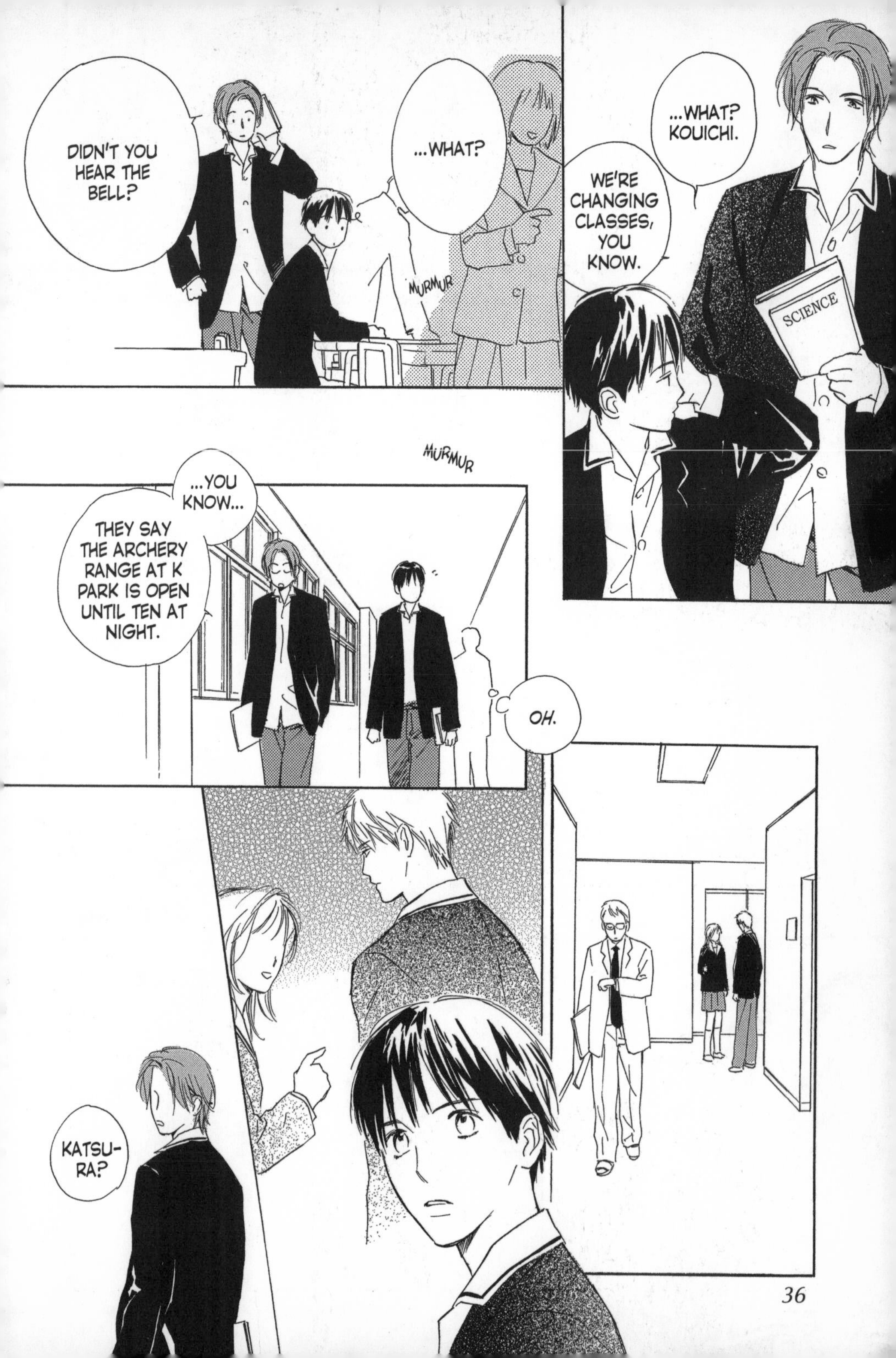
...WHAT? KOUICHI.
WE'RE CHANGING CLASSES, YOU KNOW.
...WHAT?
MURMUR
DIDN'T YOU HEAR THE BELL?
MURMUR
OH.
...YOU KNOW...
THEY SAY THE ARCHERY RANGE AT K PARK IS OPEN UNTIL TEN AT NIGHT.
KATSURA?
SCIENCE

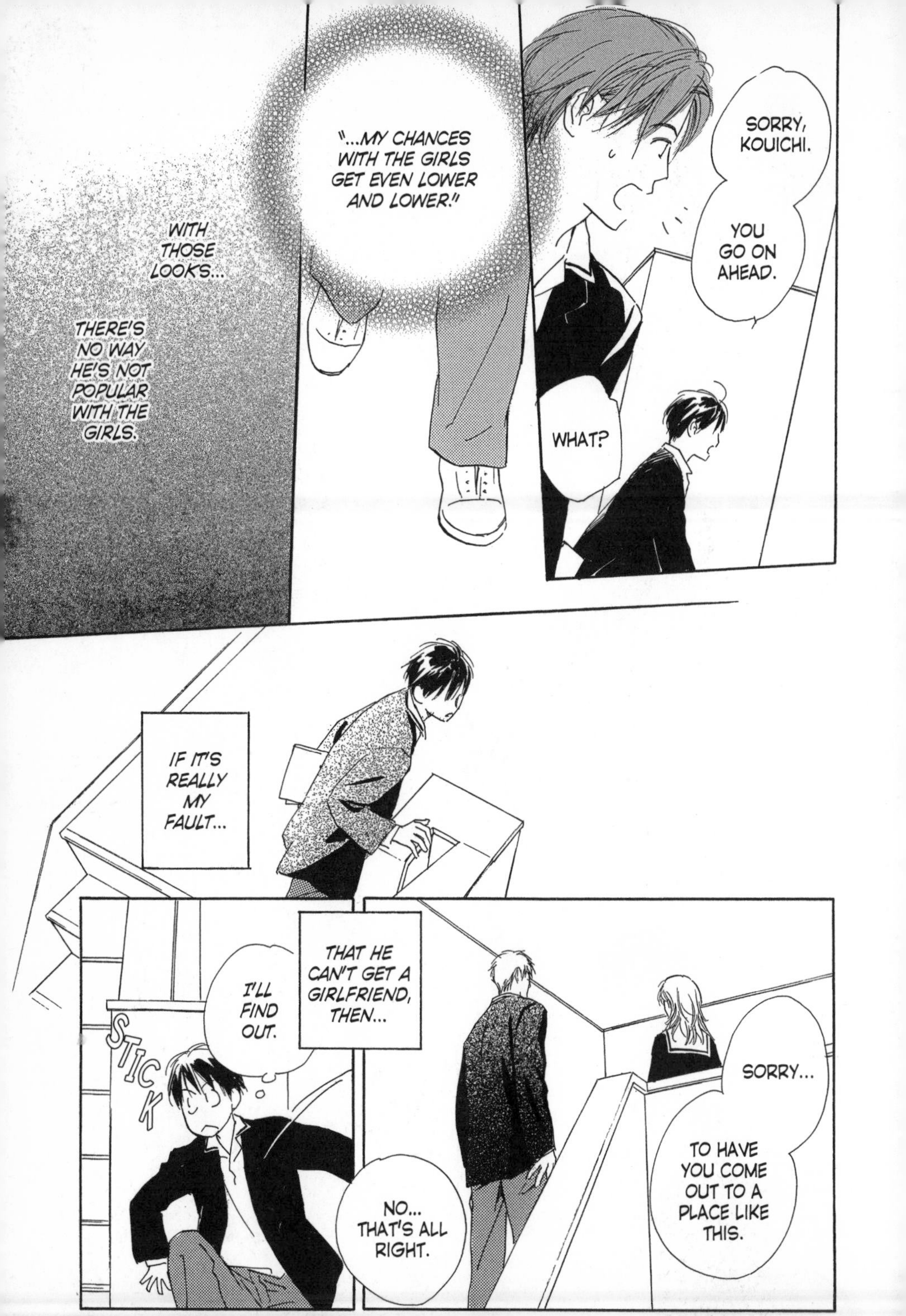
SORRY, KOUICHI.
YOU GO ON AHEAD.
WHAT?
"...MY CHANCES WITH THE GIRLS GET EVEN LOWER AND LOWER."
WITH THOSE LOOKS...
THERE'S NO WAY HE'S NOT POPULAR WITH THE GIRLS.
IF IT'S REALLY MY FAULT...
SORRY...
TO HAVE YOU COME OUT TO A PLACE LIKE THIS.
NO... THAT'S ALL RIGHT.
THAT HE CAN'T GET A GIRLFRIEND, THEN...
I'LL FIND OUT.
STICK

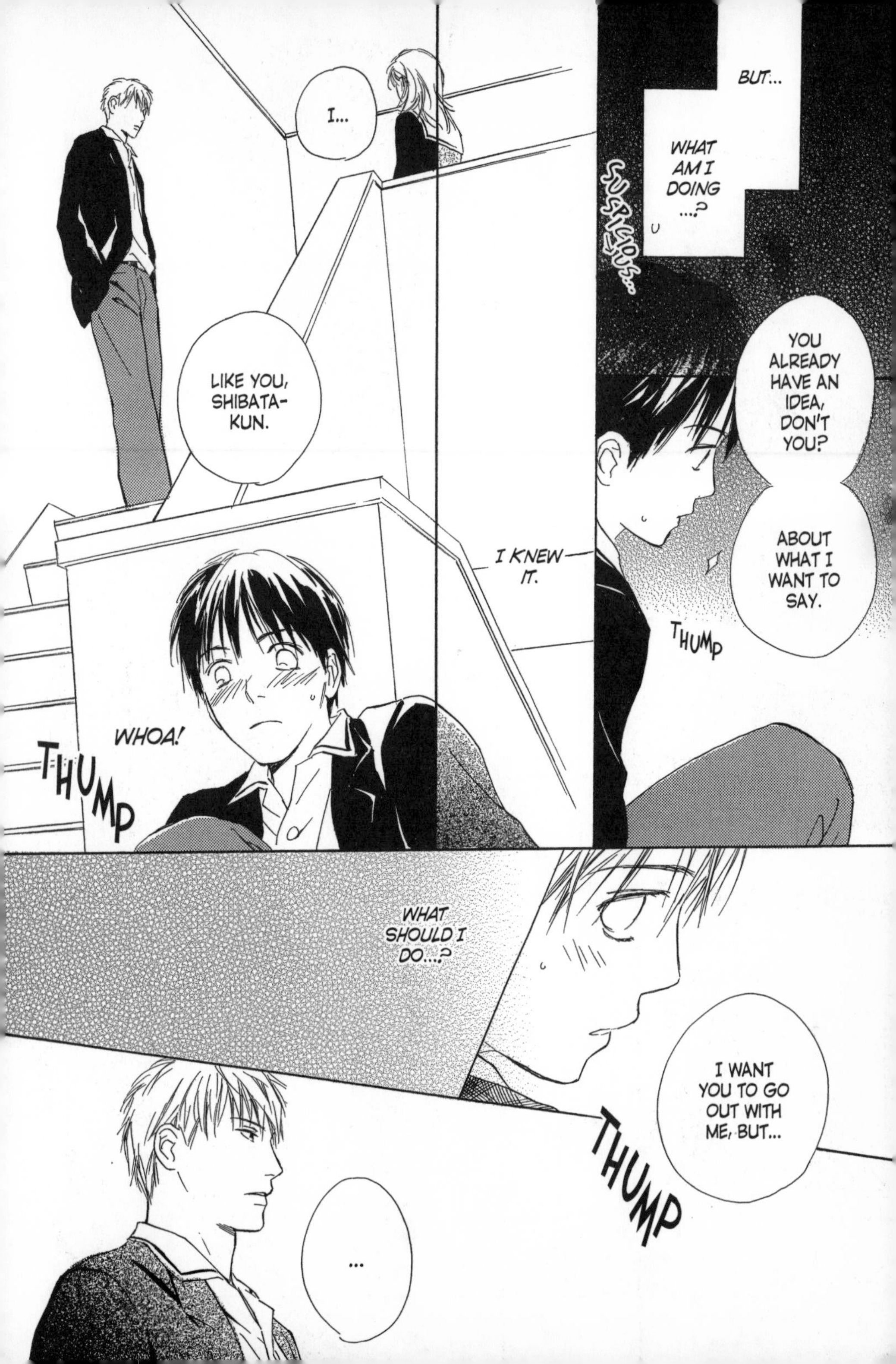
BUT...
WHAT AM I DOING ...?
SUSPICIOUS...
YOU ALREADY HAVE AN IDEA, DON'T YOU?
ABOUT WHAT I WANT TO SAY.
THUMP
I KNEW IT.
I...
LIKE YOU, SHIBATA-KUN.
WHOA!
THUMP
WHAT SHOULD I DO...?
I WANT YOU TO GO OUT WITH ME, BUT...
THUMP
...

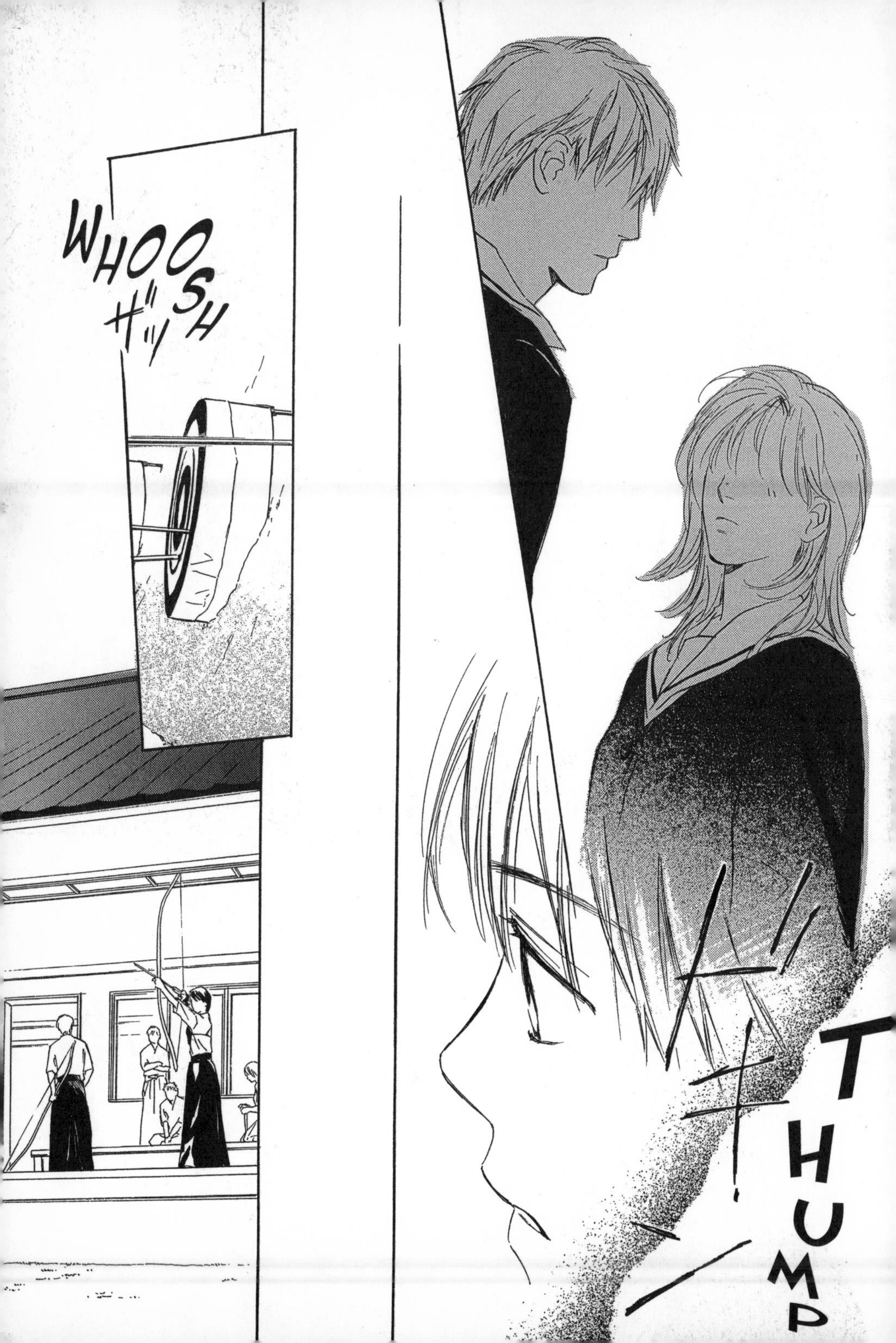
THUMP
WHOOSH
ザッ

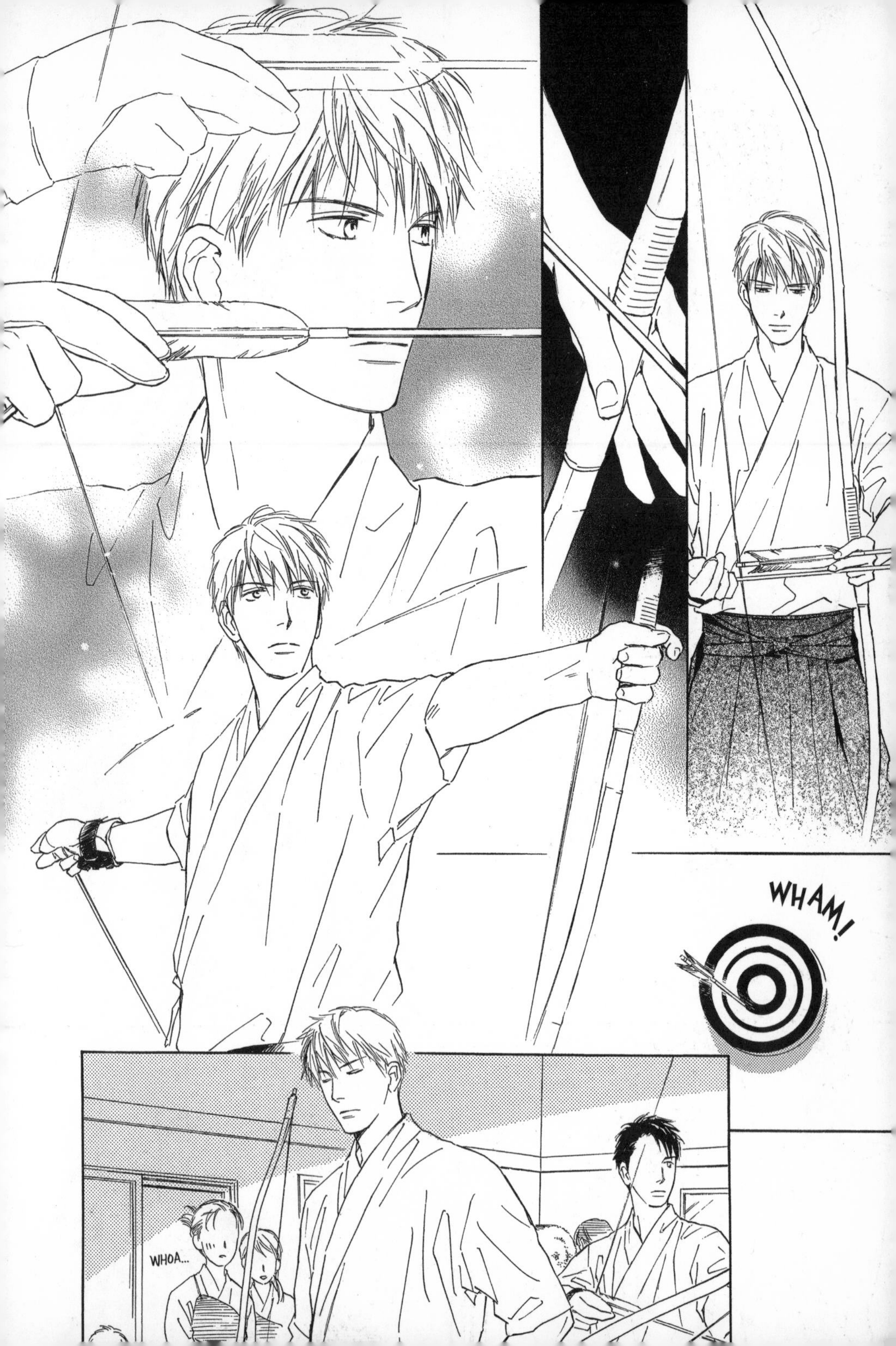
WHAM!
WHOA...

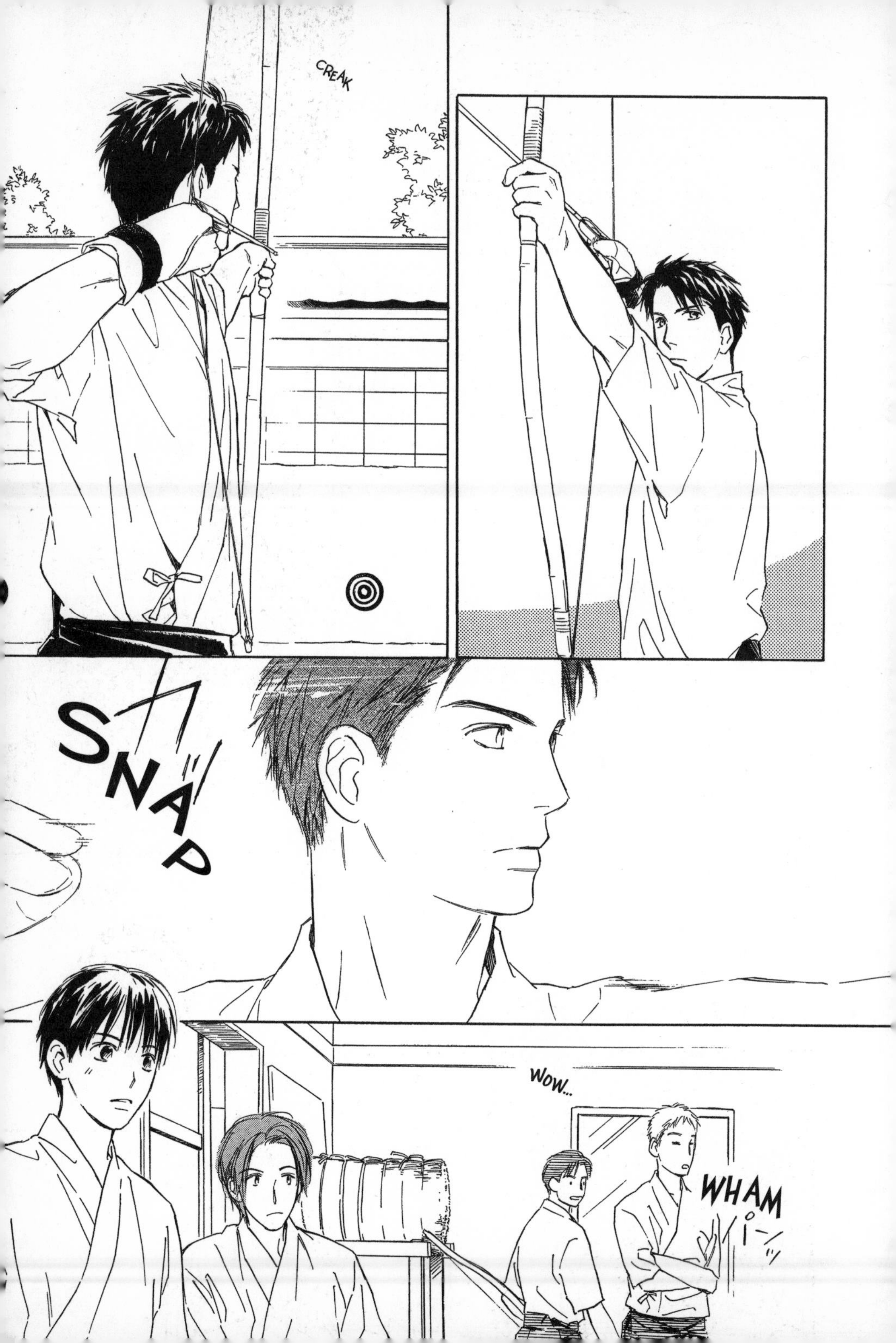
CREAK
SNAP
WOW...
WHAM

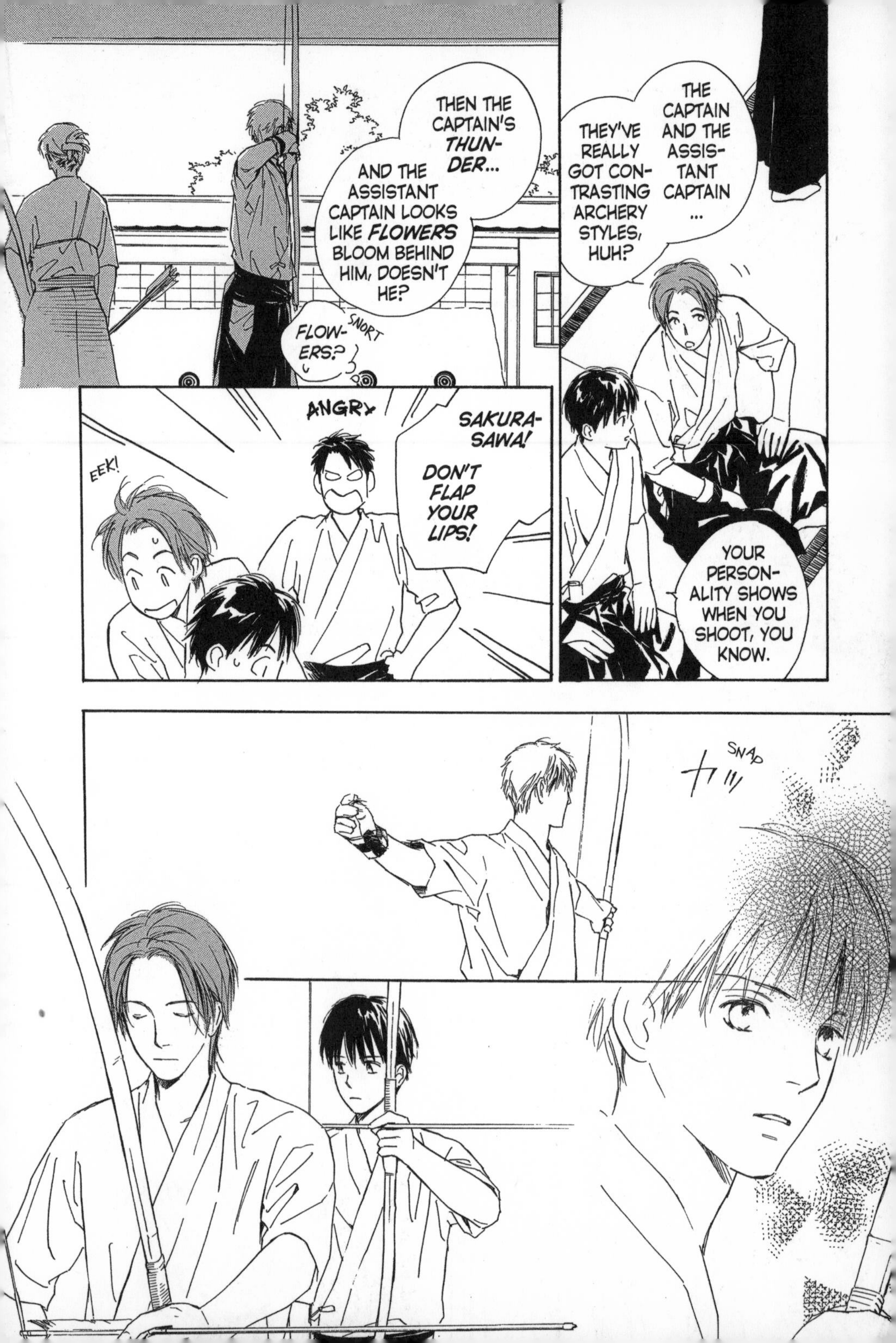
THE CAPTAIN AND THE ASSISTANT CAPTAIN ...
THEY'VE REALLY GOT CONTRASTING ARCHERY STYLES, HUH?
YOUR PERSONALITY SHOWS WHEN YOU SHOOT, YOU KNOW.
THEN THE CAPTAIN'S *THUNDER*...
AND THE ASSISTANT CAPTAIN LOOKS LIKE *FLOWERS* BLOOM BEHIND HIM, DOESN'T HE?
SNORT
FLOWERS?
SAKURASAWA!
DON'T FLAP YOUR LIPS!
ANGRY
EEK!
SNAP

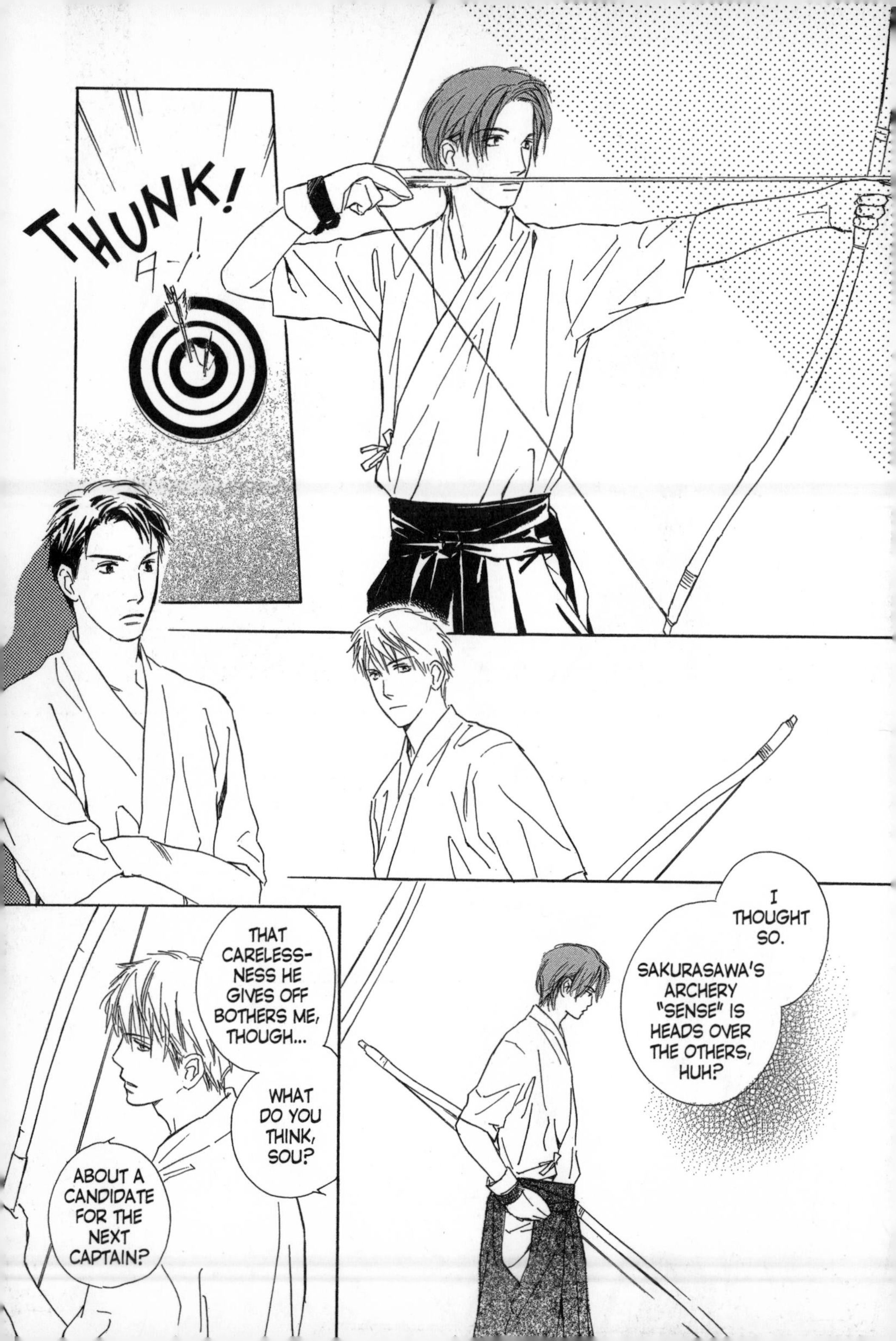
THUNK!
I THOUGHT SO.
SAKURASAWA'S ARCHERY "SENSE" IS HEADS OVER THE OTHERS, HUH?
THAT CARELESS-NESS HE GIVES OFF BOTHERS ME, THOUGH...
WHAT DO YOU THINK, SOU?
ABOUT A CANDIDATE FOR THE NEXT CAPTAIN?

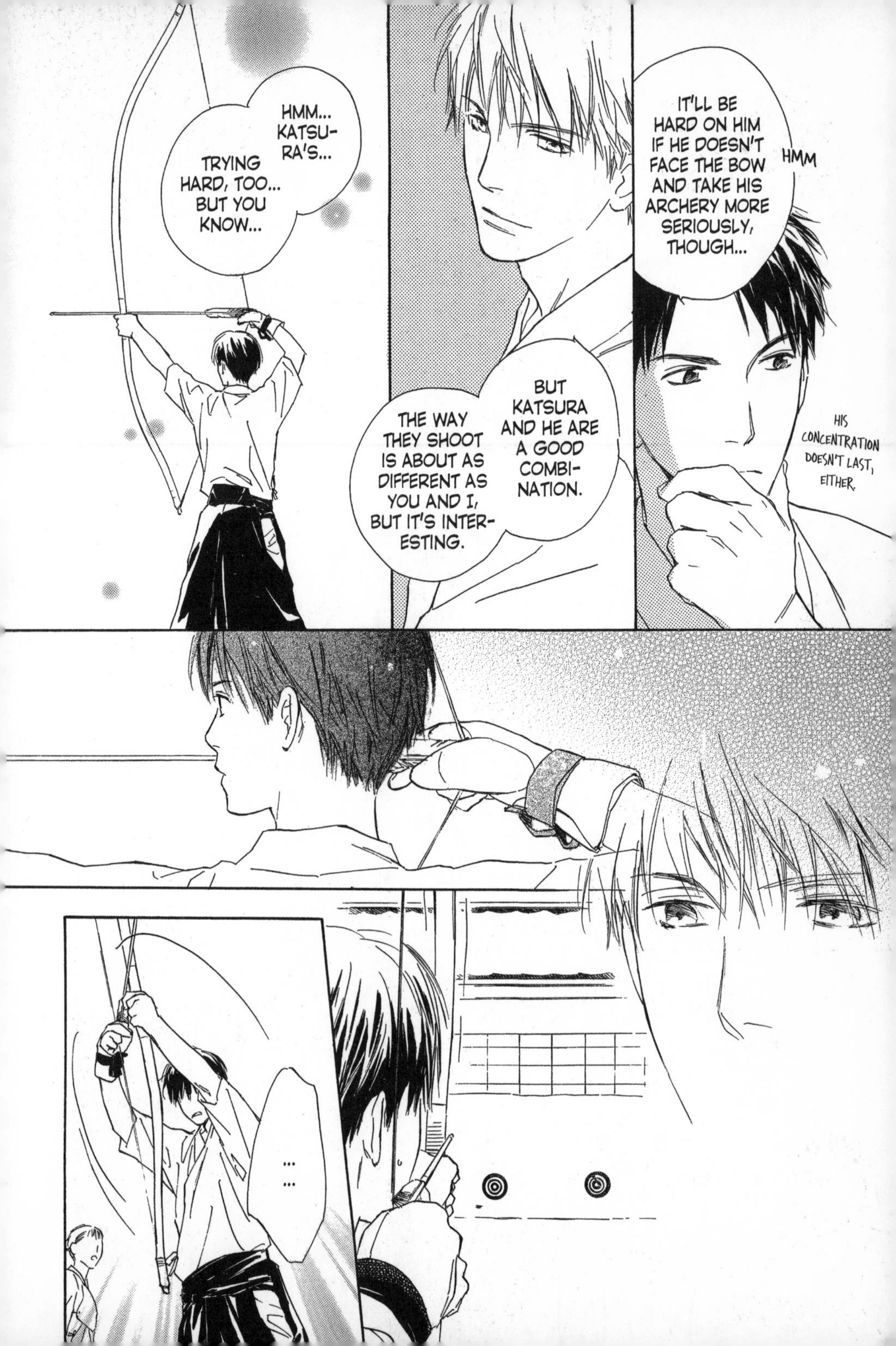
IT'LL BE HARD ON HIM IF HE DOESN'T FACE THE BOW AND TAKE HIS ARCHERY MORE SERIOUSLY, THOUGH...
HMM
HIS CONCENTRATION DOESN'T LAST, EITHER.
BUT KATSURA AND HE ARE A GOOD COMBI-NATION.
THE WAY THEY SHOOT IS ABOUT AS DIFFERENT AS YOU AND I, BUT IT'S INTER-ESTING.
HMM... KATSU-RA'S...
TRYING HARD, TOO... BUT YOU KNOW...
... ...

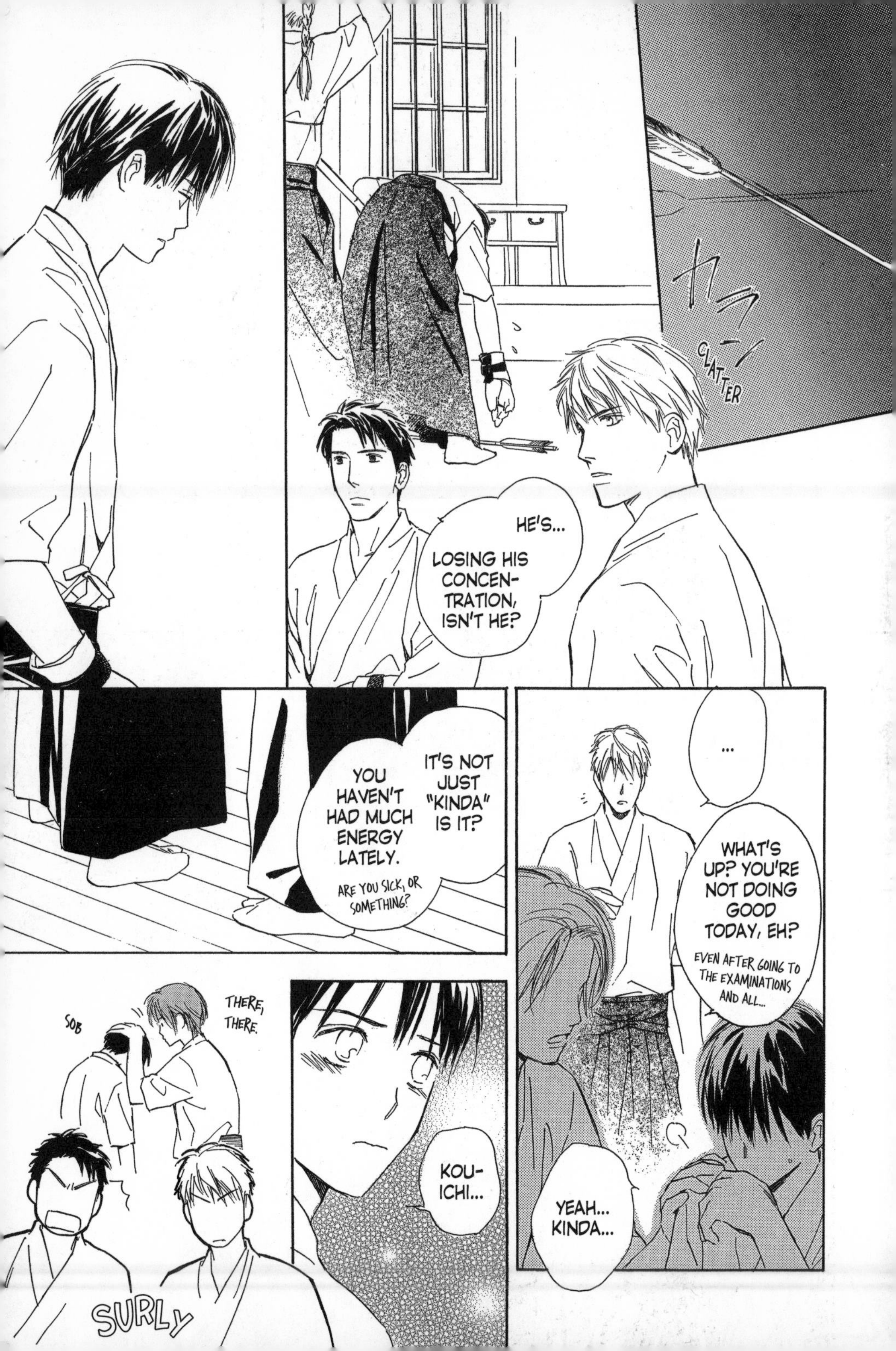
CLATTER
HE'S...
LOSING HIS CONCENTRATION, ISN'T HE?
...
WHAT'S UP? YOU'RE NOT DOING GOOD TODAY, EH?
EVEN AFTER GOING TO THE EXAMINATIONS AND ALL...
YEAH... KINDA...
IT'S NOT JUST "KINDA" IS IT?
YOU HAVEN'T HAD MUCH ENERGY LATELY.
ARE YOU SICK, OR SOMETHING?
KOU-ICHI...
THERE, THERE.
SOB
SURLY

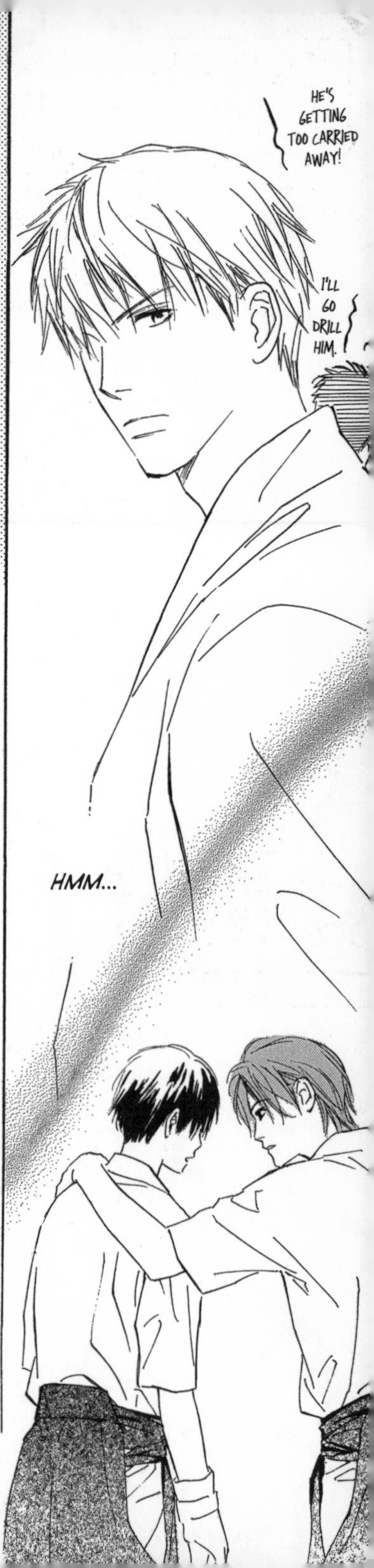
HE'S GETTING TOO CARRIED AWAY!
I'LL GO DRILL HIM.
HMM...

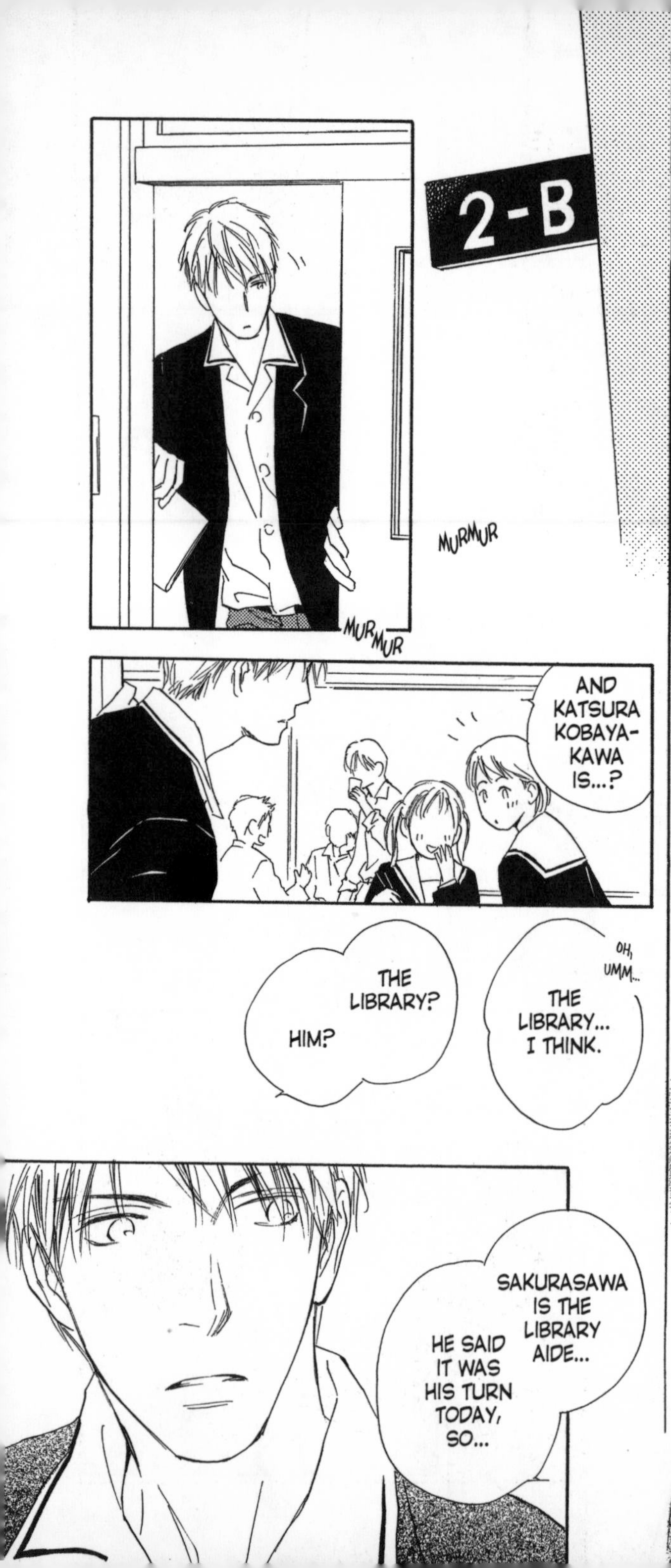
2-B
MURMUR
MURMUR
AND KATSURA KOBAYA-KAWA IS...?
OH, UMM...
THE LIBRARY... I THINK.
THE LIBRARY?
HIM?
SAKURASAWA IS THE LIBRARY AIDE...
HE SAID IT WAS HIS TURN TODAY, SO...

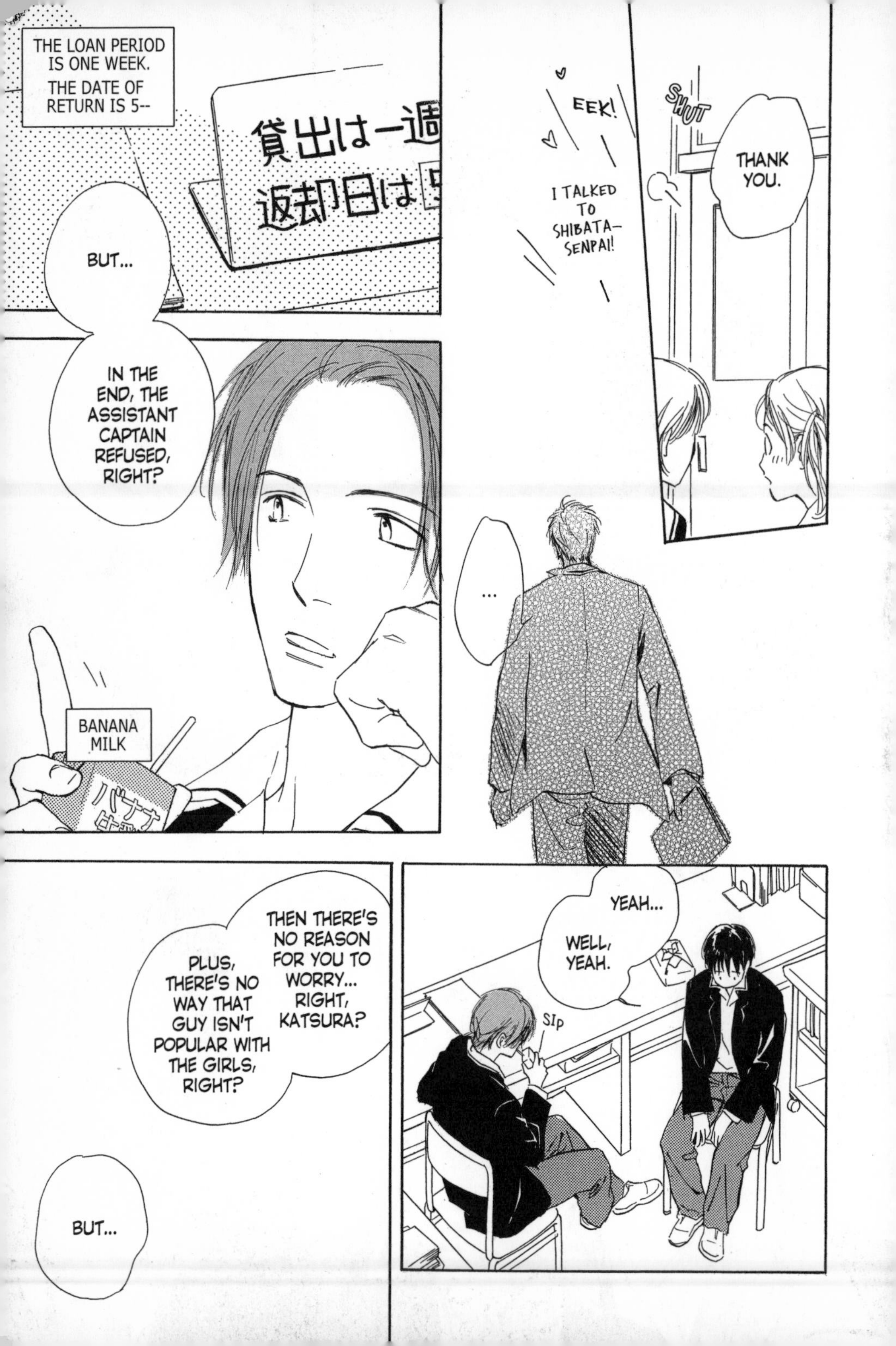
SHUT
THANK YOU.
EEK!
I TALKED TO SHIBATA-SENPAI!
...
THE LOAN PERIOD IS ONE WEEK. THE DATE OF RETURN IS 5--
貸出は一週
返却日は
BUT...
IN THE END, THE ASSISTANT CAPTAIN REFUSED, RIGHT?
BANANA MILK
YEAH... WELL, YEAH.
SIP
THEN THERE'S NO REASON FOR YOU TO WORRY... RIGHT, KATSURA?
PLUS, THERE'S NO WAY THAT GUY ISN'T POPULAR WITH THE GIRLS, RIGHT?
BUT...

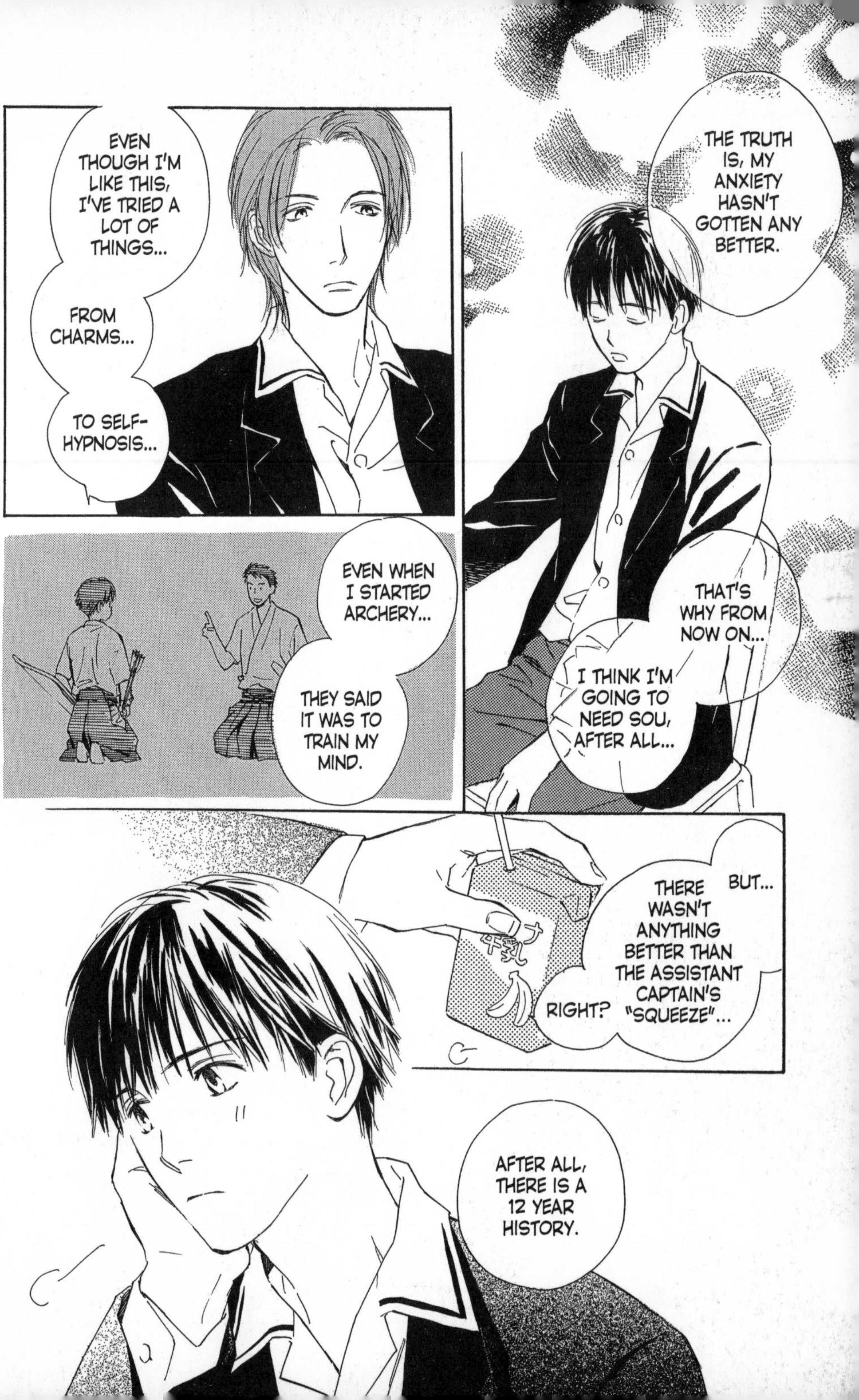
THE TRUTH IS, MY ANXIETY HASN'T GOTTEN ANY BETTER.
THAT'S WHY FROM NOW ON...
I THINK I'M GOING TO NEED SOU, AFTER ALL...
EVEN THOUGH I'M LIKE THIS, I'VE TRIED A LOT OF THINGS...
FROM CHARMS...
TO SELF-HYPNOSIS...
EVEN WHEN I STARTED ARCHERY...
THEY SAID IT WAS TO TRAIN MY MIND.
BUT...
THERE WASN'T ANYTHING BETTER THAN THE ASSISTANT CAPTAIN'S "SQUEEZE"...
RIGHT?
AFTER ALL, THERE IS A 12 YEAR HISTORY.

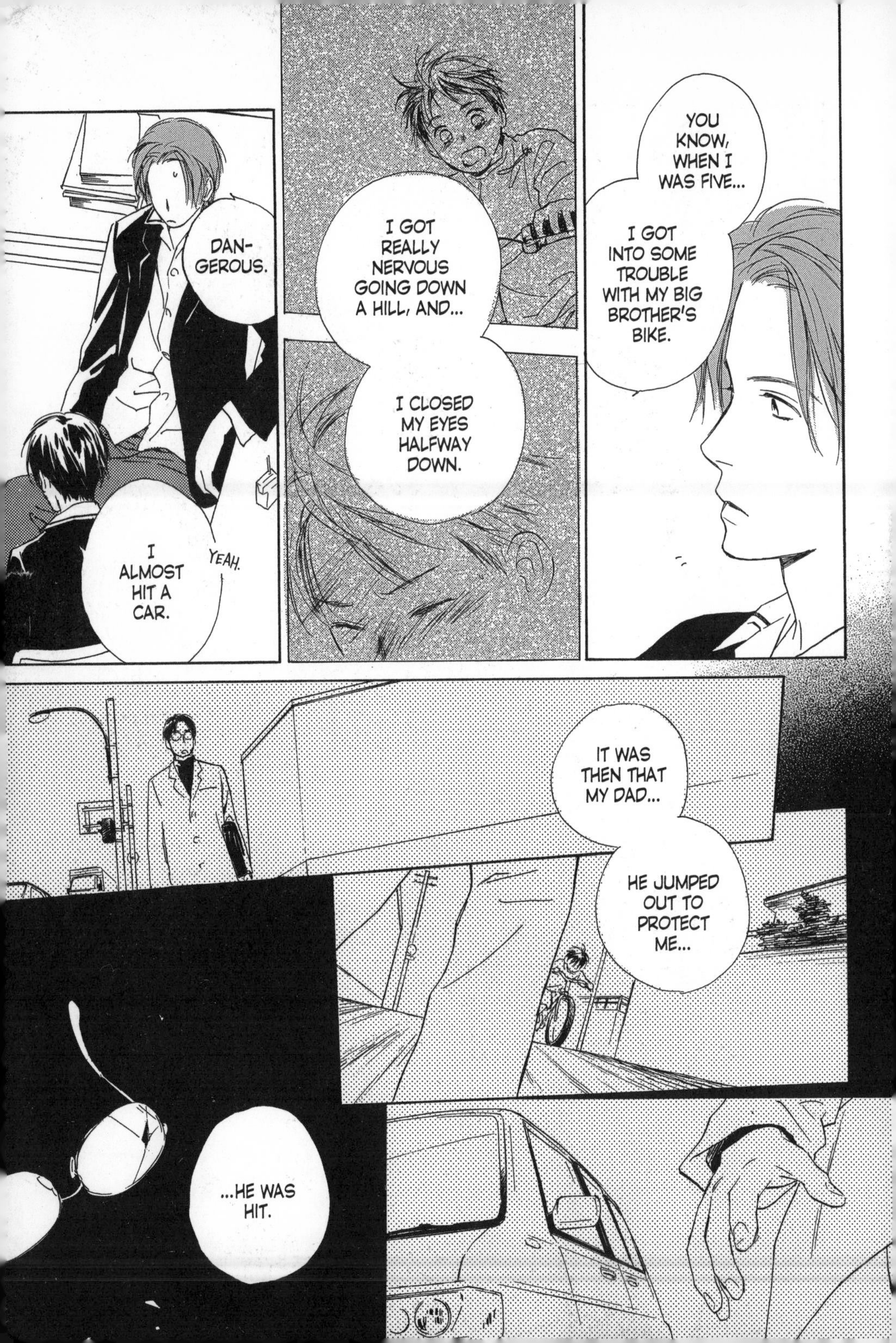
YOU KNOW, WHEN I WAS FIVE...
I GOT INTO SOME TROUBLE WITH MY BIG BROTHER'S BIKE.
I GOT REALLY NERVOUS GOING DOWN A HILL, AND...
I CLOSED MY EYES HALFWAY DOWN.
DAN-GEROUS.
YEAH.
I ALMOST HIT A CAR.
IT WAS THEN THAT MY DAD...
HE JUMPED OUT TO PROTECT ME...
...HE WAS HIT.

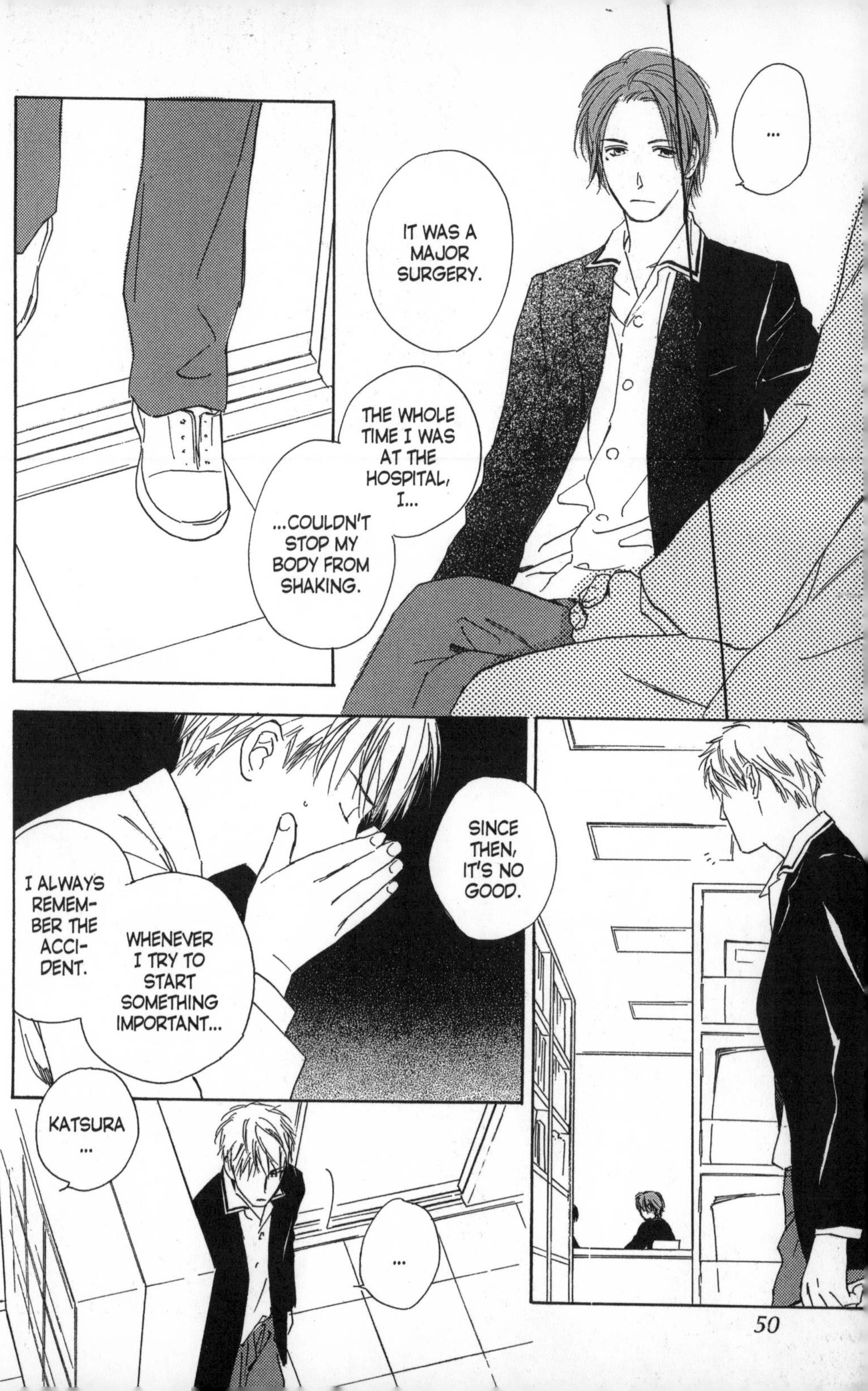
...
IT WAS A MAJOR SURGERY.
THE WHOLE TIME I WAS AT THE HOSPITAL, I...
...COULDN'T STOP MY BODY FROM SHAKING.
SINCE THEN, IT'S NO GOOD.
WHENEVER I TRY TO START SOMETHING IMPORTANT...
I ALWAYS REMEM-BER THE ACCI-DENT.
...
KATSURA ...

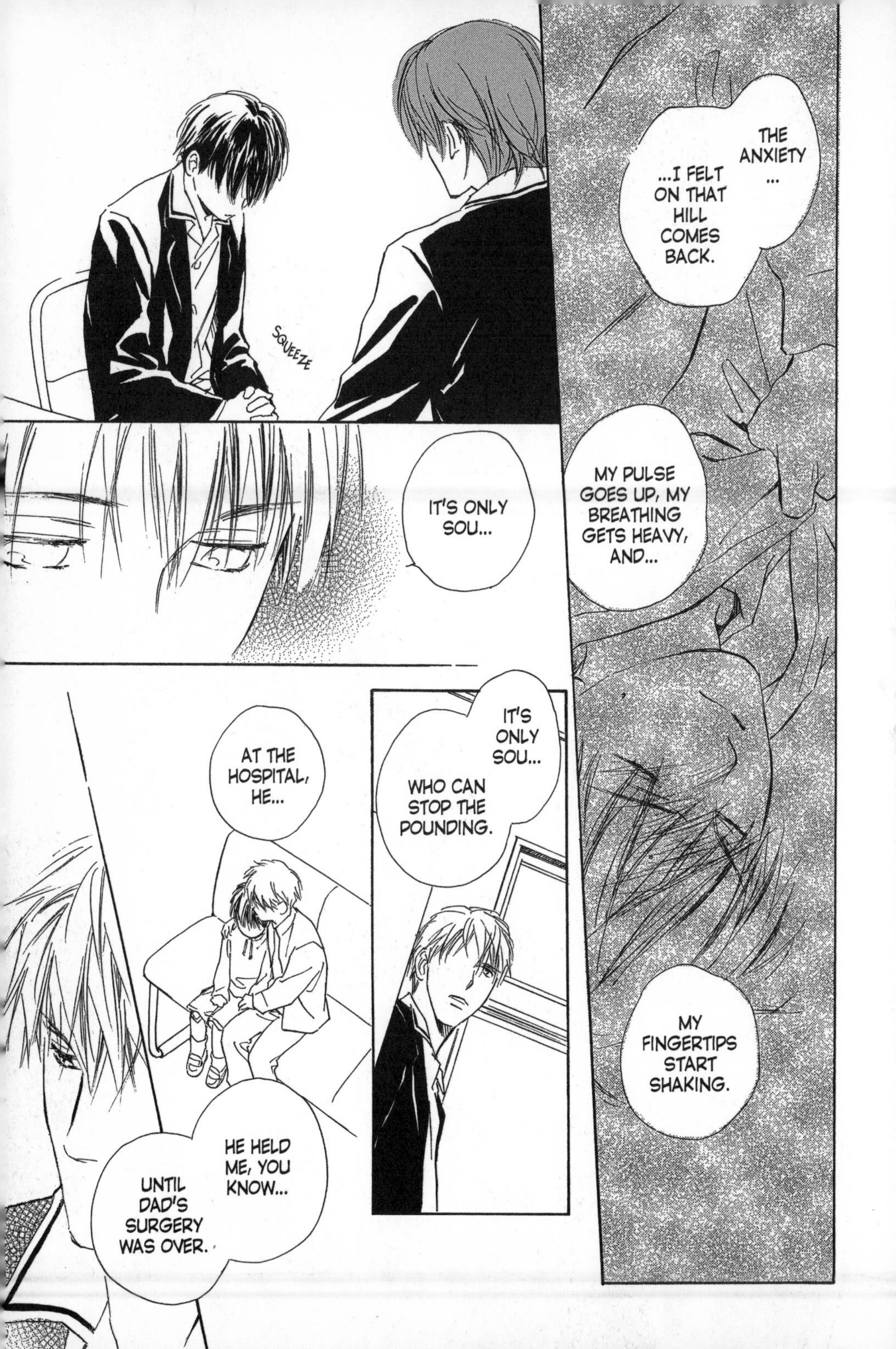
THE ANXIETY ...
...I FELT ON THAT HILL COMES BACK.
MY PULSE GOES UP, MY BREATHING GETS HEAVY, AND...
MY FINGERTIPS START SHAKING.
SQUEEZE
IT'S ONLY SOU...
IT'S ONLY SOU...
WHO CAN STOP THE POUNDING.
AT THE HOSPITAL, HE...
HE HELD ME, YOU KNOW...
UNTIL DAD'S SURGERY WAS OVER.

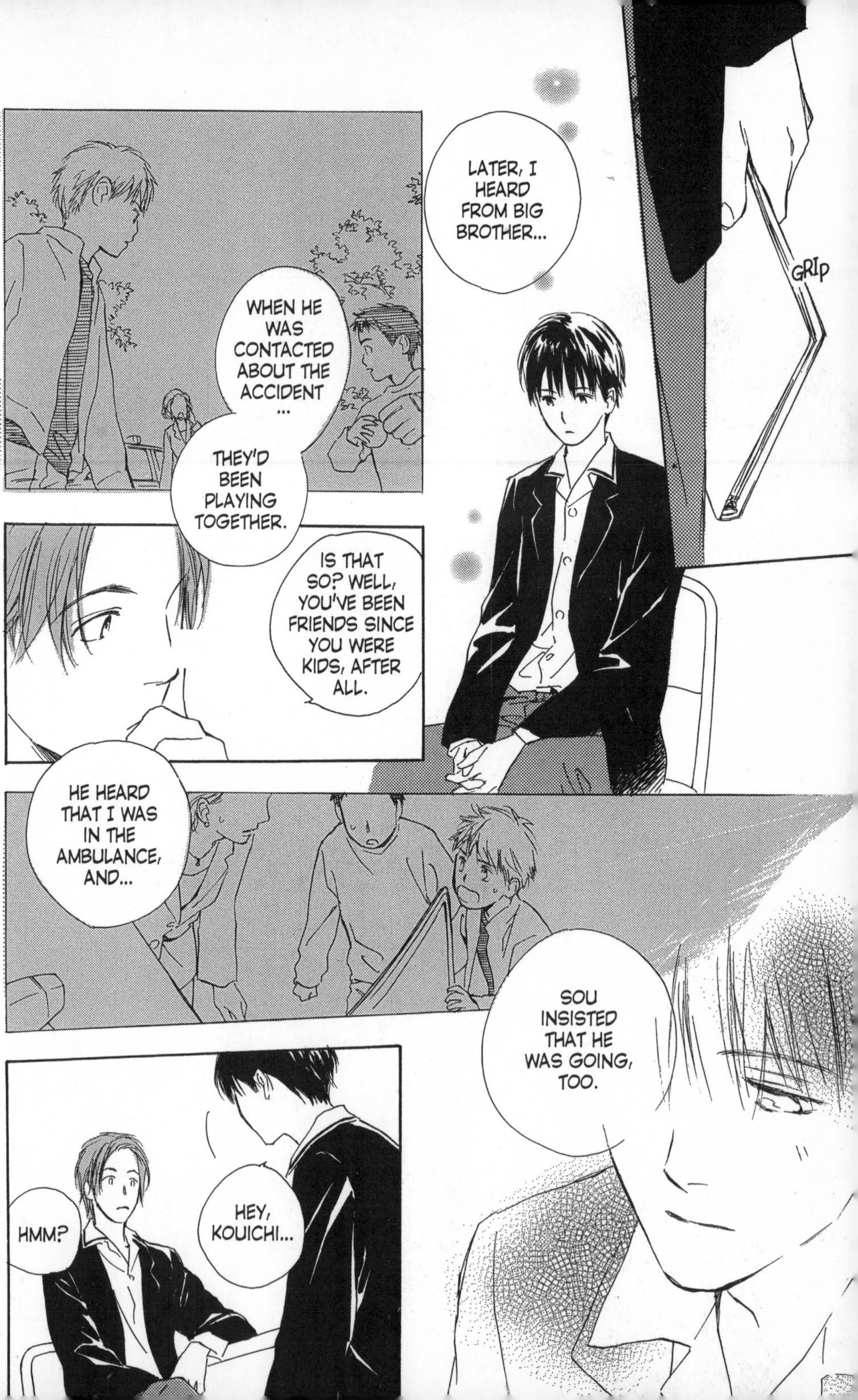
LATER, I HEARD FROM BIG BROTHER...
GRIP
WHEN HE WAS CONTACTED ABOUT THE ACCIDENT ...
THEY'D BEEN PLAYING TOGETHER.
IS THAT SO? WELL, YOU'VE BEEN FRIENDS SINCE YOU WERE KIDS, AFTER ALL.
HE HEARD THAT I WAS IN THE AMBULANCE, AND...
SOU INSISTED THAT HE WAS GOING, TOO.
HEY, KOUICHI...
HMM?

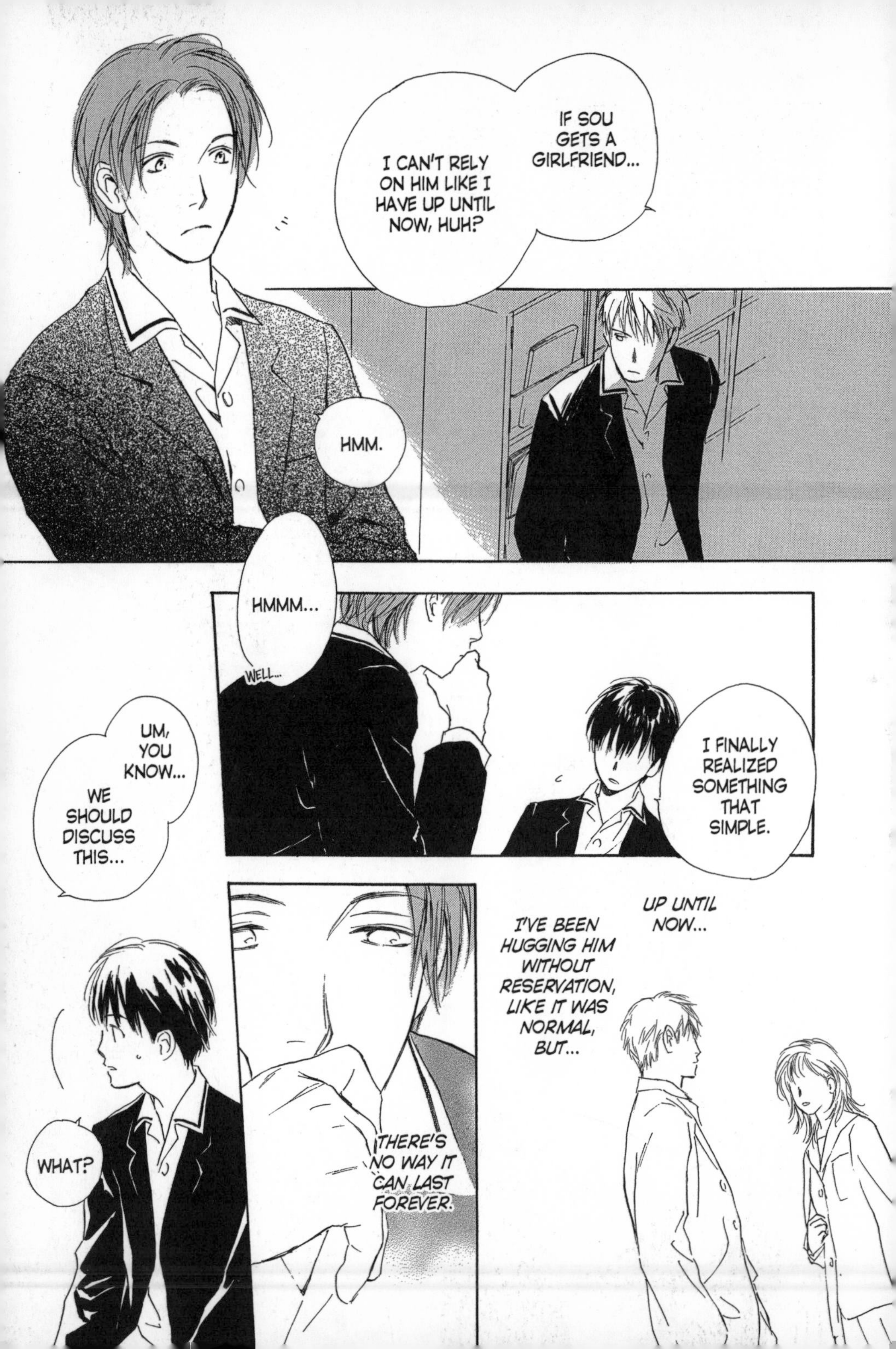
IF SOU GETS A GIRLFRIEND...
I CAN'T RELY ON HIM LIKE I HAVE UP UNTIL NOW, HUH?
HMM.
I FINALLY REALIZED SOMETHING THAT SIMPLE.
HMMM...
WELL...
UM, YOU KNOW... WE SHOULD DISCUSS THIS...
UP UNTIL NOW...
I'VE BEEN HUGGING HIM WITHOUT RESERVATION, LIKE IT WAS NORMAL, BUT...
THERE'S NO WAY IT CAN LAST FOREVER.
WHAT?

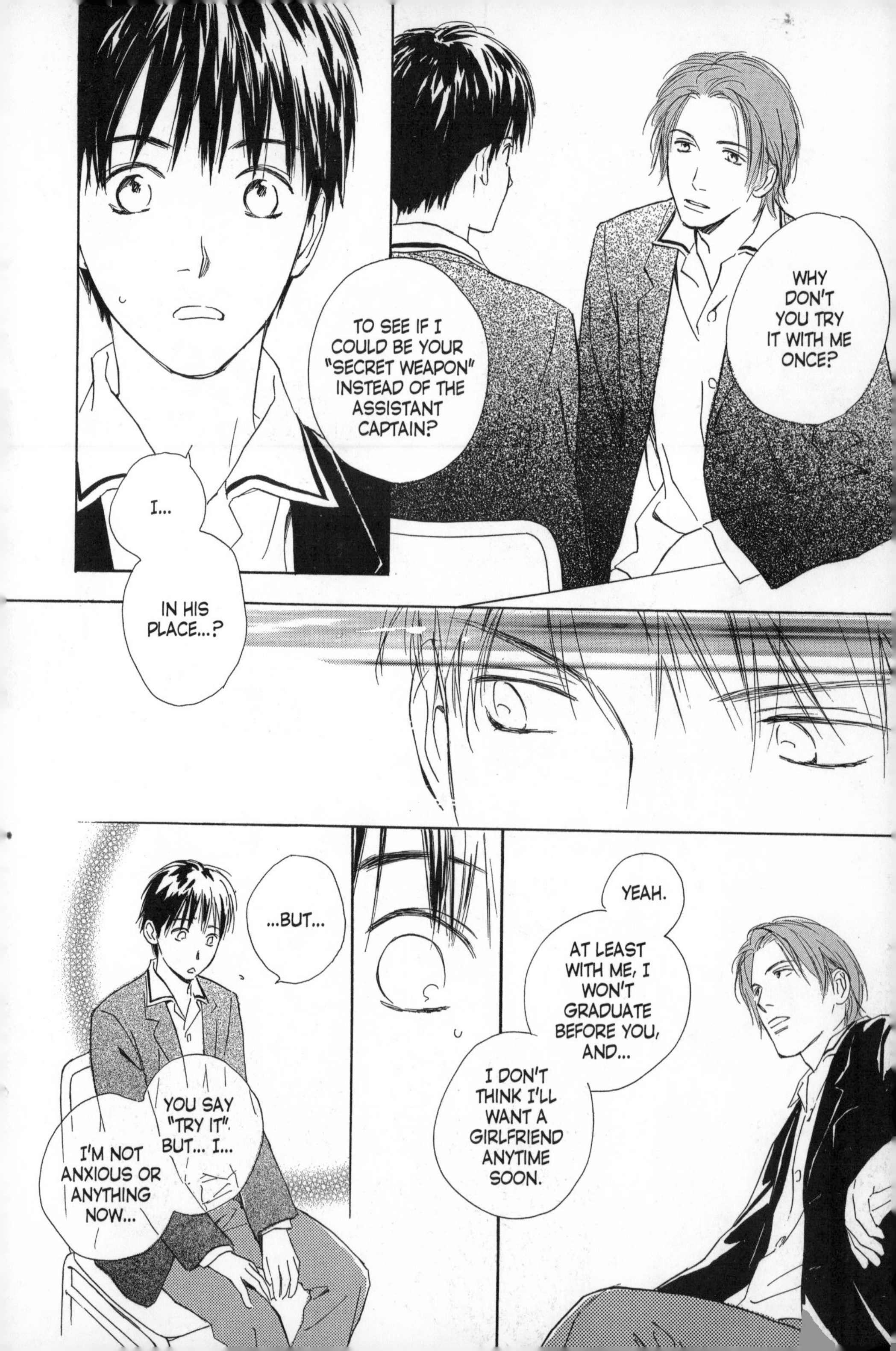
WHY DON'T YOU TRY IT WITH ME ONCE?
TO SEE IF I COULD BE YOUR "SECRET WEAPON" INSTEAD OF THE ASSISTANT CAPTAIN?
I...
IN HIS PLACE...?
YEAH.
AT LEAST WITH ME, I WON'T GRADUATE BEFORE YOU, AND...
I DON'T THINK I'LL WANT A GIRLFRIEND ANYTIME SOON.
...BUT...
YOU SAY "TRY IT". BUT... I...
I'M NOT ANXIOUS OR ANYTHING NOW...

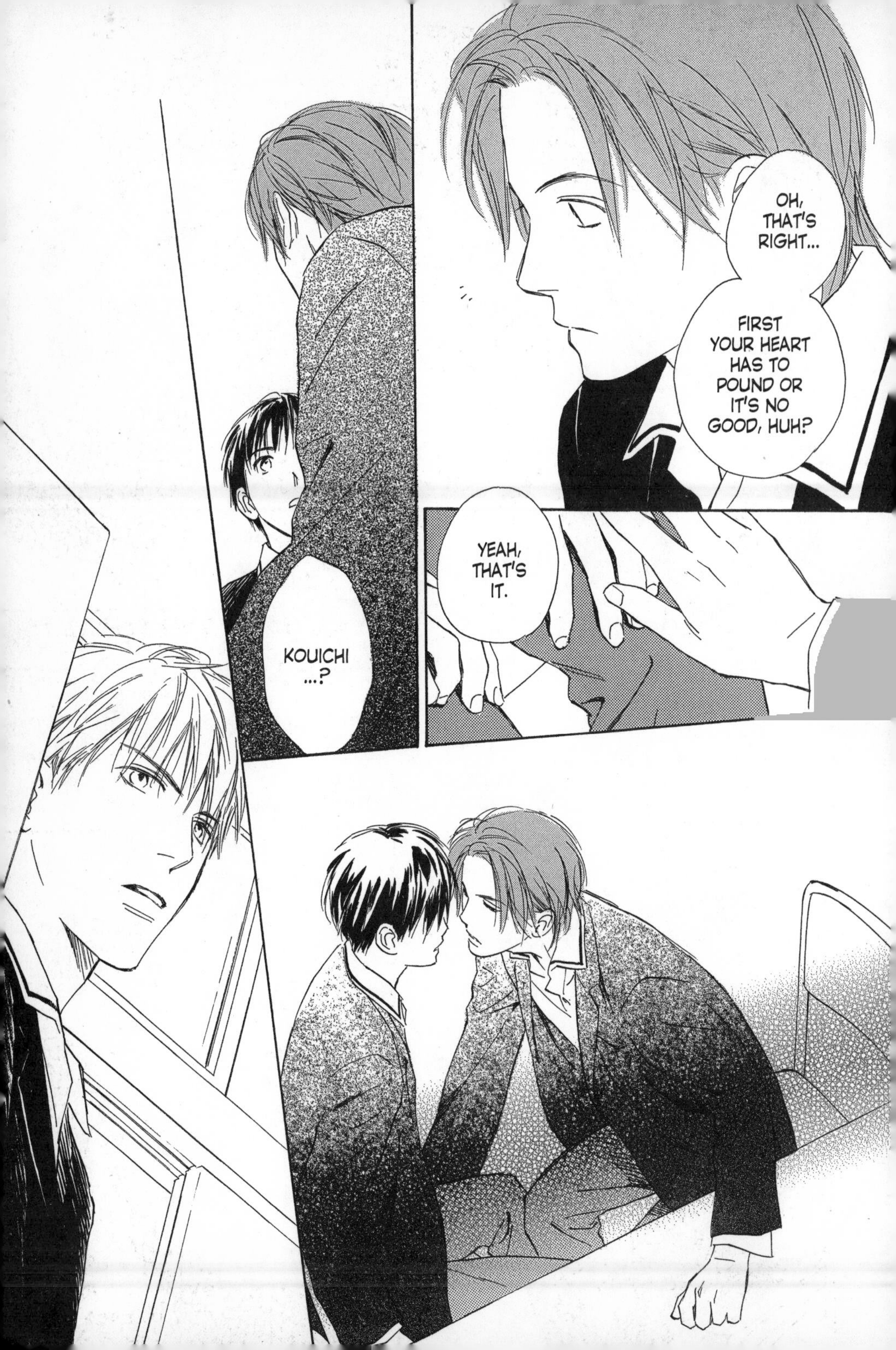
OH, THAT'S RIGHT...
FIRST YOUR HEART HAS TO POUND OR IT'S NO GOOD, HUH?
YEAH, THAT'S IT.
KOUICHI ...?

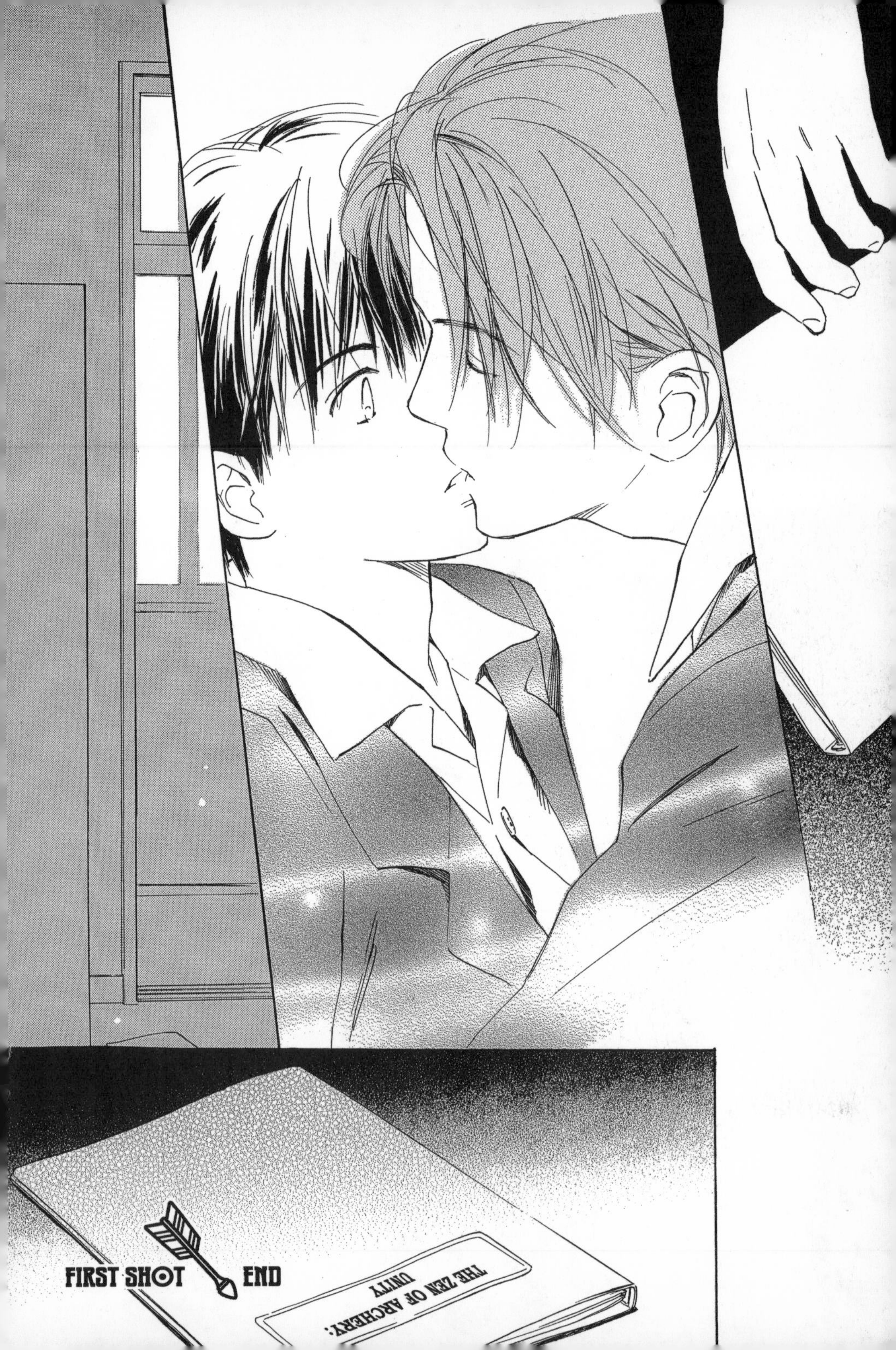
THE ZEN OF ARCHERY:
UNITY
FIRST SHOT END

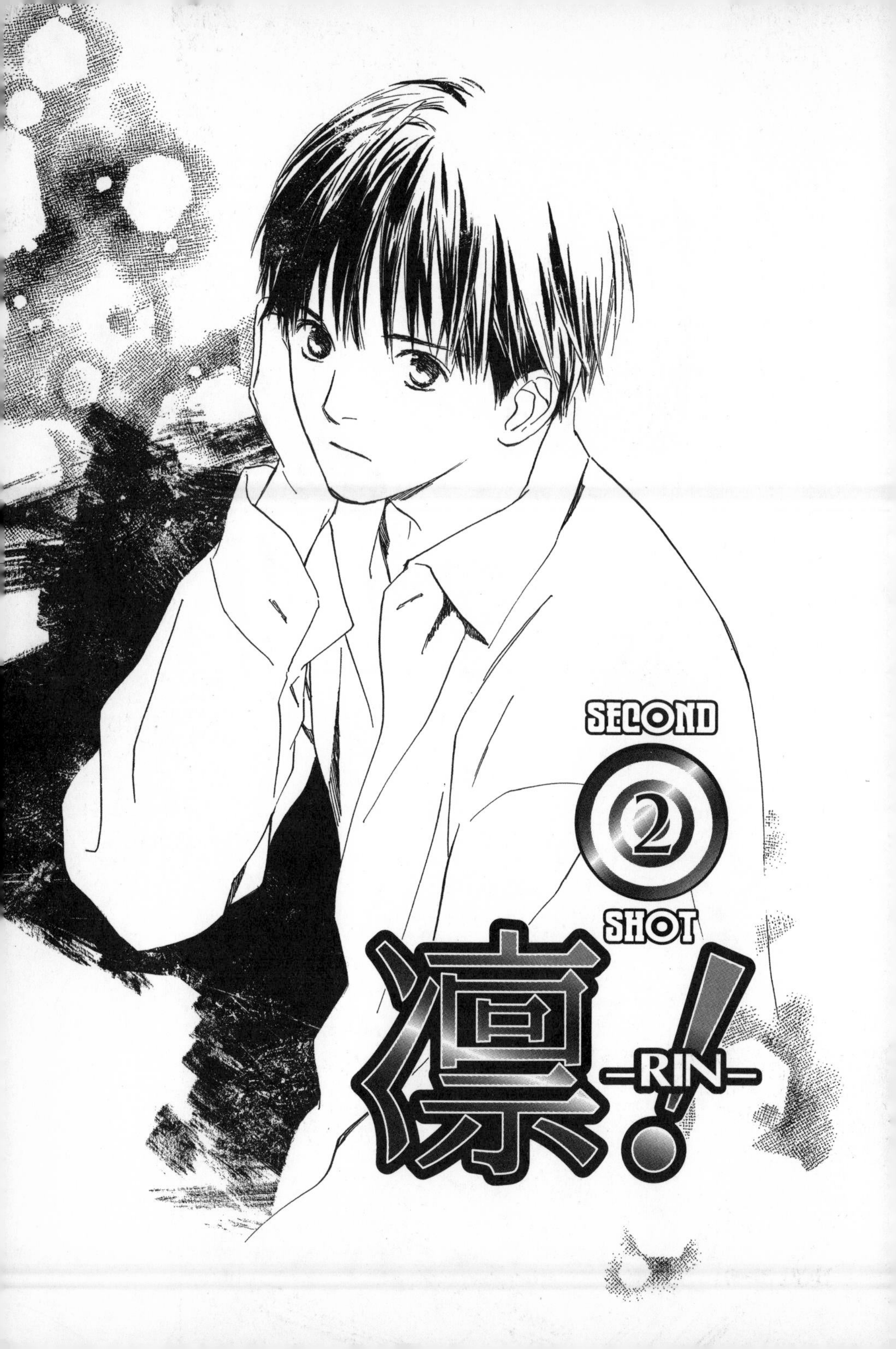
SECOND
2
SHOT
凛!
-RIN-

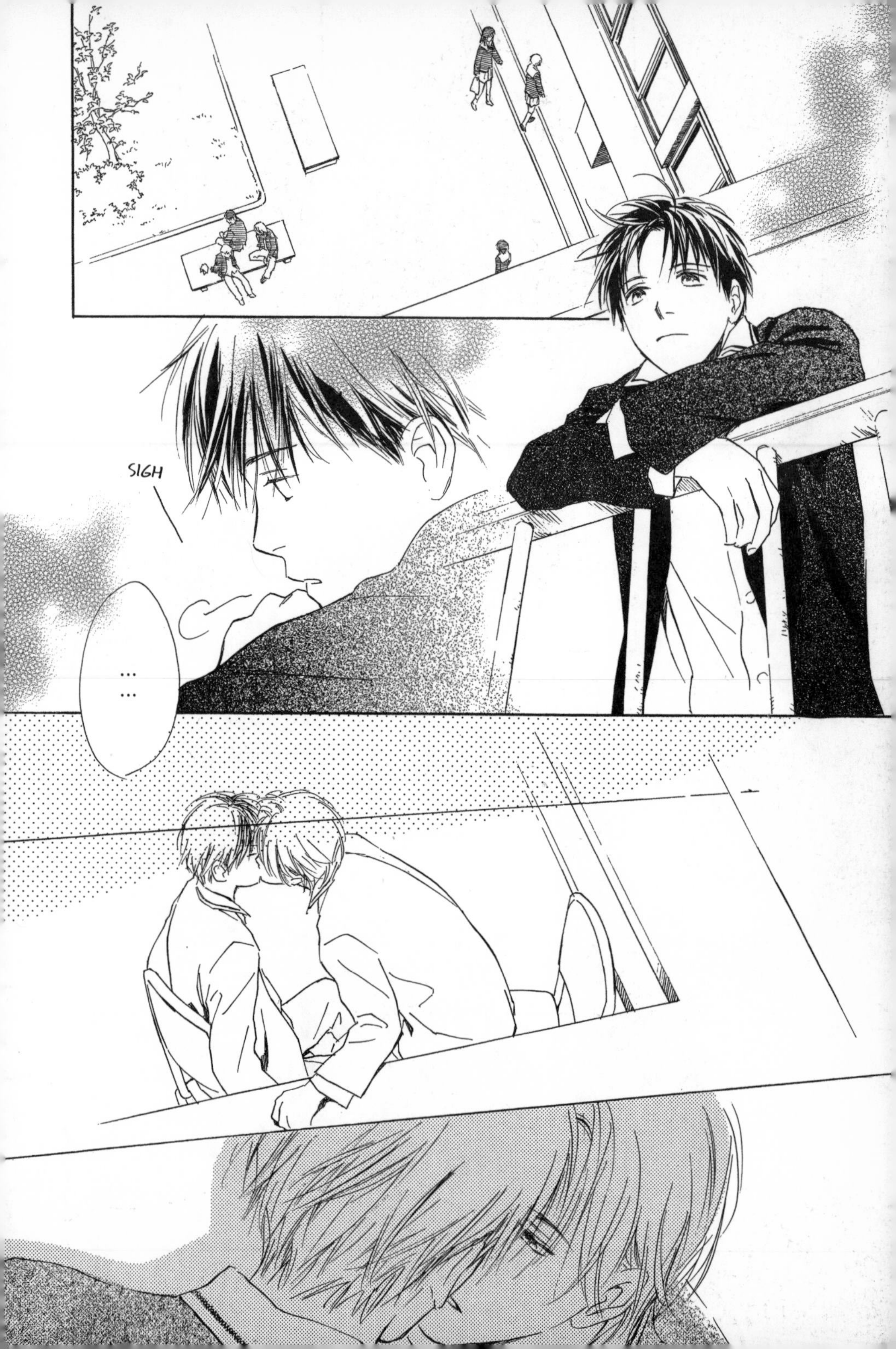
SIGH
......

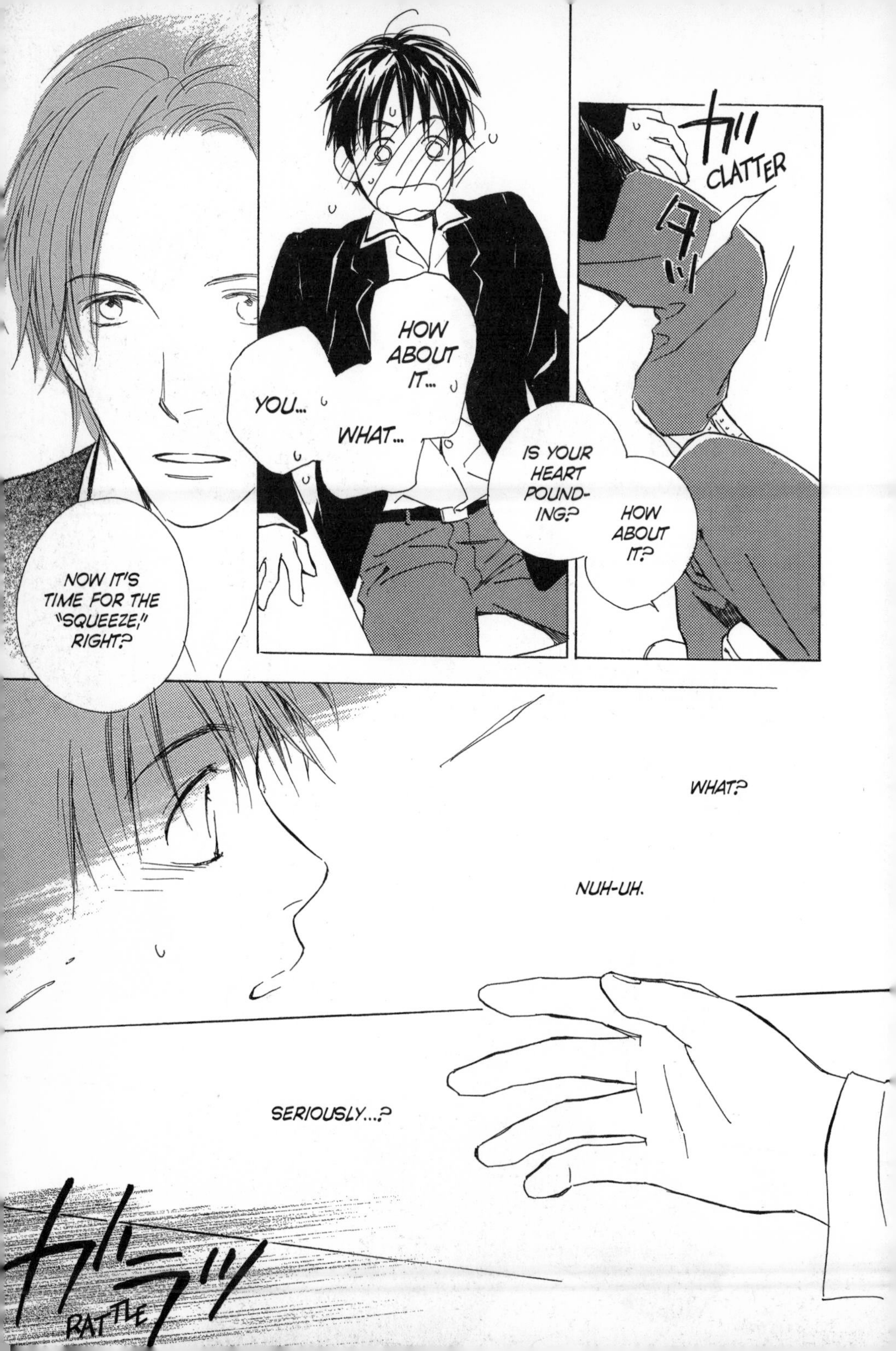
CLATTER
IS YOUR HEART POUNDING?
HOW ABOUT IT?
HOW ABOUT IT...
YOU...
WHAT...
NOW IT'S TIME FOR THE "SQUEEZE," RIGHT?
WHAT?
NUH-UH.
SERIOUSLY...?
RATTLE

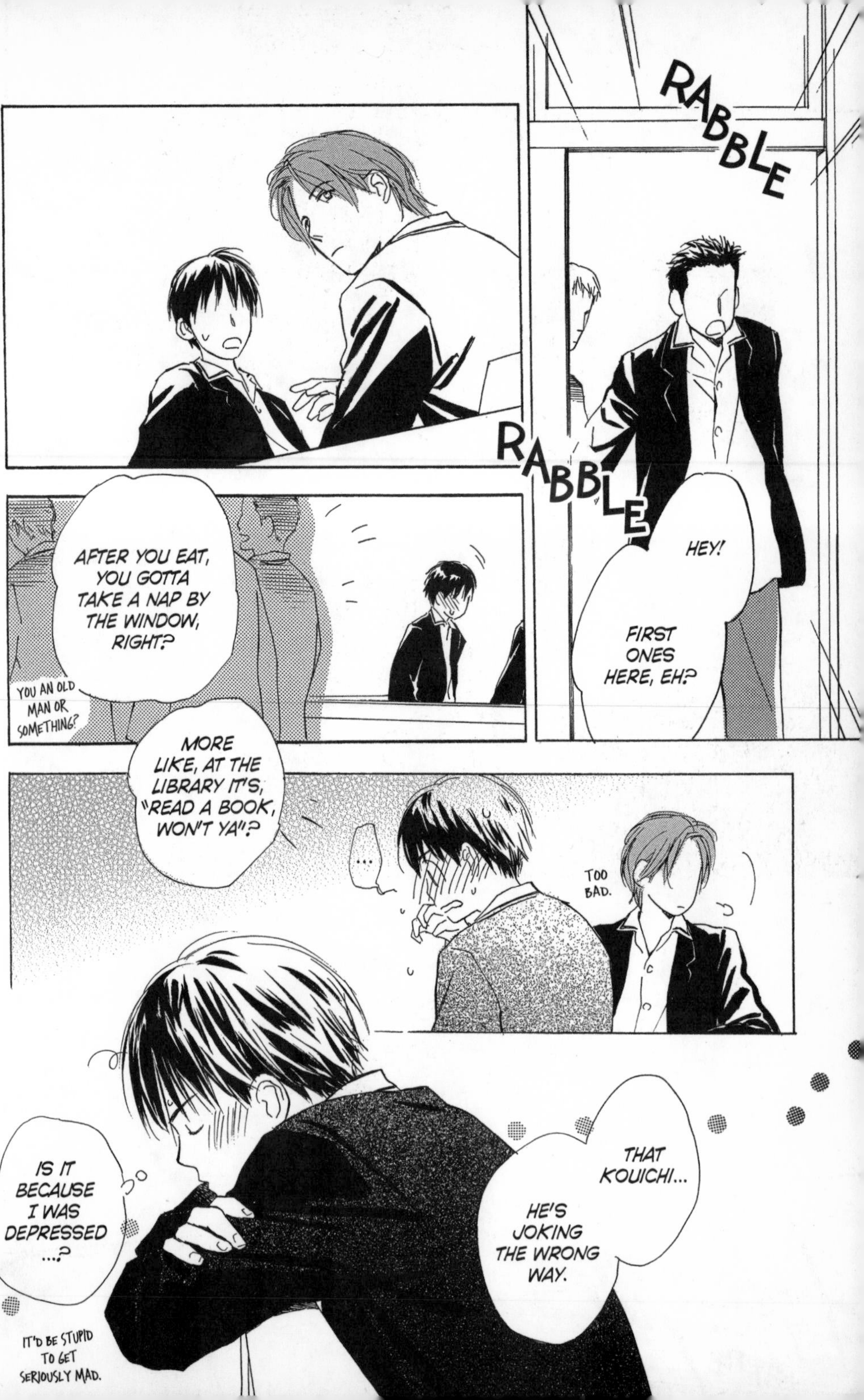
RABBLE
RABBLE
HEY!
FIRST ONES HERE, EH?
AFTER YOU EAT, YOU GOTTA TAKE A NAP BY THE WINDOW, RIGHT?
YOU AN OLD MAN OR SOMETHING?
MORE LIKE, AT THE LIBRARY IT'S, "READ A BOOK, WON'T YA"?
...
TOO BAD.
THAT KOUICHI...
HE'S JOKING THE WRONG WAY.
IS IT BECAUSE I WAS DEPRESSED ...?
IT'D BE STUPID TO GET SERIOUSLY MAD.

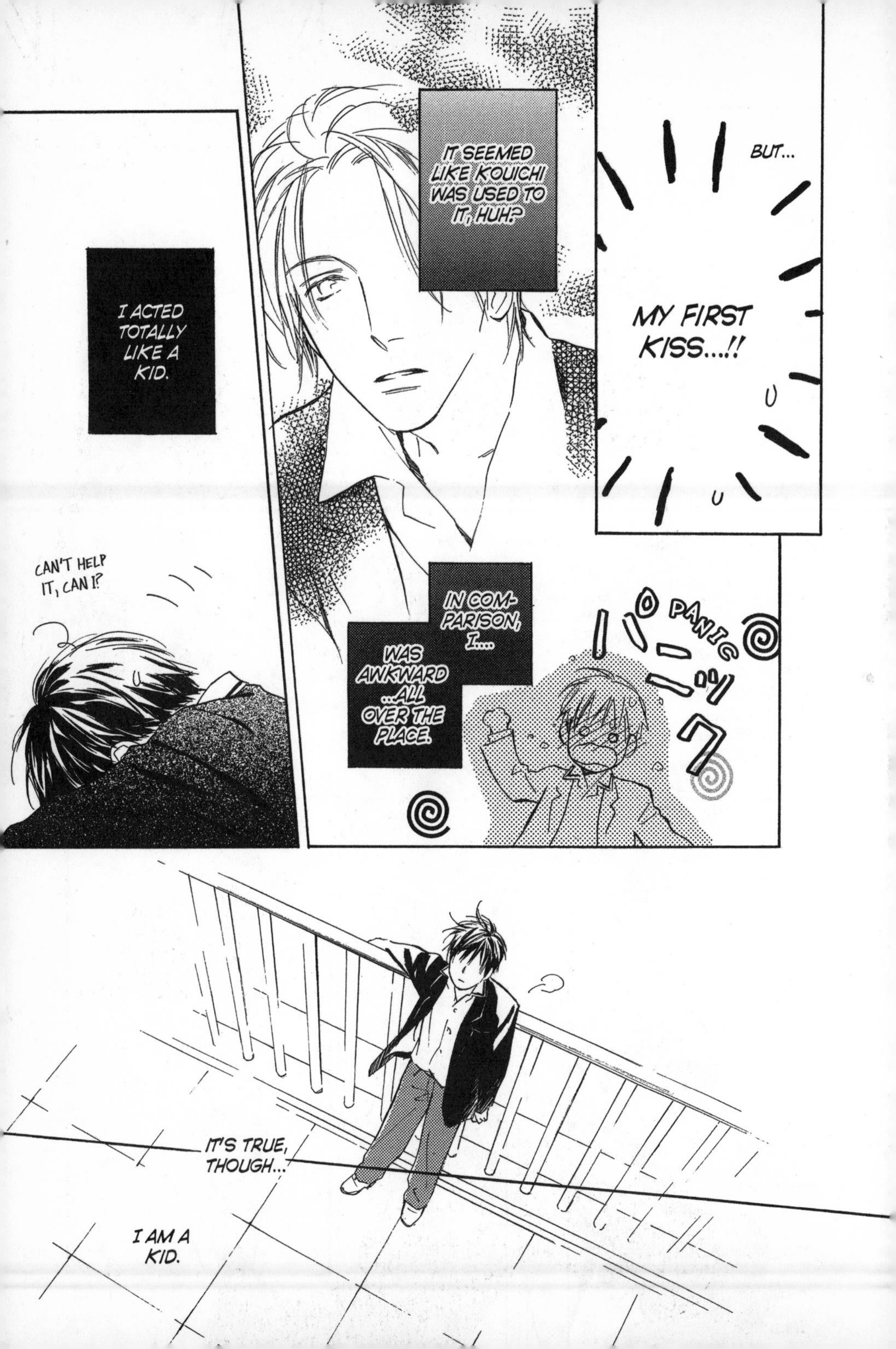
BUT...
MY FIRST KISS...!!
IT SEEMED LIKE KOUICHI WAS USED TO IT, HUH?
I ACTED TOTALLY LIKE A KID.
PANIC
IN COMPARISON, I...
WAS AWKWARD ...ALL OVER THE PLACE.
CAN'T HELP IT, CAN I?
IT'S TRUE, THOUGH...
I AM A KID.

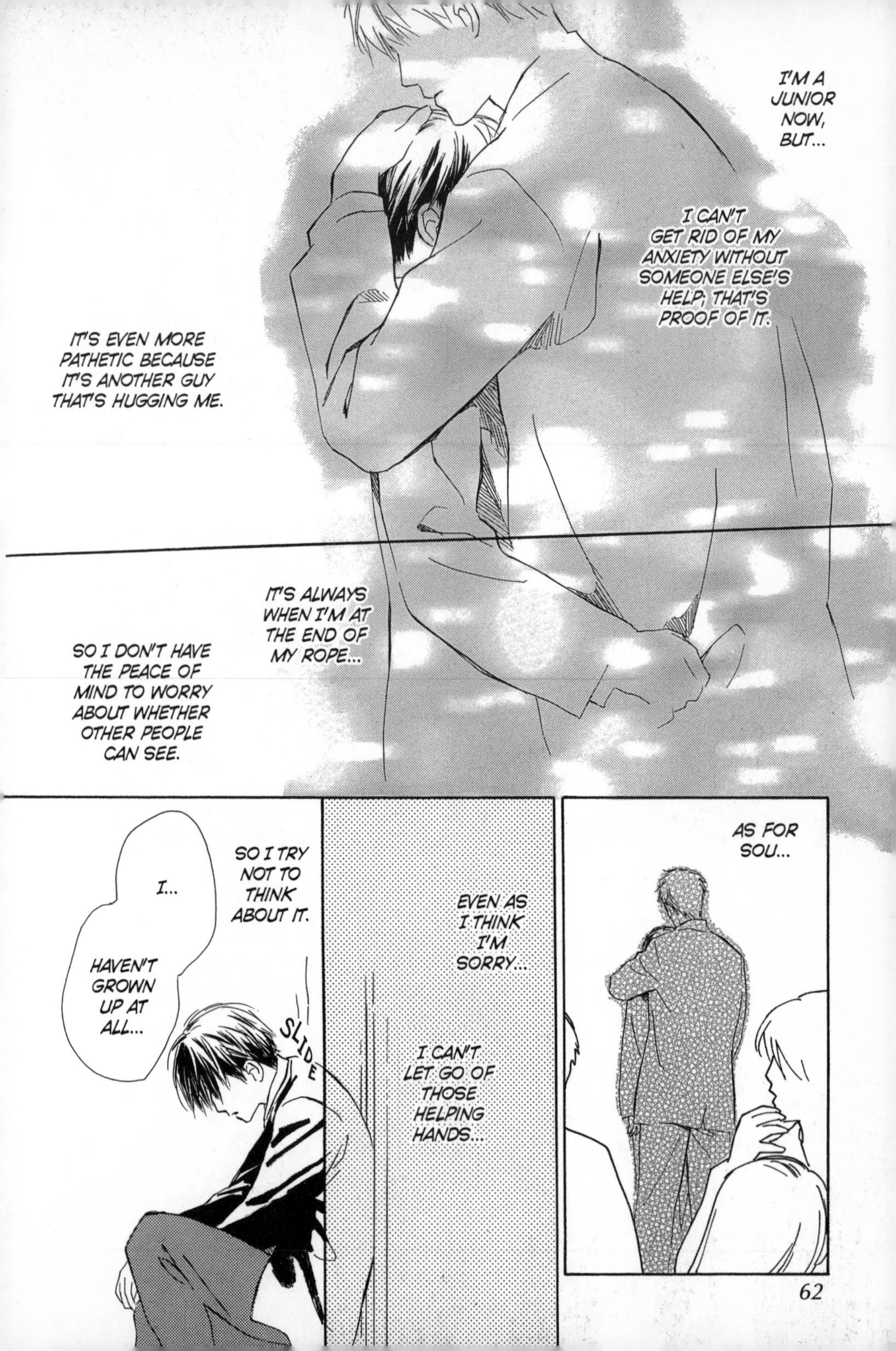
I'M A JUNIOR NOW, BUT...
I CAN'T GET RID OF MY ANXIETY WITHOUT SOMEONE ELSE'S HELP; THAT'S PROOF OF IT.
IT'S EVEN MORE PATHETIC BECAUSE IT'S ANOTHER GUY THAT'S HUGGING ME.
IT'S ALWAYS WHEN I'M AT THE END OF MY ROPE...
SO I DON'T HAVE THE PEACE OF MIND TO WORRY ABOUT WHETHER OTHER PEOPLE CAN SEE.
AS FOR SOU...
EVEN AS I THINK I'M SORRY...
I CAN'T LET GO OF THOSE HELPING HANDS...
SO I TRY NOT TO THINK ABOUT IT.
SLIDE
I...
HAVEN'T GROWN UP AT ALL...

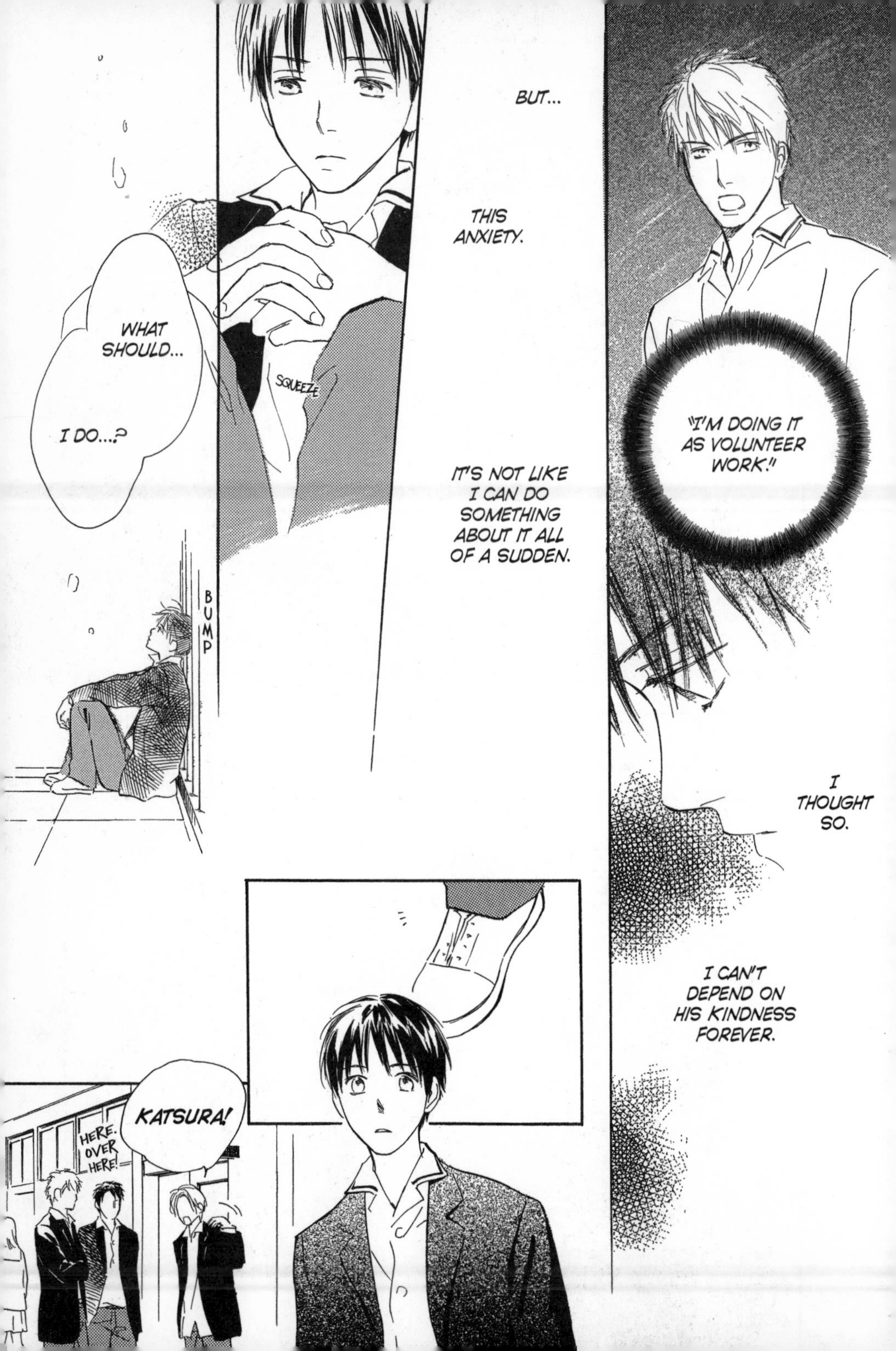
"I'M DOING IT AS VOLUNTEER WORK."
I THOUGHT SO.
I CAN'T DEPEND ON HIS KINDNESS FOREVER.
BUT...
THIS ANXIETY.
IT'S NOT LIKE I CAN DO SOMETHING ABOUT IT ALL OF A SUDDEN.
SQUEEZE
WHAT SHOULD...
I DO...?
BUMP
KATSURA!
HERE. OVER HERE!

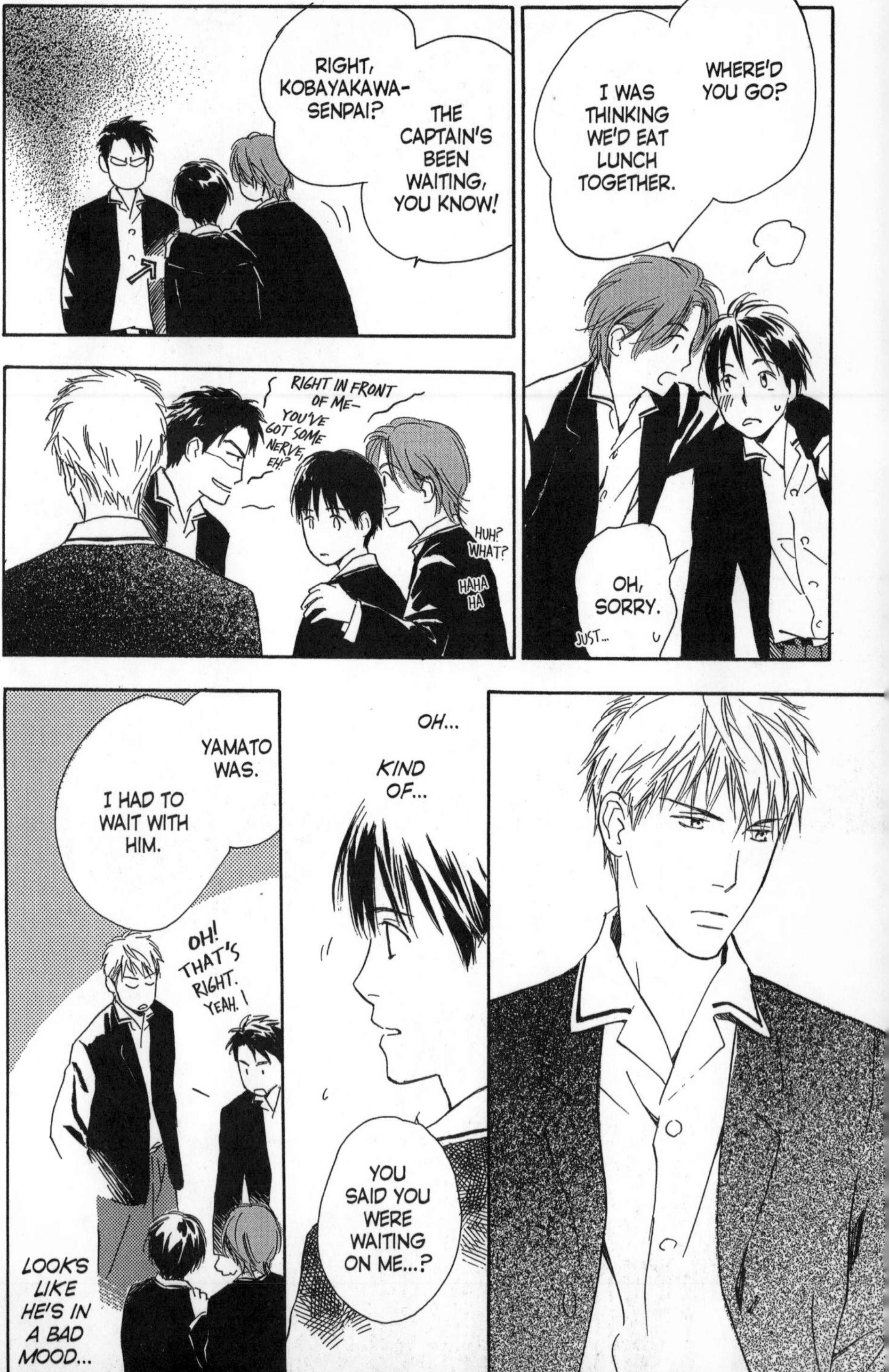
WHERE'D YOU GO?
I WAS THINKING WE'D EAT LUNCH TOGETHER.
OH, SORRY.
JUST...
RIGHT, KOBAYAKAWA-SENPAI?
THE CAPTAIN'S BEEN WAITING, YOU KNOW!
RIGHT IN FRONT OF ME-
YOU'VE GOT SOME NERVE, EH?
HUH? WHAT?
HAHA HA
OH...
KIND OF...
YOU SAID YOU WERE WAITING ON ME...?
YAMATO WAS.
I HAD TO WAIT WITH HIM.
OH! THAT'S RIGHT. YEAH.
LOOKS LIKE HE'S IN A BAD MOOD...

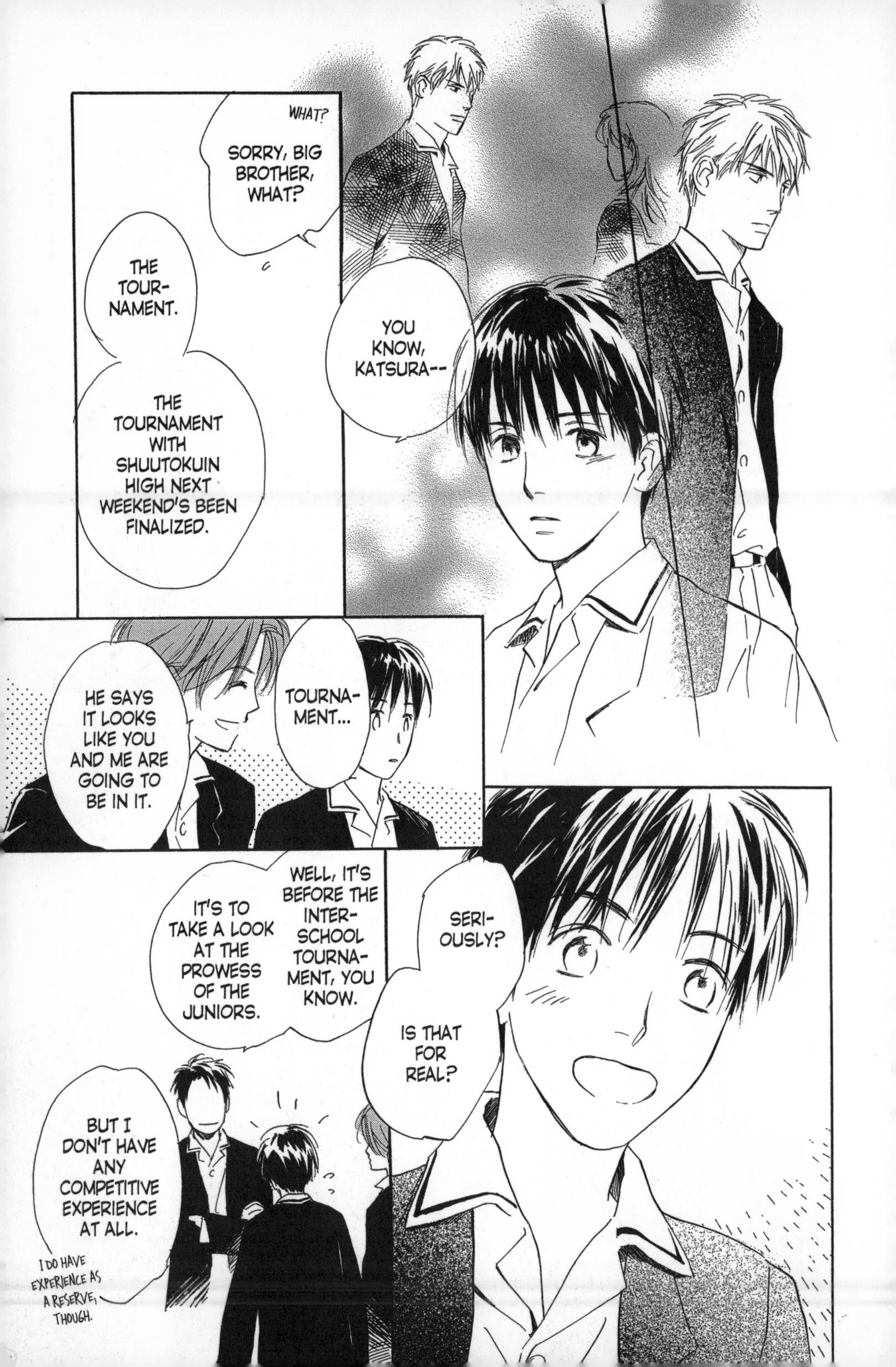
YOU KNOW, KATSURA--
WHAT?
SORRY, BIG BROTHER, WHAT?
THE TOURNAMENT.
THE TOURNAMENT WITH SHUUTOKUIN HIGH NEXT WEEKEND'S BEEN FINALIZED.
TOURNAMENT...
HE SAYS IT LOOKS LIKE YOU AND ME ARE GOING TO BE IN IT.
SERIOUSLY?
IS THAT FOR REAL?
WELL, IT'S BEFORE THE INTER-SCHOOL TOURNAMENT, YOU KNOW.
IT'S TO TAKE A LOOK AT THE PROWESS OF THE JUNIORS.
BUT I DON'T HAVE ANY COMPETITIVE EXPERIENCE AT ALL.
I DO HAVE EXPERIENCE AS A RESERVE, THOUGH.

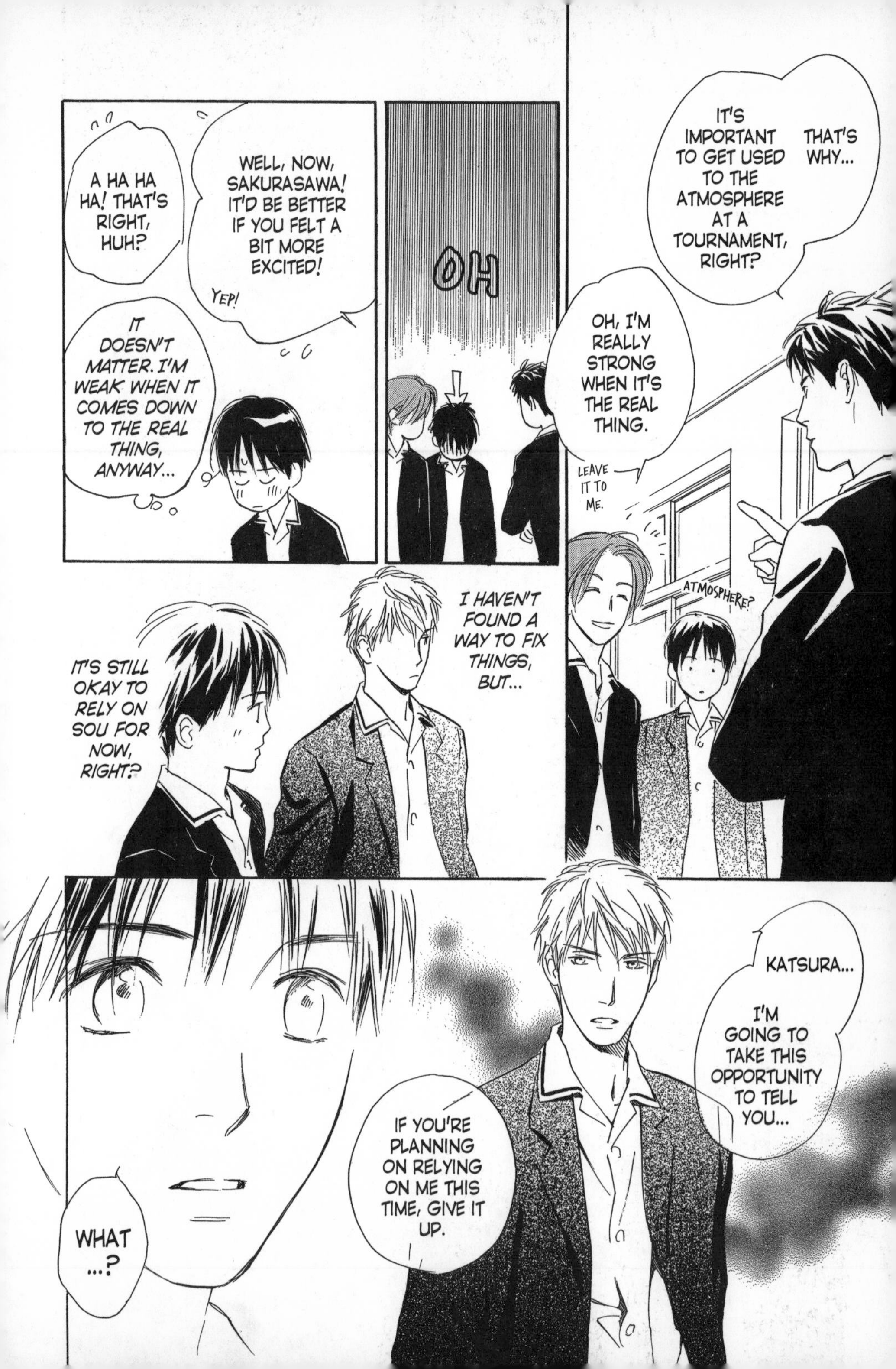
THAT'S WHY...
IT'S IMPORTANT TO GET USED TO THE ATMOSPHERE AT A TOURNAMENT, RIGHT?
OH, I'M REALLY STRONG WHEN IT'S THE REAL THING.
LEAVE IT TO ME.
ATMOSPHERE?
OH
WELL, NOW, SAKURASAWA! IT'D BE BETTER IF YOU FELT A BIT MORE EXCITED!
A HA HA HA! THAT'S RIGHT, HUH?
YEP!
IT DOESN'T MATTER. I'M WEAK WHEN IT COMES DOWN TO THE REAL THING, ANYWAY...
I HAVEN'T FOUND A WAY TO FIX THINGS, BUT...
IT'S STILL OKAY TO RELY ON SOU FOR NOW, RIGHT?
KATSURA...
I'M GOING TO TAKE THIS OPPORTUNITY TO TELL YOU...
IF YOU'RE PLANNING ON RELYING ON ME THIS TIME, GIVE IT UP.
WHAT ...?

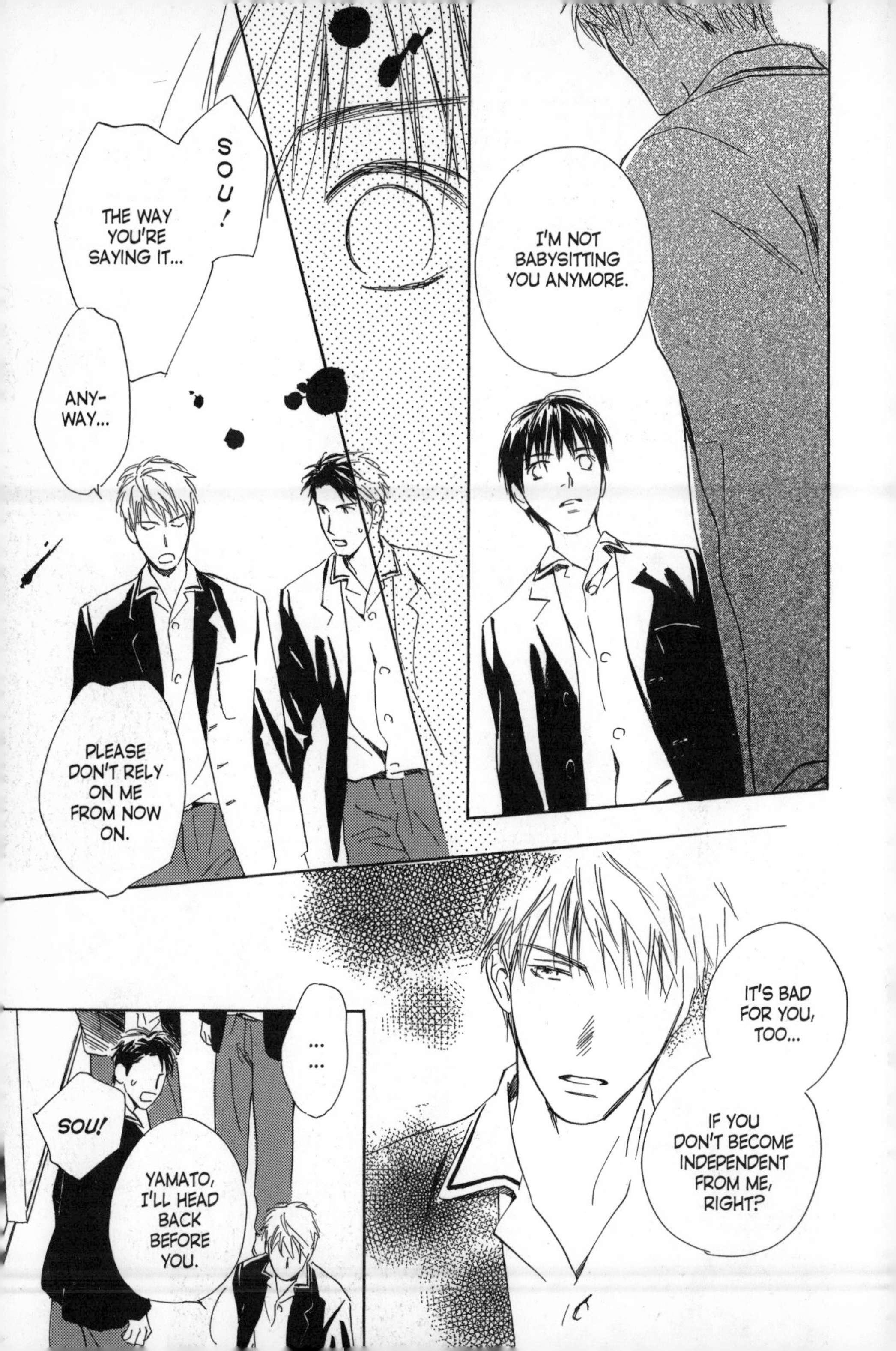
I'M NOT BABYSITTING YOU ANYMORE.
SOU!
THE WAY YOU'RE SAYING IT...
ANY-WAY...
PLEASE DON'T RELY ON ME FROM NOW ON.
IT'S BAD FOR YOU, TOO...
IF YOU DON'T BECOME INDEPENDENT FROM ME, RIGHT?
......
SOU!
YAMATO, I'LL HEAD BACK BEFORE YOU.

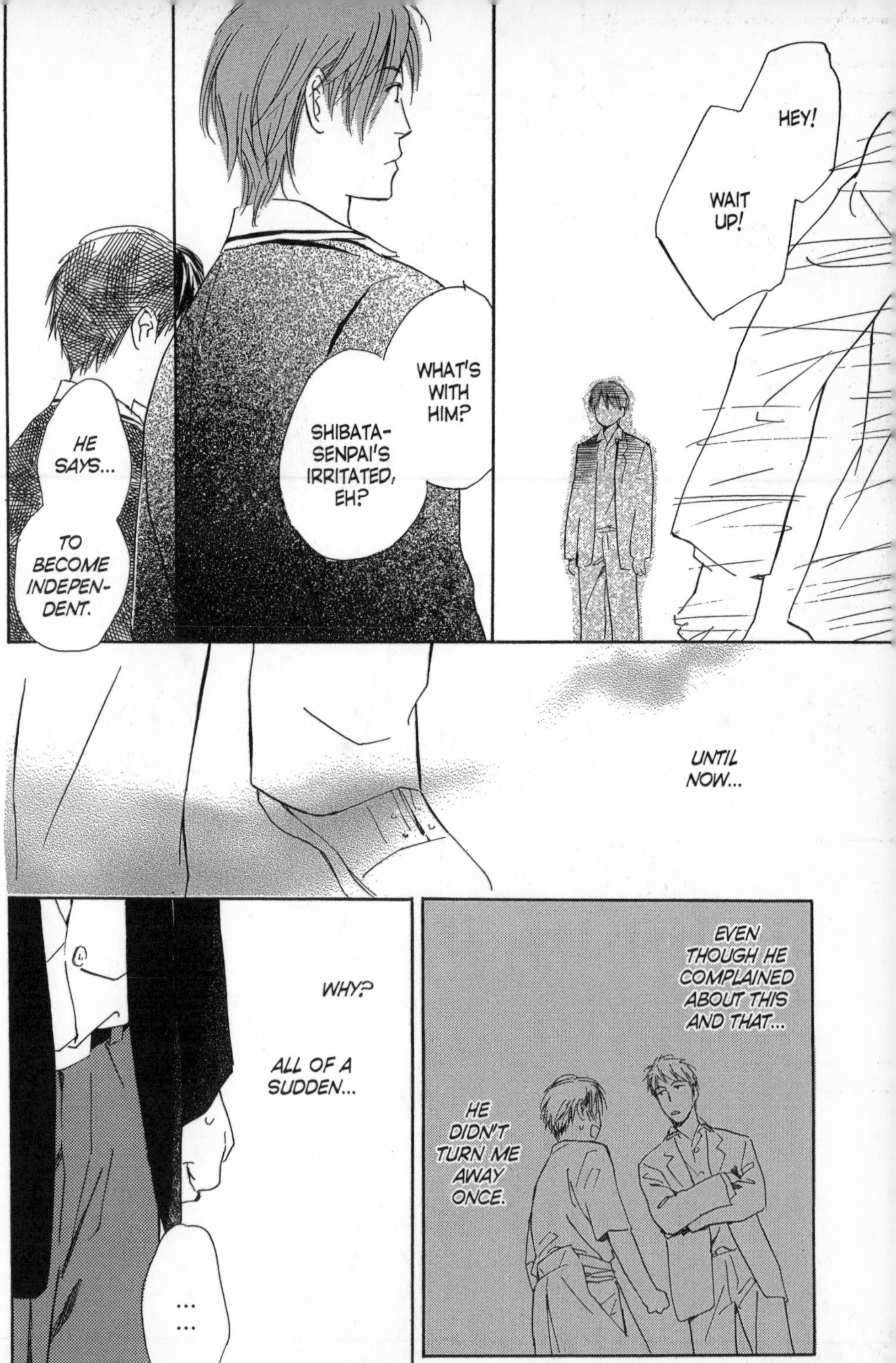
HEY!
WAIT UP!
WHAT'S WITH HIM?
SHIBATA-SENPAI'S IRRITATED, EH?
HE SAYS...
TO BECOME INDEPENDENT.
UNTIL NOW...
EVEN THOUGH HE COMPLAINED ABOUT THIS AND THAT...
HE DIDN'T TURN ME AWAY ONCE.
WHY?
ALL OF A SUDDEN...
......

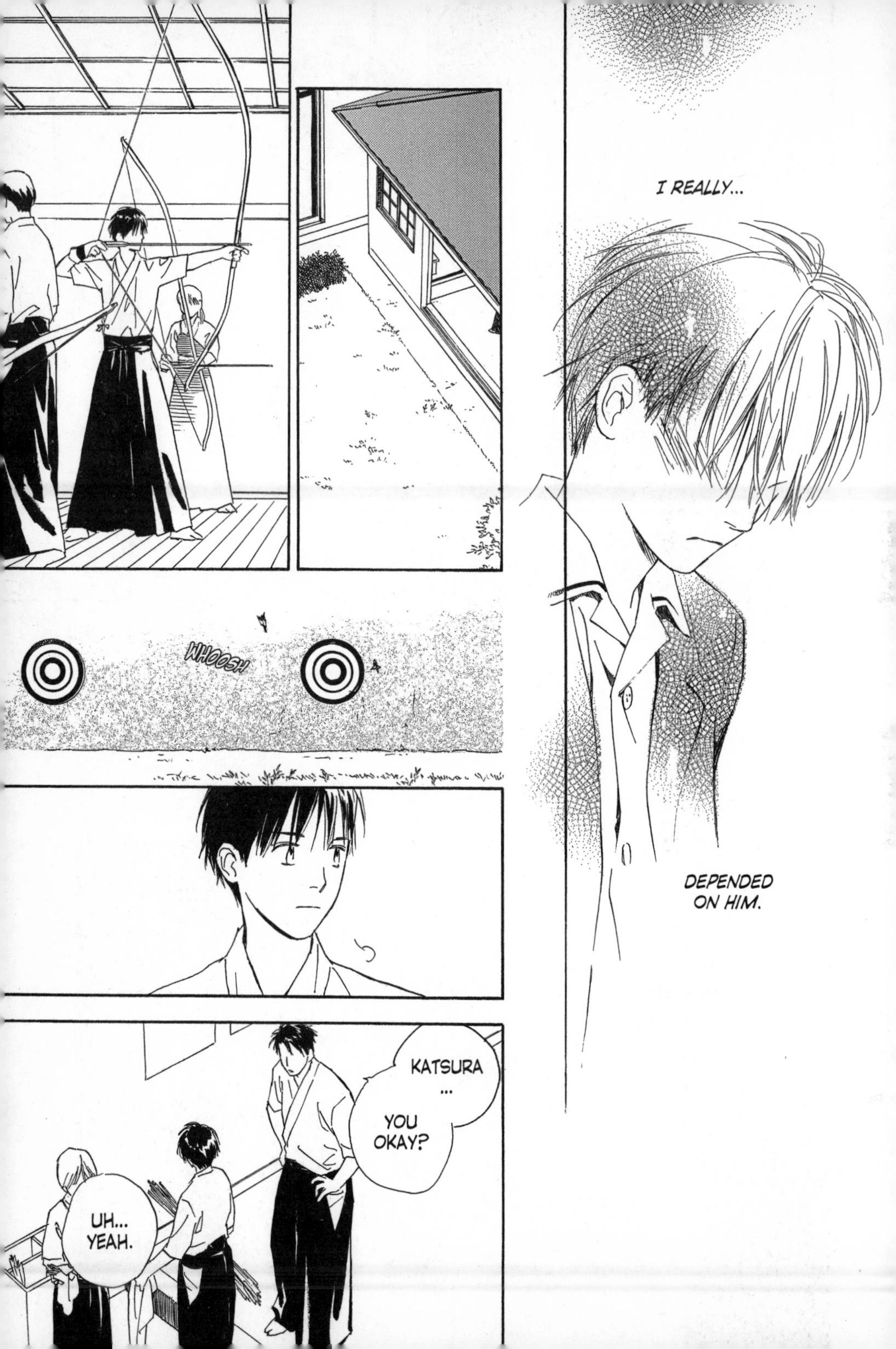
I REALLY...
DEPENDED ON HIM.
WHOOSH
KATSURA ...
YOU OKAY?
UH... YEAH.

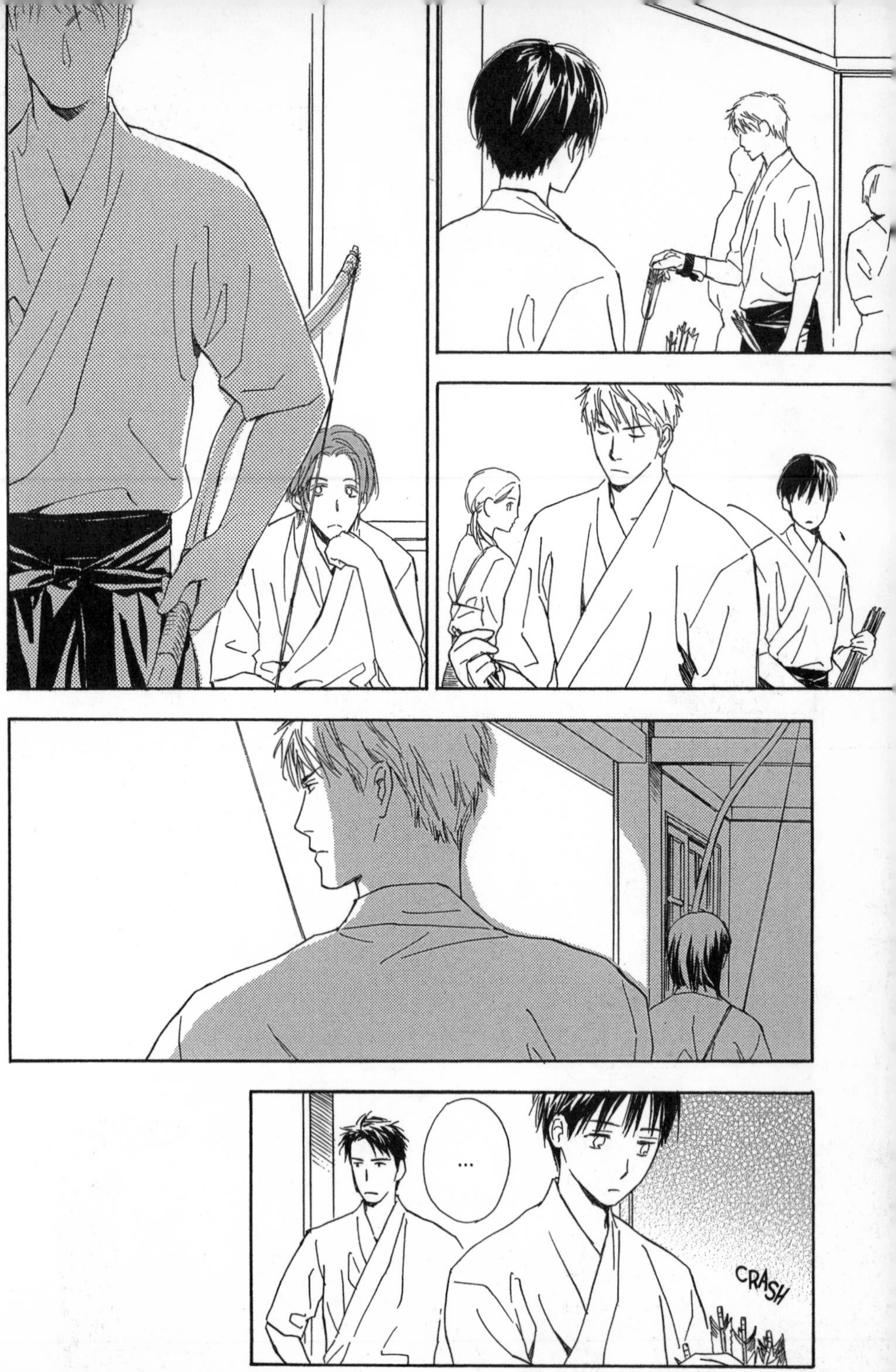
...
CRASH

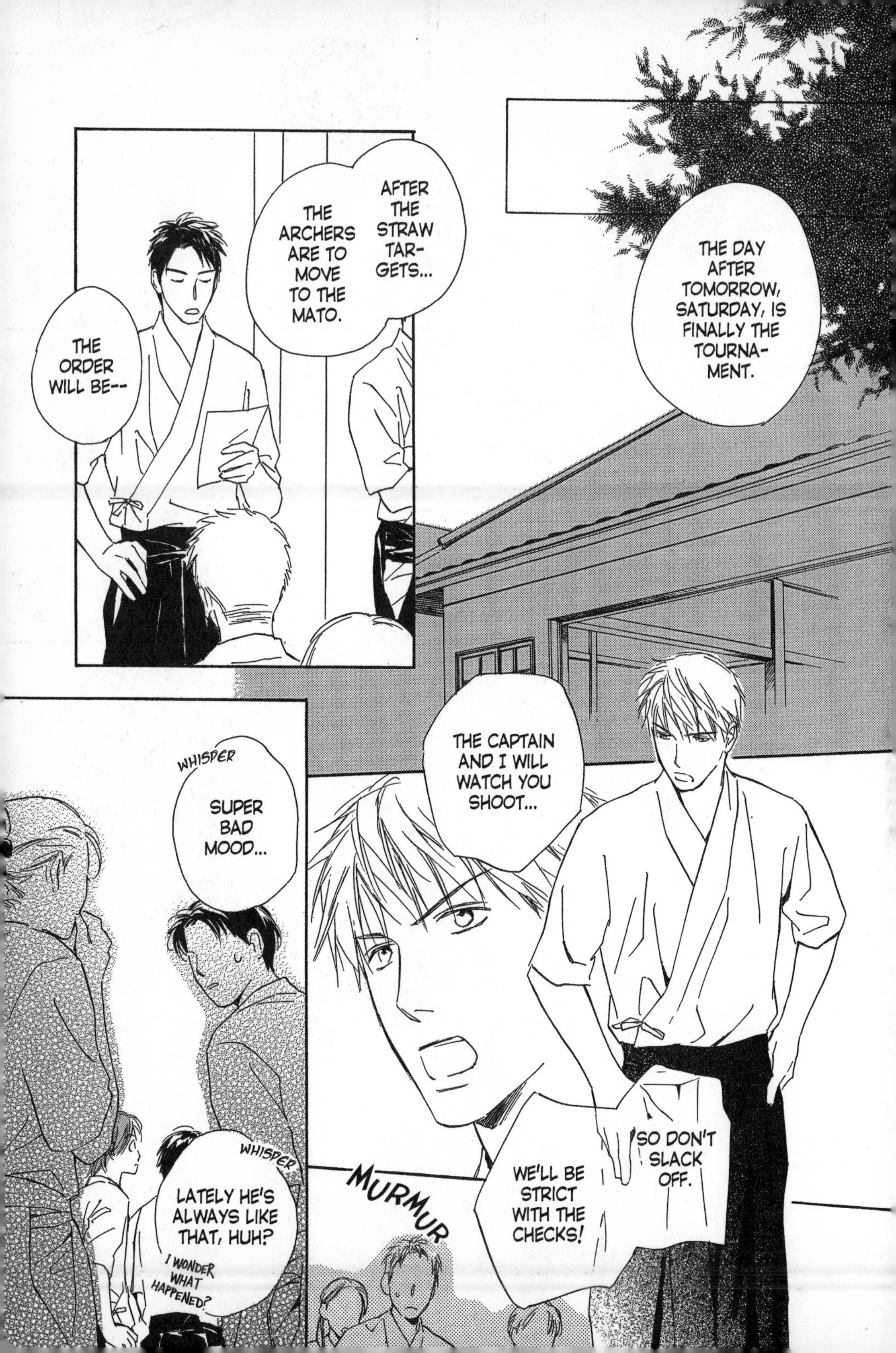
THE DAY AFTER TOMORROW, SATURDAY, IS FINALLY THE TOURNA-MENT.
AFTER THE STRAW TAR-GETS...
THE ARCHERS ARE TO MOVE TO THE MATO.
THE ORDER WILL BE--
THE CAPTAIN AND I WILL WATCH YOU SHOOT...
SO DON'T SLACK OFF.
WE'LL BE STRICT WITH THE CHECKS!
MURMUR
WHISPER
SUPER BAD MOOD...
WHISPER
LATELY HE'S ALWAYS LIKE THAT, HUH?
I WONDER WHAT HAPPENED?

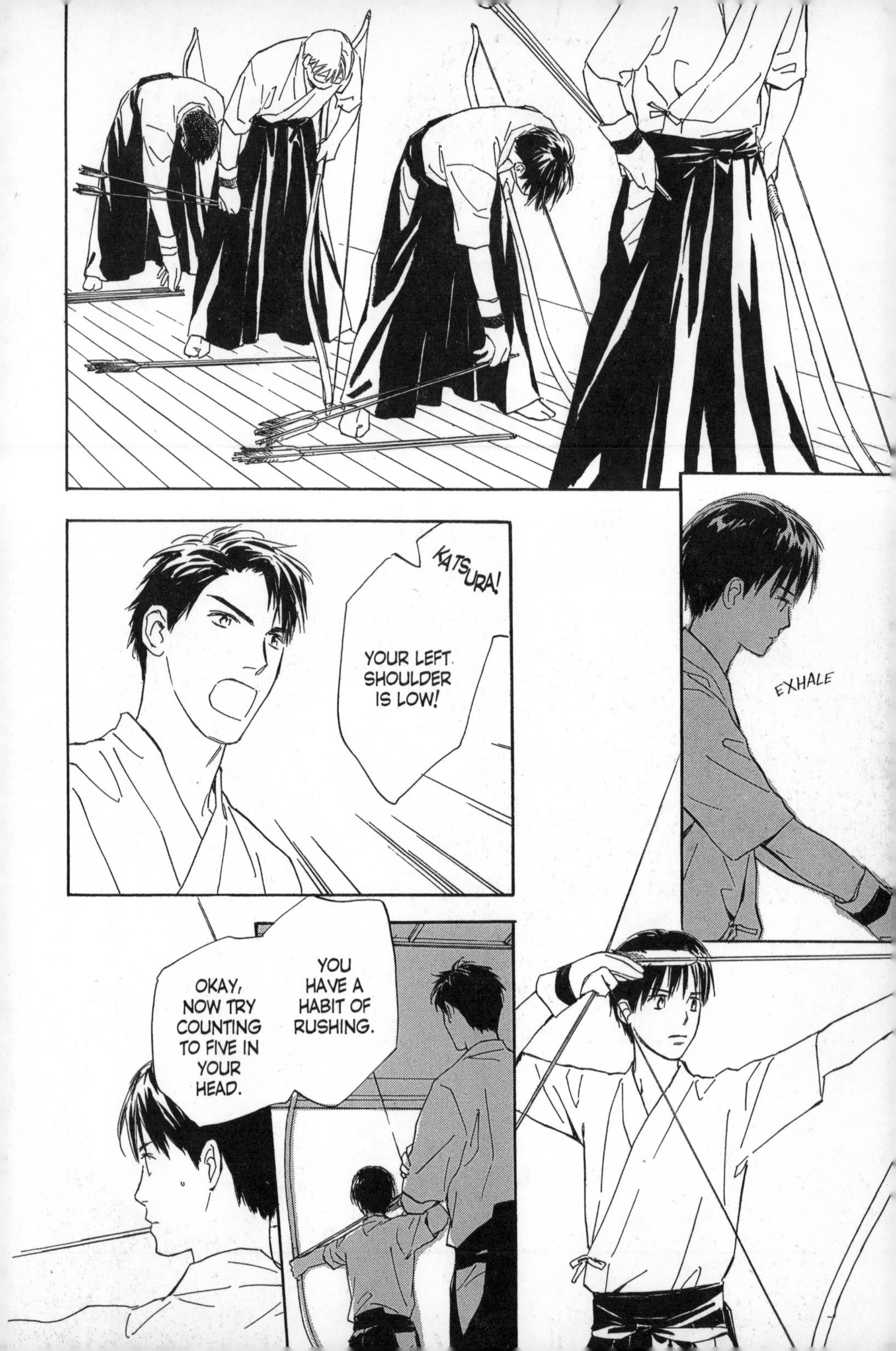
EXHALE
KATSURA!
YOUR LEFT SHOULDER IS LOW!
YOU HAVE A HABIT OF RUSHING.
OKAY, NOW TRY COUNTING TO FIVE IN YOUR HEAD.

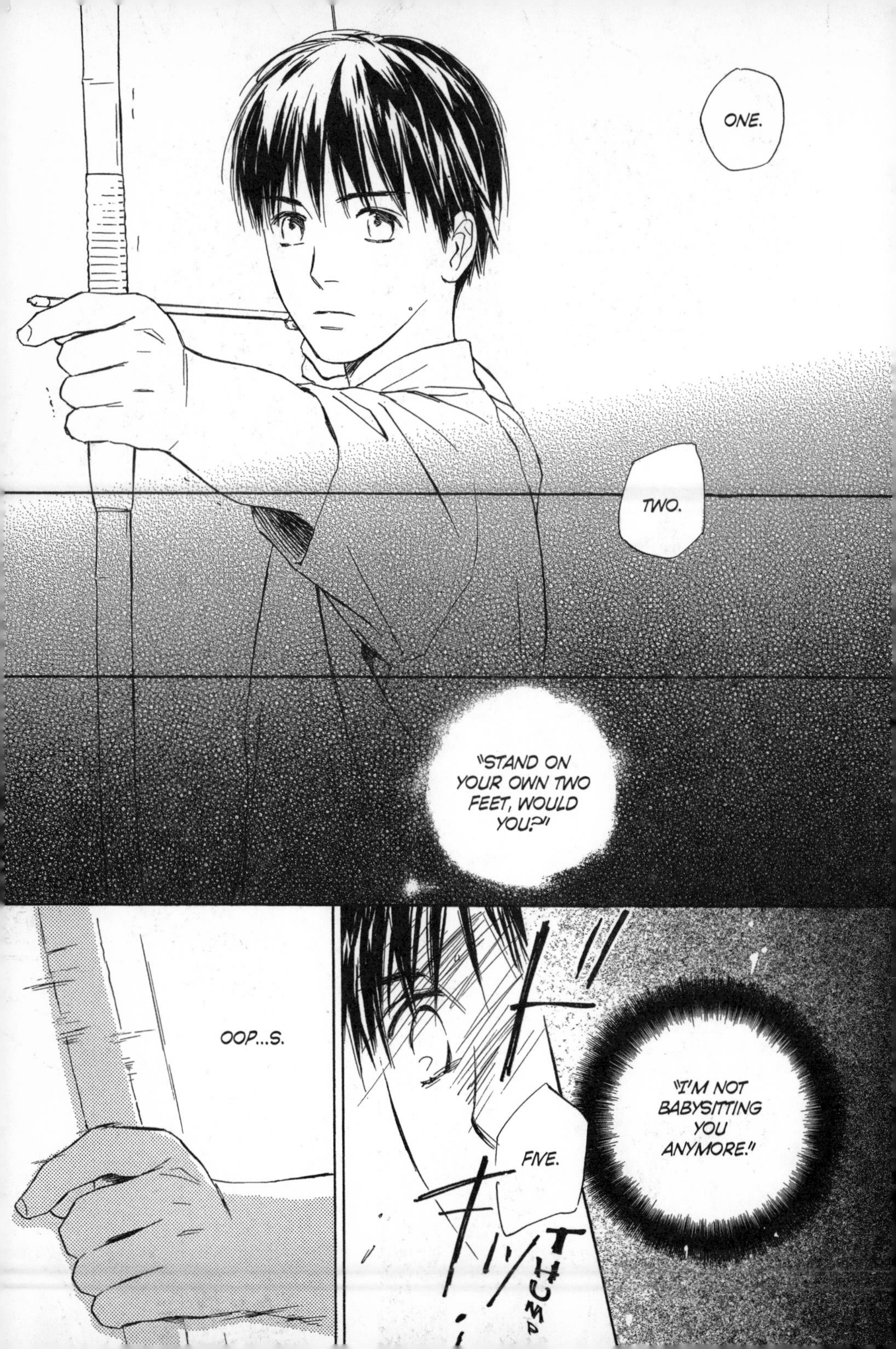
ONE.
TWO.
"STAND ON YOUR OWN TWO FEET, WOULD YOU?"
"I'M NOT BABYSITTING YOU ANYMORE."
FIVE.
THUMP
OOP...S.

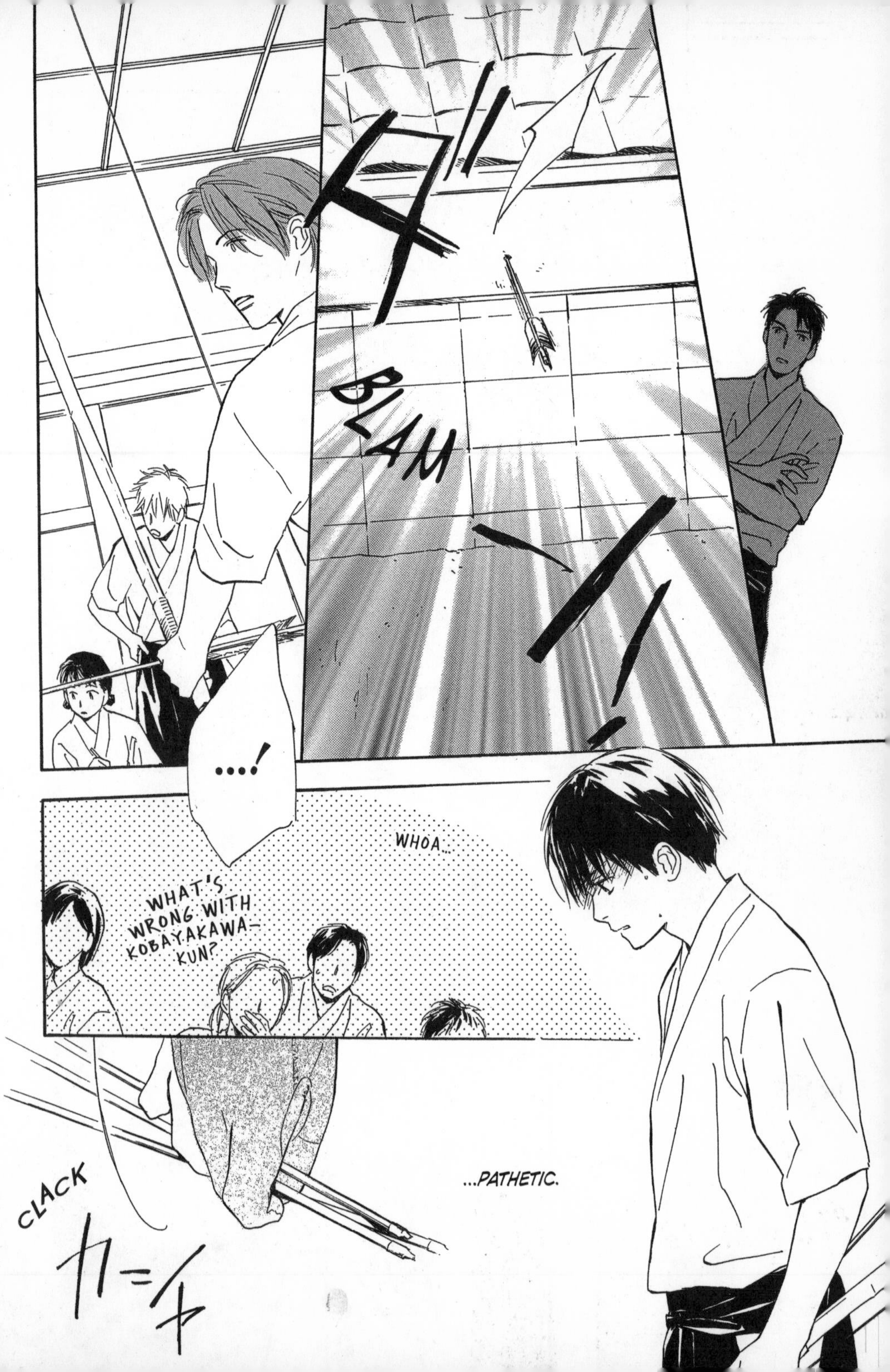
BLAM
...!
WHOA...
WHAT'S WRONG WITH KOBAYAKAWA-KUN?
...PATHETIC.
CLACK

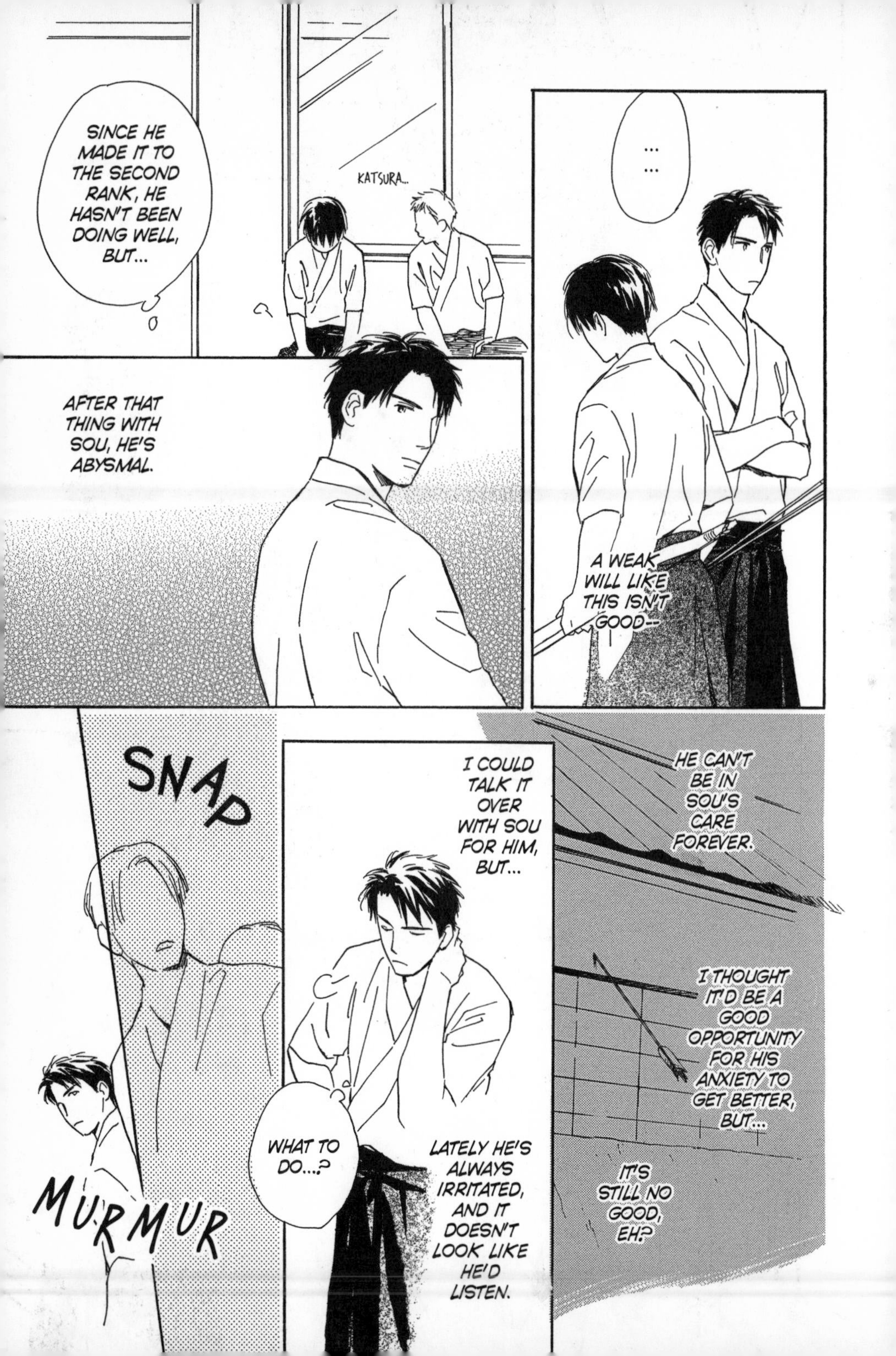
......
KATSURA...
SINCE HE MADE IT TO THE SECOND RANK, HE HASN'T BEEN DOING WELL, BUT...
A WEAK WILL LIKE THIS ISN'T GOOD--
AFTER THAT THING WITH SOU, HE'S ABYSMAL.
HE CAN'T BE IN SOU'S CARE FOREVER.
I THOUGHT IT'D BE A GOOD OPPORTUNITY FOR HIS ANXIETY TO GET BETTER, BUT...
IT'S STILL NO GOOD, EH?
I COULD TALK IT OVER WITH SOU FOR HIM, BUT...
LATELY HE'S ALWAYS IRRITATED, AND IT DOESN'T LOOK LIKE HE'D LISTEN.
WHAT TO DO...?
SNAP
MURMUR

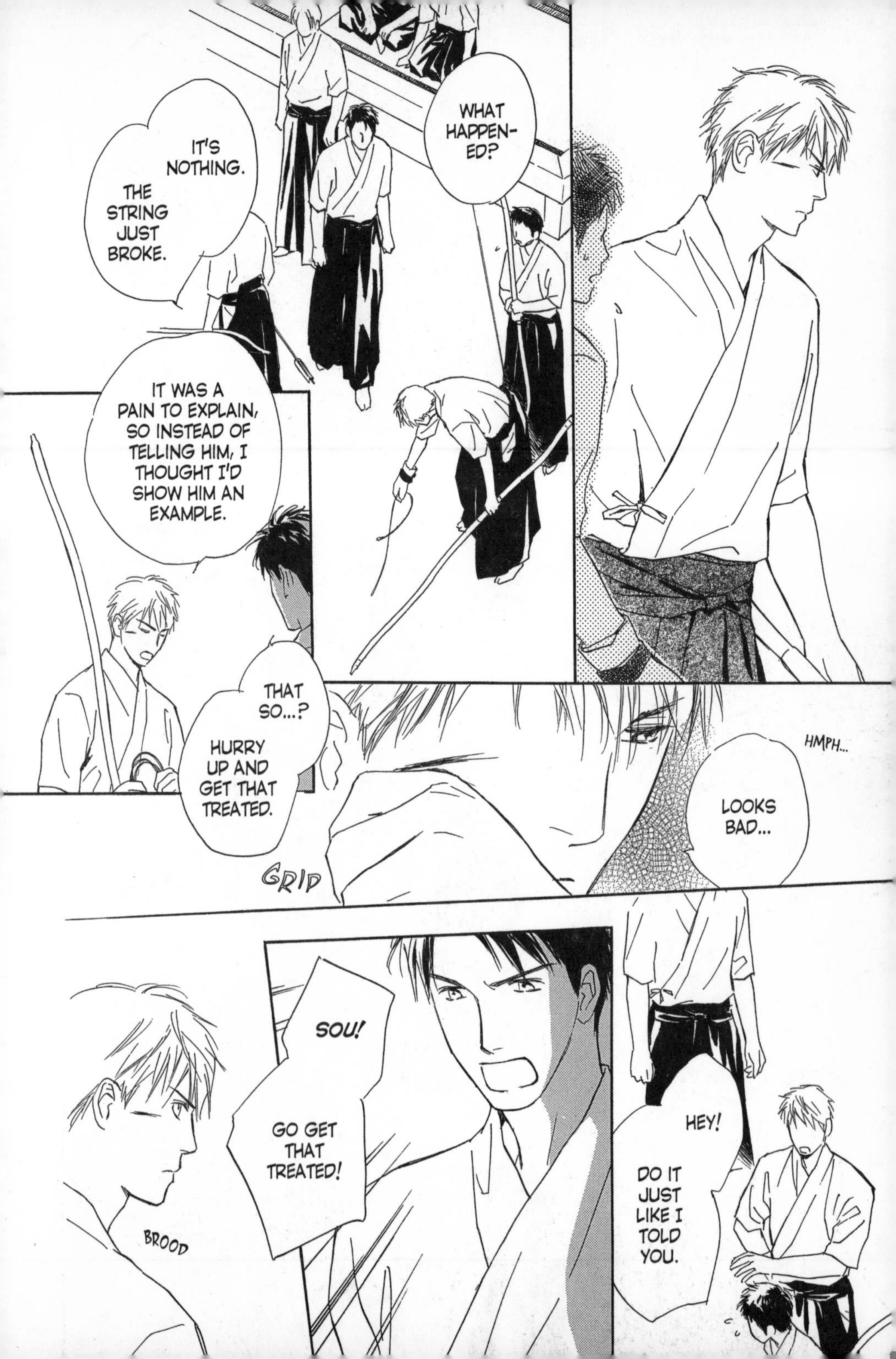
WHAT HAPPEN-ED?
IT'S NOTHING.
THE STRING JUST BROKE.
IT WAS A PAIN TO EXPLAIN, SO INSTEAD OF TELLING HIM, I THOUGHT I'D SHOW HIM AN EXAMPLE.
THAT SO...?
HURRY UP AND GET THAT TREATED.
HMPH...
LOOKS BAD...
GRIP
HEY!
DO IT JUST LIKE I TOLD YOU.
SOU!
GO GET THAT TREATED!
BROOD

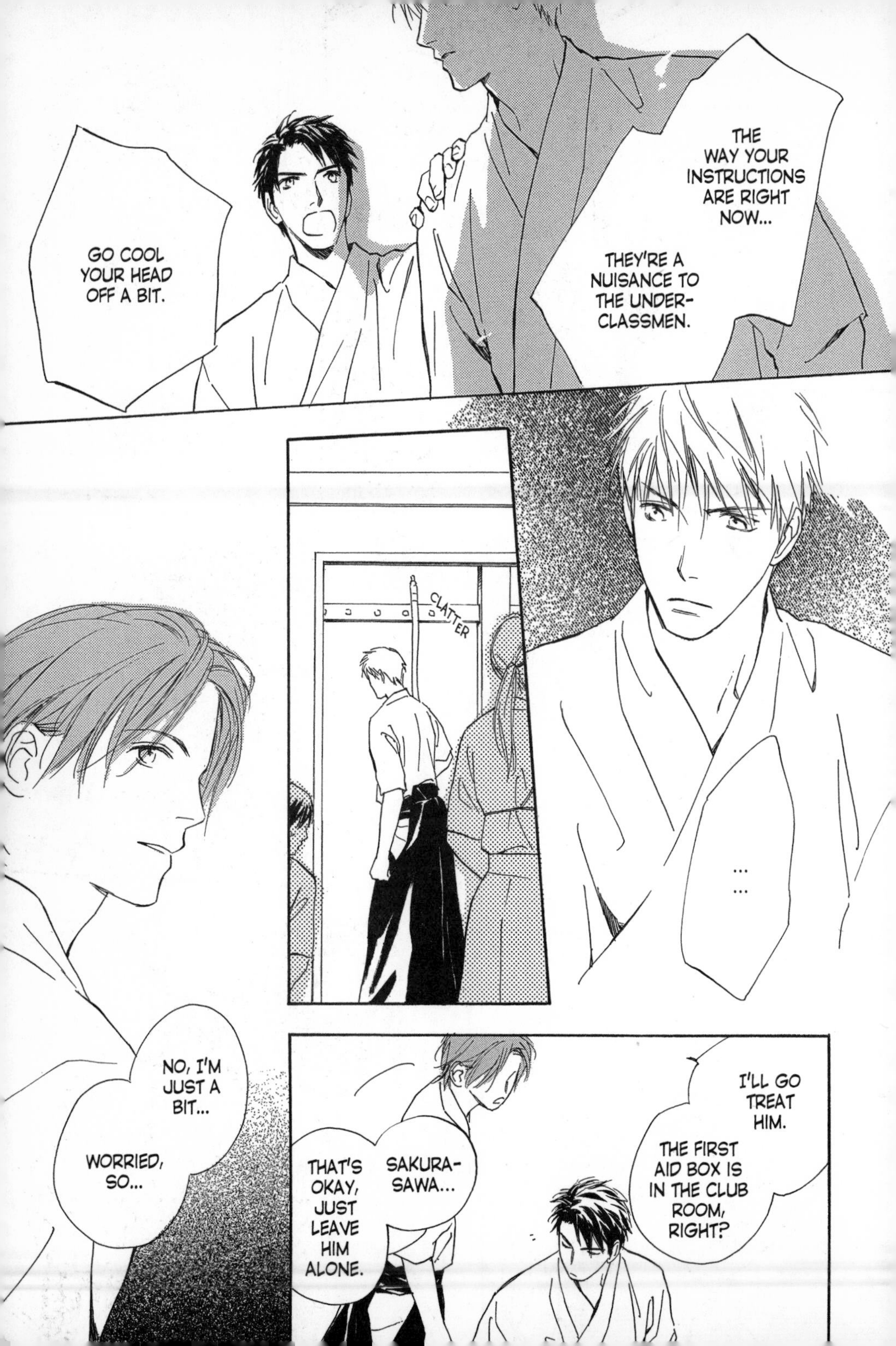
THE WAY YOUR INSTRUCTIONS ARE RIGHT NOW...
THEY'RE A NUISANCE TO THE UNDER-CLASSMEN.
GO COOL YOUR HEAD OFF A BIT.
......
CLATTER
I'LL GO TREAT HIM.
THE FIRST AID BOX IS IN THE CLUB ROOM, RIGHT?
SAKURA-SAWA...
THAT'S OKAY, JUST LEAVE HIM ALONE.
NO, I'M JUST A BIT...
WORRIED, SO...

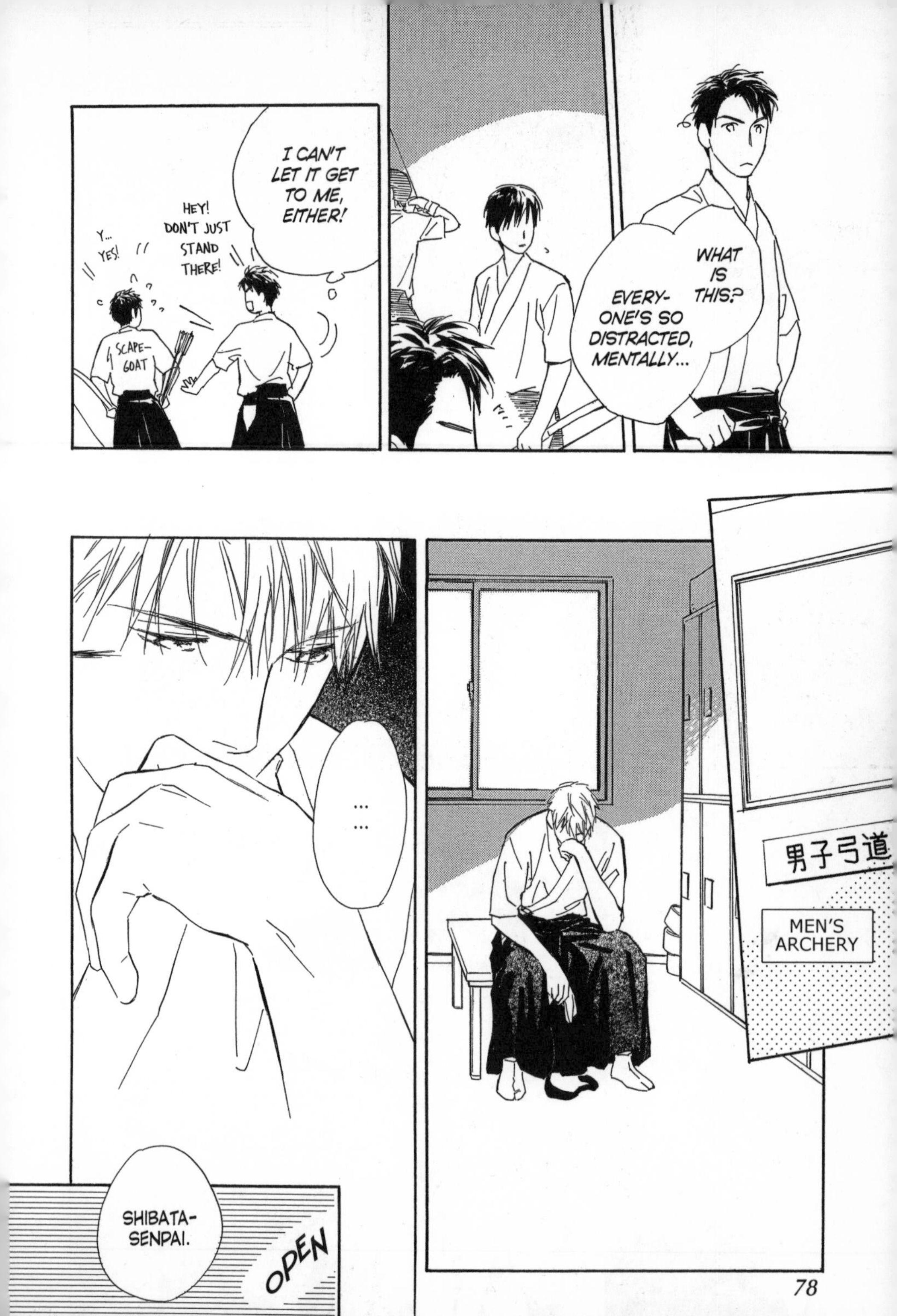

WHAT IS THIS?
EVERY-ONE'S SO DISTRACTED, MENTALLY...
I CAN'T LET IT GET TO ME, EITHER!
HEY! DON'T JUST STAND THERE!
Y... YES!
SCAPE-GOAT
男子弓道
MEN'S ARCHERY
... ...
SHIBATA-SENPAI.
OPEN

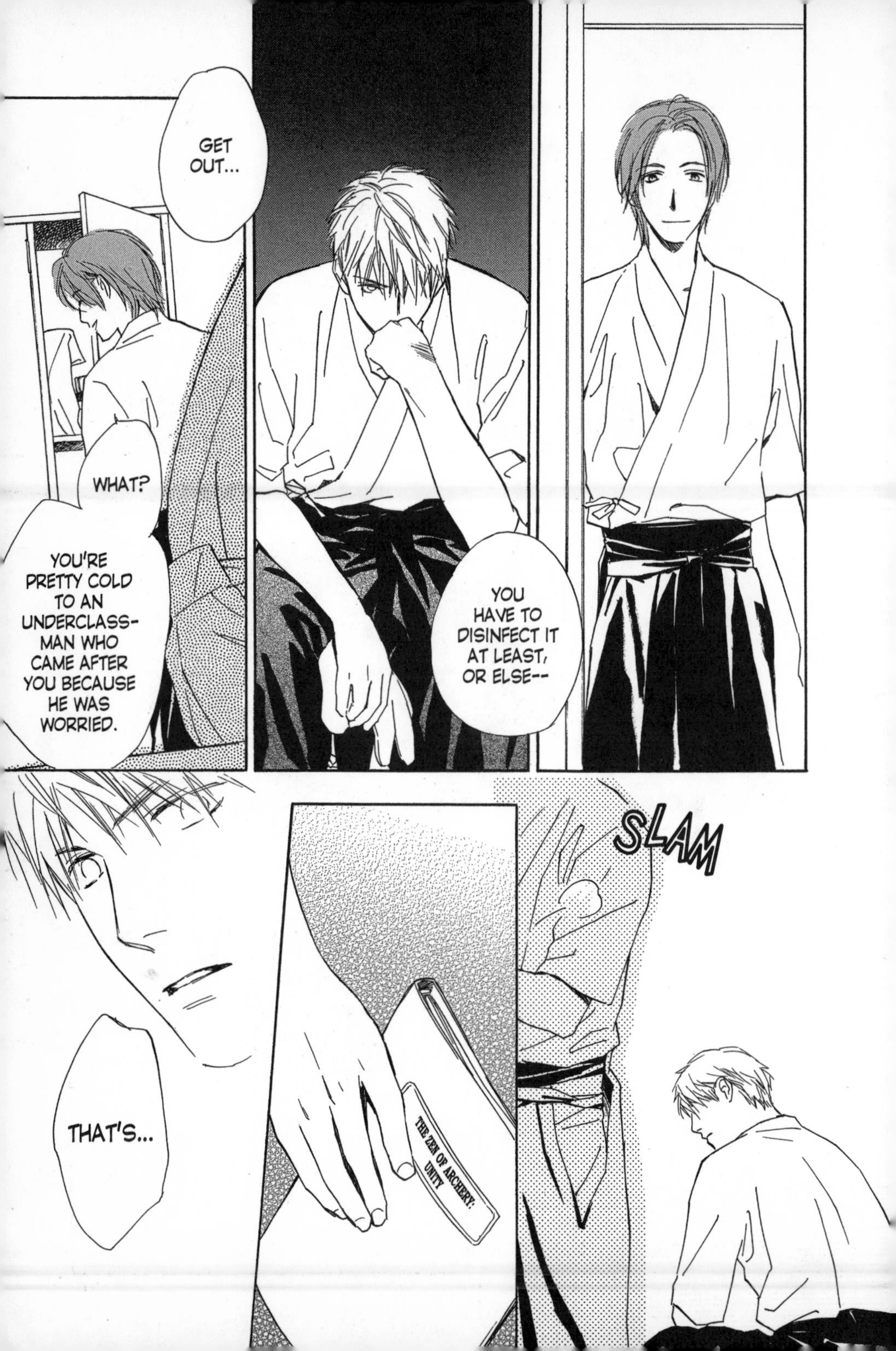
YOU HAVE TO DISINFECT IT AT LEAST, OR ELSE--
GET OUT...
WHAT?
YOU'RE PRETTY COLD TO AN UNDERCLASSMAN WHO CAME AFTER YOU BECAUSE HE WAS WORRIED.
SLAM
THE ZEN OF ARCHERY: UNITY
THAT'S...

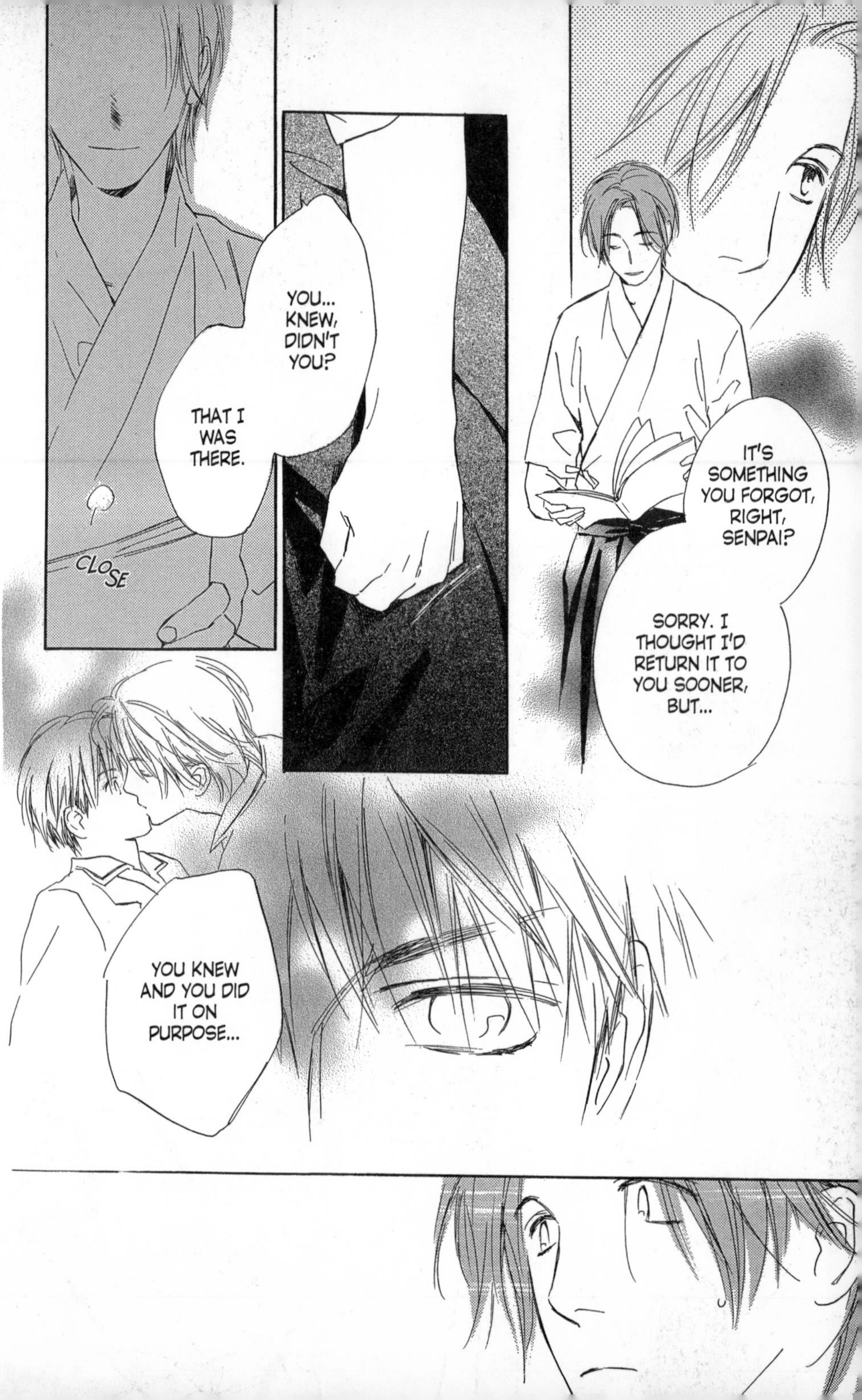
IT'S SOMETHING YOU FORGOT, RIGHT, SENPAI?
SORRY. I THOUGHT I'D RETURN IT TO YOU SOONER, BUT...
YOU... KNEW, DIDN'T YOU?
THAT I WAS THERE.
CLOSE
YOU KNEW AND YOU DID IT ON PURPOSE...

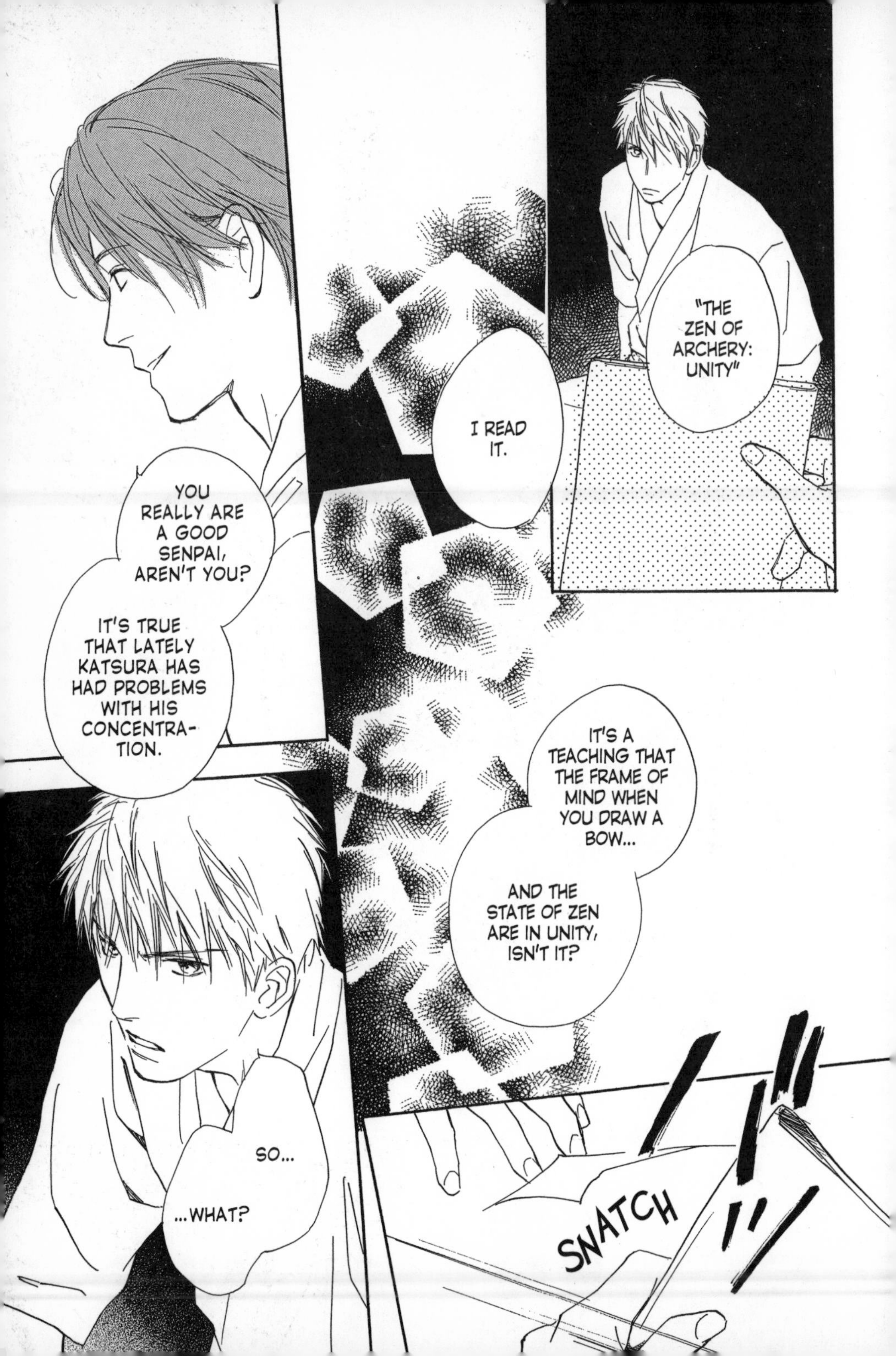

"THE ZEN OF ARCHERY: UNITY"
I READ IT.
YOU REALLY ARE A GOOD SENPAI, AREN'T YOU?
IT'S TRUE THAT LATELY KATSURA HAS HAD PROBLEMS WITH HIS CONCENTRATION.
IT'S A TEACHING THAT THE FRAME OF MIND WHEN YOU DRAW A BOW...
AND THE STATE OF ZEN ARE IN UNITY, ISN'T IT?
SNATCH
SO...
...WHAT?

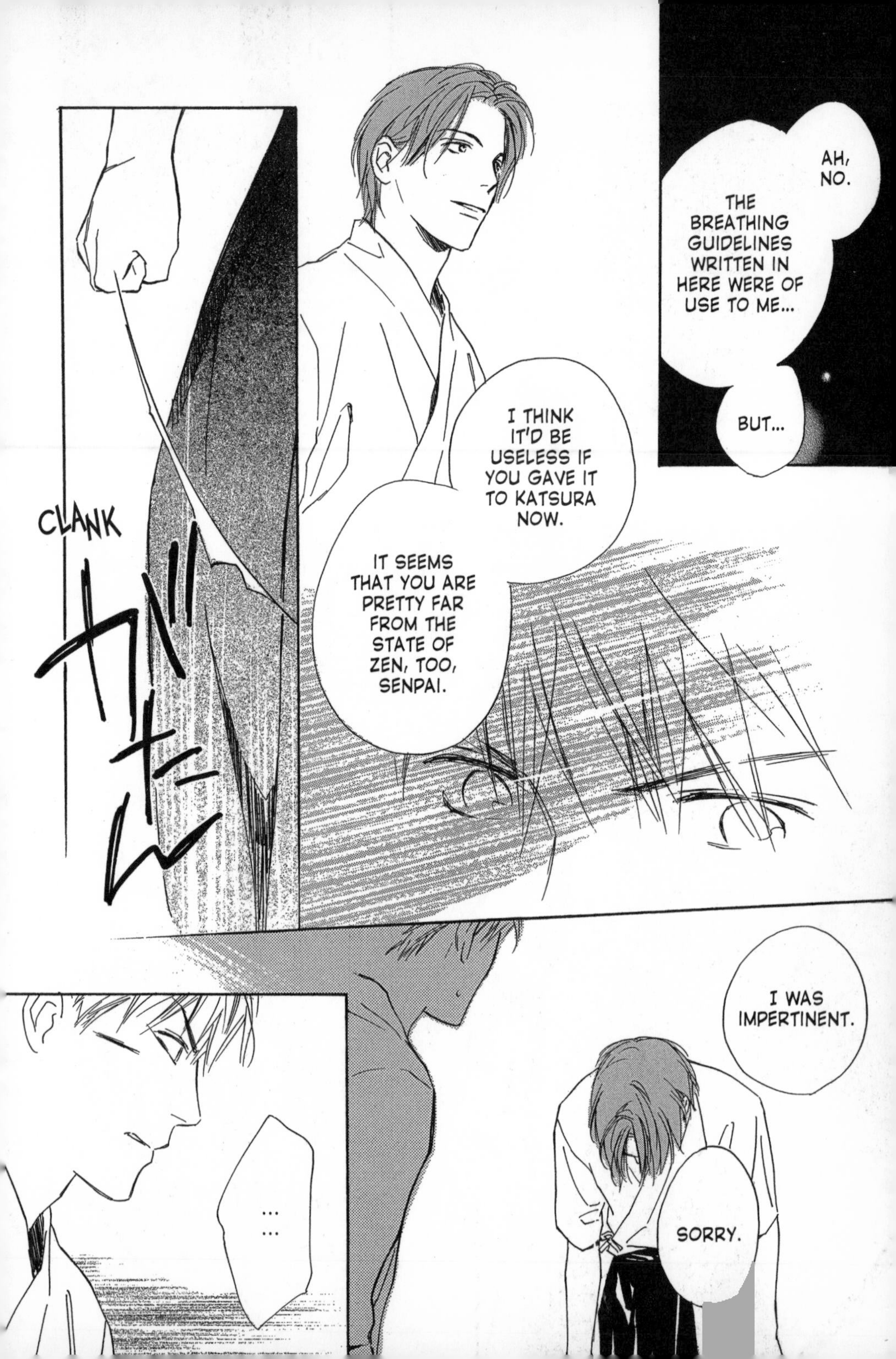

AH, NO.
THE BREATHING GUIDELINES WRITTEN IN HERE WERE OF USE TO ME...
BUT...
I THINK IT'D BE USELESS IF YOU GAVE IT TO KATSURA NOW.
IT SEEMS THAT YOU ARE PRETTY FAR FROM THE STATE OF ZEN, TOO, SENPAI.
CLANK
I WAS IMPERTINENT.
SORRY.
...
...

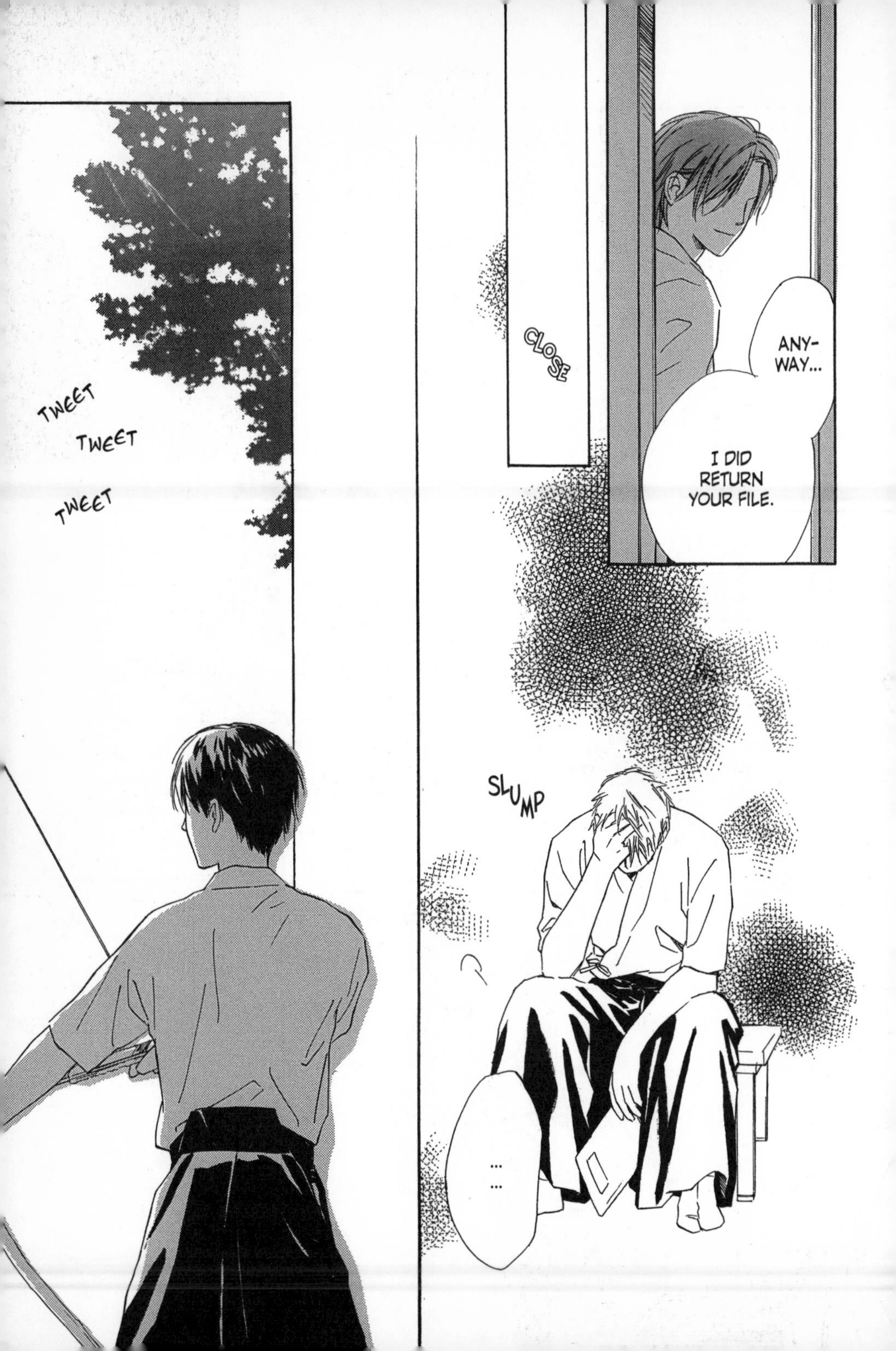
ANY-WAY...
I DID RETURN YOUR FILE.
CLOSE
SLUMP
... ...
TWEET
TWEET
TWEET

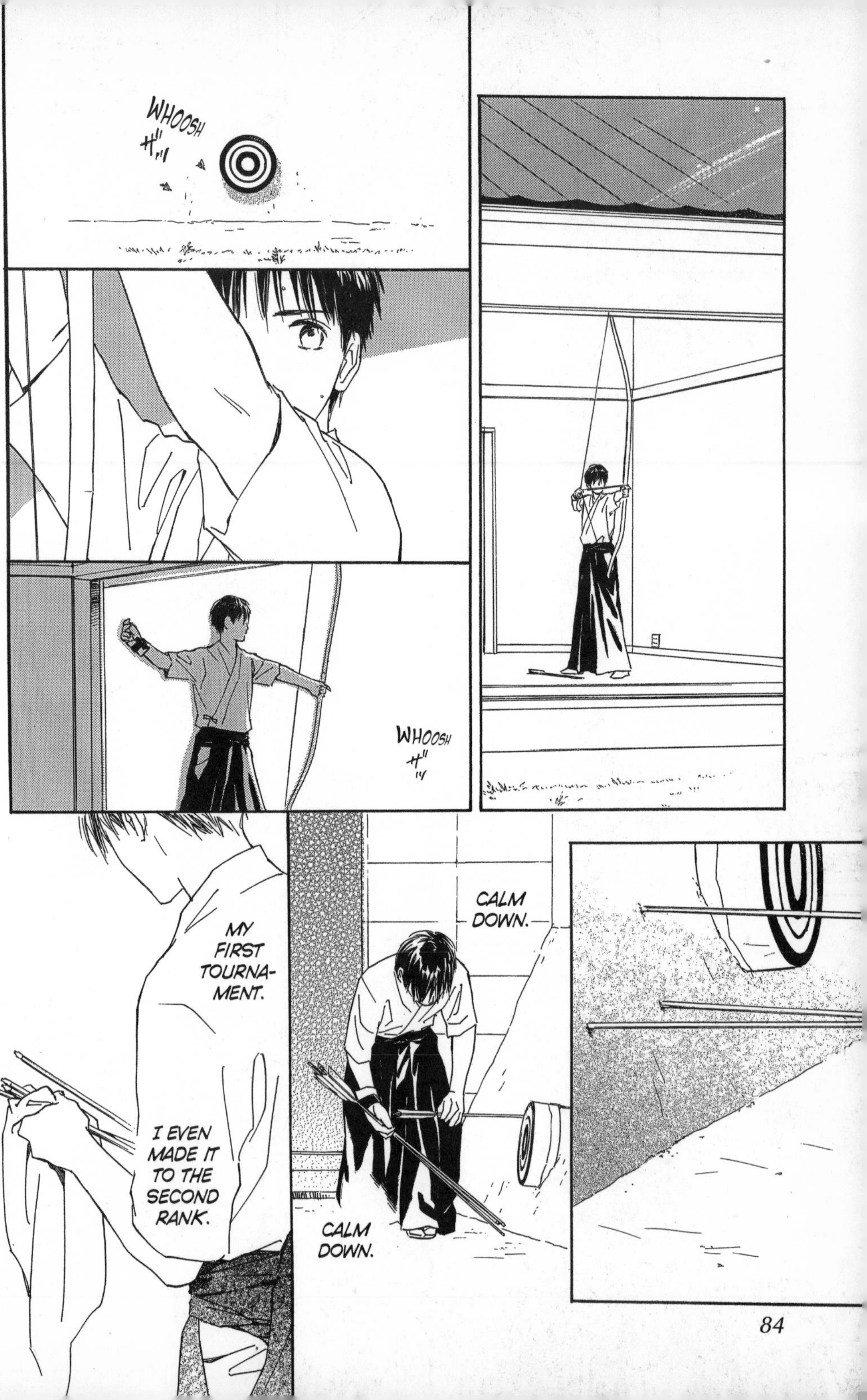
WHOOSH
WHOOSH
CALM DOWN.
CALM DOWN.
MY FIRST TOURNAMENT.
I EVEN MADE IT TO THE SECOND RANK.

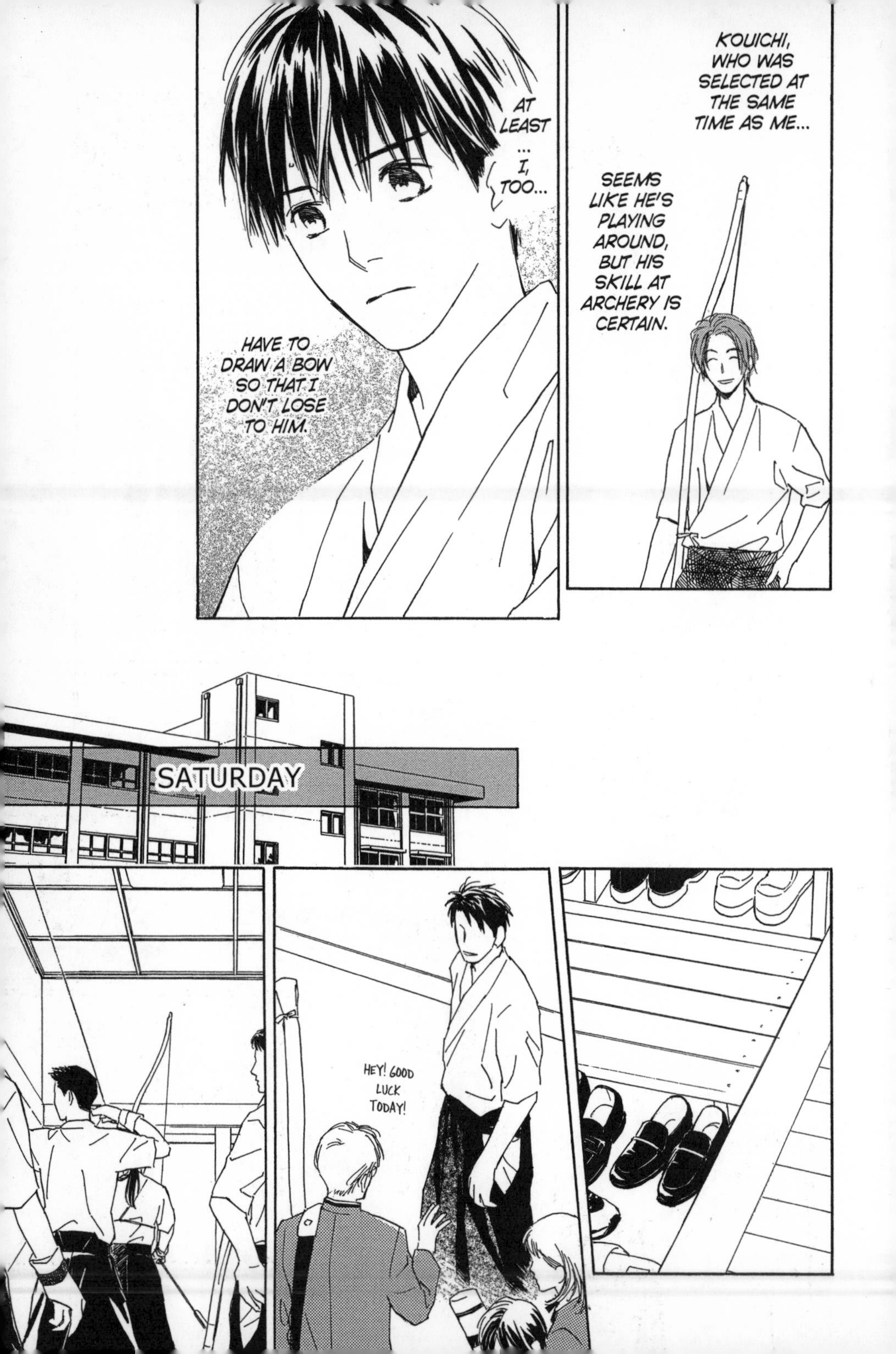
KOUICHI, WHO WAS SELECTED AT THE SAME TIME AS ME...
SEEMS LIKE HE'S PLAYING AROUND, BUT HIS SKILL AT ARCHERY IS CERTAIN.
AT LEAST ... I, TOO...
HAVE TO DRAW A BOW SO THAT I DON'T LOSE TO HIM.
SATURDAY
HEY! GOOD LUCK TODAY!

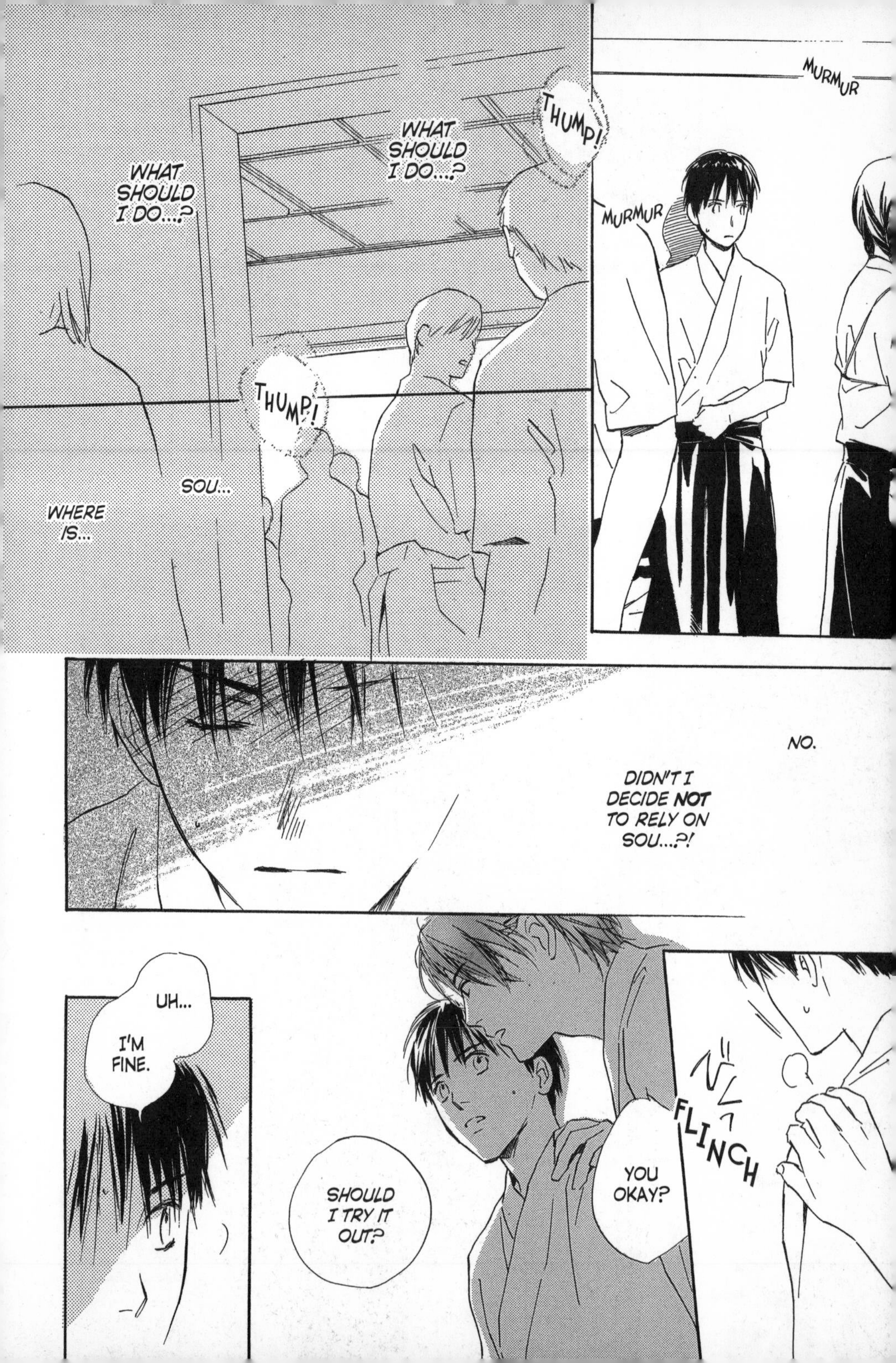
MURMUR
MURMUR
THUMP!
WHAT SHOULD I DO...?
WHAT SHOULD I DO...?
THUMP!
SOU...
WHERE IS...
NO.
DIDN'T I DECIDE **NOT** TO RELY ON SOU...?!
FLINCH
YOU OKAY?
SHOULD I TRY IT OUT?
UH...
I'M FINE.

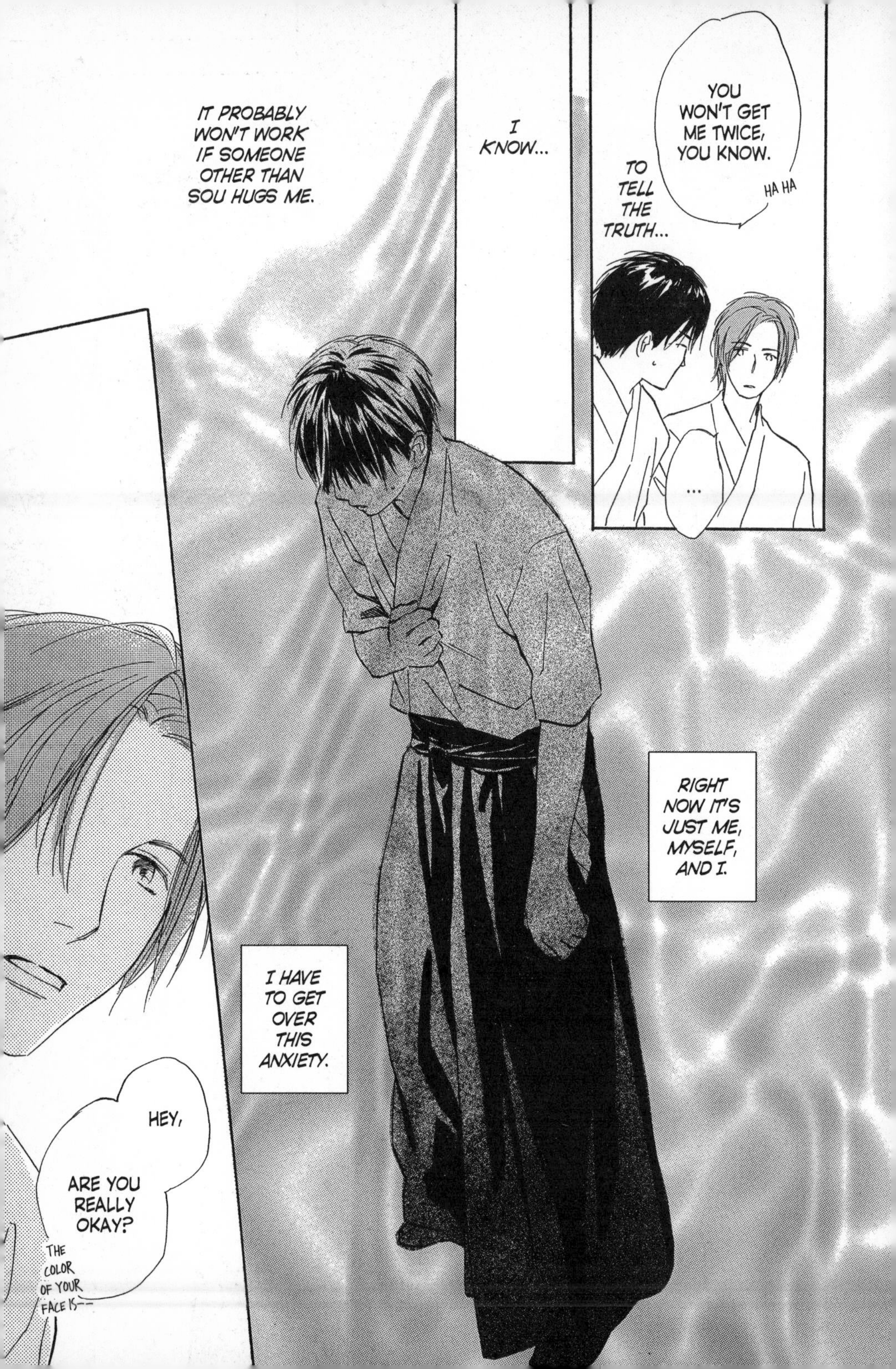

YOU WON'T GET ME TWICE, YOU KNOW.
HA HA
TO TELL THE TRUTH...
...
I KNOW...
IT PROBABLY WON'T WORK IF SOMEONE OTHER THAN SOU HUGS ME.
RIGHT NOW IT'S JUST ME, MYSELF, AND I.
I HAVE TO GET OVER THIS ANXIETY.
HEY,
ARE YOU REALLY OKAY?
THE COLOR OF YOUR FACE IS—

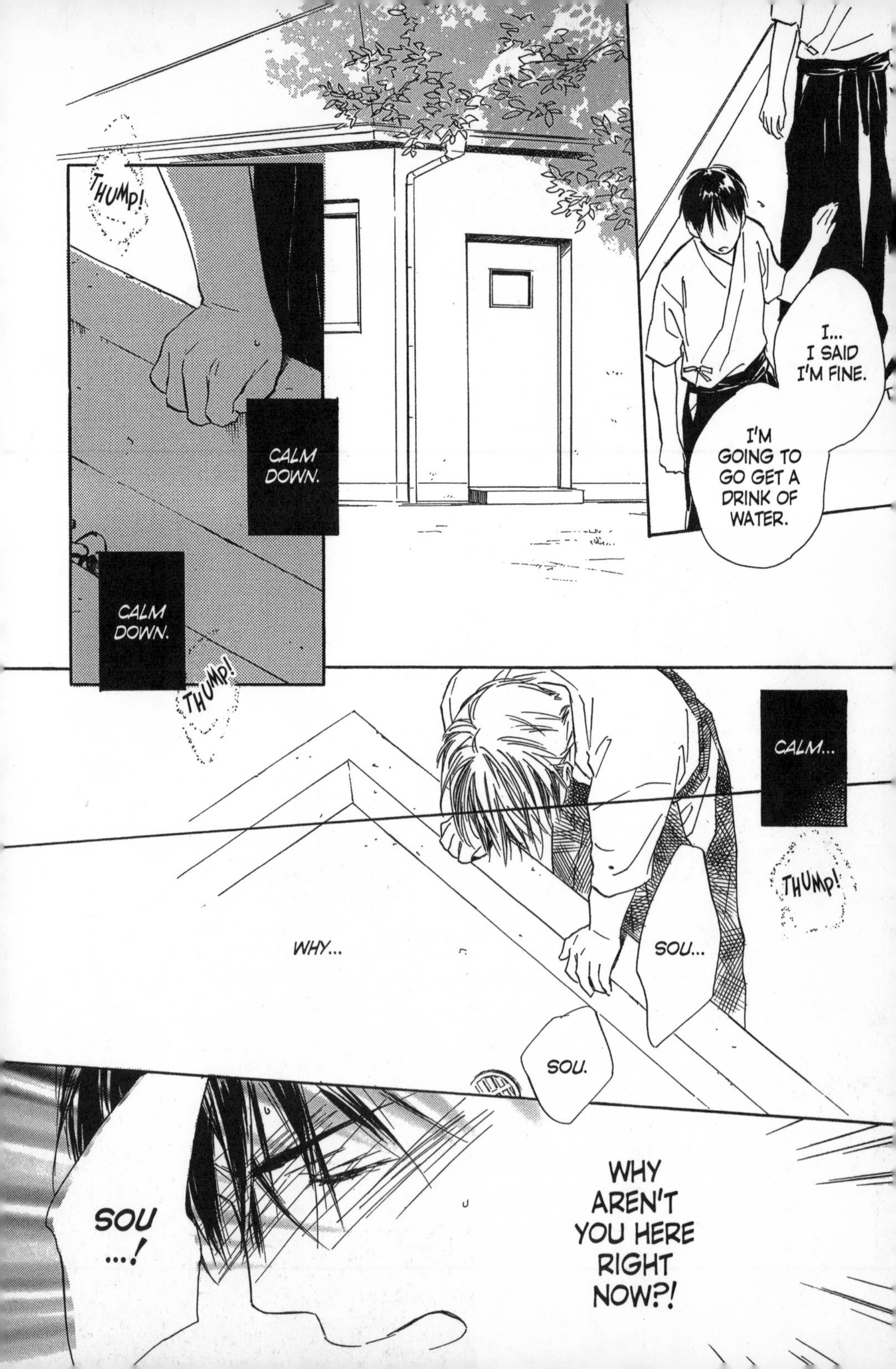
I... I SAID I'M FINE.
I'M GOING TO GO GET A DRINK OF WATER.
THUMP!
CALM DOWN.
CALM DOWN.
THUMP!
CALM...
THUMP!
SOU...
WHY...
SOU.
WHY AREN'T YOU HERE RIGHT NOW?!
SOU ...!

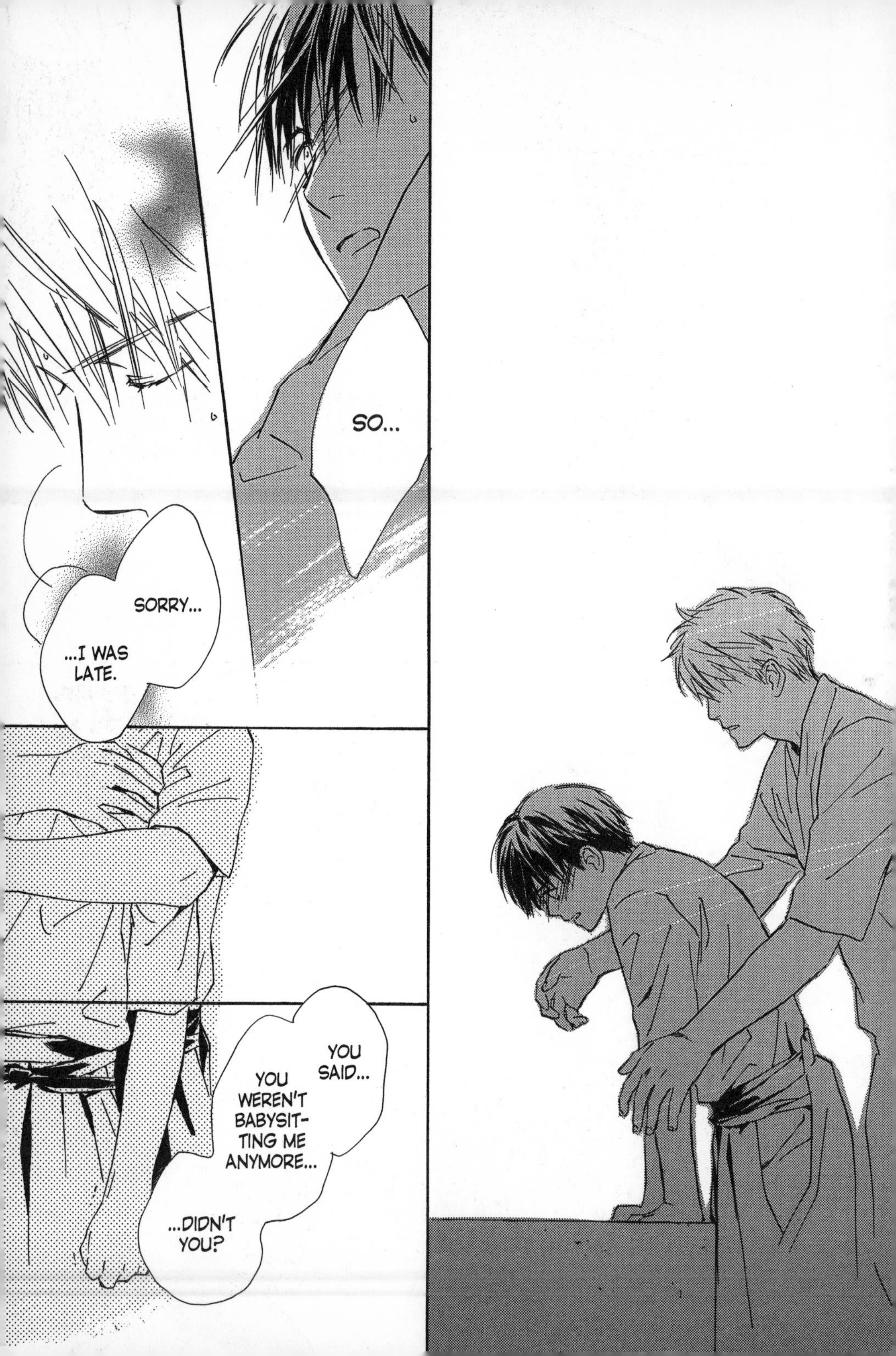
SO...
SORRY...
...I WAS LATE.
YOU SAID...
YOU WEREN'T BABYSIT-TING ME ANYMORE...
...DIDN'T YOU?

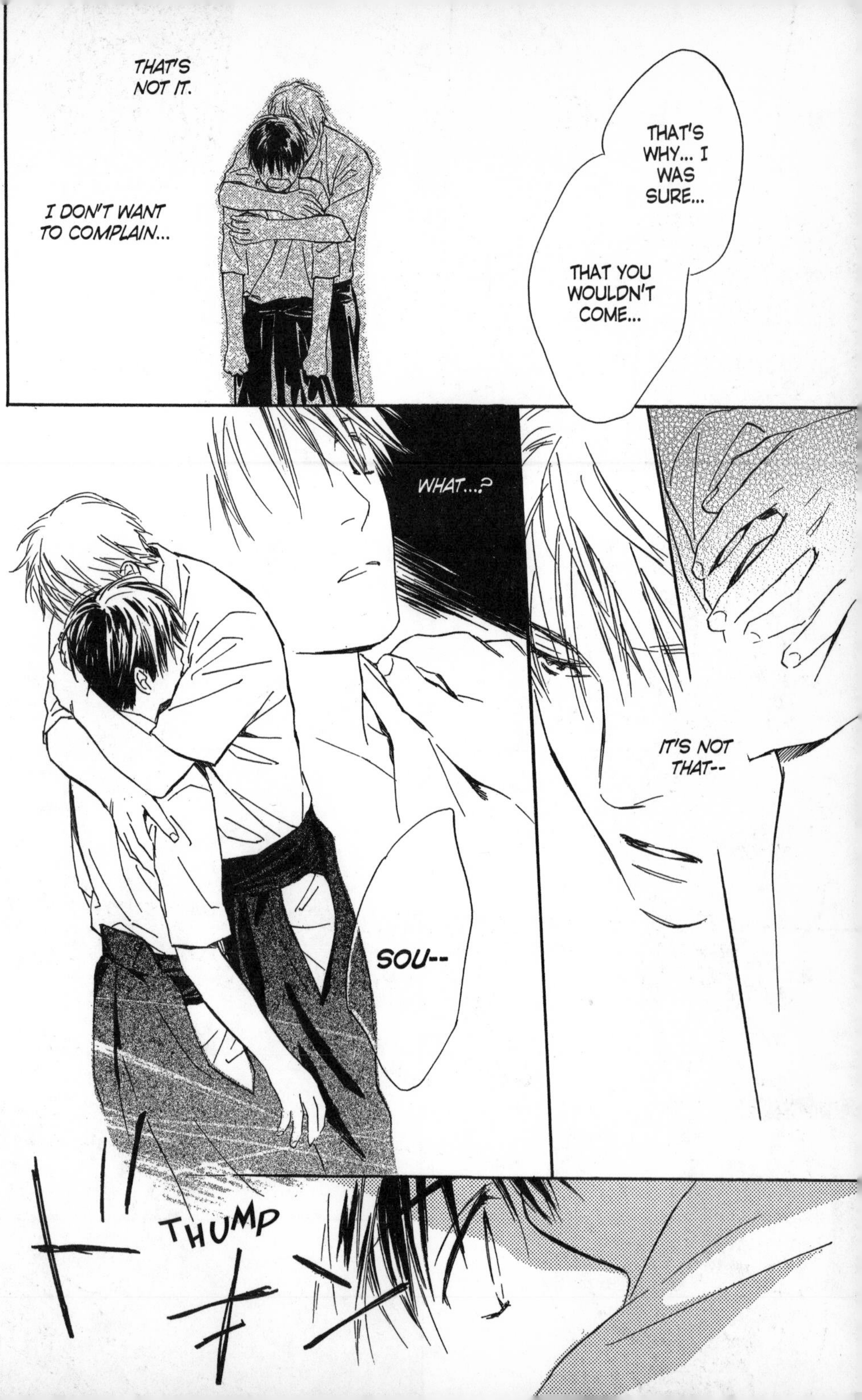
THAT'S WHY... I WAS SURE...
THAT YOU WOULDN'T COME...
THAT'S NOT IT.
I DON'T WANT TO COMPLAIN...
IT'S NOT THAT--
WHAT...?
SOU--
THUMP

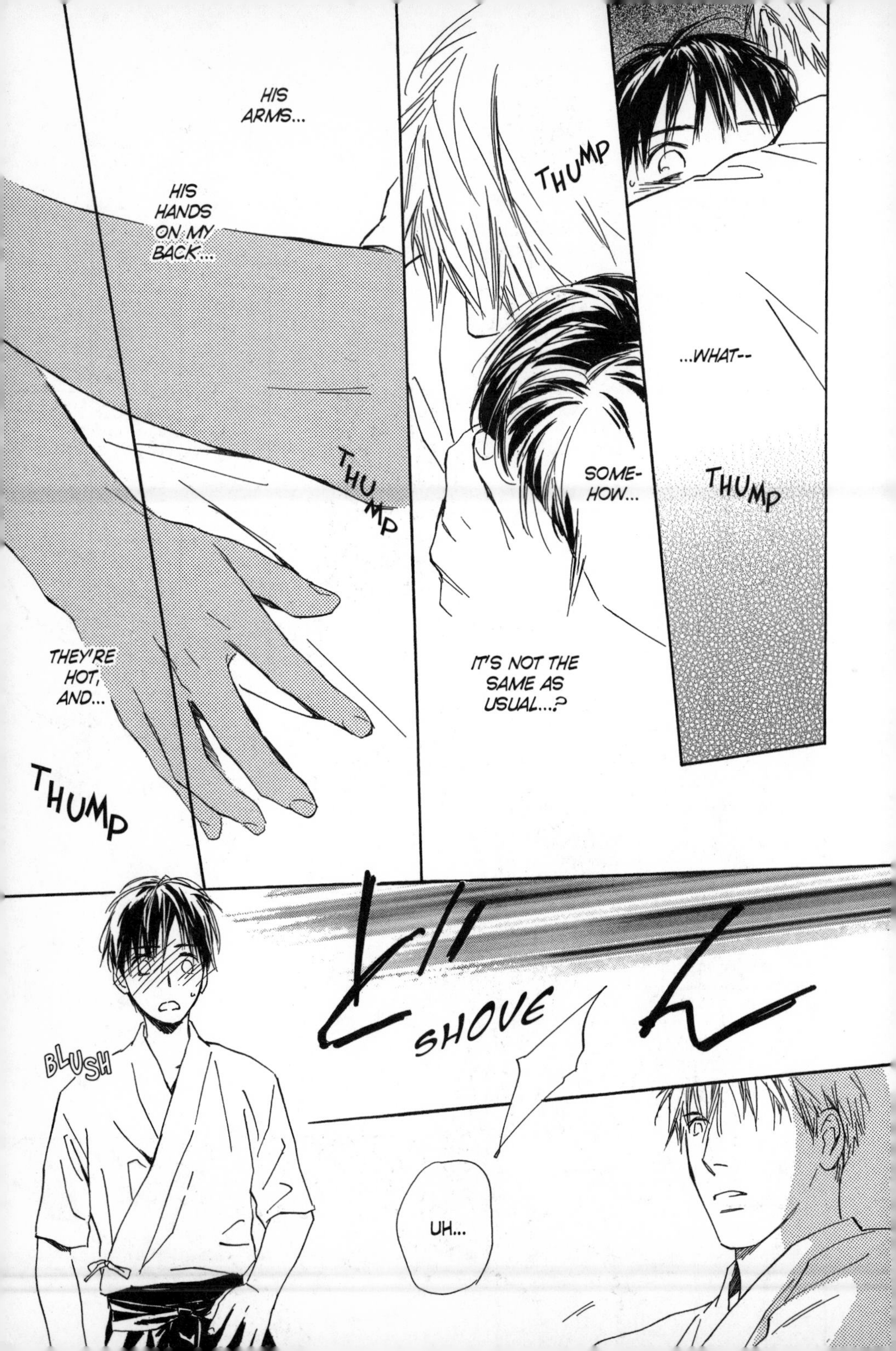
...WHAT--
THUMP
THUMP
SOME-HOW...
IT'S NOT THE SAME AS USUAL...?
HIS ARMS...
HIS HANDS ON MY BACK...
THUMP
THEY'RE HOT, AND...
THUMP
SHOVE
UH...
BLUSH

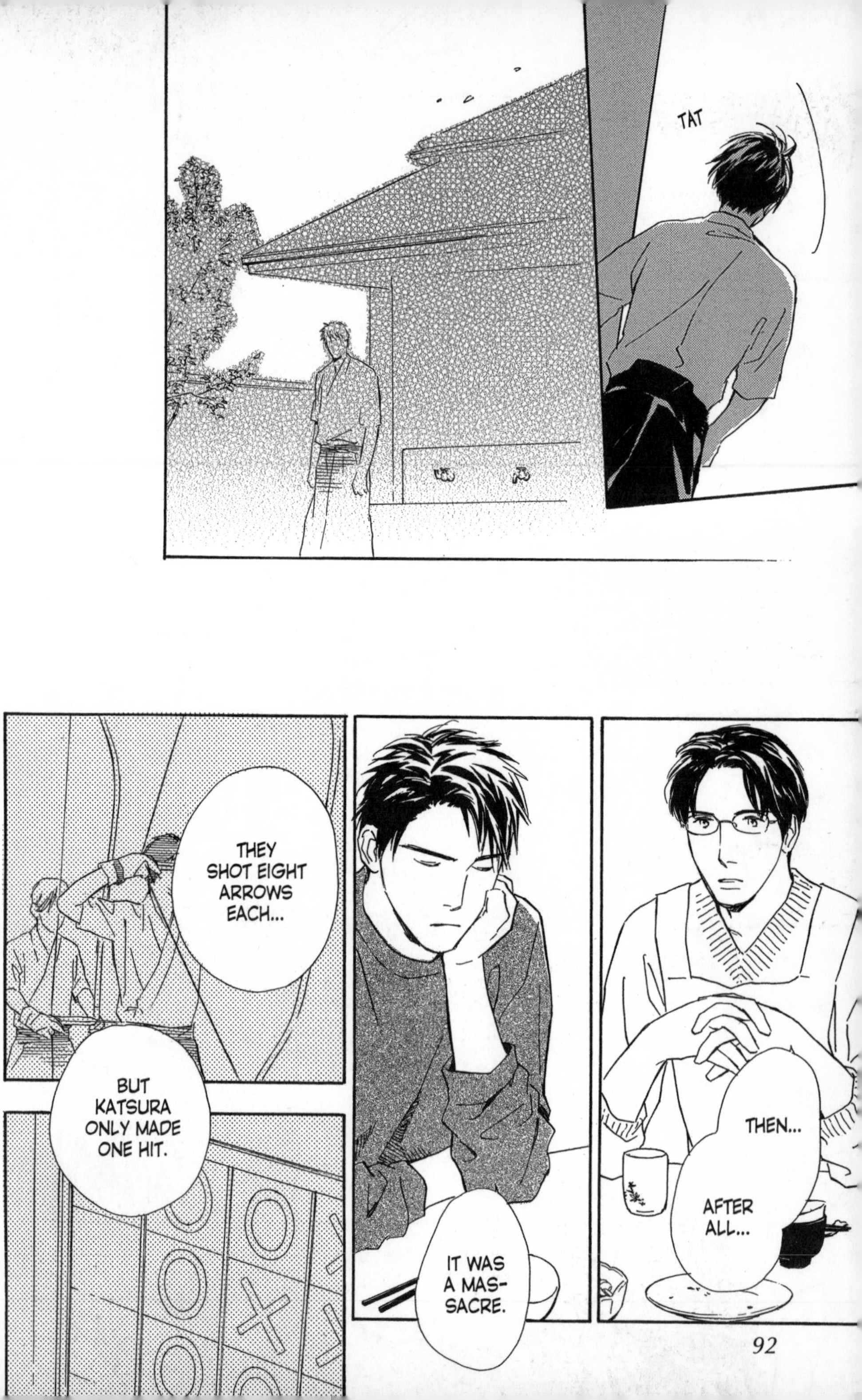

TAT
THEN...
AFTER ALL...
IT WAS A MAS-SACRE.
THEY SHOT EIGHT ARROWS EACH...
BUT KATSURA ONLY MADE ONE HIT.

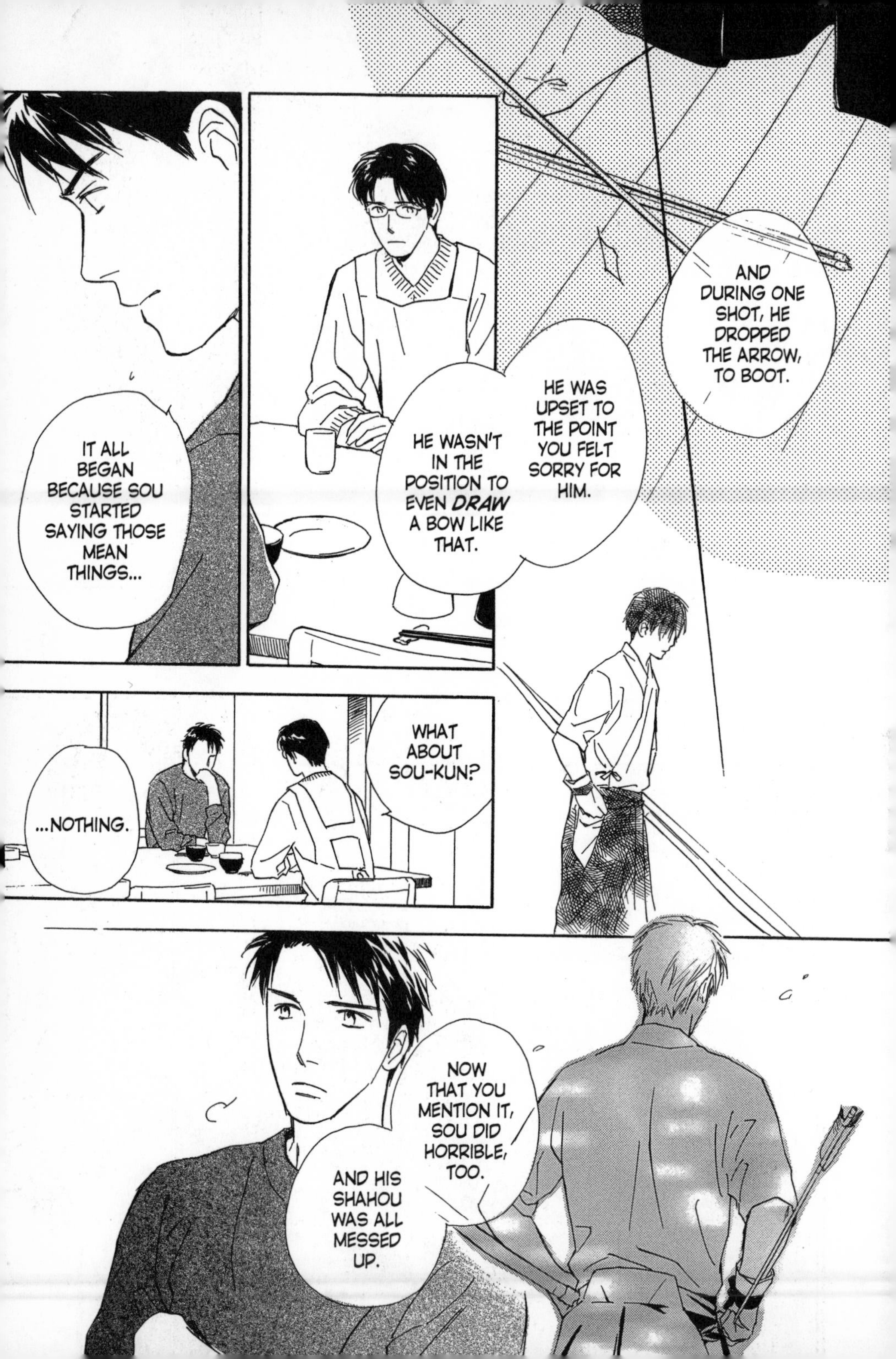
AND DURING ONE SHOT, HE DROPPED THE ARROW, TO BOOT.
HE WAS UPSET TO THE POINT YOU FELT SORRY FOR HIM.
HE WASN'T IN THE POSITION TO EVEN *DRAW* A BOW LIKE THAT.
IT ALL BEGAN BECAUSE SOU STARTED SAYING THOSE MEAN THINGS...
WHAT ABOUT SOU-KUN?
...NOTHING.
NOW THAT YOU MENTION IT, SOU DID HORRIBLE, TOO.
AND HIS SHAHOU WAS ALL MESSED UP.

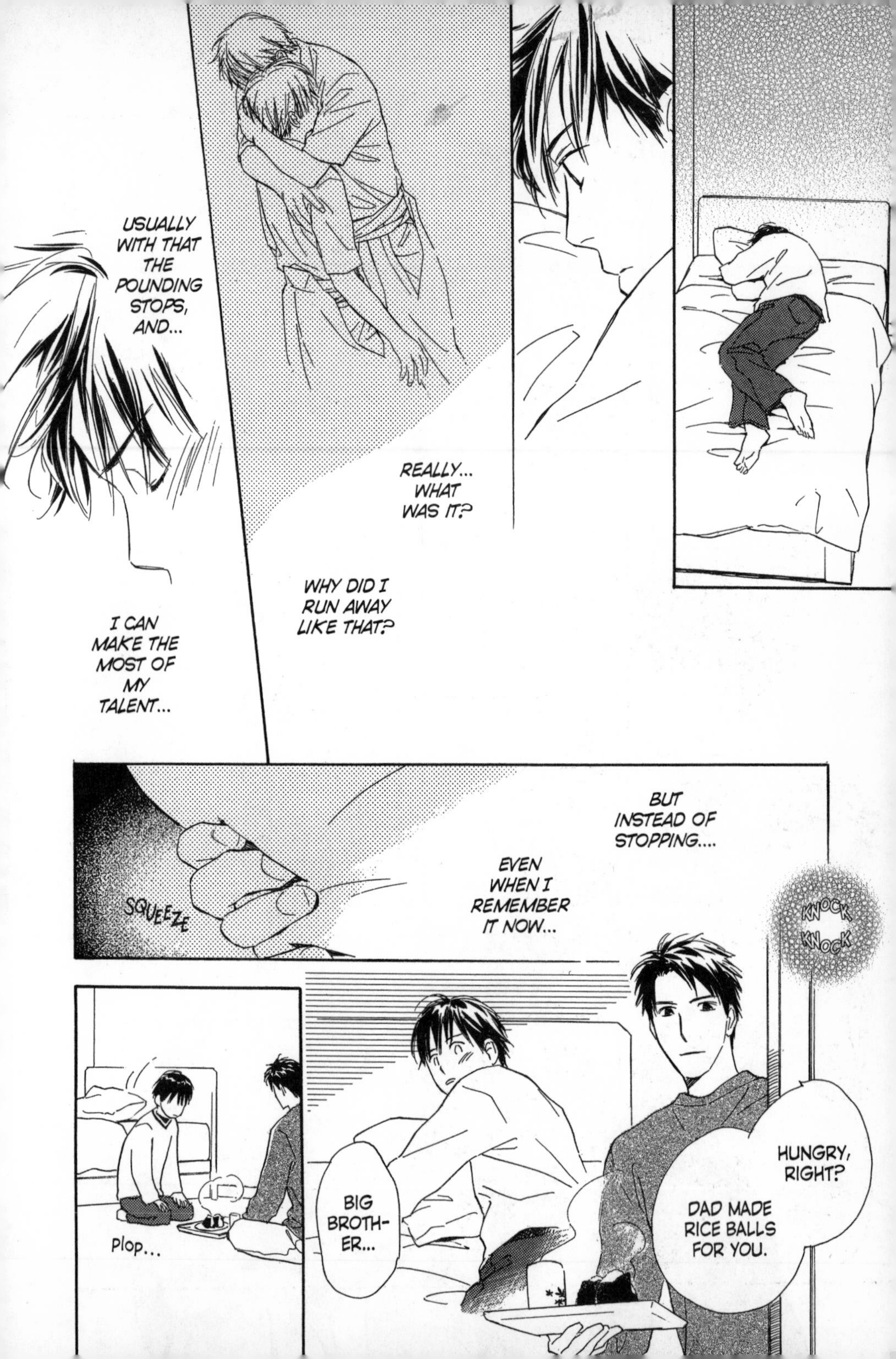
REALLY... WHAT WAS IT?
WHY DID I RUN AWAY LIKE THAT?
USUALLY WITH THAT THE POUNDING STOPS, AND...
I CAN MAKE THE MOST OF MY TALENT...
BUT INSTEAD OF STOPPING....
EVEN WHEN I REMEMBER IT NOW...
SQUEEZE
KNOCK KNOCK
HUNGRY, RIGHT?
DAD MADE RICE BALLS FOR YOU.
BIG BROTH-ER...
Plop...

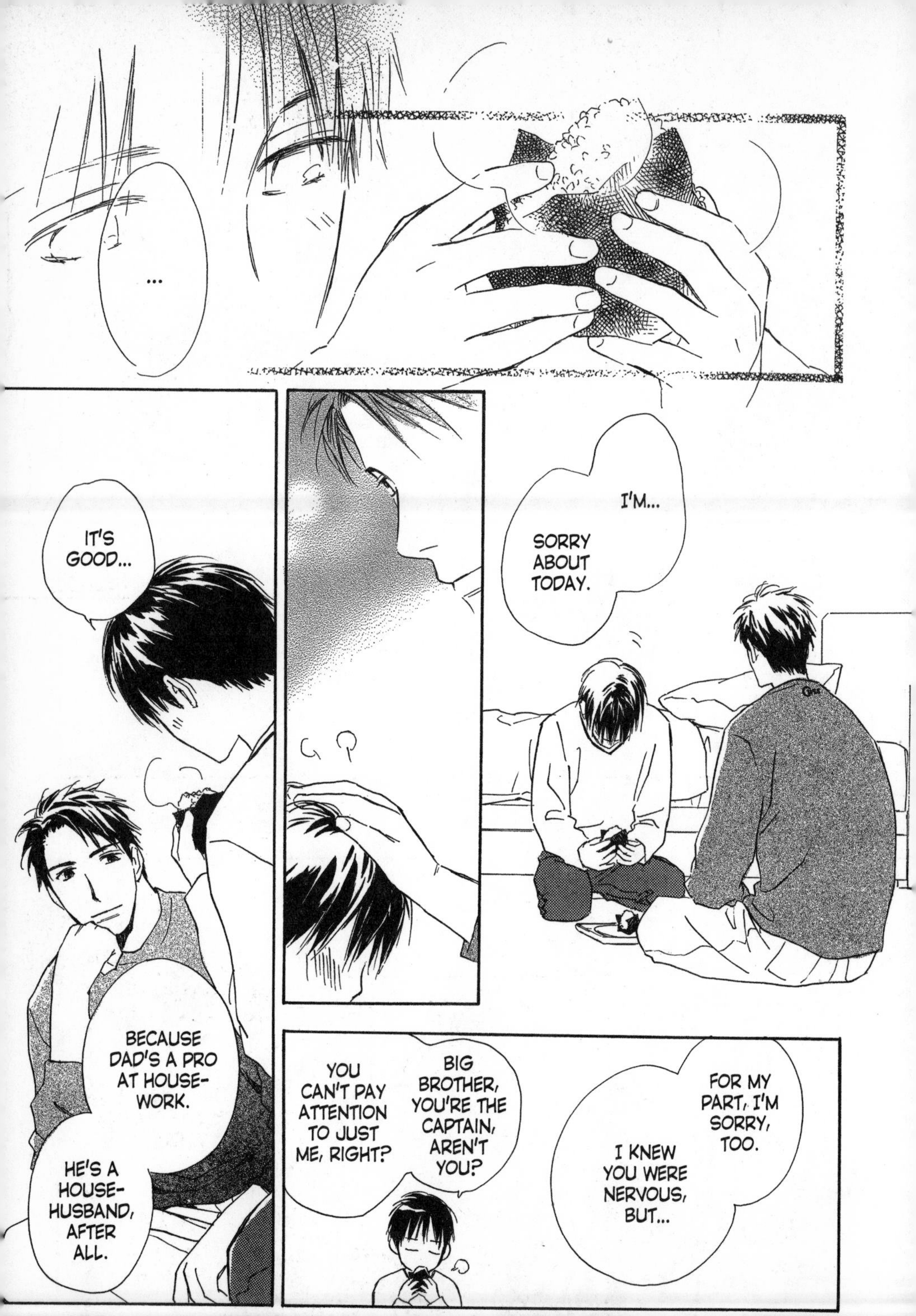
...
I'M...
SORRY ABOUT TODAY.
FOR MY PART, I'M SORRY, TOO.
I KNEW YOU WERE NERVOUS, BUT...
BIG BROTHER, YOU'RE THE CAPTAIN, AREN'T YOU?
YOU CAN'T PAY ATTENTION TO JUST ME, RIGHT?
IT'S GOOD...
BECAUSE DAD'S A PRO AT HOUSE-WORK.
HE'S A HOUSE-HUSBAND, AFTER ALL.

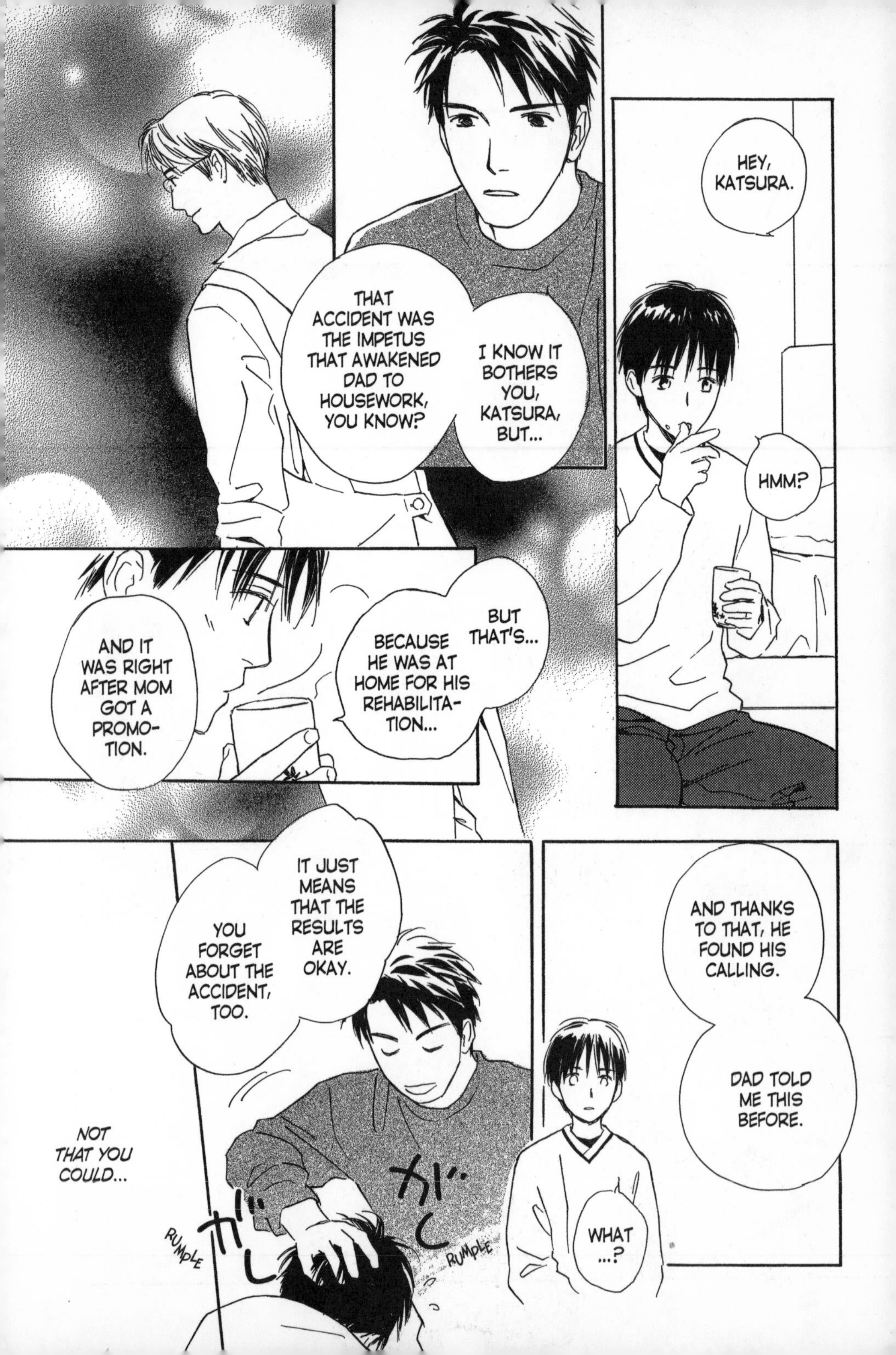
HEY, KATSURA.
HMM?
I KNOW IT BOTHERS YOU, KATSURA, BUT...
THAT ACCIDENT WAS THE IMPETUS THAT AWAKENED DAD TO HOUSEWORK, YOU KNOW?
BUT THAT'S...
BECAUSE HE WAS AT HOME FOR HIS REHABILITATION...
AND IT WAS RIGHT AFTER MOM GOT A PROMOTION.
AND THANKS TO THAT, HE FOUND HIS CALLING.
DAD TOLD ME THIS BEFORE.
WHAT ...?
IT JUST MEANS THAT THE RESULTS ARE OKAY.
YOU FORGET ABOUT THE ACCIDENT, TOO.
がし
RUMPLE
がし
RUMPLE
NOT THAT YOU COULD...

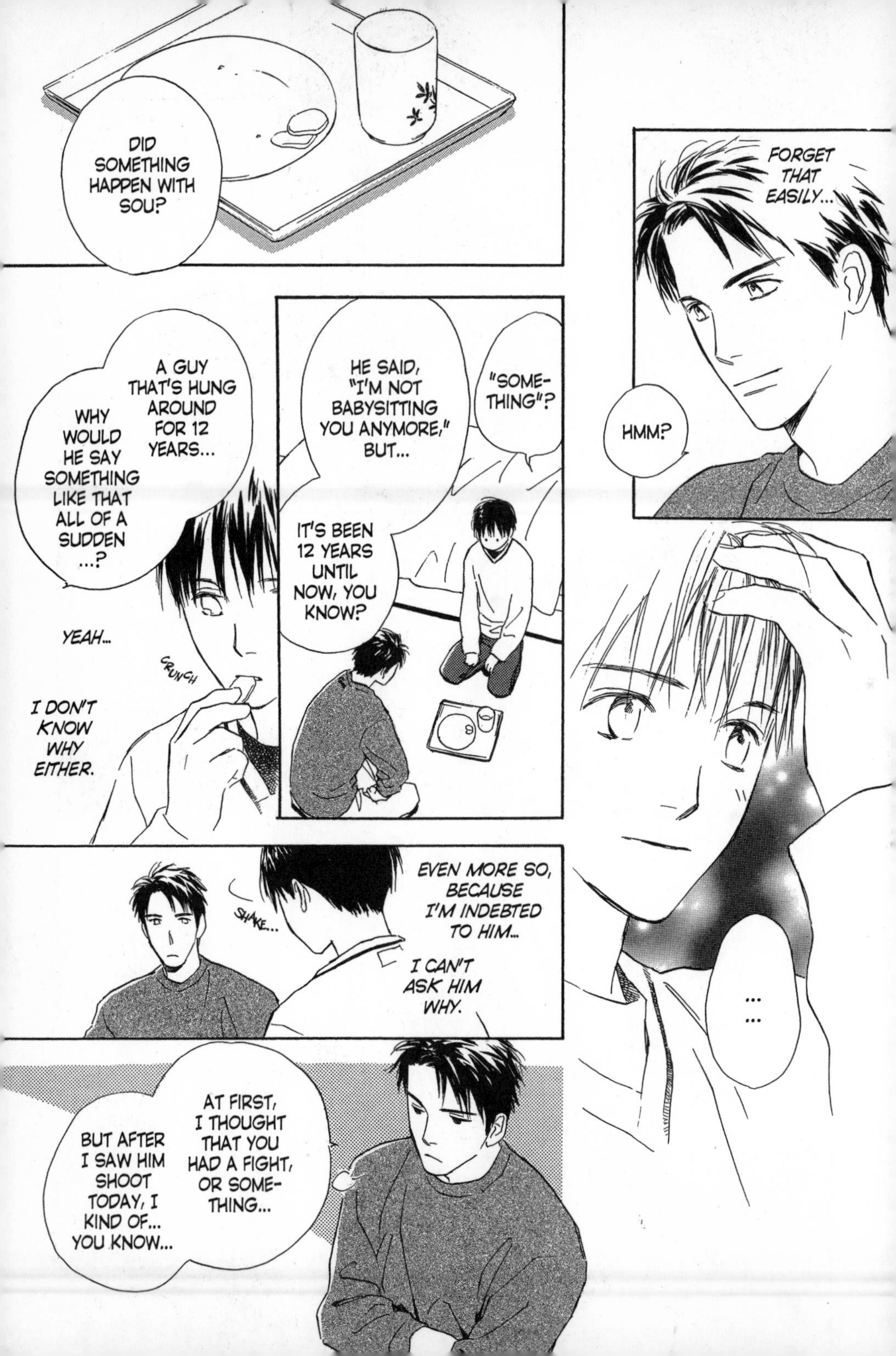
FORGET THAT EASILY...
HMM?
DID SOMETHING HAPPEN WITH SOU?
......
"SOME-THING"?
HE SAID, "I'M NOT BABYSITTING YOU ANYMORE," BUT...
IT'S BEEN 12 YEARS UNTIL NOW, YOU KNOW?
A GUY THAT'S HUNG AROUND FOR 12 YEARS...
WHY WOULD HE SAY SOMETHING LIKE THAT ALL OF A SUDDEN ...?
YEAH...
CRUNCH
I DON'T KNOW WHY EITHER.
EVEN MORE SO, BECAUSE I'M INDEBTED TO HIM...
I CAN'T ASK HIM WHY.
SHAKE...
AT FIRST, I THOUGHT THAT YOU HAD A FIGHT, OR SOME-THING...
BUT AFTER I SAW HIM SHOOT TODAY, I KIND OF... YOU KNOW...

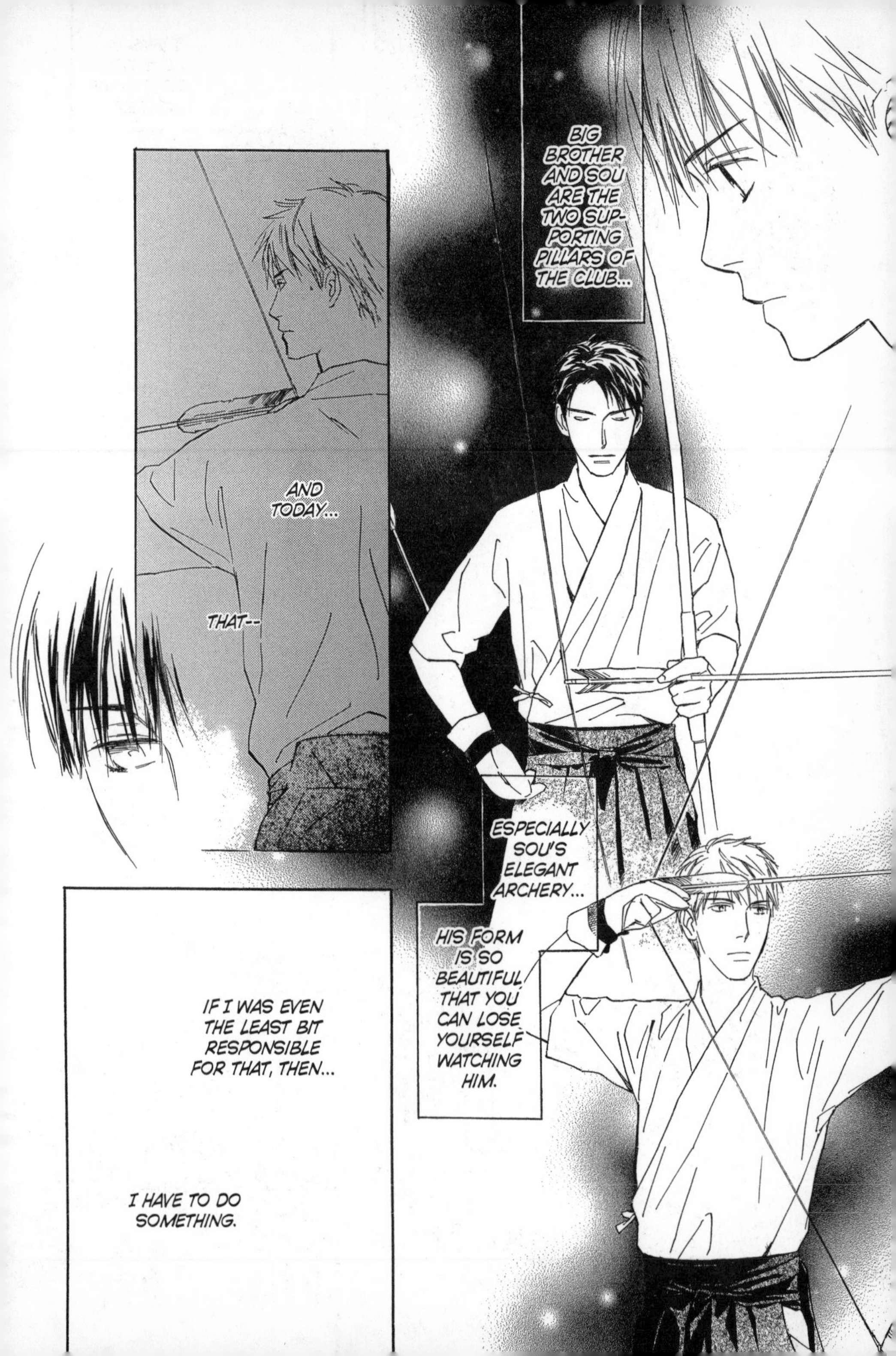
BIG BROTHER AND SOU ARE THE TWO SUP-PORTING PILLARS OF THE CLUB...
ESPECIALLY SOU'S ELEGANT ARCHERY...
HIS FORM IS SO BEAUTIFUL THAT YOU CAN LOSE YOURSELF WATCHING HIM.
AND TODAY...
THAT--
IF I WAS EVEN THE LEAST BIT RESPONSIBLE FOR THAT, THEN...
I HAVE TO DO SOMETHING.

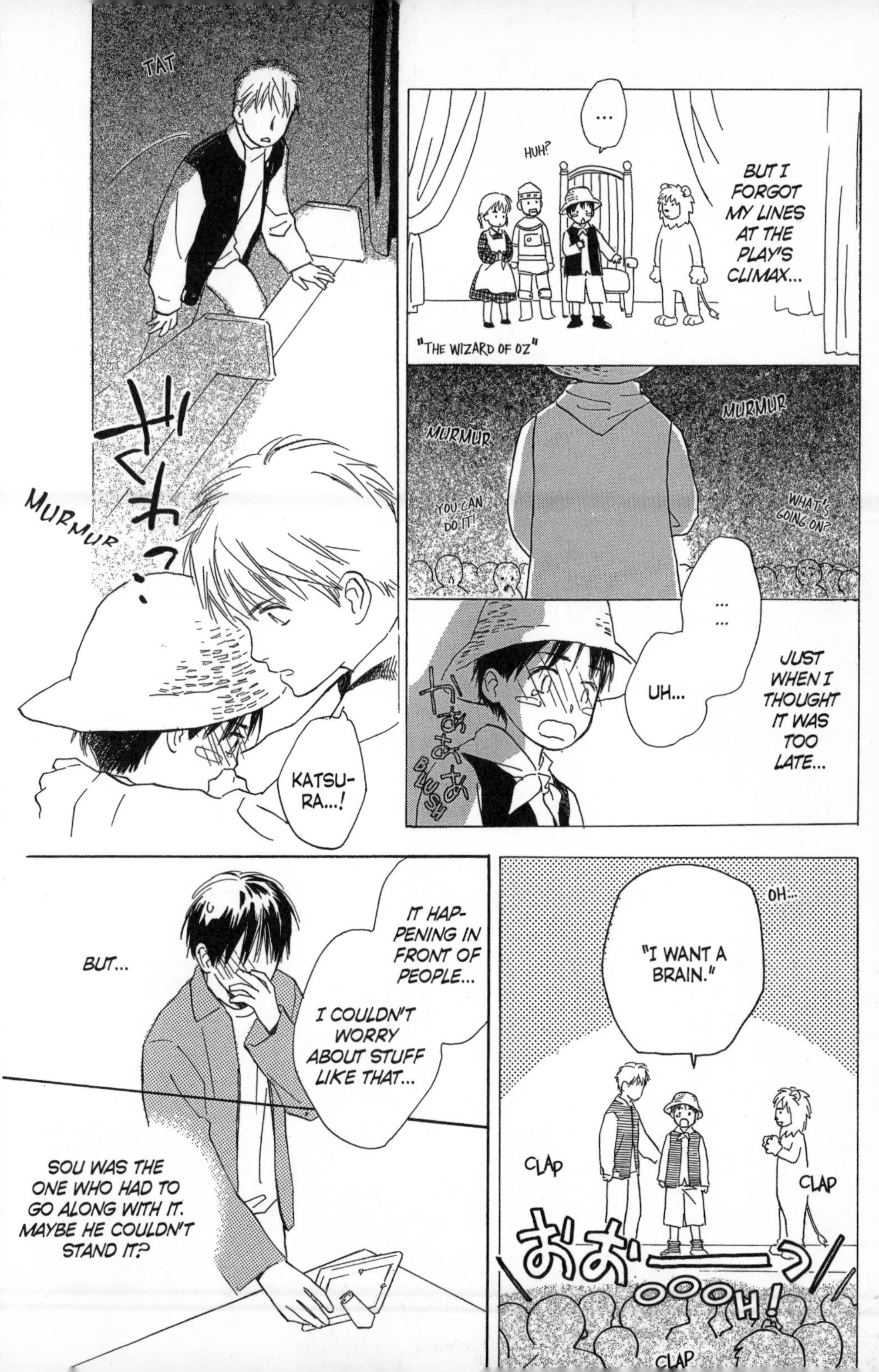
...
HUH?
BUT I FORGOT MY LINES AT THE PLAY'S CLIMAX...
"THE WIZARD OF OZ"
MURMUR
MURMUR
YOU CAN DO IT!
WHAT'S GOING ON?
... ...
UH...
JUST WHEN I THOUGHT IT WAS TOO LATE...
BLUSH
TAT
MURMUR
KATSU-RA...!
OH...
"I WANT A BRAIN."
CLAP
CLAP
おおーーっ
OOOOH!
CLAP
IT HAP-PENING IN FRONT OF PEOPLE...
I COULDN'T WORRY ABOUT STUFF LIKE THAT...
BUT...
SOU WAS THE ONE WHO HAD TO GO ALONG WITH IT. MAYBE HE COULDN'T STAND IT?

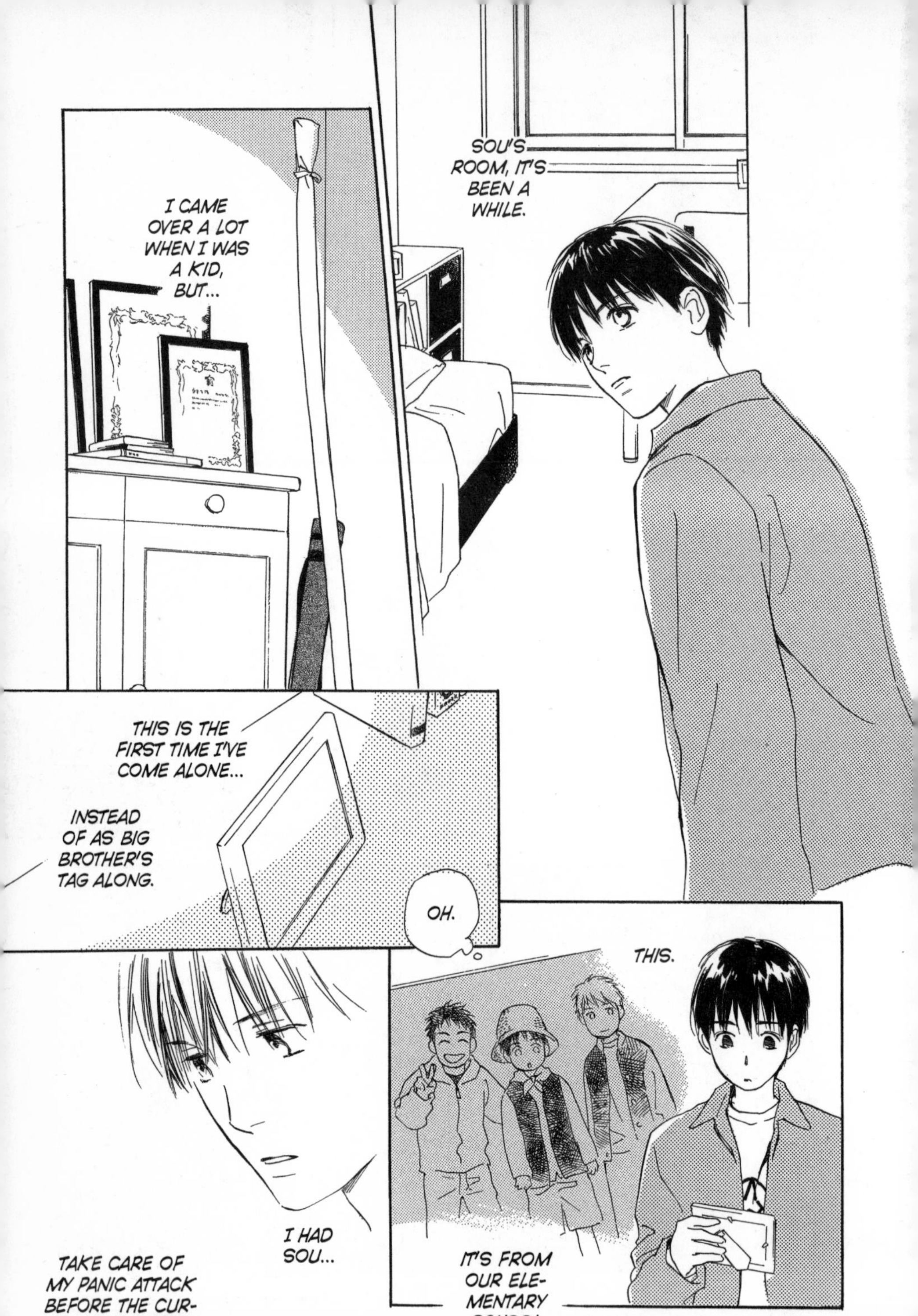
SOU'S ROOM, IT'S BEEN A WHILE.
I CAME OVER A LOT WHEN I WAS A KID, BUT...
THIS IS THE FIRST TIME I'VE COME ALONE...
INSTEAD OF AS BIG BROTHER'S TAG ALONG.
OH.
THIS.
IT'S FROM OUR ELE-MENTARY SCHOOL PLAY...
I HAD SOU...
TAKE CARE OF MY PANIC ATTACK BEFORE THE CUR-TAINS WENT UP THEN, TOO.

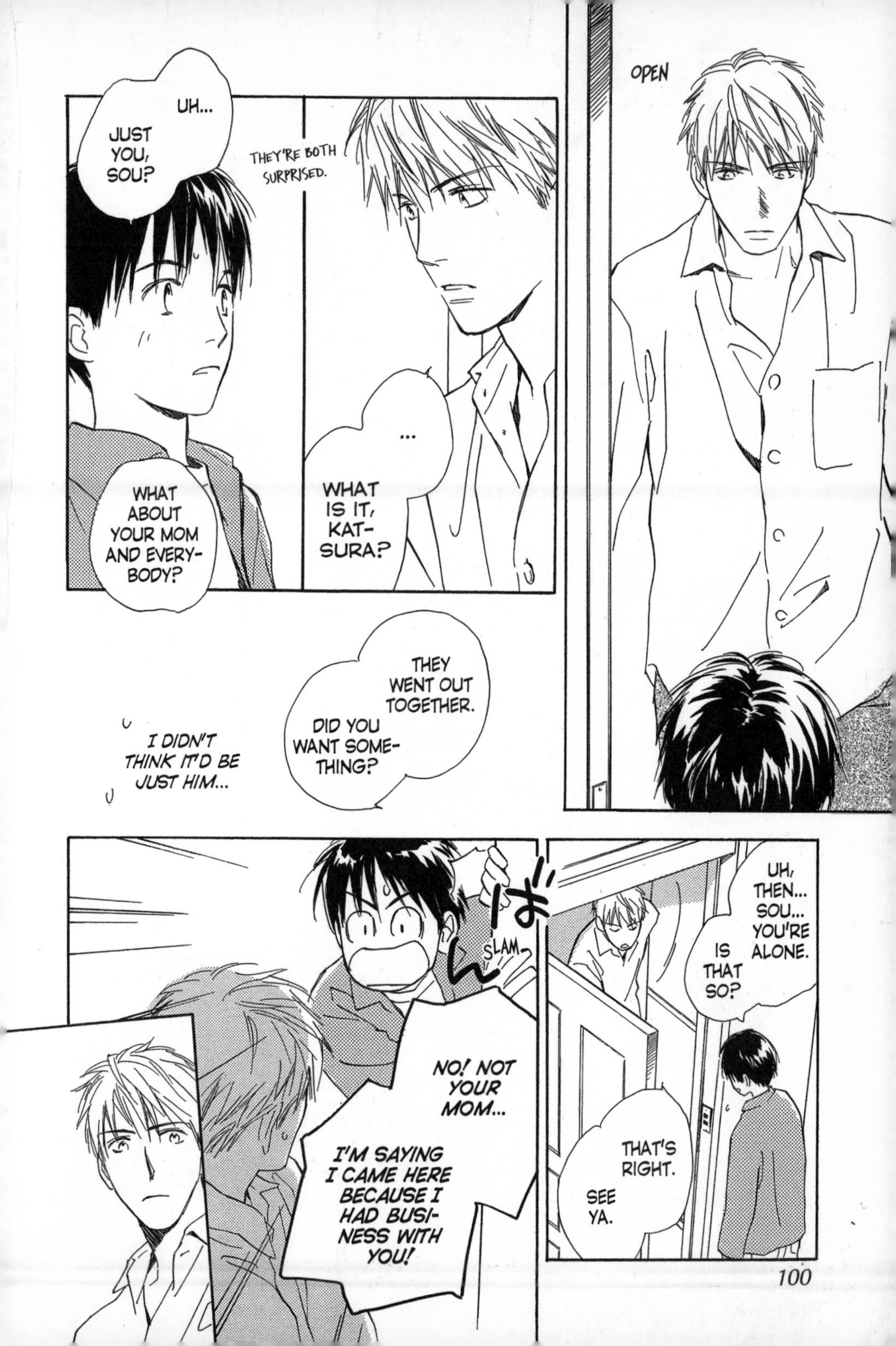
OPEN
UH...
JUST YOU, SOU?
THEY'RE BOTH SURPRISED.
...
WHAT IS IT, KAT-SURA?
WHAT ABOUT YOUR MOM AND EVERY-BODY?
THEY WENT OUT TOGETHER.
DID YOU WANT SOME-THING?
I DIDN'T THINK IT'D BE JUST HIM...
UH, THEN... SOU... YOU'RE ALONE.
IS THAT SO?
THAT'S RIGHT.
SEE YA.
SLAM
NO! NOT YOUR MOM...
I'M SAYING I CAME HERE BECAUSE I HAD BUSI-NESS WITH YOU!

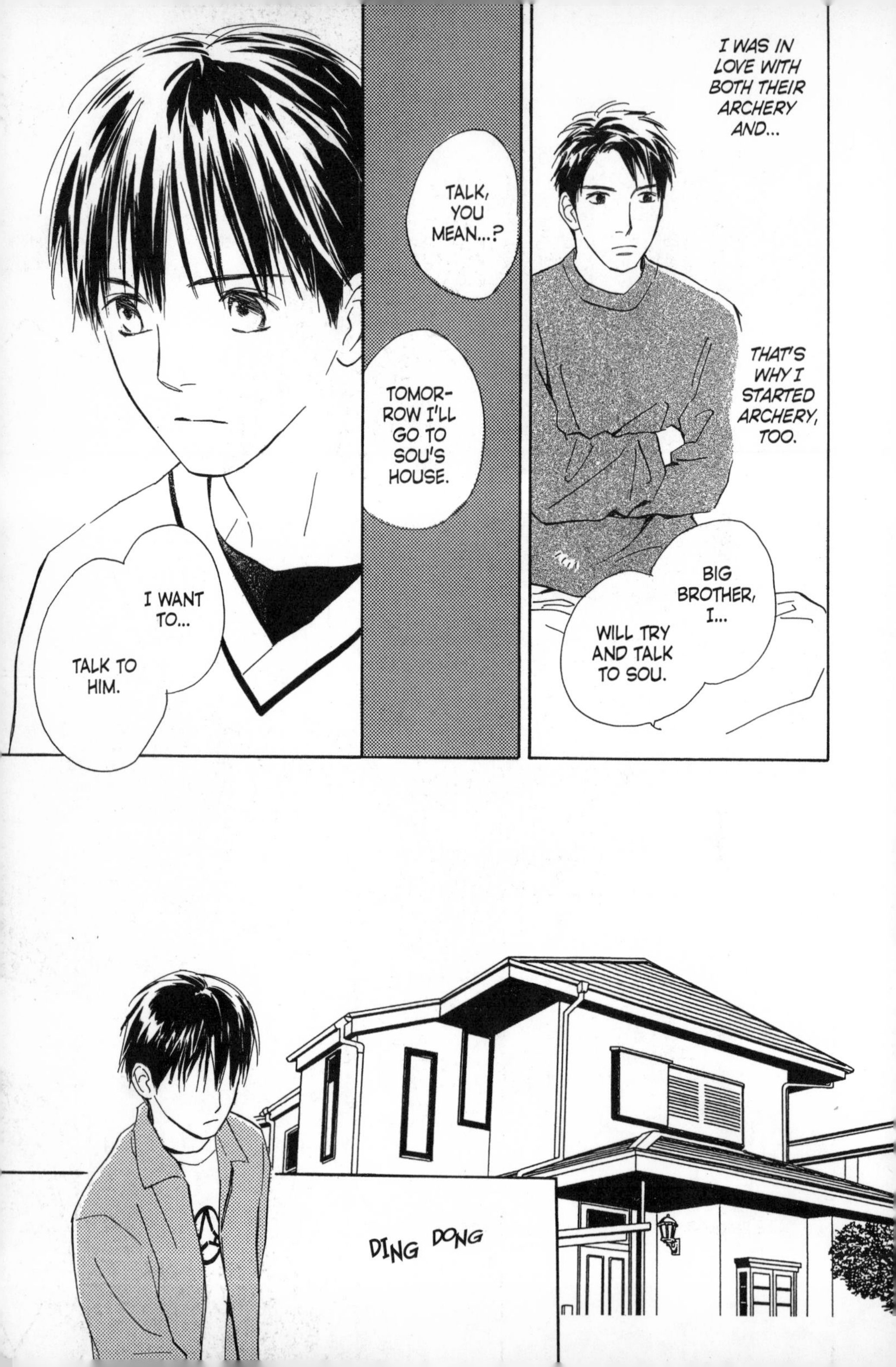
I WAS IN LOVE WITH BOTH THEIR ARCHERY AND...
THAT'S WHY I STARTED ARCHERY, TOO.
BIG BROTHER, I...
WILL TRY AND TALK TO SOU.
TALK, YOU MEAN...?
TOMOR-ROW I'LL GO TO SOU'S HOUSE.
I WANT TO...
TALK TO HIM.
DING DONG

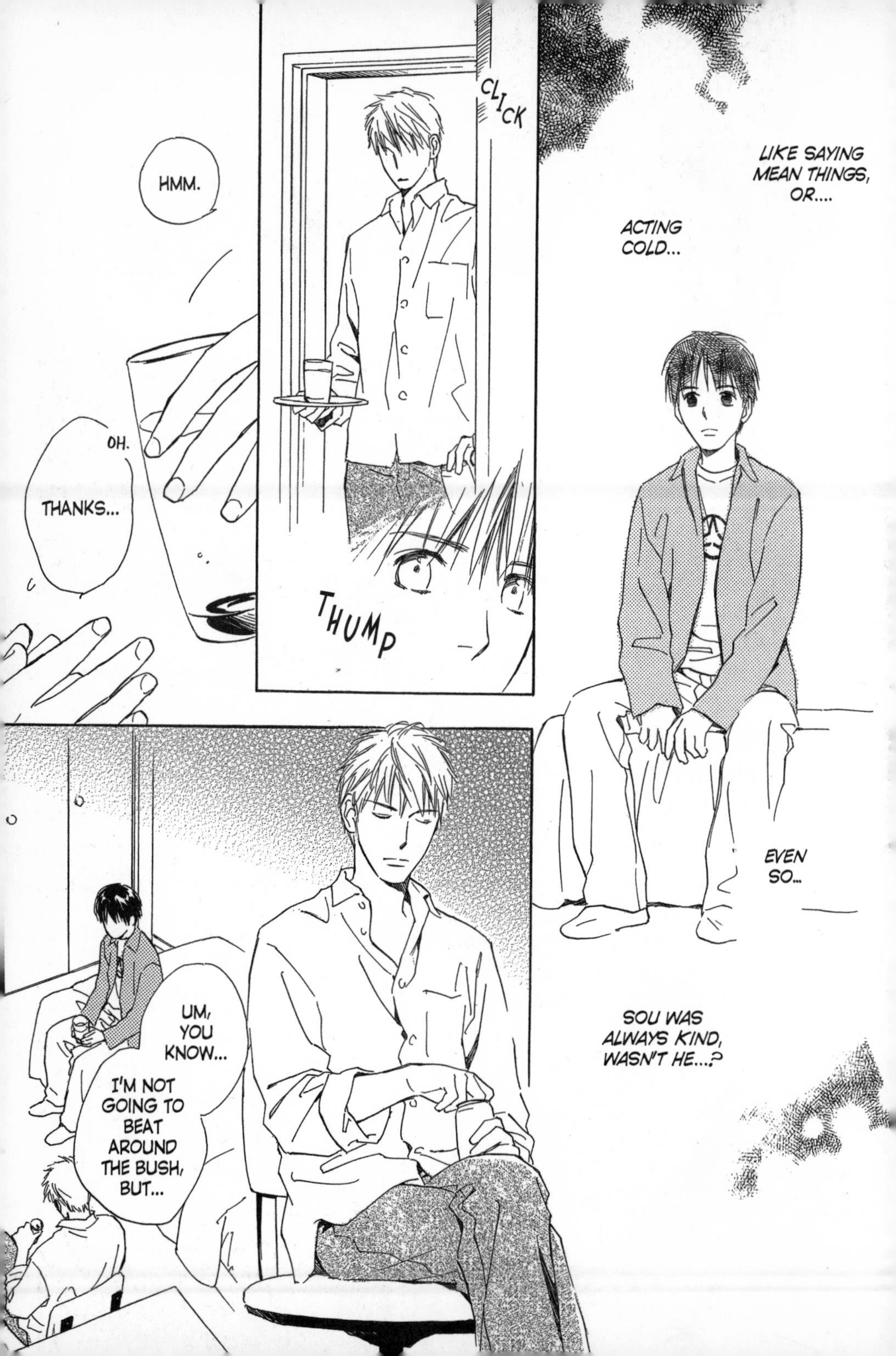
LIKE SAYING MEAN THINGS, OR....
ACTING COLD...
EVEN SO...
SOU WAS ALWAYS KIND, WASN'T HE...?
CLICK
THUMP
HMM.
OH. THANKS...
UM, YOU KNOW...
I'M NOT GOING TO BEAT AROUND THE BUSH, BUT...

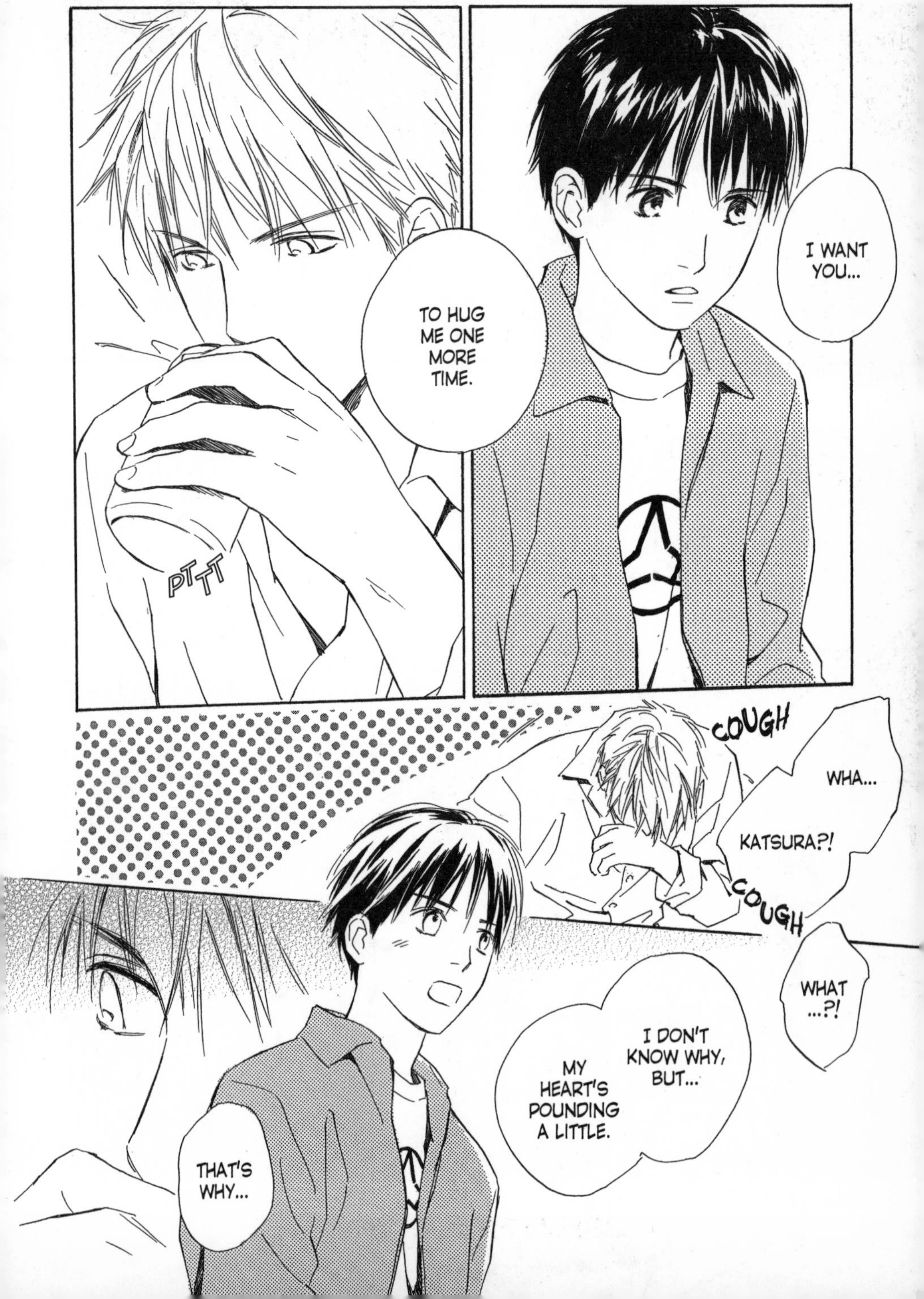
I WANT YOU...
TO HUG ME ONE MORE TIME.
PTTT
COUGH
WHA...
KATSURA?!
COUGH
WHAT ...?!
I DON'T KNOW WHY, BUT...
MY HEART'S POUNDING A LITTLE.
THAT'S WHY...

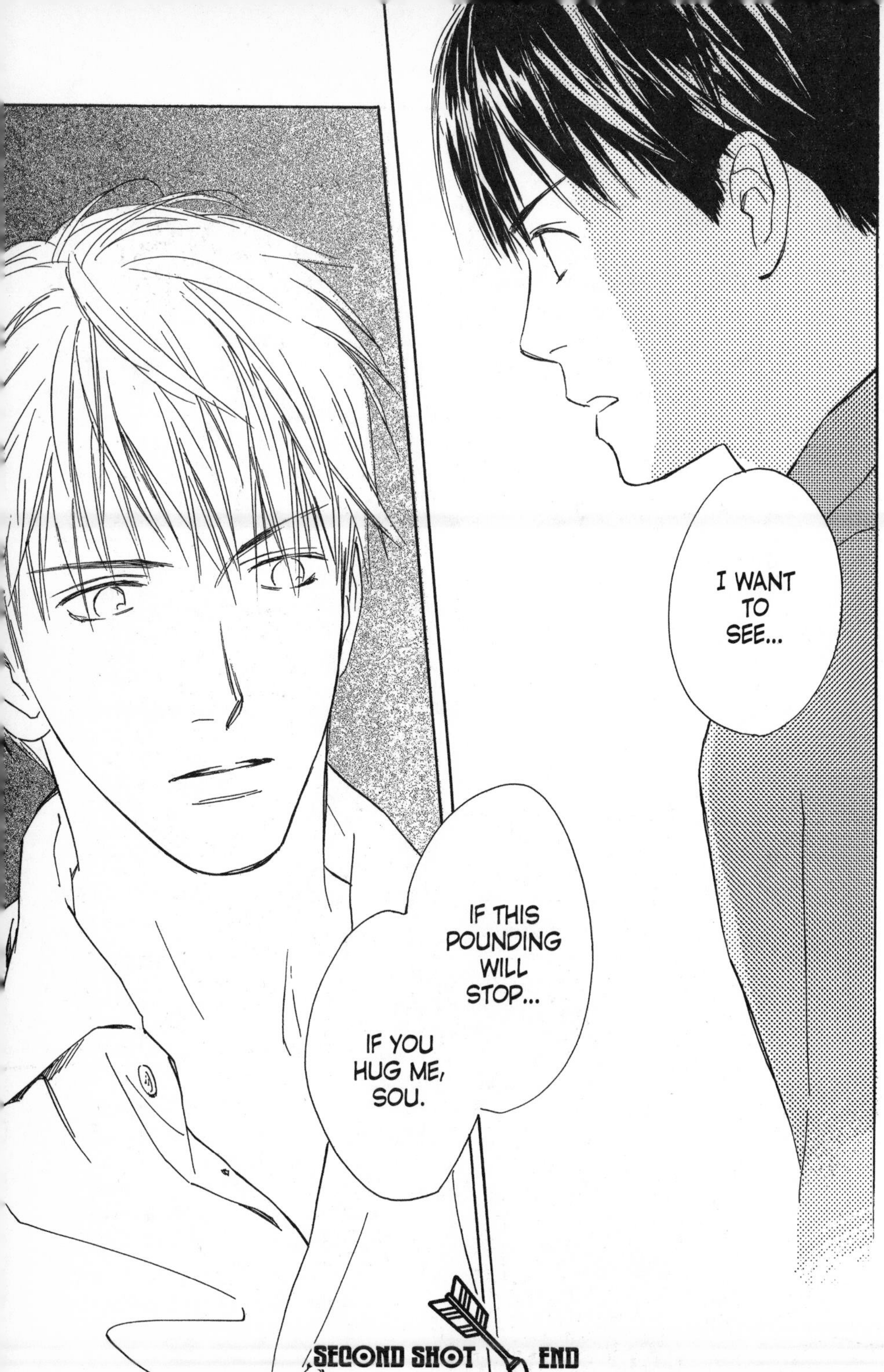
I WANT TO SEE...
IF THIS POUNDING WILL STOP...
IF YOU HUG ME, SOU.
SECOND SHOT END

NONSENSICAL TALK

✤ THANK YOU FOR TAKING THIS INTO YOUR HANDS! IT'S MANGA ABOUT ARCHERY. BY SOME PROVIDENCE OF GOD, I HAD EXPERIENCE WITH JAPANESE ARCHERY IN HIGH SCHOOL. HOWEVER, WHEN TALKING ABOUT THE MANGA THIS TIME, FOR SOME REASON I KEPT THAT A SECRET. WHY? BECAUSE I HADN'T DONE ARCHERY IN A LONG TIME AND AT THE TIME (I DID), OUR CLUB DIDN'T HAVE A REAL INSTRUCTOR, SO MY KNOWLEDGE IS A BIT SKETCHY. THEN I HAD KIND OF HAD HIGH HOPES FOR THIS. ⟶

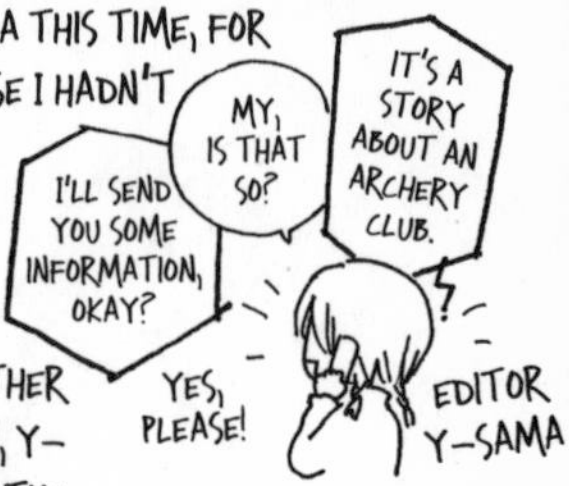
IT'S A STORY ABOUT AN ARCHERY CLUB.
MY, IS THAT SO?
I'LL SEND YOU SOME INFORMATION, OKAY?
YES, PLEASE!
EDITOR Y-SAMA

I'M AN HONEST PERSON, SO I CONFESSED RATHER QUICKLY, BUT I DON'T KNOW IF MY CONTACT PERSON, Y-SAMA, HAD PEACE OF MIND, OR JUST FORGOT, BUT IN THE END I DIDN'T GET THE INFORMATION...(LAUGHS). IT'S LIKE, GET IT YOURSELF FROM THE START! ✤ EVEN IF IT'S HAPHAZARD, I DO HAVE SOME EXPERIENCE, SO... I REALLY PAY ATTENTION TO DETAILS LIKE THE WAY THE HANDS ARE ON A BOW OR ARROW, GESTURES AND POSTURES, ETC. HOWEVER, I DON'T HAVE CONFIDENCE IN MY AMBIGUOUS KNOWLEDGE. THIS IS MY DILEMMA. I'D FINISH SOMEHOW, WHILE THINKING ABOUT HOW DIFFICULT IT WAS TO DRAW. IF THERE ARE ANY PARTS WHERE YOU THINK, "THIS IS WRONG!" PLEASE LET ME KNOW!

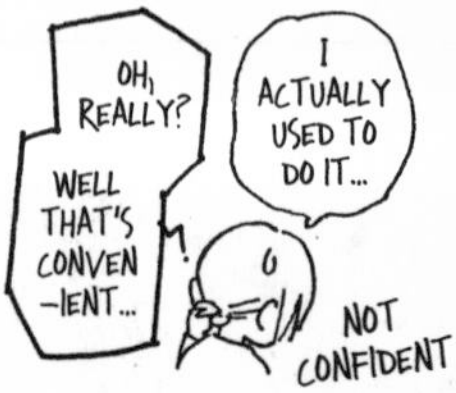
I ACTUALLY USED TO DO IT...
OH, REALLY?
WELL THAT'S CONVEN-IENT...
NOT CONFIDENT

✤ KATSURA AND THE REST OF THEM ARE SHOOTING HOLDING THEIR BOWS AT AN ANGLE, BUT COULD IT BE THAT THERE ARE FEW PEOPLE WHO REALLY USE THIS SHAHOU? I DID GO AND LOOK AT TOURNAMENTS HERE AND THERE, BUT AMONG THOSE THAT I SAW, THERE WAS ONLY ONE PERSON (A BEAR-LIKE OLD MAN). I DIDN'T SEE IT VERY MUCH DURING MY SCHOOL YEARS EITHER, BUT WHEN I DID SEE SOMEONE LIKE THAT DURING A TOURNAMENT, THEY LOOKED REALLY STRONG. THE REASON WHY I HAD KATSURA AND COMPANY USE THIS HOLD IS JUST BECAUSE IT LOOKED GOOD FROM AN ILLUSTRATIVE POINT OF VIEW!

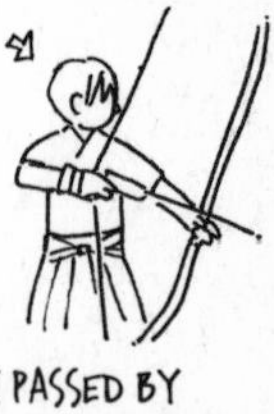

✤ WHEN I PASSED BY MY OLD HIGH SCHOOL FOR THE FIRST TIME IN A WHILE, I WAS SURPRISED BECAUSE THE APPEARANCE OF THE ARCHERY RANGE HAD IMPROVED QUITE A BIT. WHEN I FIRST JOINED THE CLUB, WE USED THE SPACE BETWEEN THE SCHOOL BUILDINGS AND IT WAS JUST A FIELD WITH ARCHERY MOUNDS (AT FIRST I THINK THE RANGE DIDN'T EVEN HAVE A ROOF...) BUT NOW THERE'S WALLS AND EVEN A GATE?! IT'S BECOME MORE DOJO-LIKE! IT SEEMS LIKE ONE OF MY OLD CLASSMATES IS NOW THE TEACHER IN CHARGE. I KEENLY FELT THAT TIMES DO CHANGE, OR SOMETHING?!

✤ THANK YOU VERY MUCH, KANNAGI-SENSEI. I ALWAYS FALL FOR THE MINOR CHARACTERS, BUT IT'S UNUSUAL; THIS TIME I'M PRETTY LOVELY-DOVEY ABOUT SOU. Y-SAMA, I'M SORRY I ALWAYS PUSH YOU TO THE LIMITS OF THE DEADLINES. EVERY TIME I ALWAYS THINK, "WELL, NEXT TIME..." BUT...(PLEASE BELIEVE ME...). I'LL TRY REALLY HARD. TO EVERYONE READING THIS, I'LL BE HAPPY TO SEE YOU AGAIN.

MANY THANKS! KAJI:RA N-CHAMA

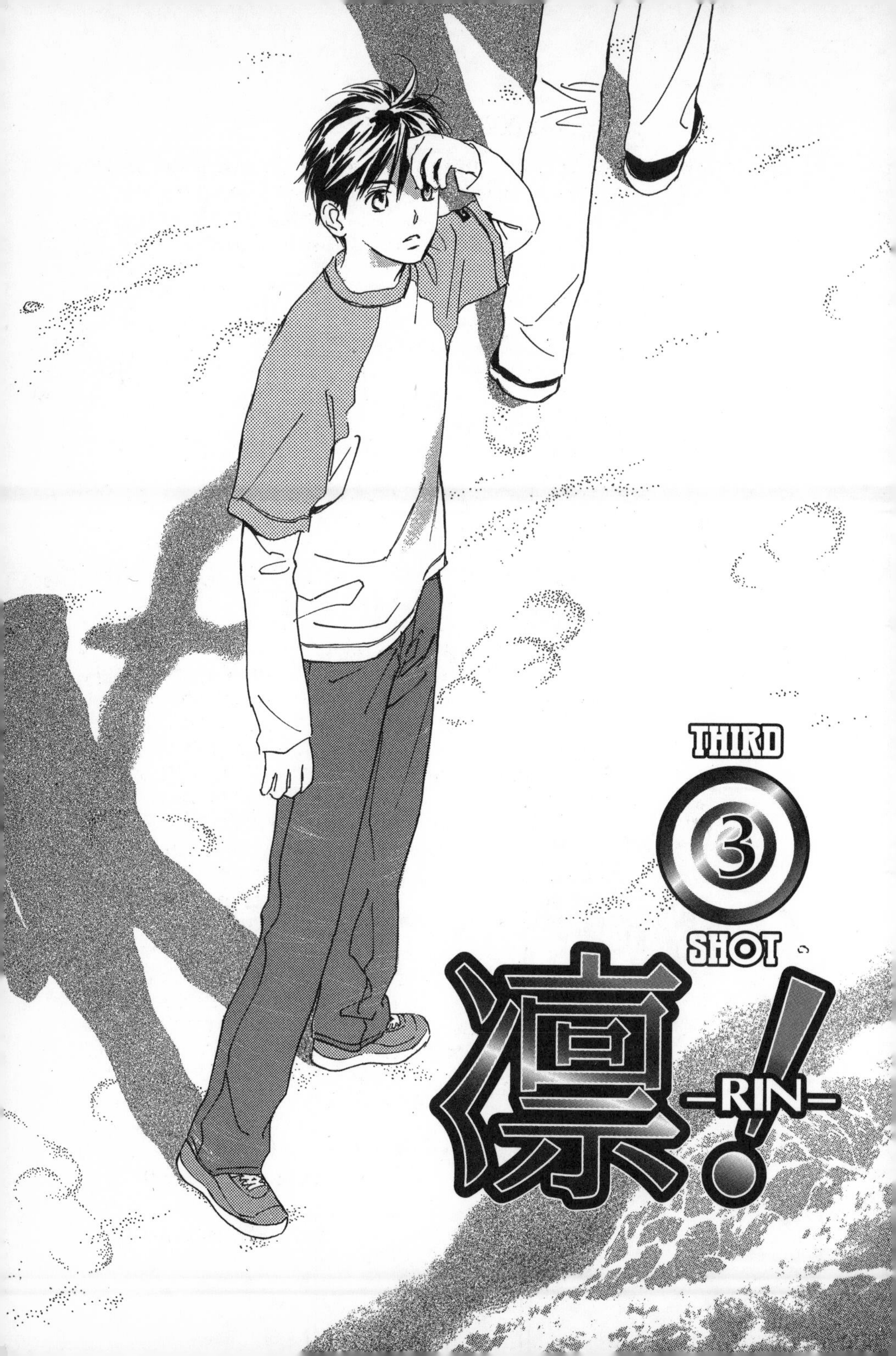
THIRD
3
SHOT
凛!
-RIN-

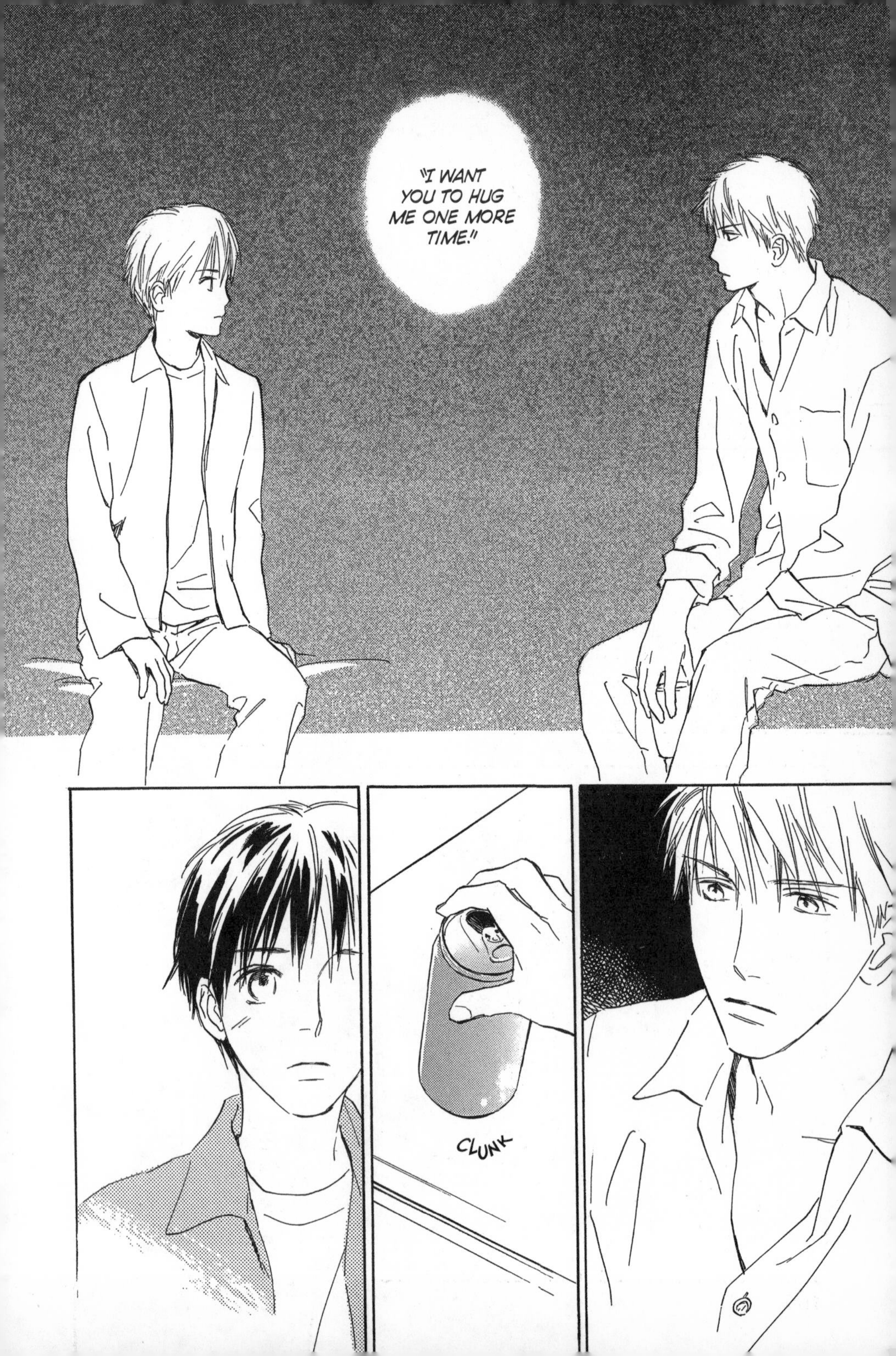
"I WANT YOU TO HUG ME ONE MORE TIME."
CLUNK

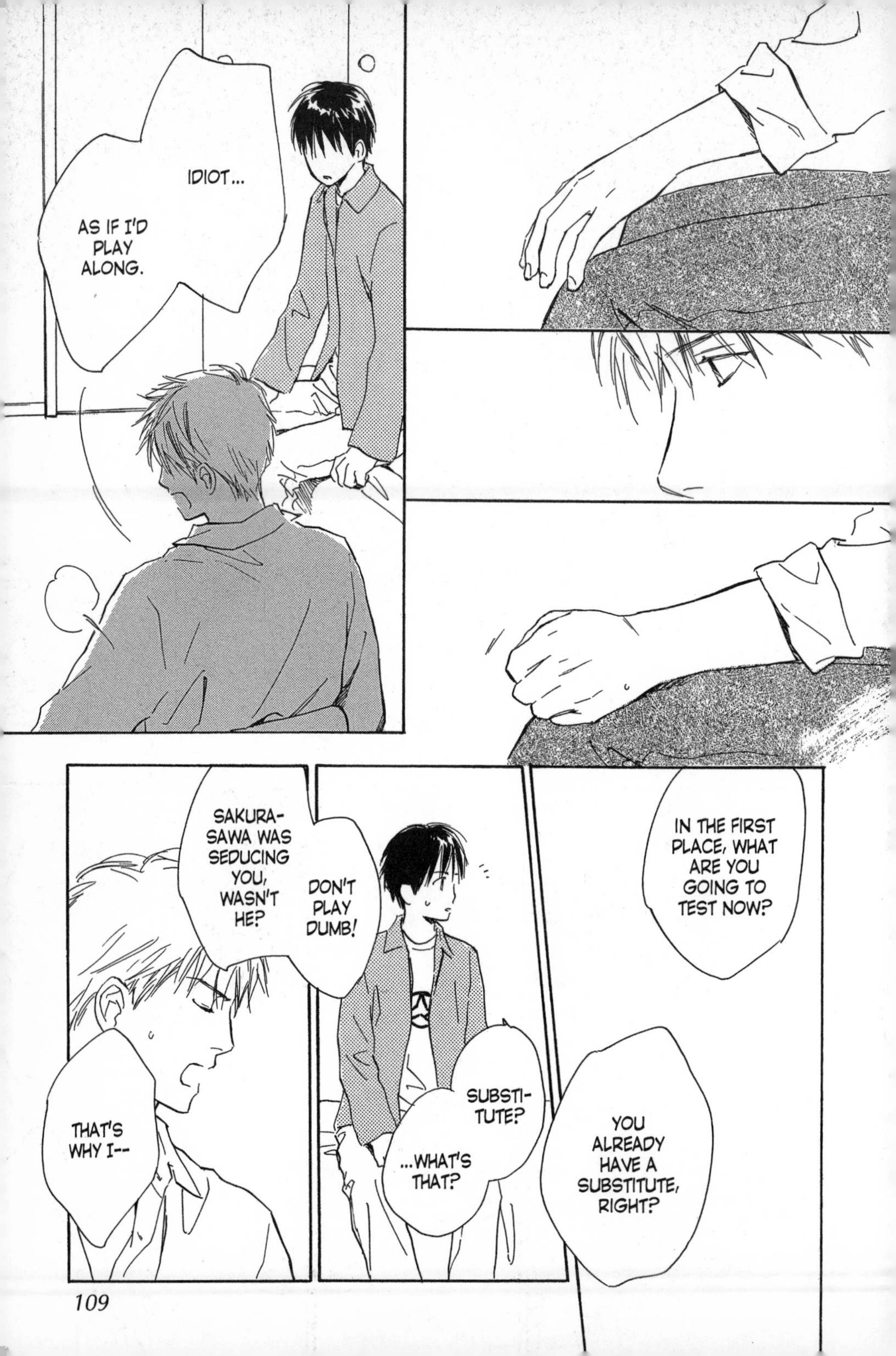
IDIOT...
AS IF I'D PLAY ALONG.
IN THE FIRST PLACE, WHAT ARE YOU GOING TO TEST NOW?
YOU ALREADY HAVE A SUBSTITUTE, RIGHT?
SUBSTI-TUTE?
...WHAT'S THAT?
DON'T PLAY DUMB!
SAKURA-SAWA WAS SEDUCING YOU, WASN'T HE?
THAT'S WHY I--

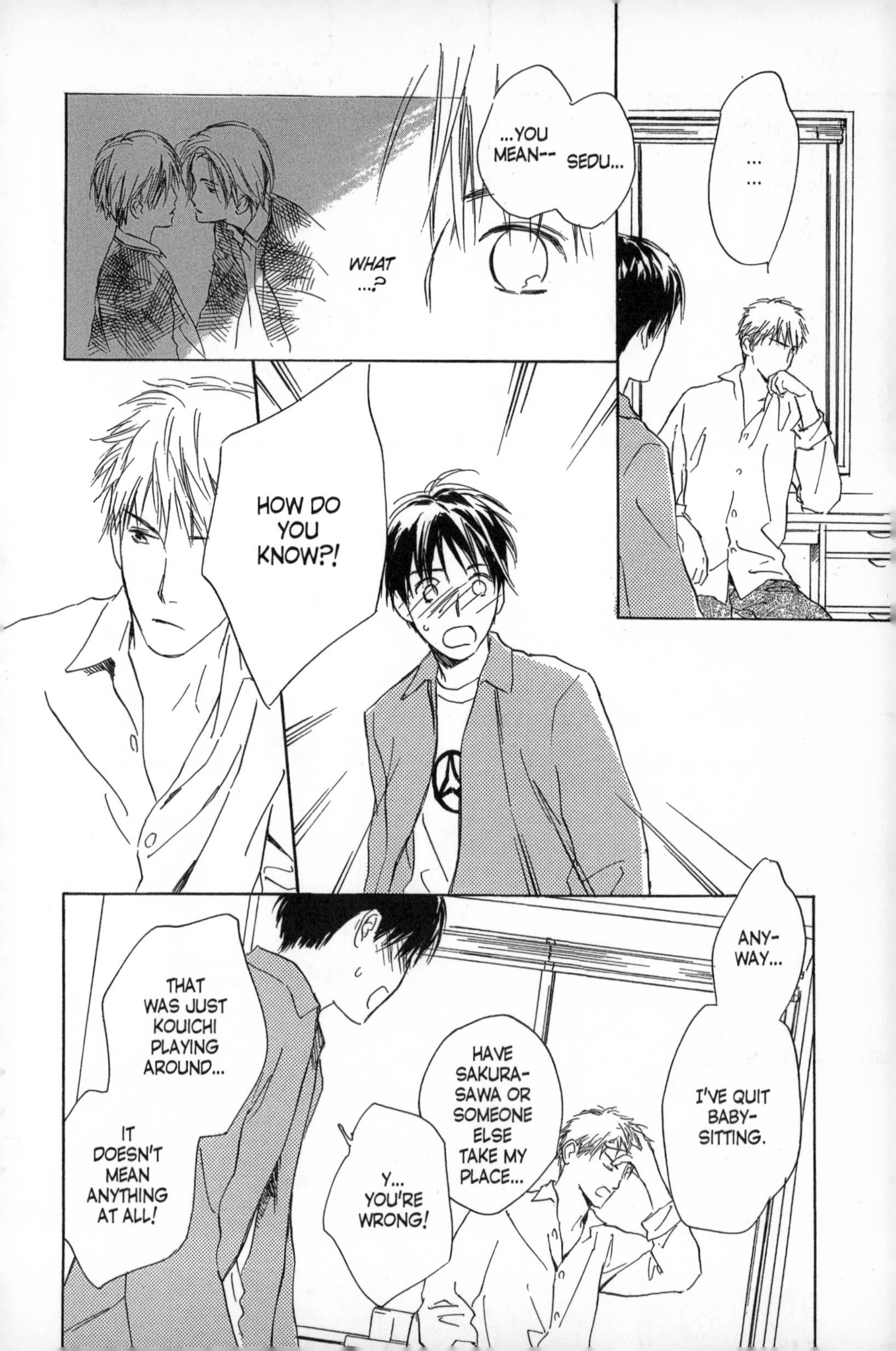

...
...
...YOU MEAN-- SEDU...
WHAT ...?
HOW DO YOU KNOW?!
ANY-WAY...
I'VE QUIT BABY-SITTING.
HAVE SAKURA-SAWA OR SOMEONE ELSE TAKE MY PLACE...
Y... YOU'RE WRONG!
THAT WAS JUST KOUICHI PLAYING AROUND...
IT DOESN'T MEAN ANYTHING AT ALL!

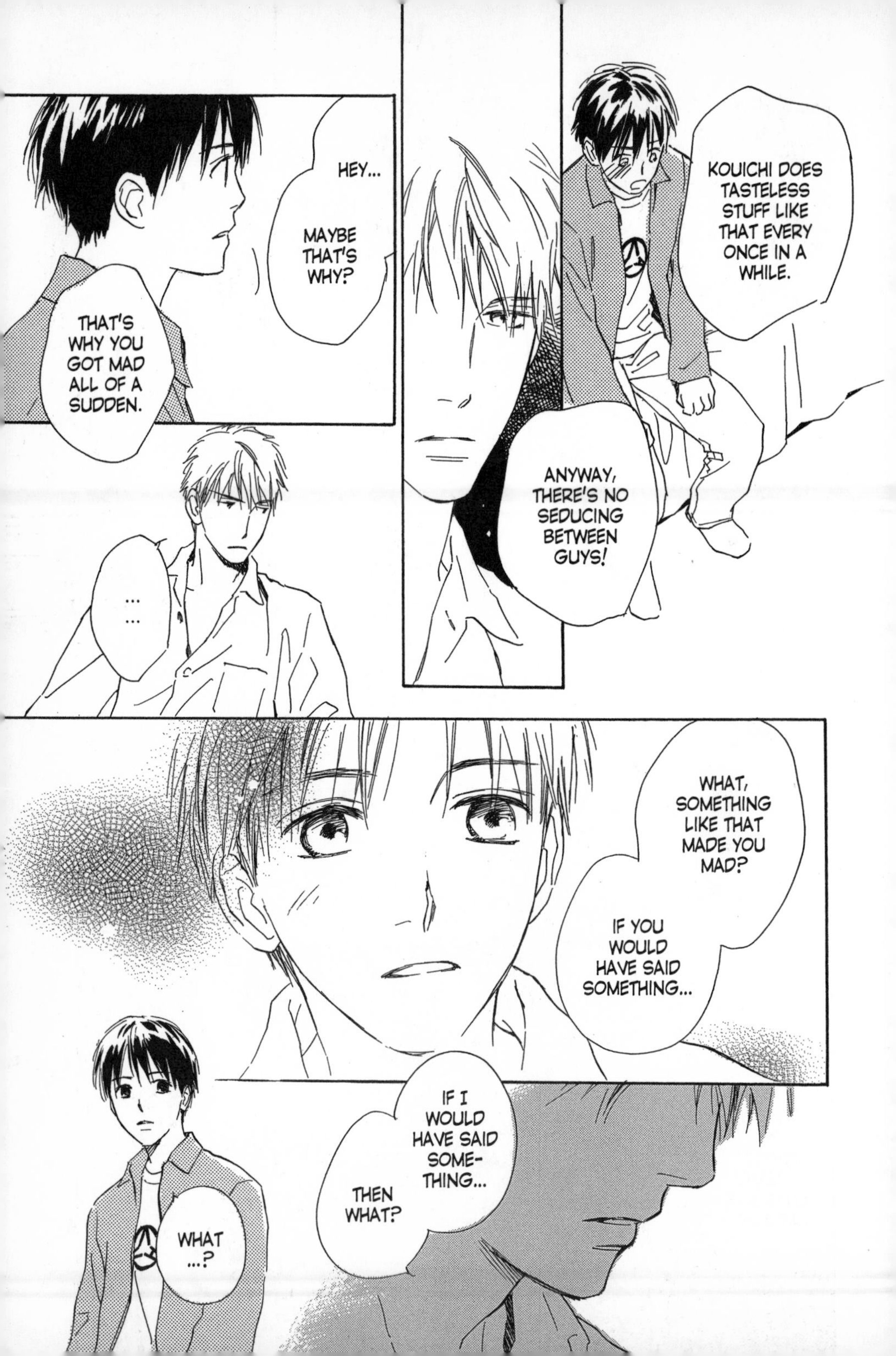
KOUICHI DOES TASTELESS STUFF LIKE THAT EVERY ONCE IN A WHILE.
ANYWAY, THERE'S NO SEDUCING BETWEEN GUYS!
HEY...
MAYBE THAT'S WHY?
THAT'S WHY YOU GOT MAD ALL OF A SUDDEN.
......
WHAT, SOMETHING LIKE THAT MADE YOU MAD?
IF YOU WOULD HAVE SAID SOMETHING...
IF I WOULD HAVE SAID SOME-THING...
THEN WHAT?
WHAT...?

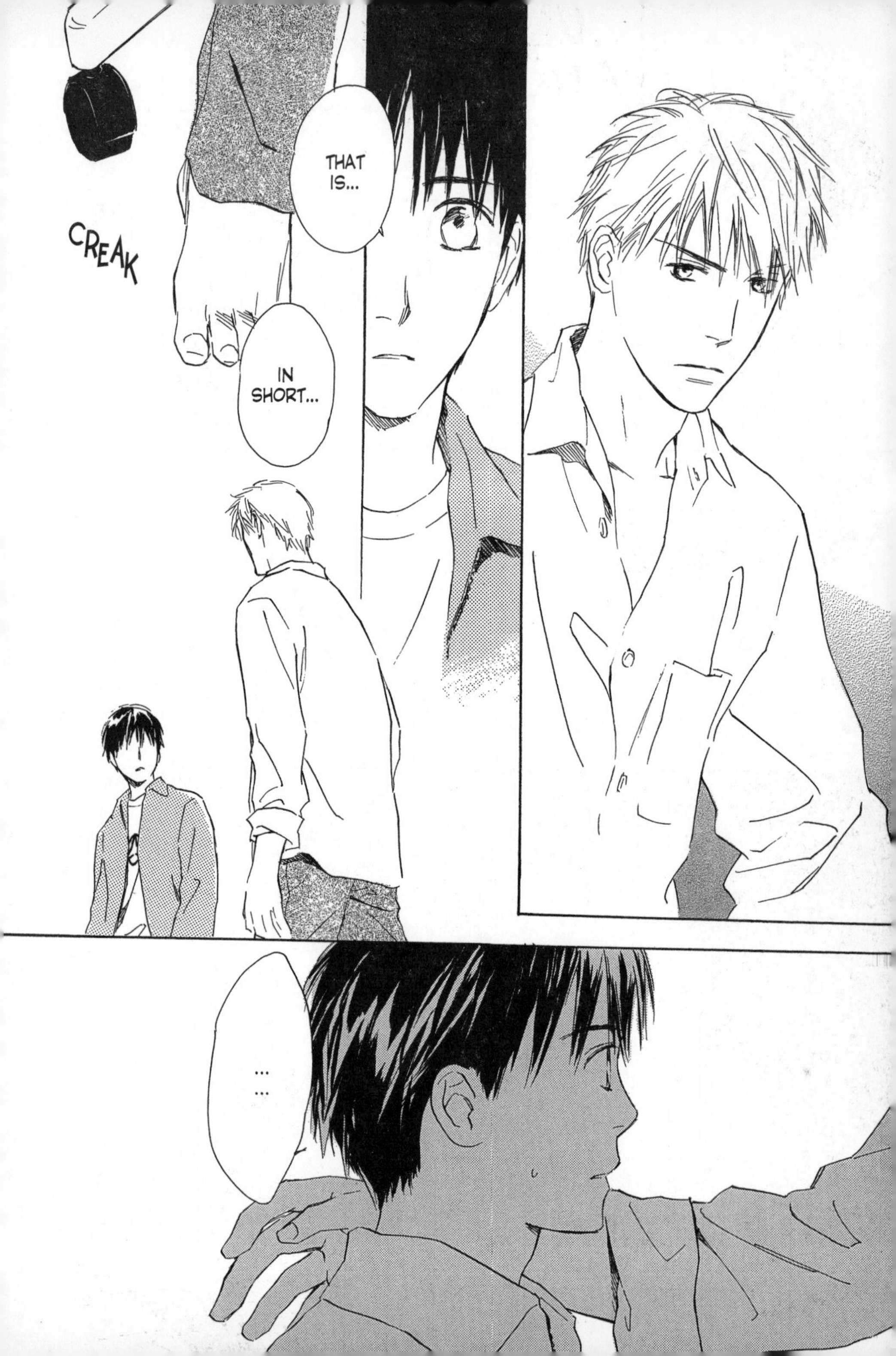
THAT IS...
IN SHORT...
CREAK
......

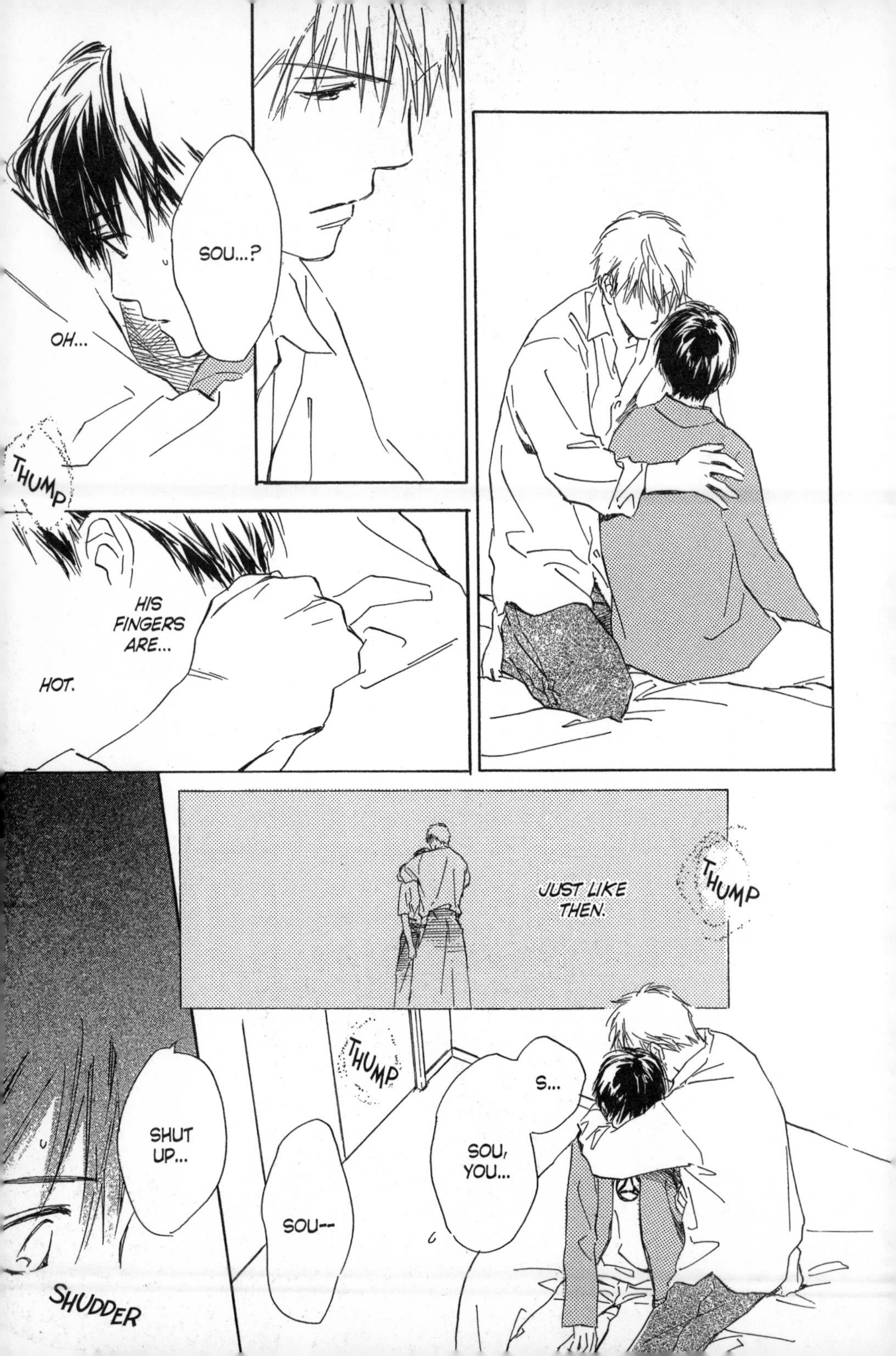
SOU...?
OH...
THUMP
HIS FINGERS ARE...
HOT.
THUMP
JUST LIKE THEN.
S...
SOU, YOU...
THUMP
SOU--
SHUT UP...
SHUDDER

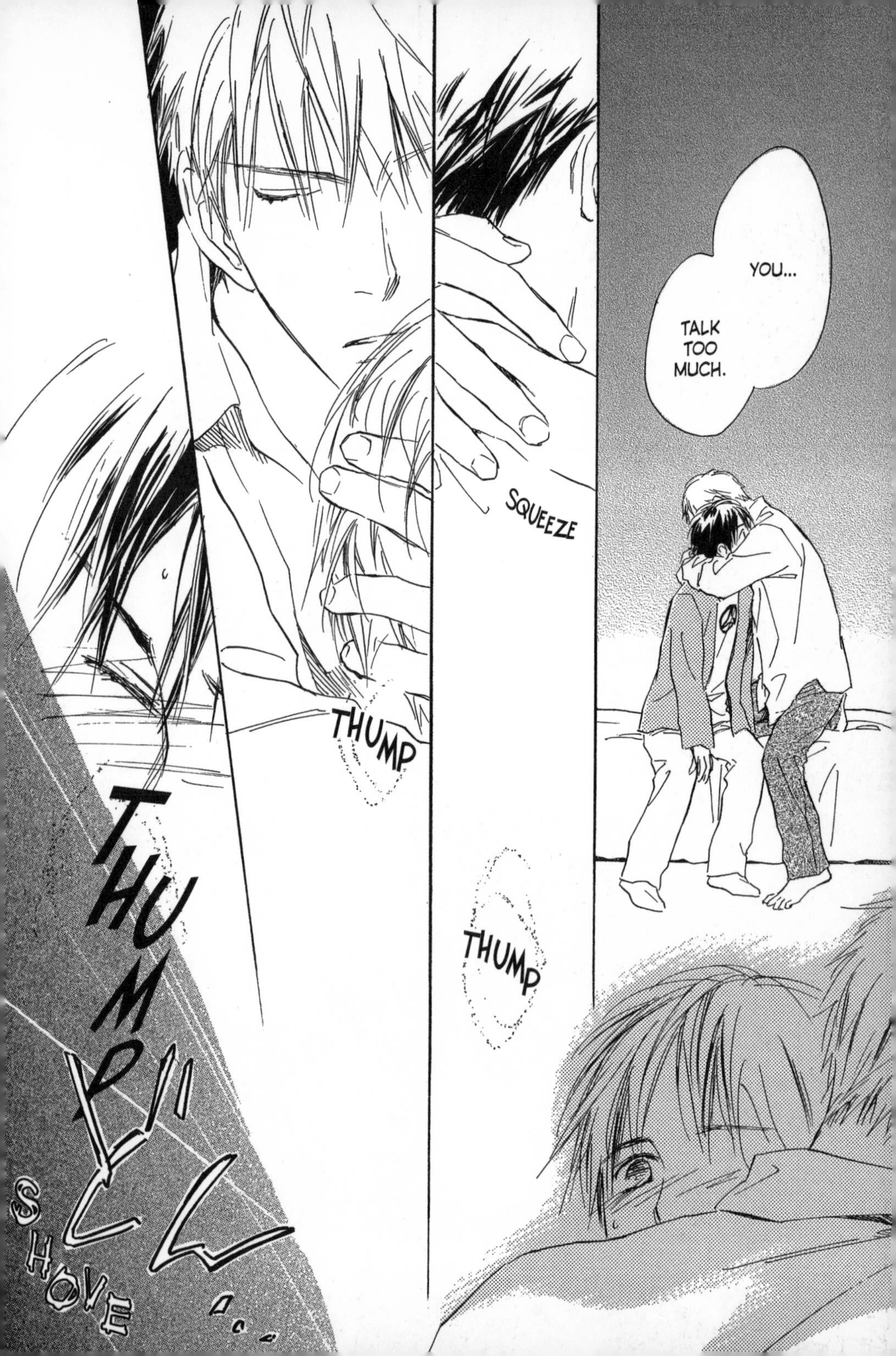
YOU...
TALK TOO MUCH.
SQUEEZE
THUMP
THUMP
THUMP!!
SHOVE

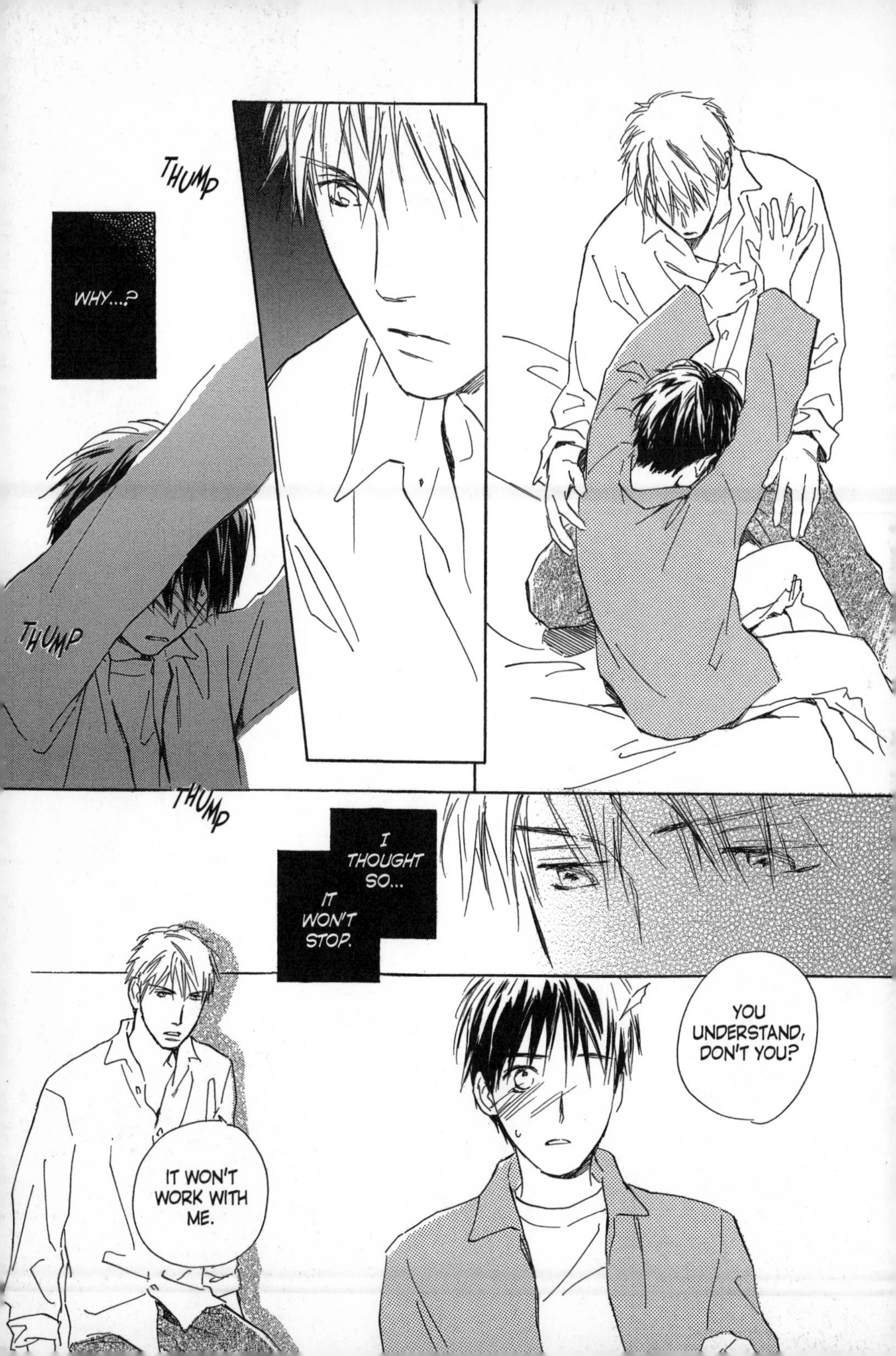
THUMP
WHY...?
THUMP
I THOUGHT SO...
IT WON'T STOP.
THUMP
YOU UNDERSTAND, DON'T YOU?
IT WON'T WORK WITH ME.

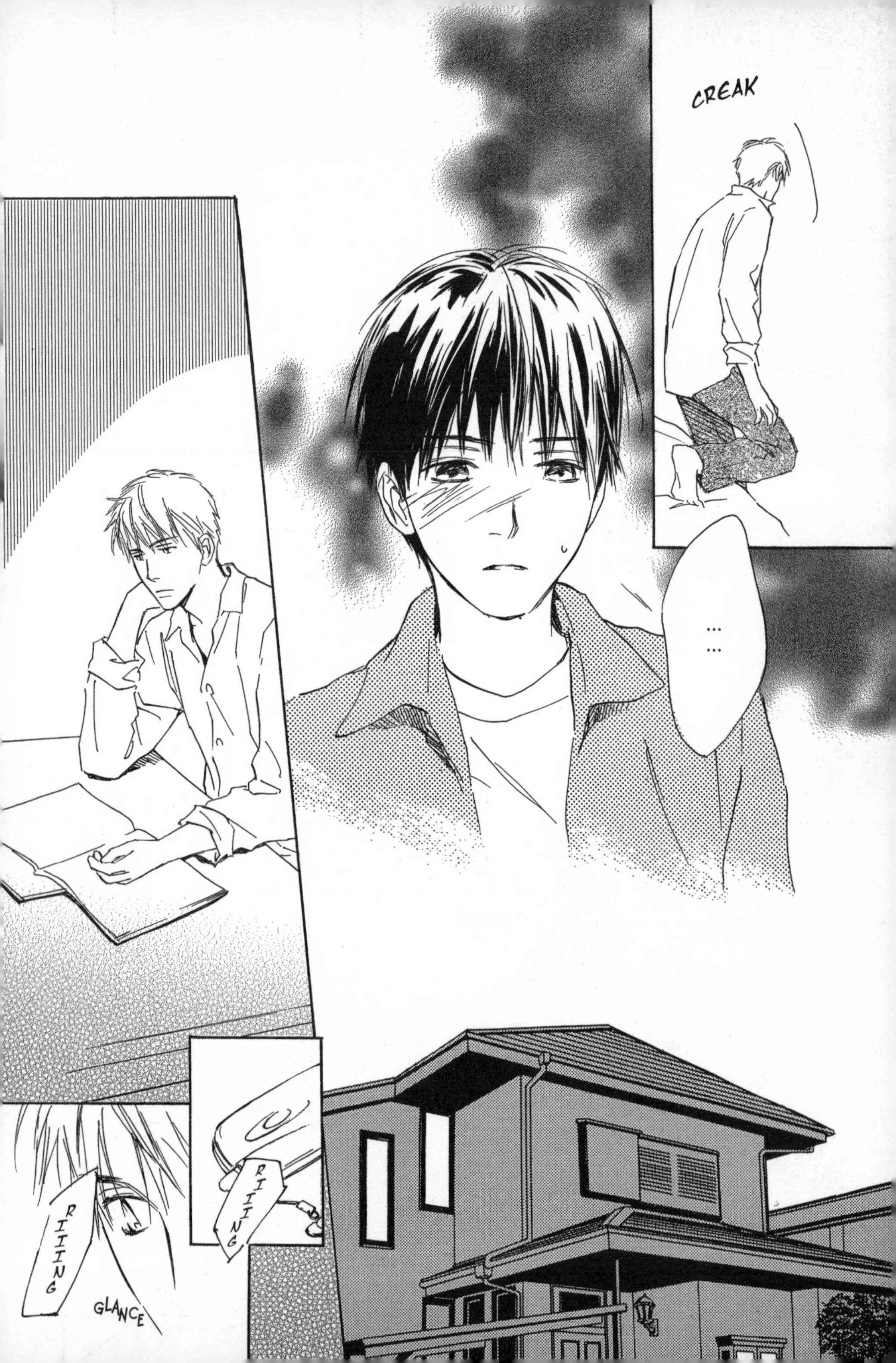
CREAK
... ...
RIIING
RIIING
GLANCE

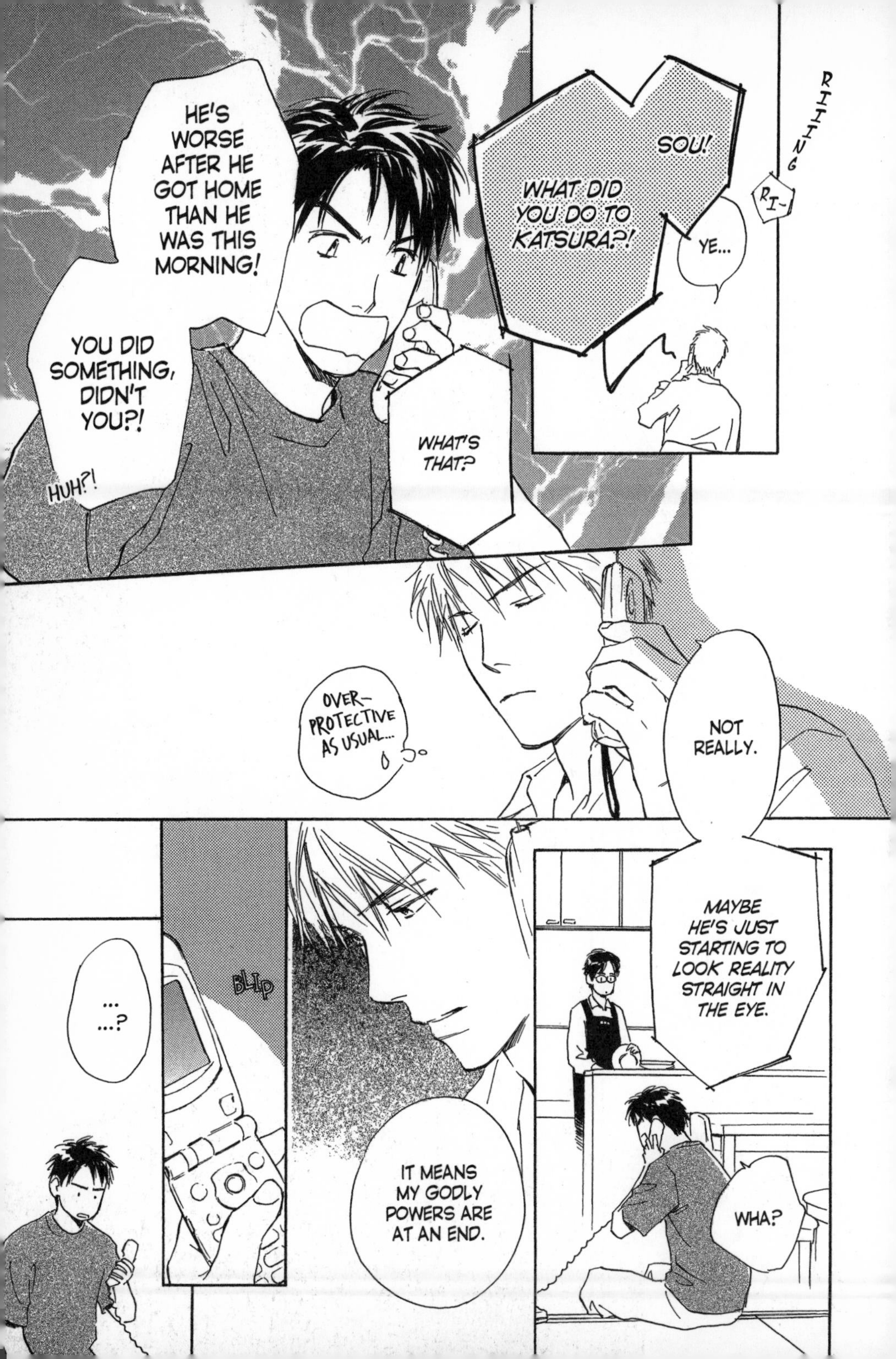
RIIIING
RI-
YE...
SOU! WHAT DID YOU DO TO KATSURA?!
HE'S WORSE AFTER HE GOT HOME THAN HE WAS THIS MORNING!
YOU DID SOMETHING, DIDN'T YOU?!
HUH?!
WHAT'S THAT?
NOT REALLY.
OVER-PROTECTIVE AS USUAL...
MAYBE HE'S JUST STARTING TO LOOK REALITY STRAIGHT IN THE EYE.
WHA?
IT MEANS MY GODLY POWERS ARE AT AN END.
BLIP
... ...?

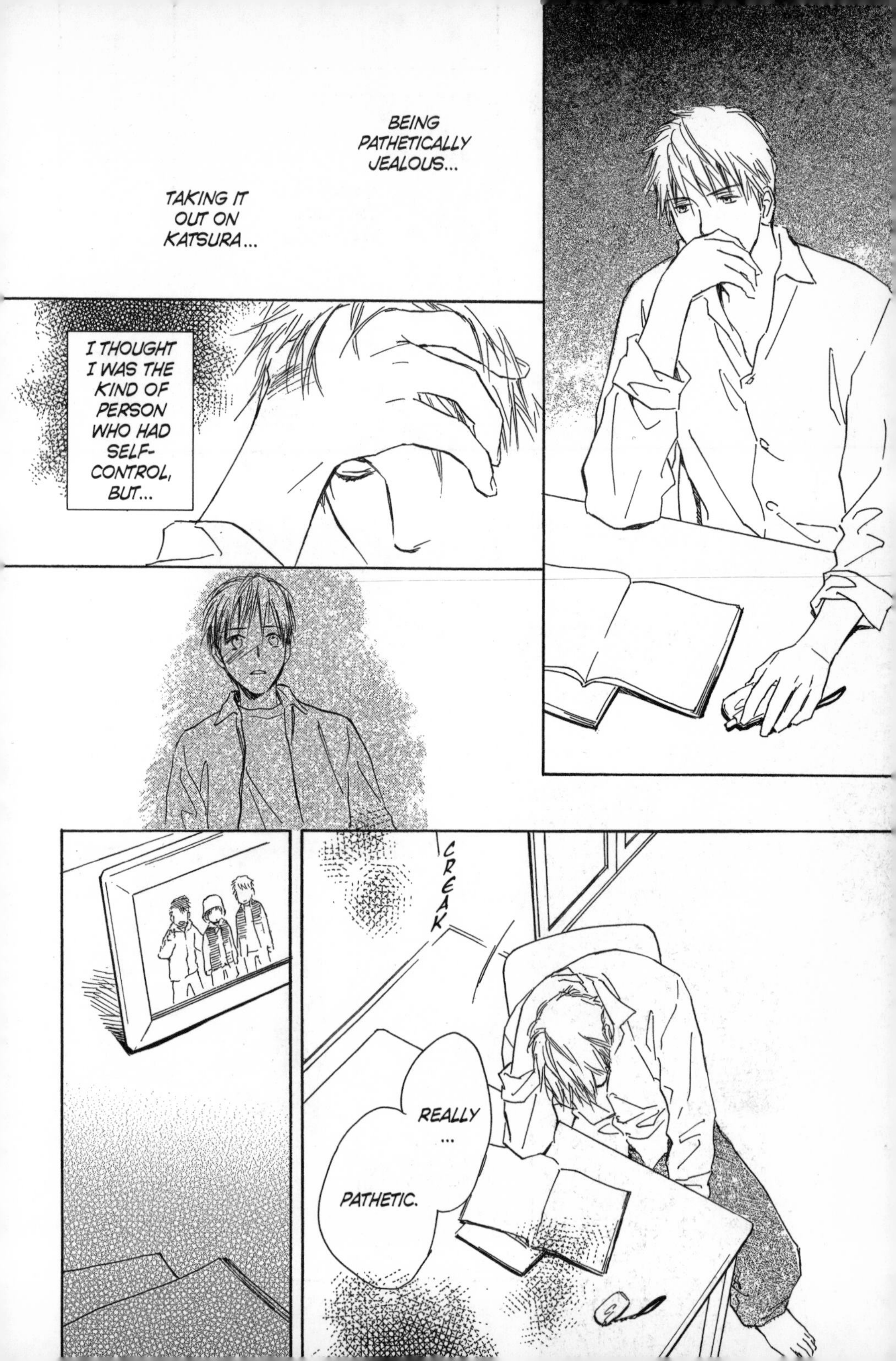
BEING PATHETICALLY JEALOUS...
TAKING IT OUT ON KATSURA...
I THOUGHT I WAS THE KIND OF PERSON WHO HAD SELF-CONTROL, BUT...
CREAK
REALLY ...
PATHETIC.

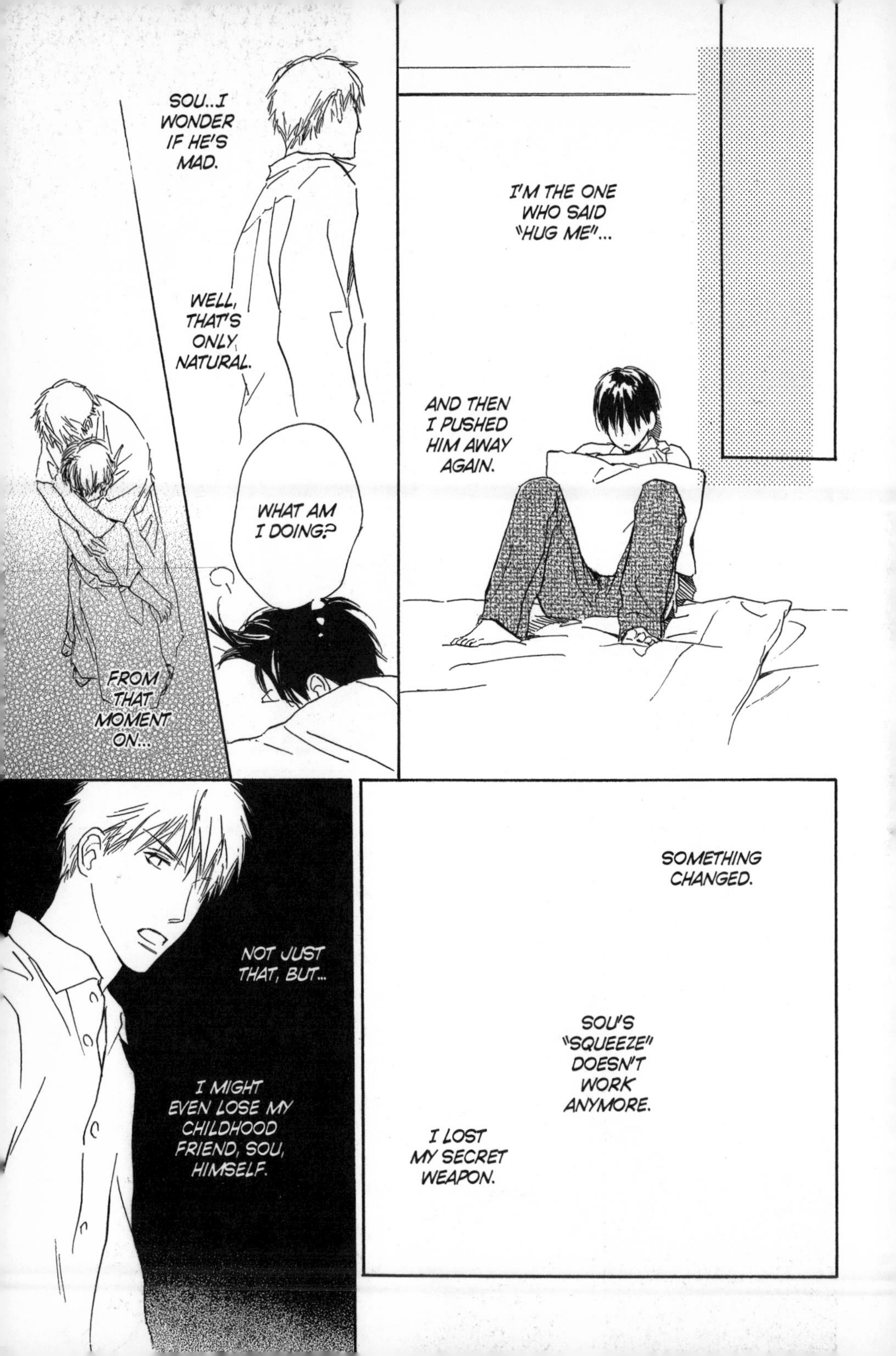
I'M THE ONE WHO SAID "HUG ME"...
AND THEN I PUSHED HIM AWAY AGAIN.
SOU..I WONDER IF HE'S MAD.
WELL, THAT'S ONLY NATURAL.
WHAT AM I DOING?
FROM THAT MOMENT ON...
SOMETHING CHANGED.
SOU'S "SQUEEZE" DOESN'T WORK ANYMORE.
I LOST MY SECRET WEAPON.
NOT JUST THAT, BUT...
I MIGHT EVEN LOSE MY CHILDHOOD FRIEND, SOU, HIMSELF.

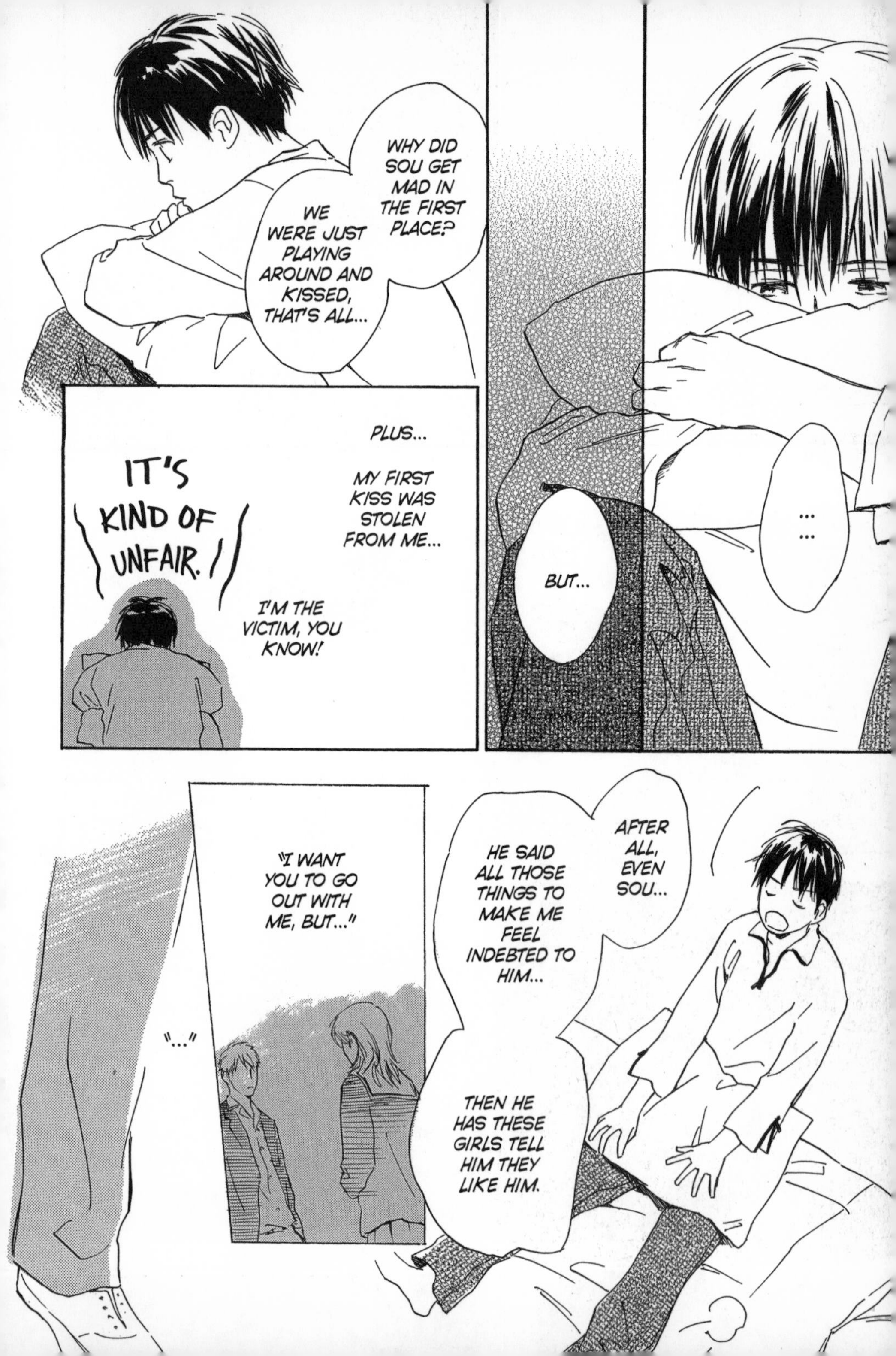

...
...
BUT...
WHY DID SOU GET MAD IN THE FIRST PLACE?
WE WERE JUST PLAYING AROUND AND KISSED, THAT'S ALL...
PLUS...
MY FIRST KISS WAS STOLEN FROM ME...
IT'S KIND OF UNFAIR.
I'M THE VICTIM, YOU KNOW!
AFTER ALL, EVEN SOU...
HE SAID ALL THOSE THINGS TO MAKE ME FEEL INDEBTED TO HIM...
THEN HE HAS THESE GIRLS TELL HIM THEY LIKE HIM.
"I WANT YOU TO GO OUT WITH ME, BUT..."
"..."

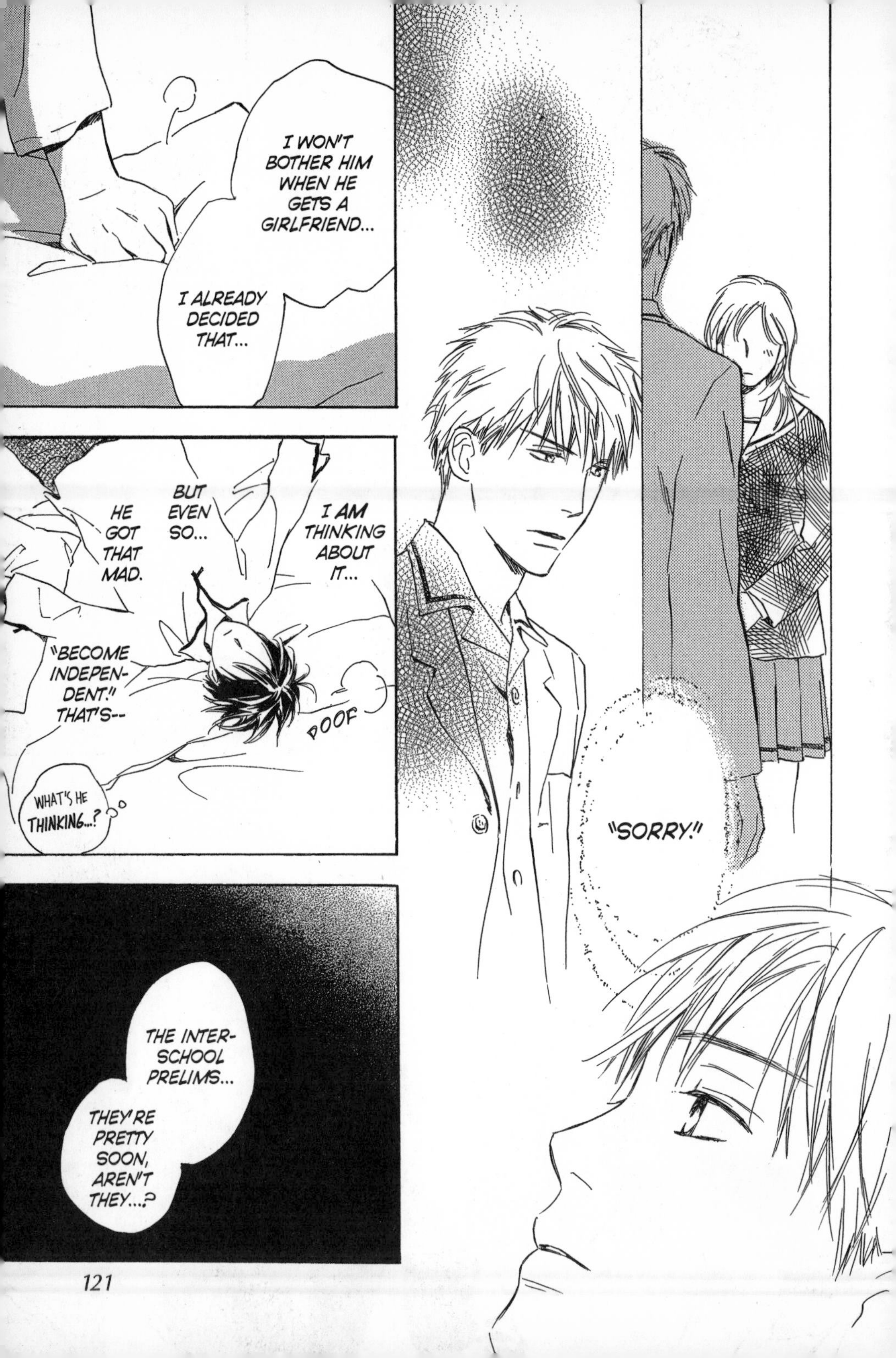
"SORRY!"
I WON'T BOTHER HIM WHEN HE GETS A GIRLFRIEND...
I ALREADY DECIDED THAT...
I AM THINKING ABOUT IT...
BUT EVEN SO...
HE GOT THAT MAD.
"BECOME INDEPENDENT!" THAT'S--
POOF
WHAT'S HE THINKING...?
THE INTER-SCHOOL PRELIMS...
THEY'RE PRETTY SOON, AREN'T THEY...?

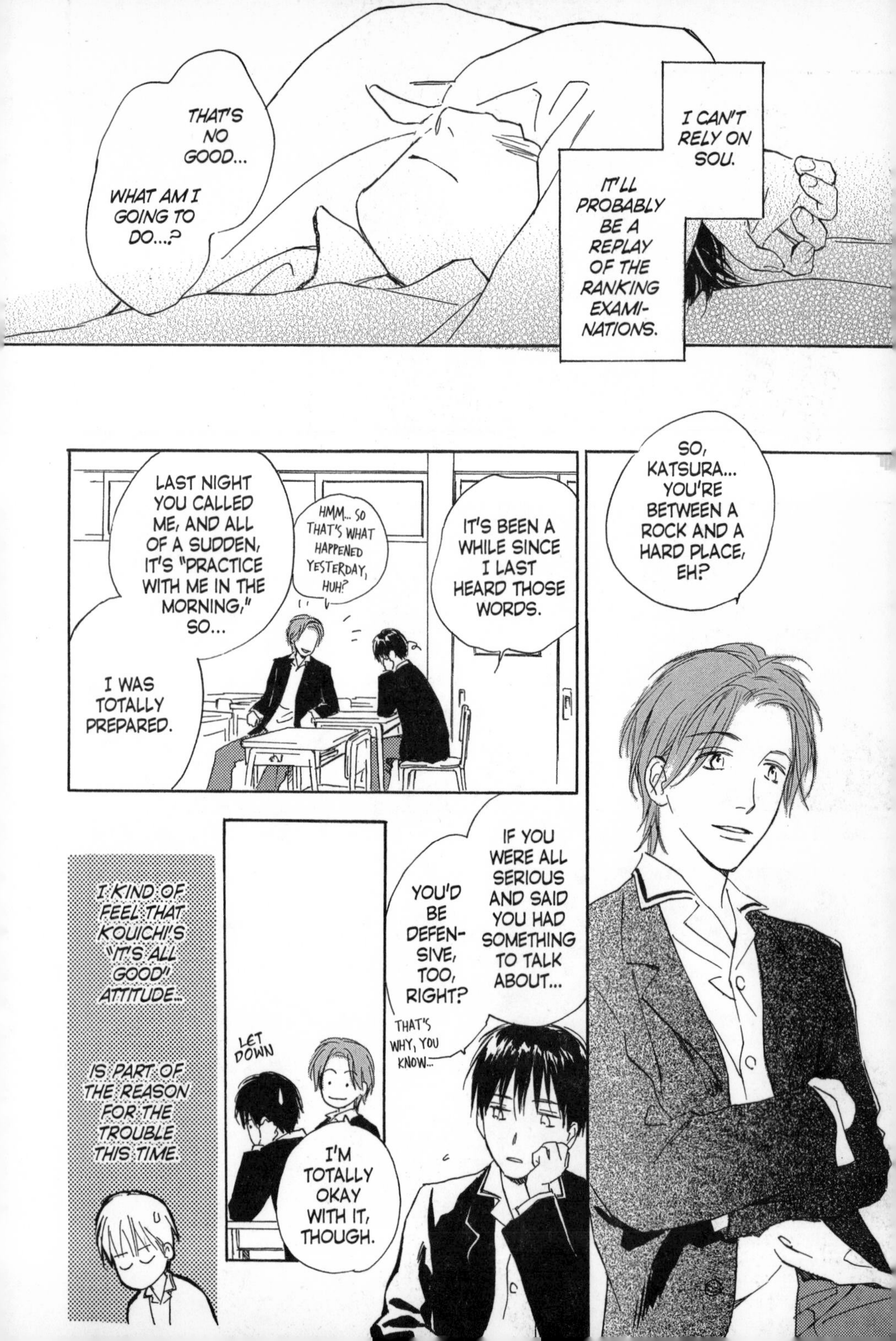
I CAN'T RELY ON SOU.
IT'LL PROBABLY BE A REPLAY OF THE RANKING EXAMI-NATIONS.
THAT'S NO GOOD...
WHAT AM I GOING TO DO...?
SO, KATSURA... YOU'RE BETWEEN A ROCK AND A HARD PLACE, EH?
IT'S BEEN A WHILE SINCE I LAST HEARD THOSE WORDS.
HMM... SO THAT'S WHAT HAPPENED YESTERDAY, HUH?
LAST NIGHT YOU CALLED ME, AND ALL OF A SUDDEN, IT'S "PRACTICE WITH ME IN THE MORNING," SO...
I WAS TOTALLY PREPARED.
IF YOU WERE ALL SERIOUS AND SAID YOU HAD SOMETHING TO TALK ABOUT...
YOU'D BE DEFEN-SIVE, TOO, RIGHT?
THAT'S WHY, YOU KNOW...
LET DOWN
I'M TOTALLY OKAY WITH IT, THOUGH.
I KIND OF FEEL THAT KOUICHI'S "IT'S ALL GOOD" ATTITUDE...
IS PART OF THE REASON FOR THE TROUBLE THIS TIME.

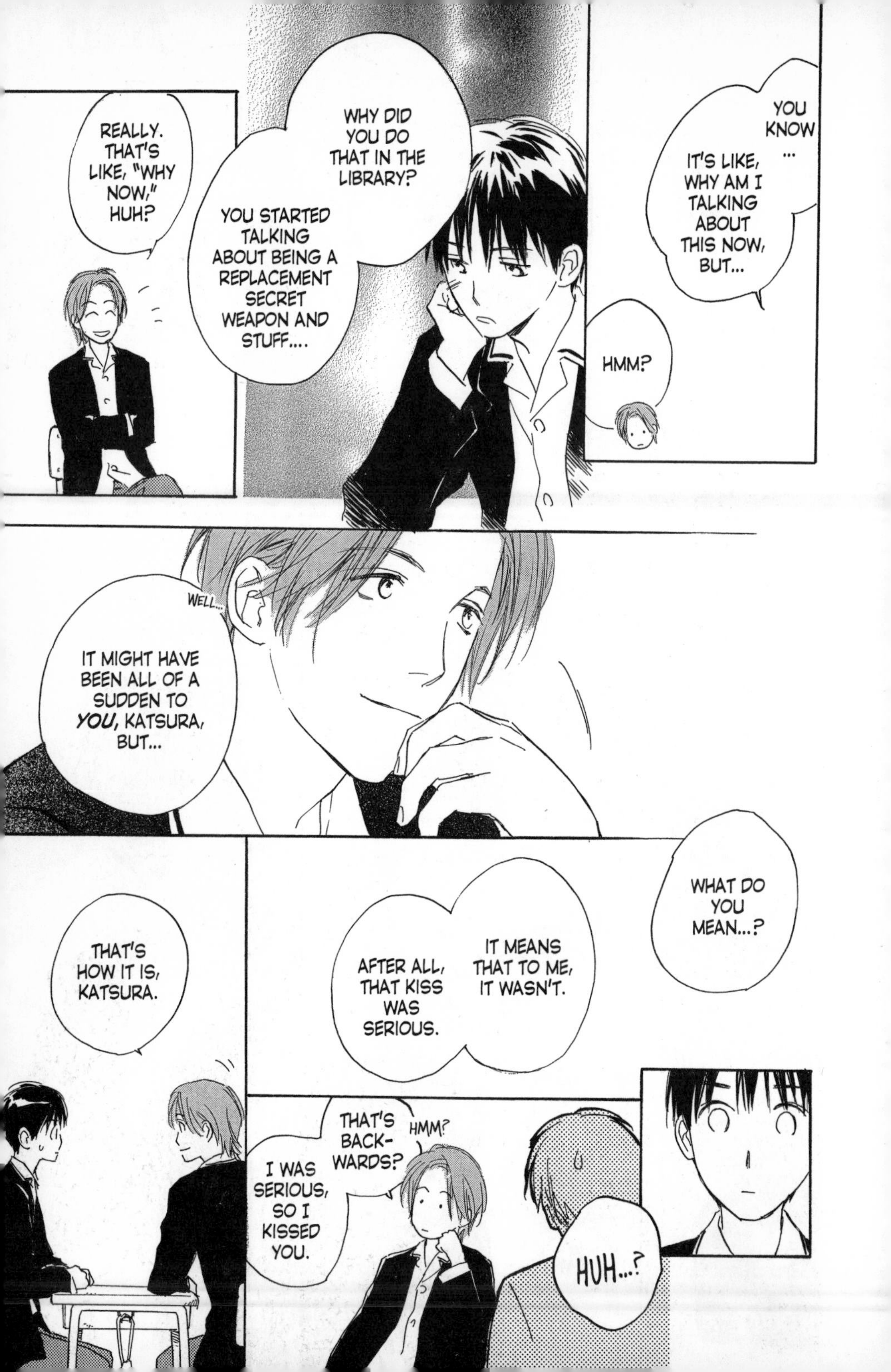
YOU KNOW ...
IT'S LIKE, WHY AM I TALKING ABOUT THIS NOW, BUT...
HMM?
WHY DID YOU DO THAT IN THE LIBRARY?
YOU STARTED TALKING ABOUT BEING A REPLACEMENT SECRET WEAPON AND STUFF....
REALLY. THAT'S LIKE, "WHY NOW," HUH?
WELL...
IT MIGHT HAVE BEEN ALL OF A SUDDEN TO *YOU*, KATSURA, BUT...
WHAT DO YOU MEAN...?
IT MEANS THAT TO ME, IT WASN'T.
AFTER ALL, THAT KISS WAS SERIOUS.
HUH...?
HMM?
THAT'S BACKWARDS?
I WAS SERIOUS, SO I KISSED YOU.
THAT'S HOW IT IS, KATSURA.

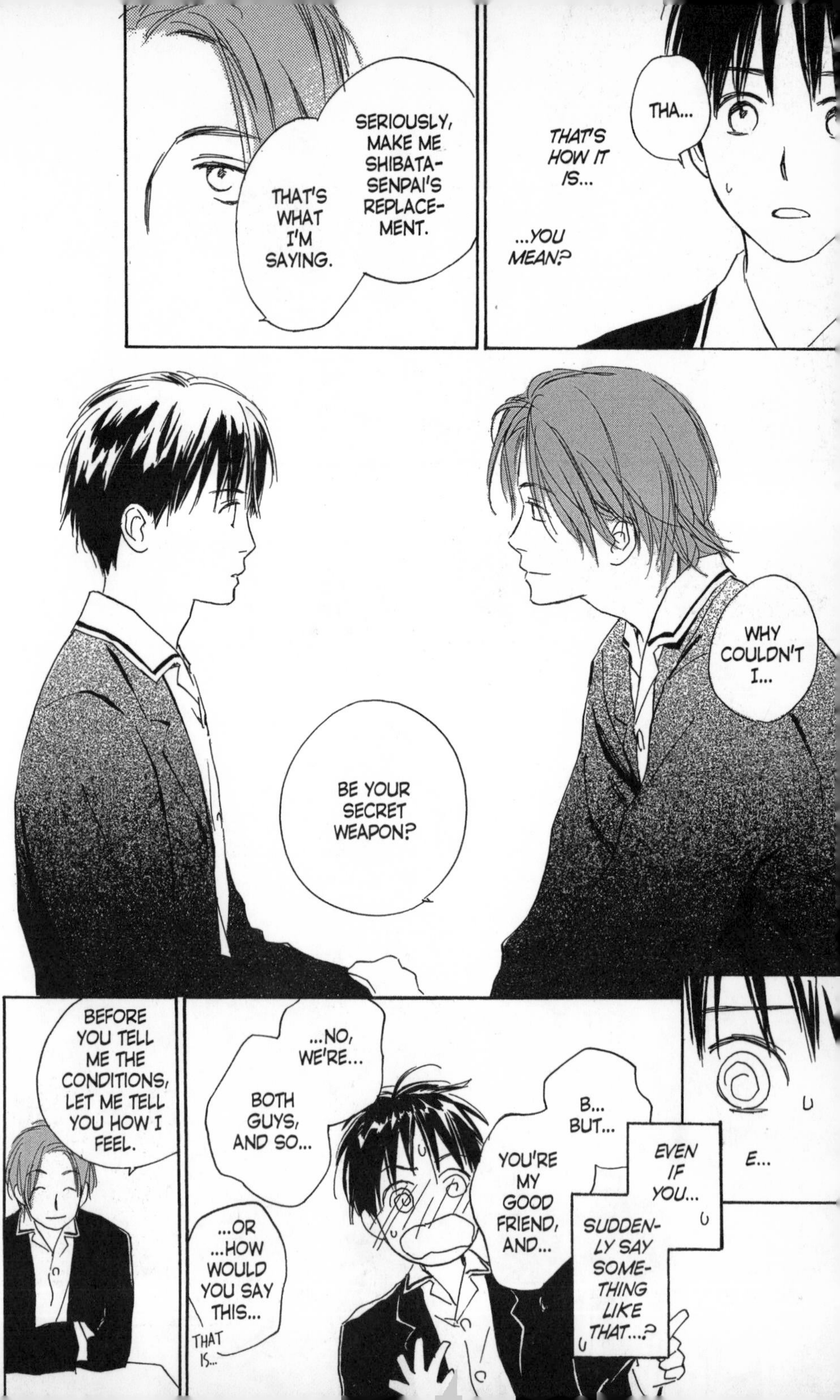
THA...
THAT'S HOW IT IS...
...YOU MEAN?
SERIOUSLY, MAKE ME SHIBATA-SENPAI'S REPLACEMENT.
THAT'S WHAT I'M SAYING.
WHY COULDN'T I...
BE YOUR SECRET WEAPON?
E...
EVEN IF YOU...
SUDDENLY SAY SOMETHING LIKE THAT...?
B... BUT...
YOU'RE MY GOOD FRIEND, AND...
...NO, WE'RE...
BOTH GUYS, AND SO...
...OR ...HOW WOULD YOU SAY THIS...
THAT IS...
BEFORE YOU TELL ME THE CONDITIONS, LET ME TELL YOU HOW I FEEL.

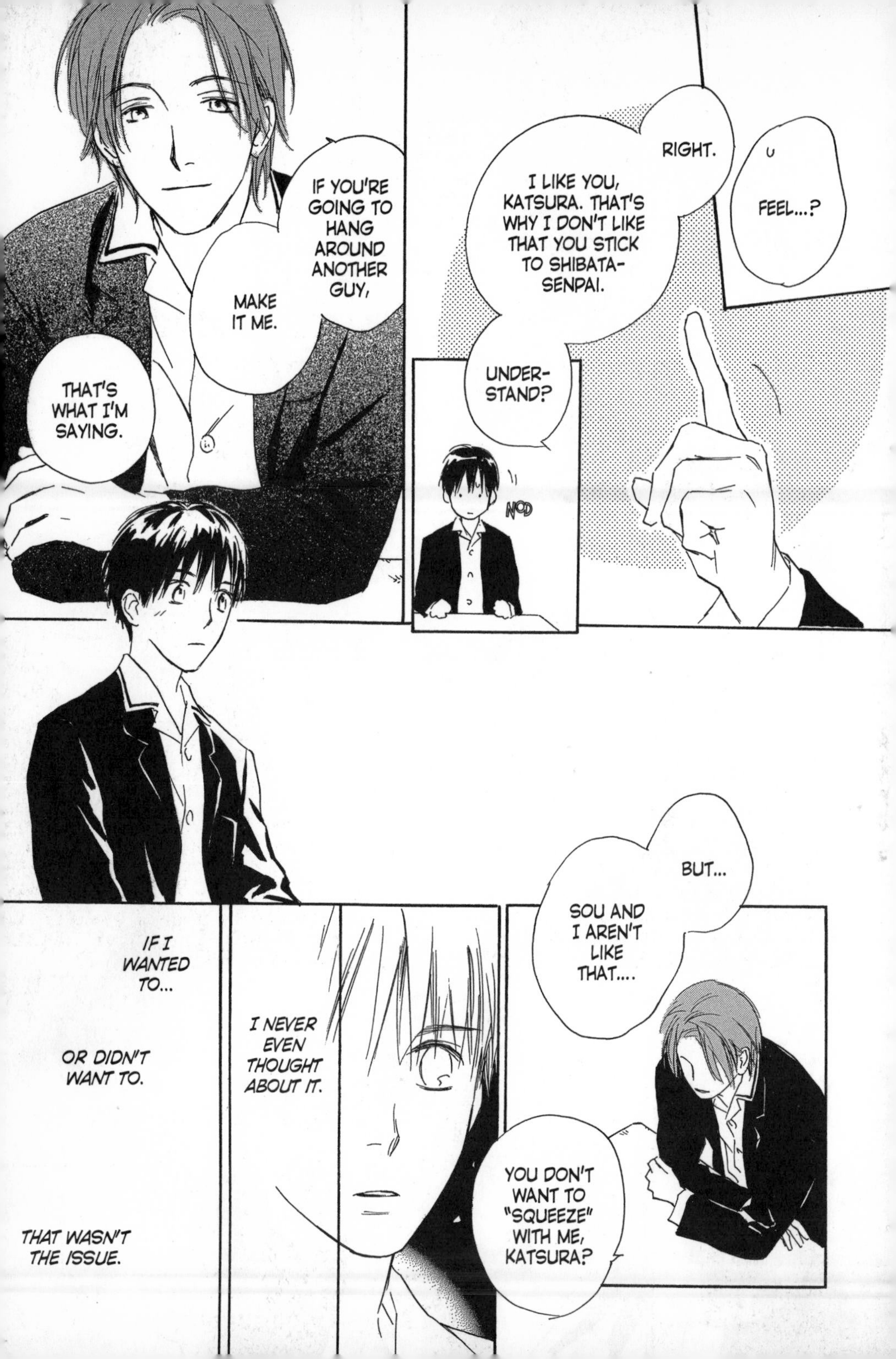
FEEL...?
RIGHT.
I LIKE YOU, KATSURA. THAT'S WHY I DON'T LIKE THAT YOU STICK TO SHIBATA-SENPAI.
UNDER-STAND?
NOD
IF YOU'RE GOING TO HANG AROUND ANOTHER GUY,
MAKE IT ME.
THAT'S WHAT I'M SAYING.
BUT...
SOU AND I AREN'T LIKE THAT....
YOU DON'T WANT TO "SQUEEZE" WITH ME, KATSURA?
I NEVER EVEN THOUGHT ABOUT IT.
IF I WANTED TO...
OR DIDN'T WANT TO.
THAT WASN'T THE ISSUE.

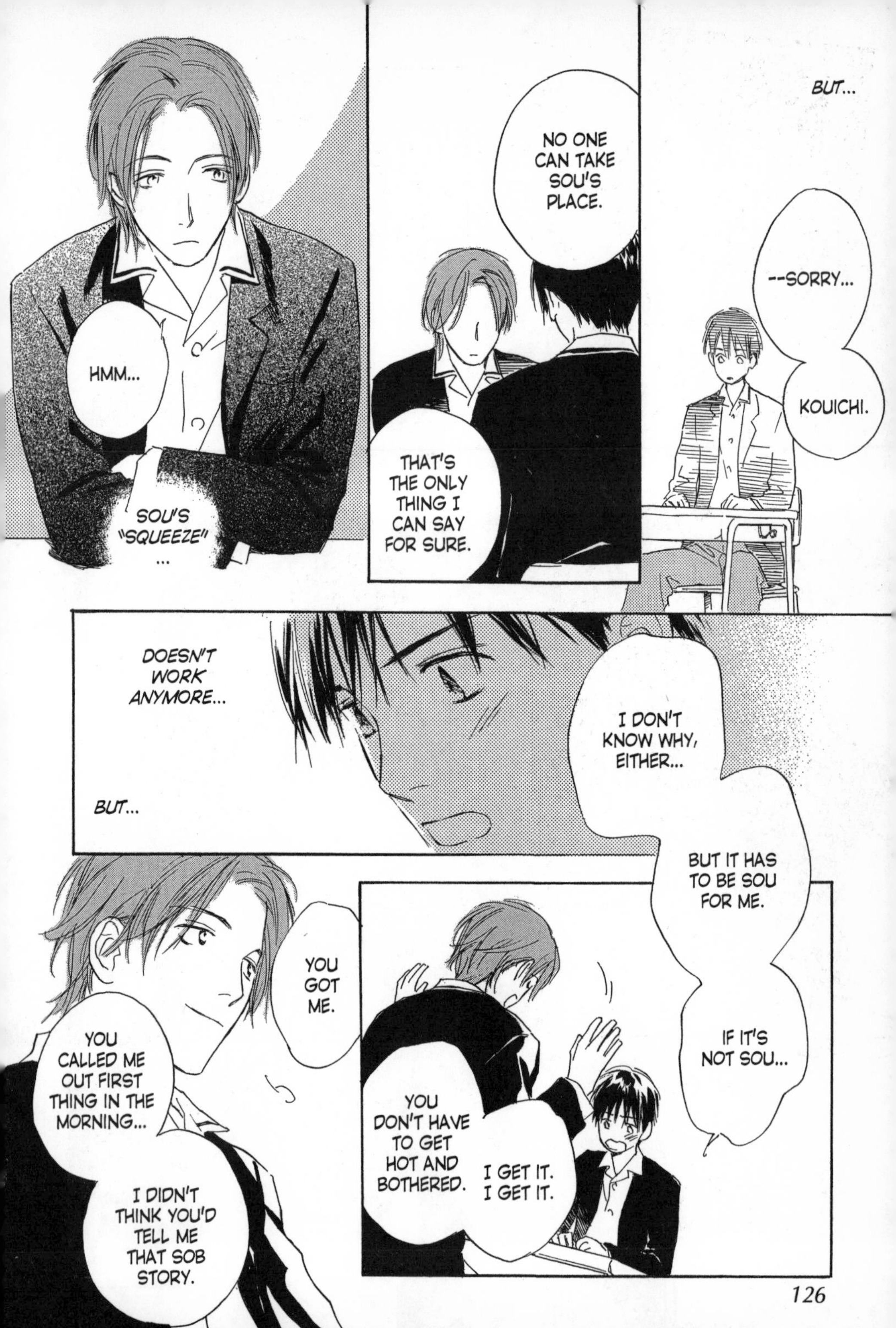
BUT...
--SORRY...
KOUICHI.
NO ONE CAN TAKE SOU'S PLACE.
THAT'S THE ONLY THING I CAN SAY FOR SURE.
HMM...
SOU'S "SQUEEZE" ...
I DON'T KNOW WHY, EITHER...
DOESN'T WORK ANYMORE...
BUT...
BUT IT HAS TO BE SOU FOR ME.
IF IT'S NOT SOU...
I GET IT. I GET IT.
YOU DON'T HAVE TO GET HOT AND BOTHERED.
YOU GOT ME.
YOU CALLED ME OUT FIRST THING IN THE MORNING...
I DIDN'T THINK YOU'D TELL ME THAT SOB STORY.

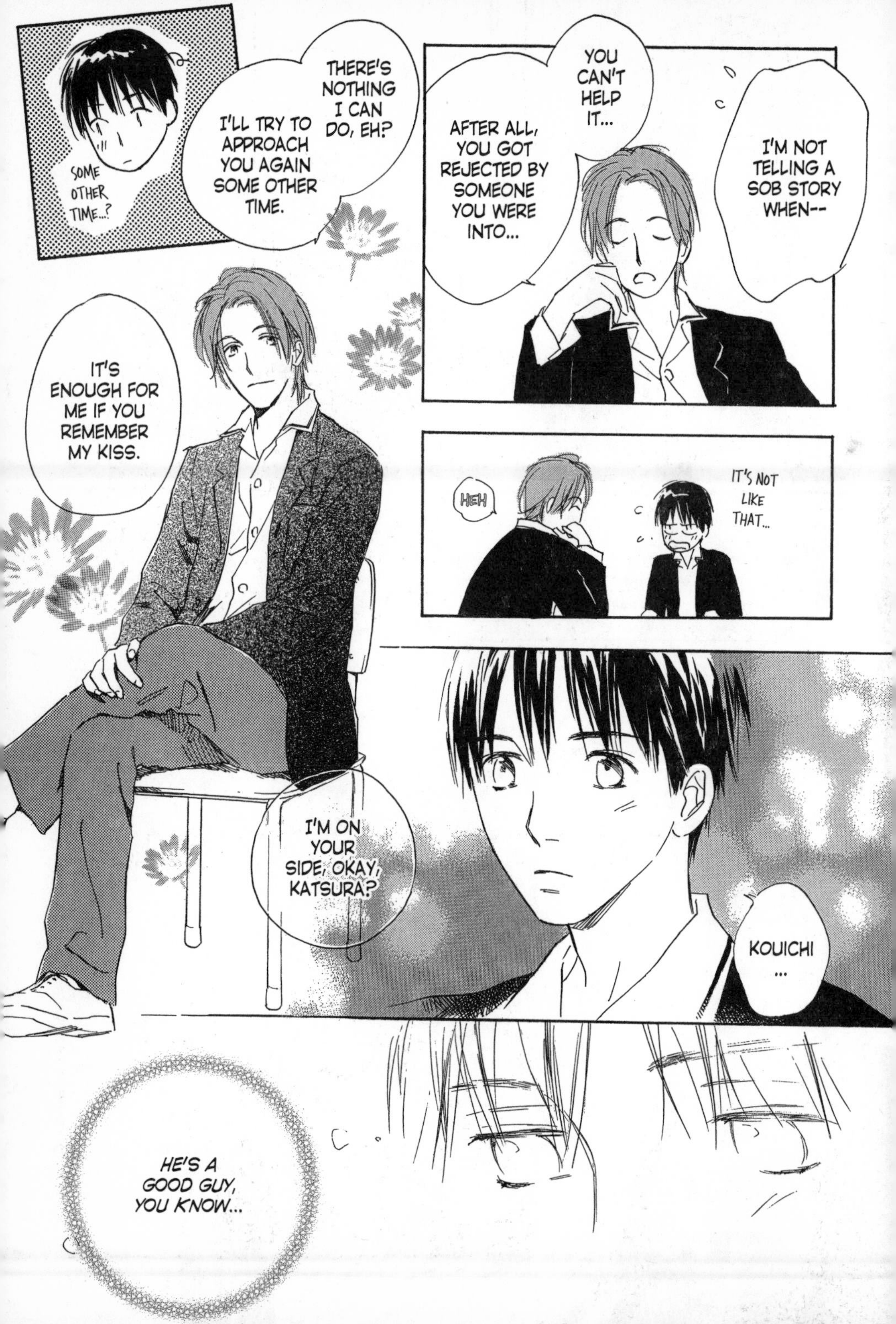
I'M NOT TELLING A SOB STORY WHEN--
YOU CAN'T HELP IT...
AFTER ALL, YOU GOT REJECTED BY SOMEONE YOU WERE INTO...
IT'S NOT LIKE THAT...
HEH
THERE'S NOTHING I CAN DO, EH?
I'LL TRY TO APPROACH YOU AGAIN SOME OTHER TIME.
SOME OTHER TIME...?
IT'S ENOUGH FOR ME IF YOU REMEMBER MY KISS.
I'M ON YOUR SIDE, OKAY, KATSURA?
KOUICHI ...
HE'S A GOOD GUY, YOU KNOW...

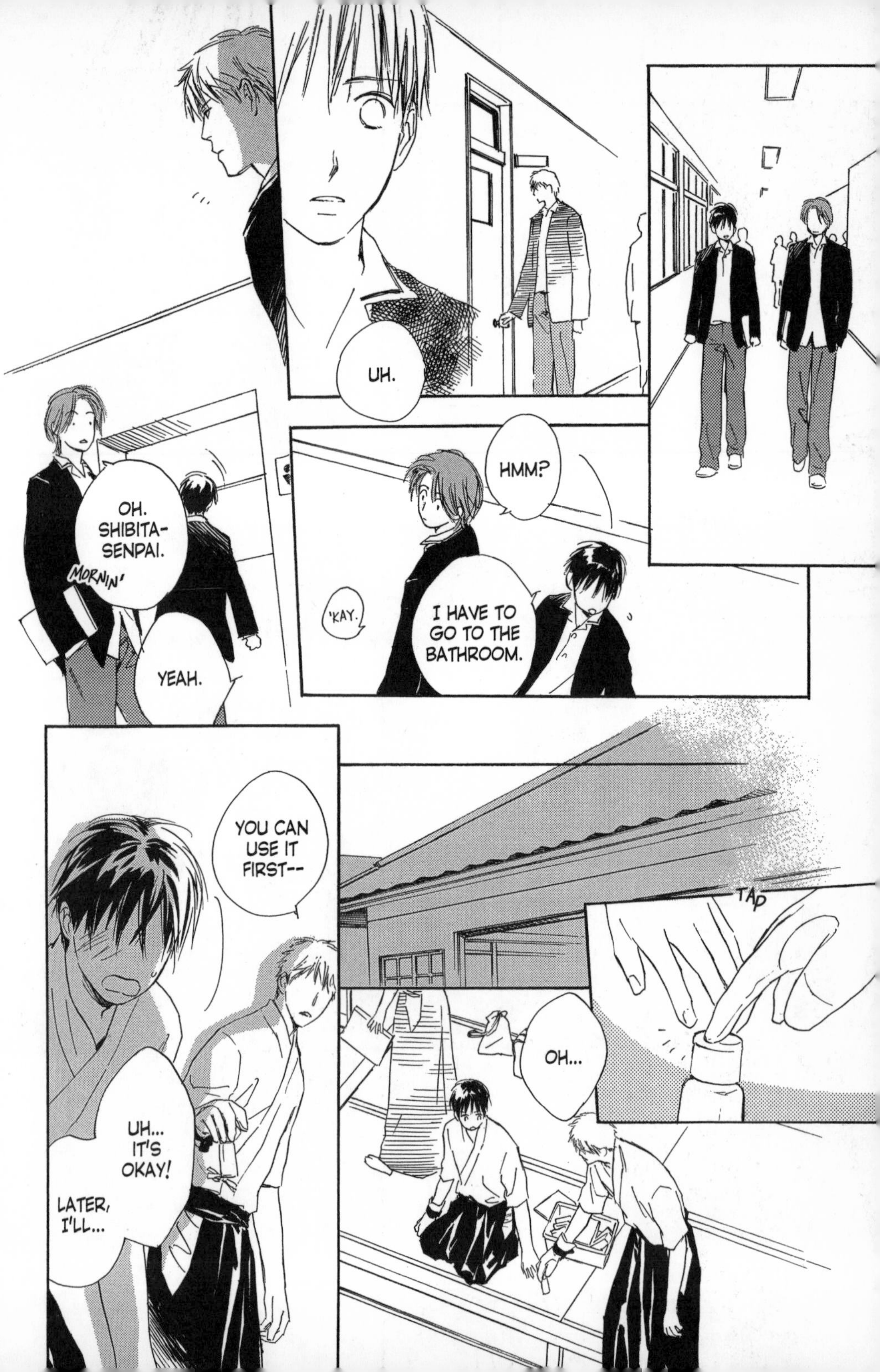
UH.
HMM?
I HAVE TO GO TO THE BATHROOM.
'KAY.
OH. SHIBITA-SENPAI.
MORNIN'
YEAH.
TAP
OH...
YOU CAN USE IT FIRST--
UH... IT'S OKAY!
LATER, I'LL...

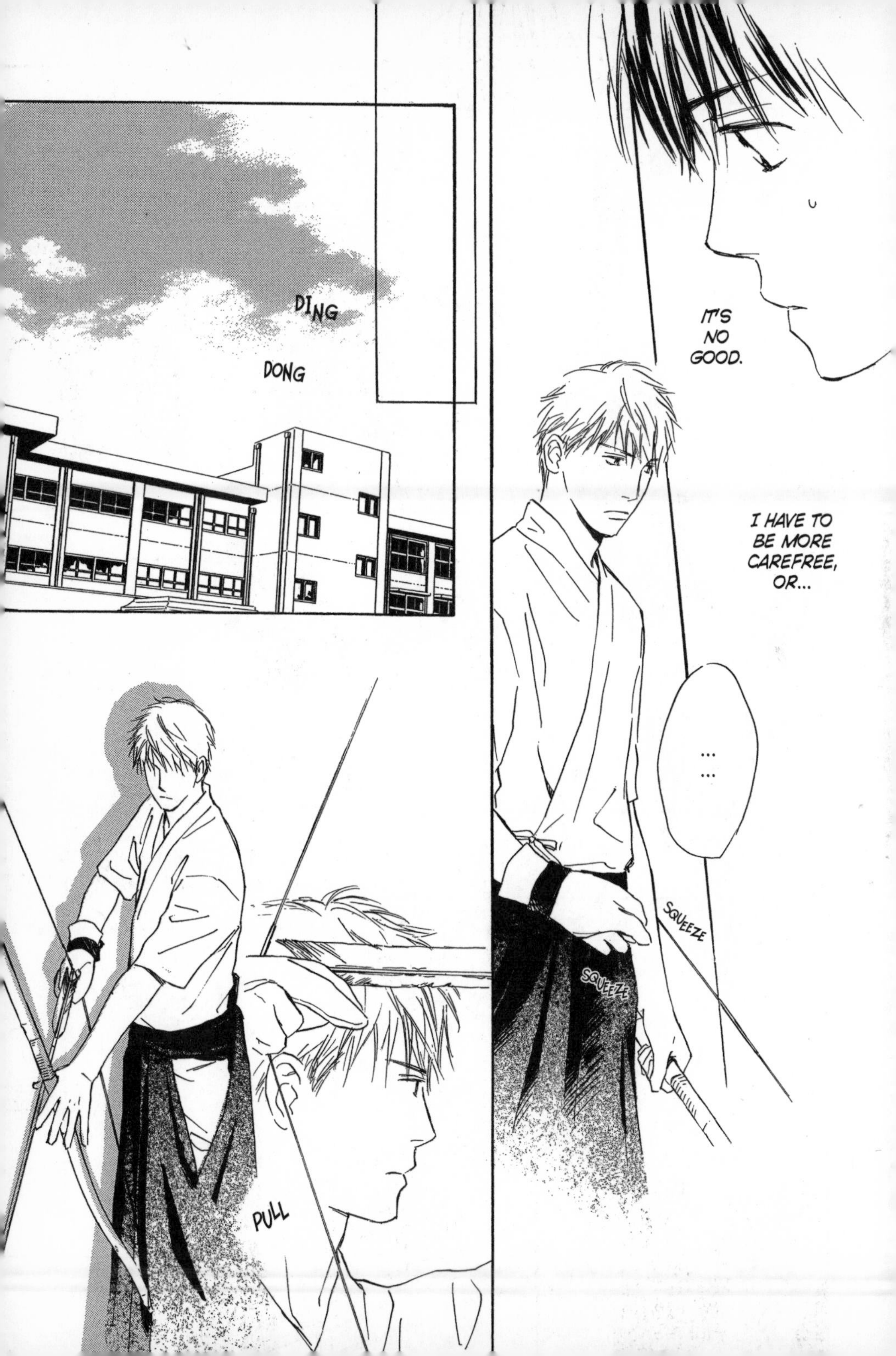

IT'S NO GOOD.
I HAVE TO BE MORE CAREFREE, OR...
......
SQUEEZE
SQUEEZE
DING
DONG
PULL

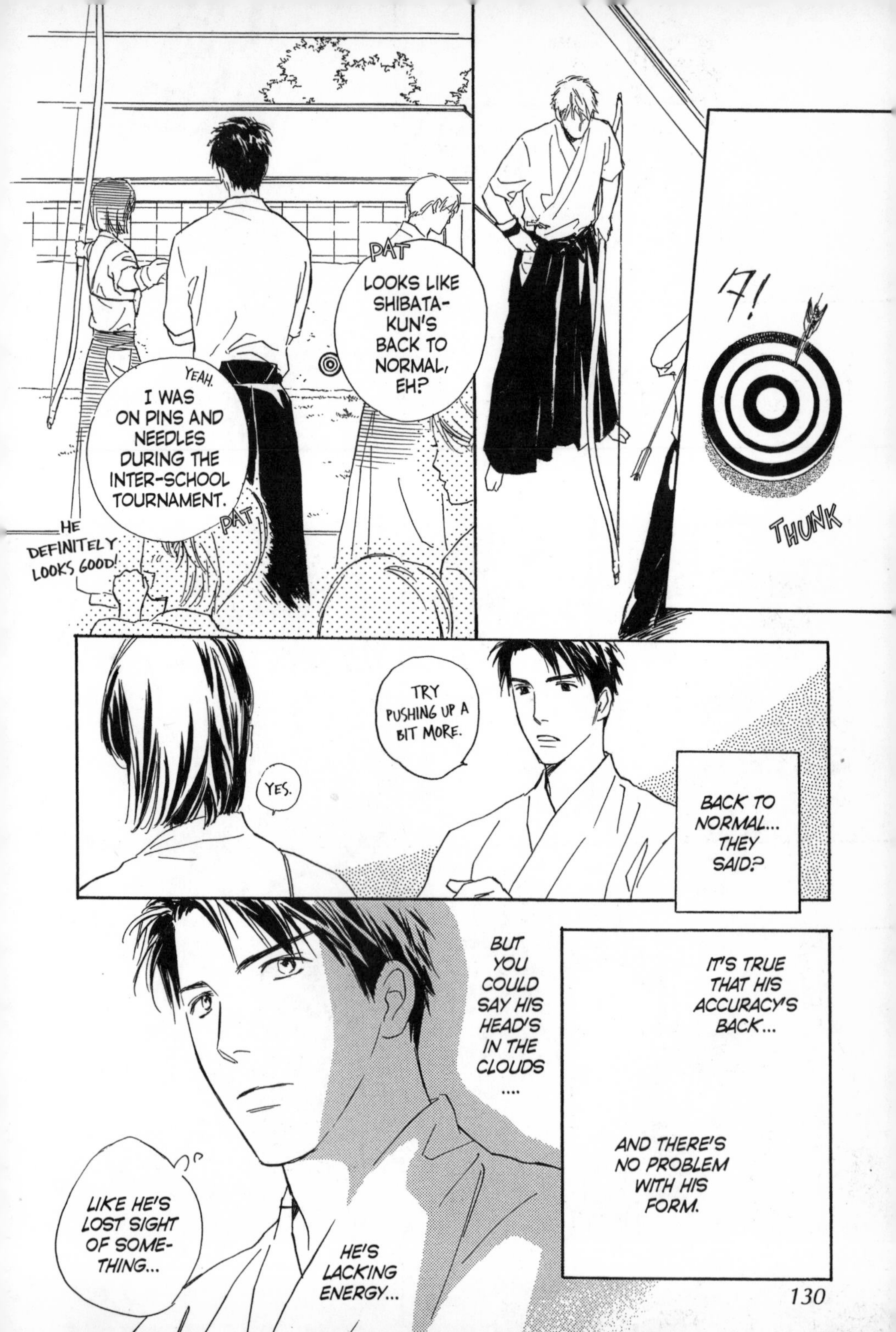
7!
THUNK
PAT
LOOKS LIKE SHIBATA-KUN'S BACK TO NORMAL, EH?
YEAH.
I WAS ON PINS AND NEEDLES DURING THE INTER-SCHOOL TOURNAMENT.
PAT
HE DEFINITELY LOOKS GOOD!
TRY PUSHING UP A BIT MORE.
YES.
BACK TO NORMAL... THEY SAID?
IT'S TRUE THAT HIS ACCURACY'S BACK...
AND THERE'S NO PROBLEM WITH HIS FORM.
BUT YOU COULD SAY HIS HEAD'S IN THE CLOUDS ....
HE'S LACKING ENERGY...
LIKE HE'S LOST SIGHT OF SOME-THING...

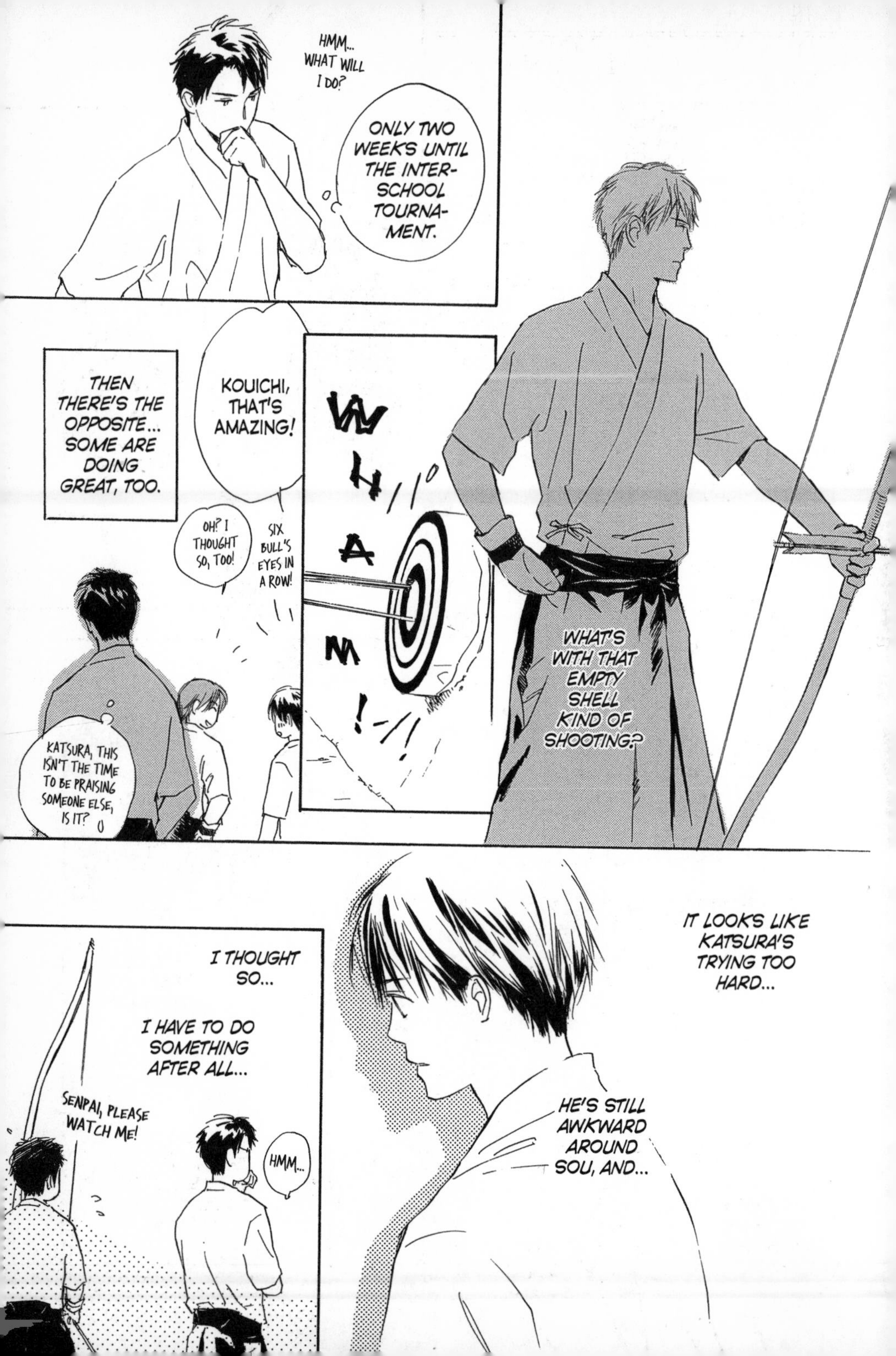

HMM... WHAT WILL I DO?
ONLY TWO WEEKS UNTIL THE INTER-SCHOOL TOURNAMENT.
THEN THERE'S THE OPPOSITE... SOME ARE DOING GREAT, TOO.
WHAT'S WITH THAT EMPTY SHELL KIND OF SHOOTING?
WHAM!
KOUICHI, THAT'S AMAZING!
SIX BULL'S EYES IN A ROW!
OH? I THOUGHT SO, TOO!
KATSURA, THIS ISN'T THE TIME TO BE PRAISING SOMEONE ELSE, IS IT?
IT LOOKS LIKE KATSURA'S TRYING TOO HARD...
HE'S STILL AWKWARD AROUND SOU, AND...
I THOUGHT SO...
I HAVE TO DO SOMETHING AFTER ALL...
SENPAI, PLEASE WATCH ME!
HMM...

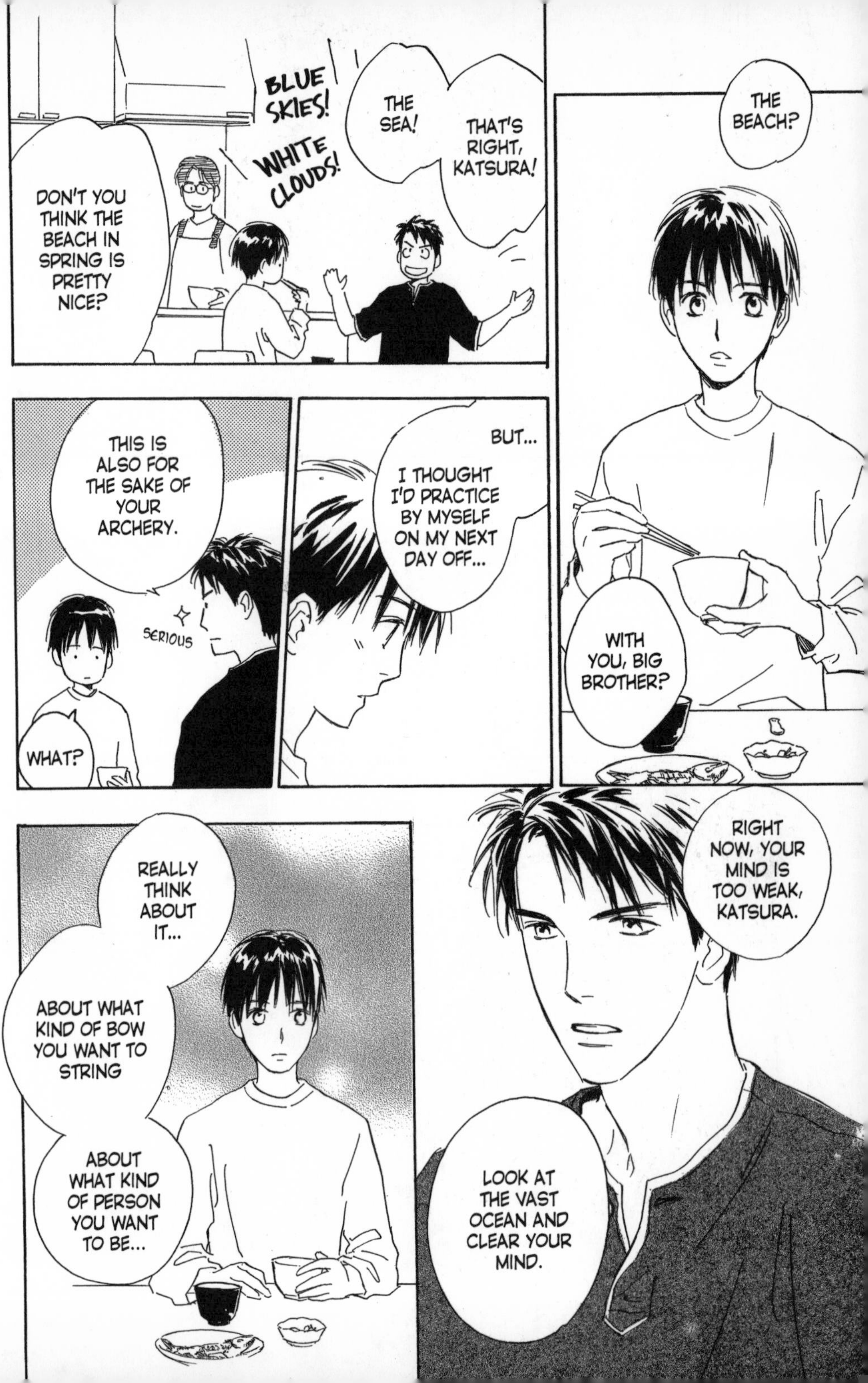
THE BEACH?
WITH YOU, BIG BROTHER?
THE SEA!
THAT'S RIGHT, KATSURA!
BLUE SKIES!
WHITE CLOUDS!
DON'T YOU THINK THE BEACH IN SPRING IS PRETTY NICE?
BUT...
I THOUGHT I'D PRACTICE BY MYSELF ON MY NEXT DAY OFF...
THIS IS ALSO FOR THE SAKE OF YOUR ARCHERY.
SERIOUS
WHAT?
RIGHT NOW, YOUR MIND IS TOO WEAK, KATSURA.
LOOK AT THE VAST OCEAN AND CLEAR YOUR MIND.
REALLY THINK ABOUT IT...
ABOUT WHAT KIND OF BOW YOU WANT TO STRING
ABOUT WHAT KIND OF PERSON YOU WANT TO BE...

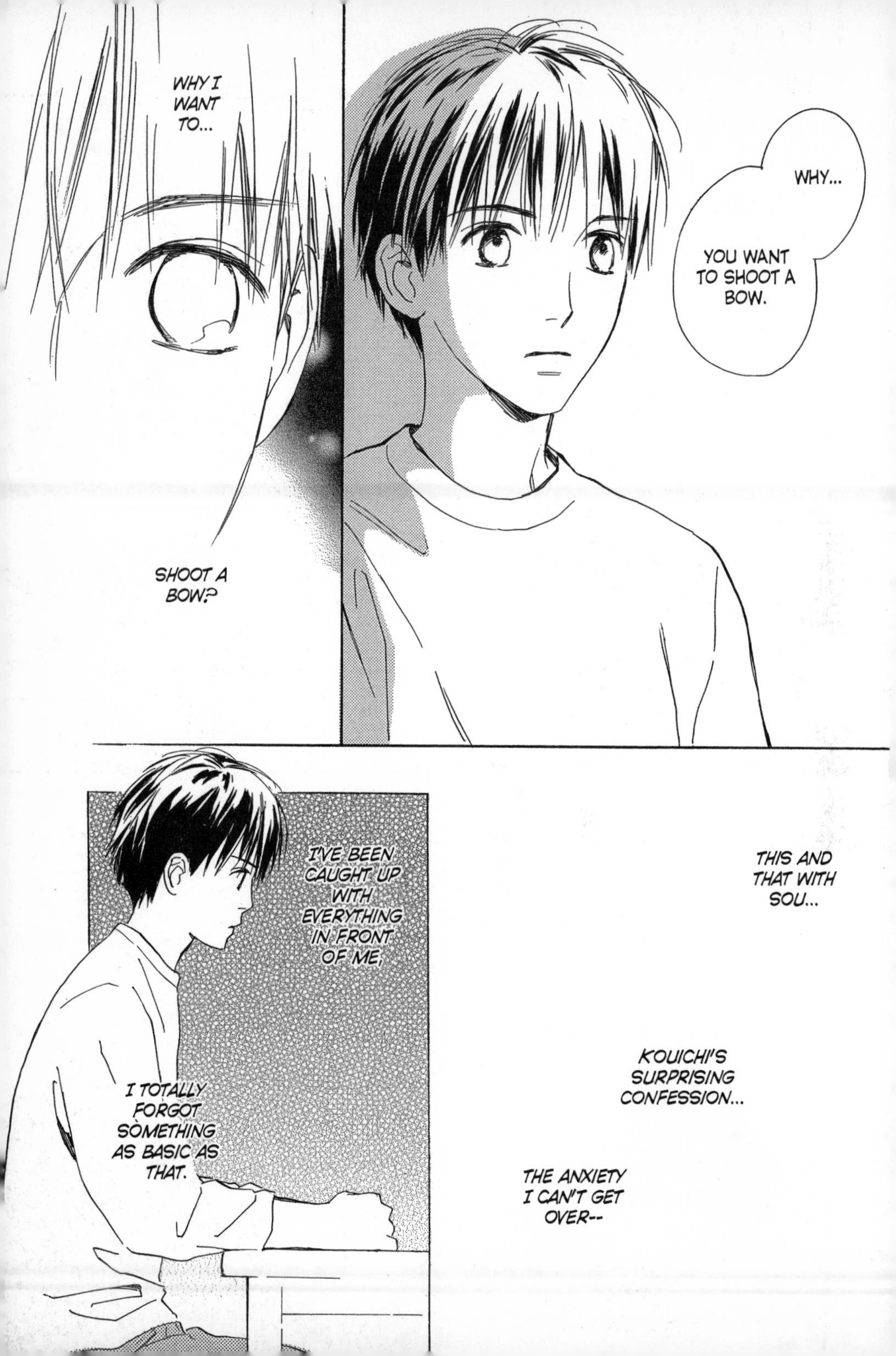
WHY...
YOU WANT TO SHOOT A BOW.
WHY I WANT TO...
SHOOT A BOW?
THIS AND THAT WITH SOU...
KOUICHI'S SURPRISING CONFESSION...
THE ANXIETY I CAN'T GET OVER--
I'VE BEEN CAUGHT UP WITH EVERYTHING IN FRONT OF ME,
I TOTALLY FORGOT SOMETHING AS BASIC AS THAT.

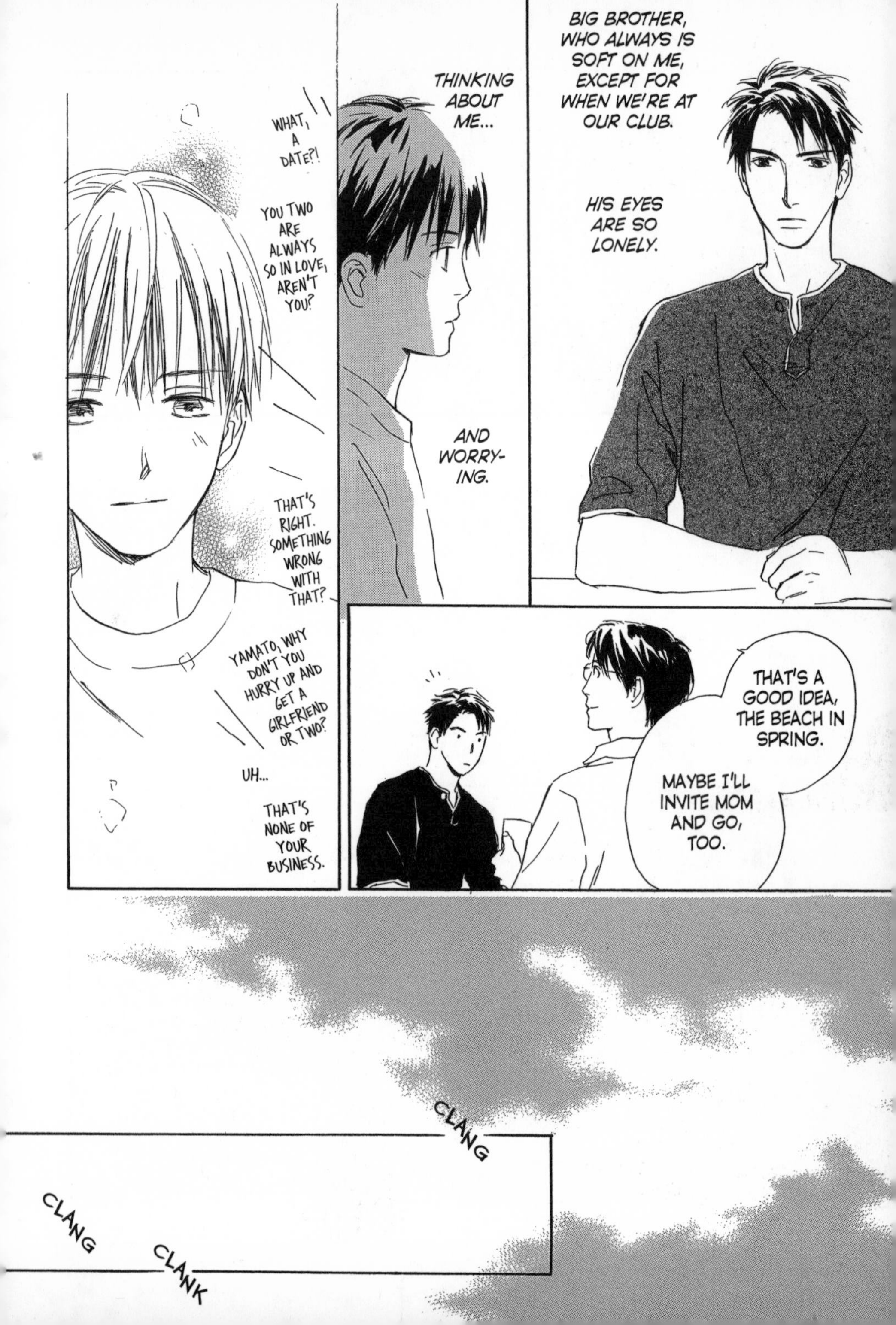
BIG BROTHER, WHO ALWAYS IS SOFT ON ME, EXCEPT FOR WHEN WE'RE AT OUR CLUB.
HIS EYES ARE SO LONELY.
THINKING ABOUT ME...
AND WORRY-ING.
THAT'S A GOOD IDEA, THE BEACH IN SPRING.
MAYBE I'LL INVITE MOM AND GO, TOO.
WHAT, A DATE?!
YOU TWO ARE ALWAYS SO IN LOVE, AREN'T YOU?
THAT'S RIGHT. SOMETHING WRONG WITH THAT?
YAMATO, WHY DON'T YOU HURRY UP AND GET A GIRLFRIEND OR TWO?
UH...
THAT'S NONE OF YOUR BUSINESS.
CLANG
CLANG
CLANG
CLANK

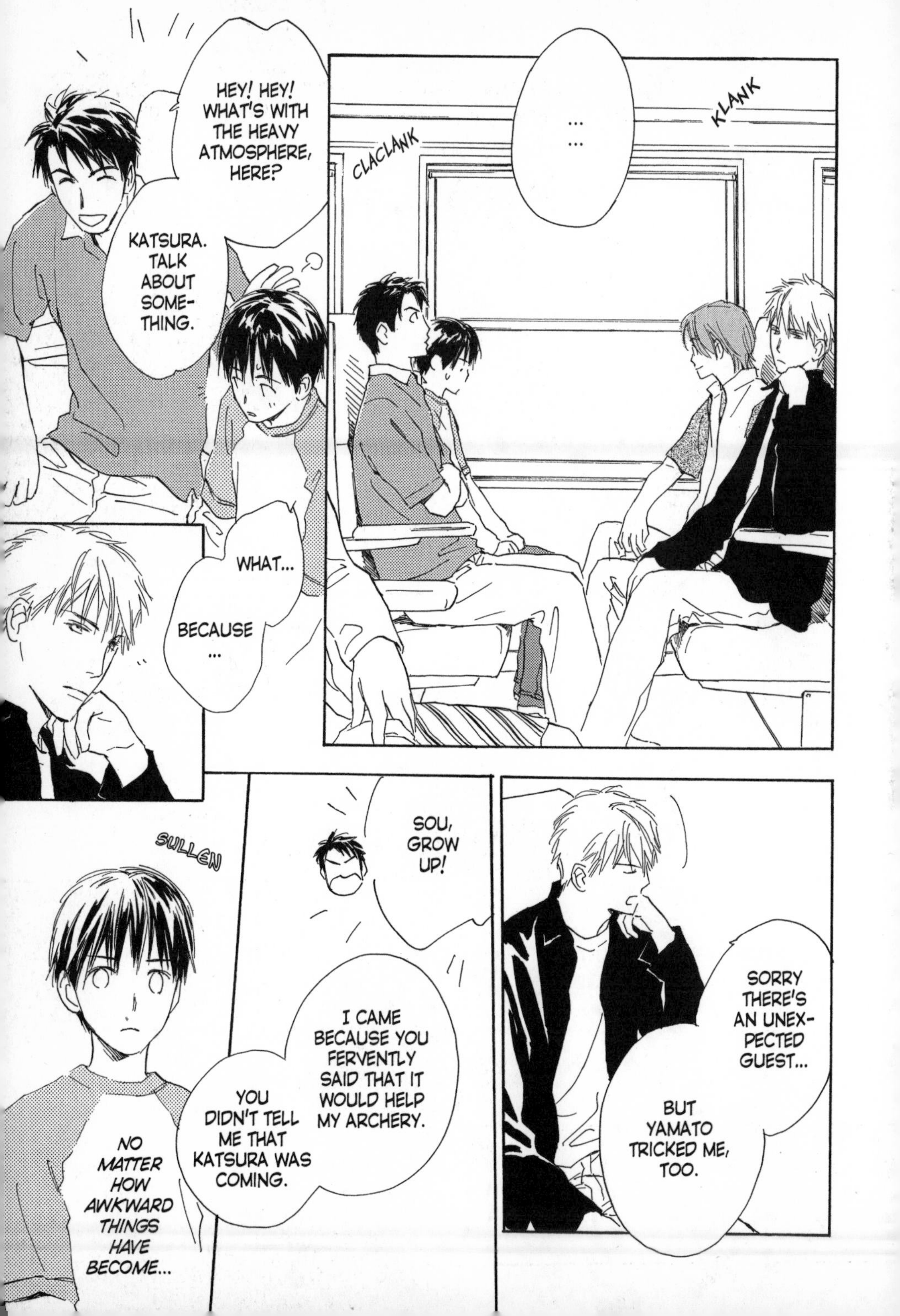

......
KLANK
CLACLANK
HEY! HEY! WHAT'S WITH THE HEAVY ATMOSPHERE, HERE?
KATSURA. TALK ABOUT SOME-THING.
WHAT... BECAUSE ...
SORRY THERE'S AN UNEX-PECTED GUEST...
BUT YAMATO TRICKED ME, TOO.
SOU, GROW UP!
I CAME BECAUSE YOU FERVENTLY SAID THAT IT WOULD HELP MY ARCHERY.
YOU DIDN'T TELL ME THAT KATSURA WAS COMING.
SULLEN
NO MATTER HOW AWKWARD THINGS HAVE BECOME...

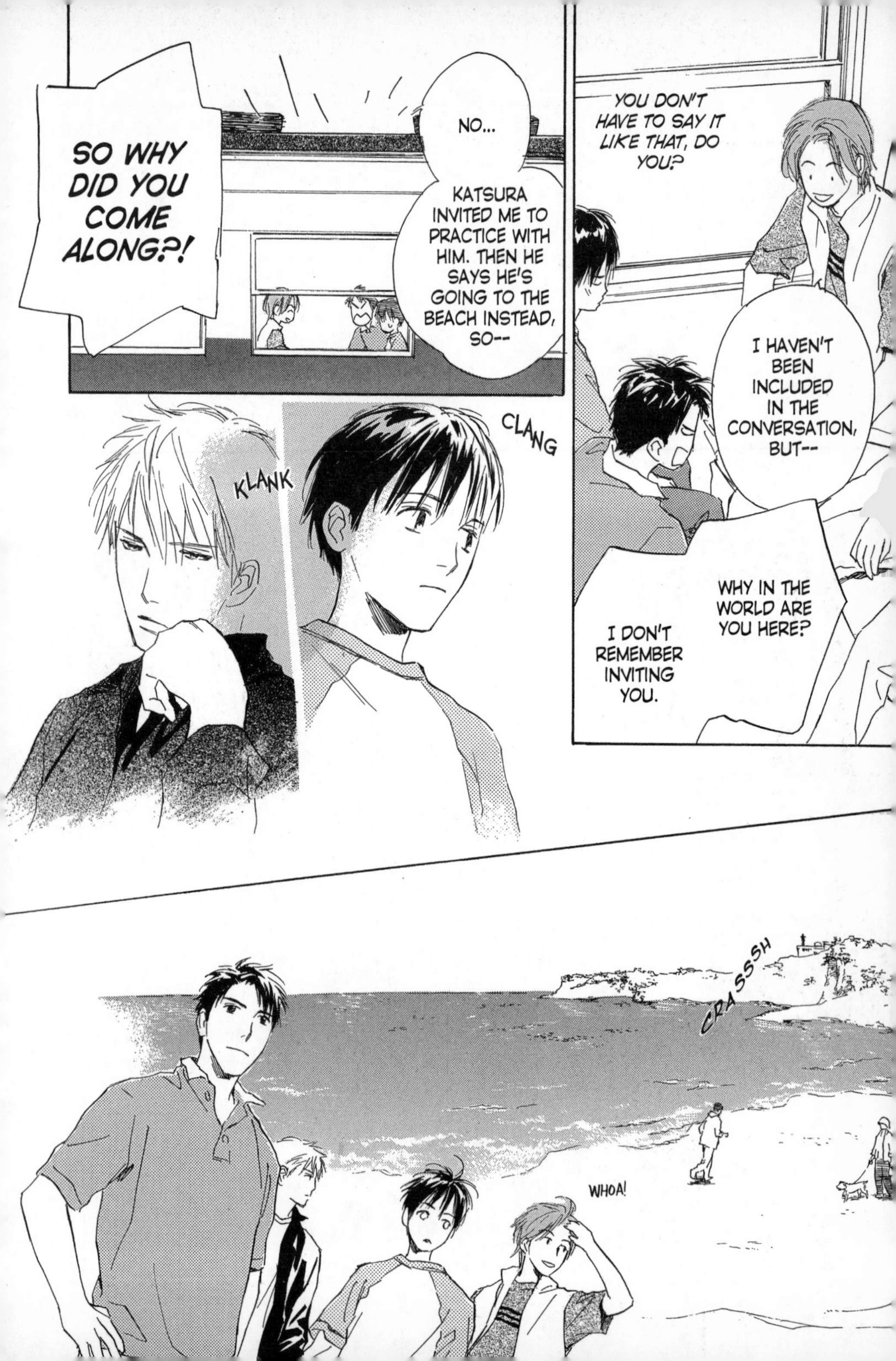

YOU DON'T HAVE TO SAY IT LIKE THAT, DO YOU?
I HAVEN'T BEEN INCLUDED IN THE CONVERSATION, BUT--
WHY IN THE WORLD ARE YOU HERE?
I DON'T REMEMBER INVITING YOU.
NO...
KATSURA INVITED ME TO PRACTICE WITH HIM. THEN HE SAYS HE'S GOING TO THE BEACH INSTEAD, SO--
SO WHY DID YOU COME ALONG?!
CLANG
KLANK
CRASSSH
WHOA!

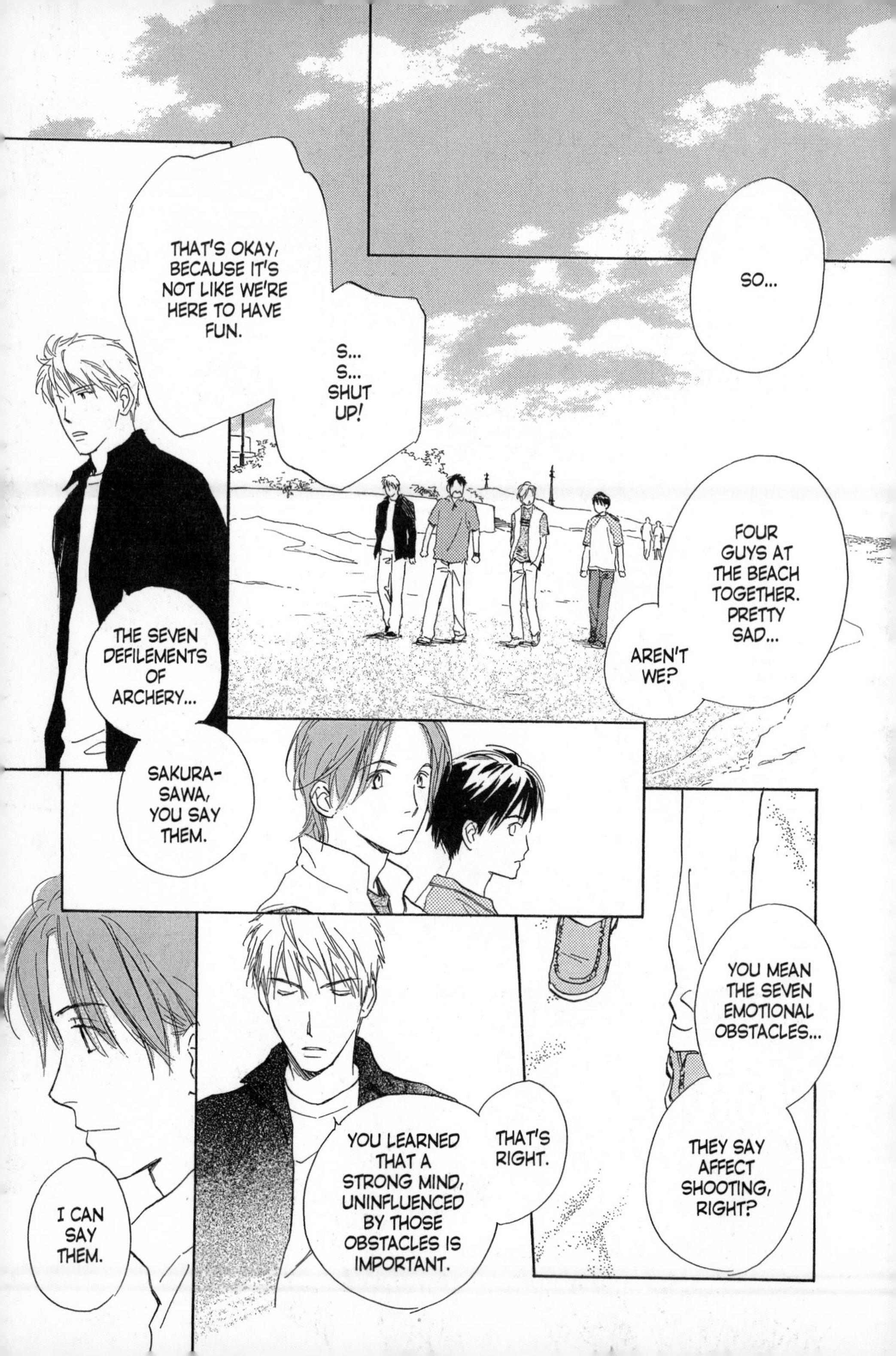
SO...
FOUR GUYS AT THE BEACH TOGETHER. PRETTY SAD...
AREN'T WE?
THAT'S OKAY, BECAUSE IT'S NOT LIKE WE'RE HERE TO HAVE FUN.
S... S... SHUT UP!
THE SEVEN DEFILEMENTS OF ARCHERY...
SAKURA-SAWA, YOU SAY THEM.
YOU MEAN THE SEVEN EMOTIONAL OBSTACLES...
THEY SAY AFFECT SHOOTING, RIGHT?
THAT'S RIGHT.
YOU LEARNED THAT A STRONG MIND, UNINFLUENCED BY THOSE OBSTACLES IS IMPORTANT.
I CAN SAY THEM.

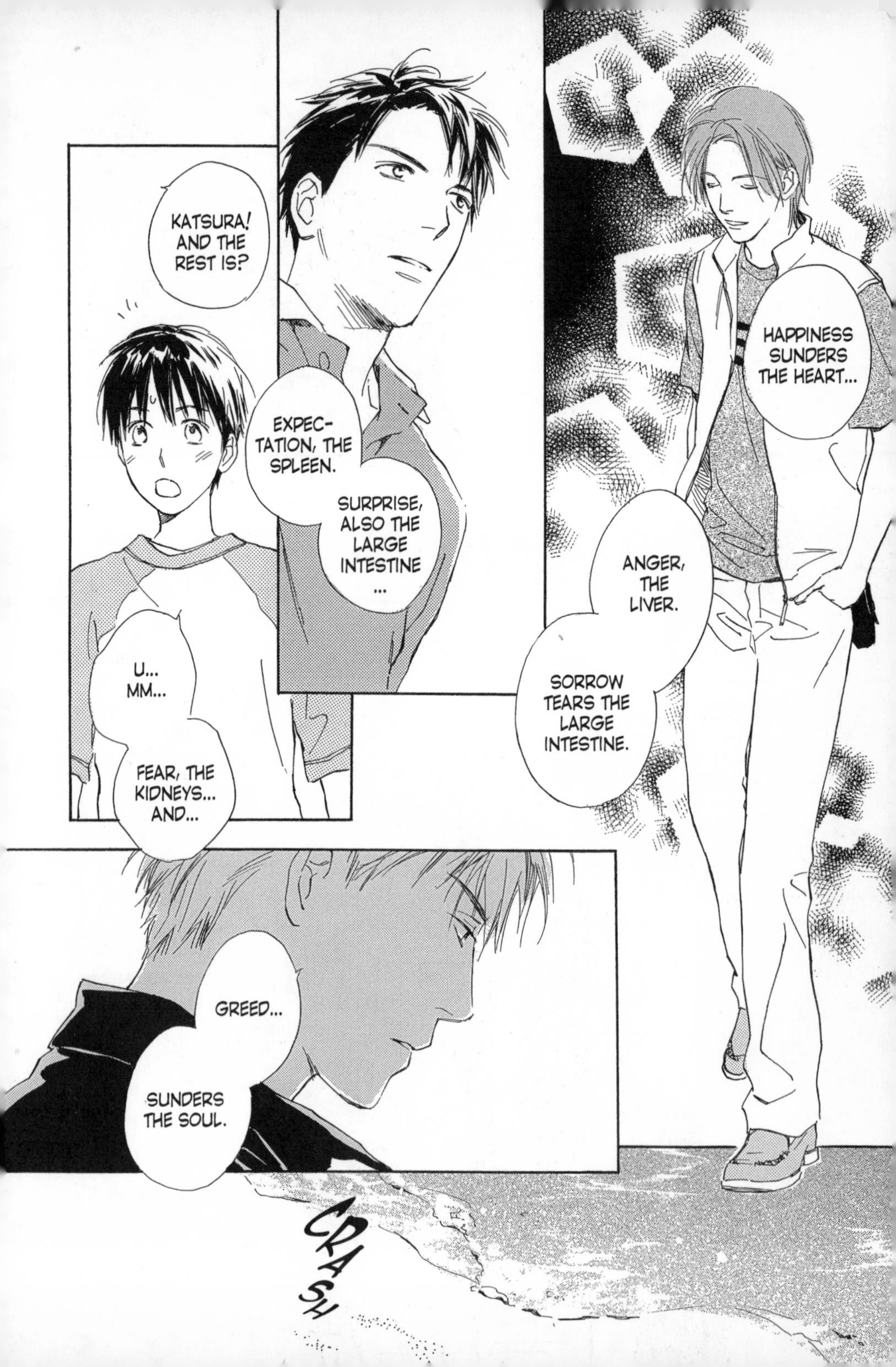

HAPPINESS SUNDERS THE HEART...
ANGER, THE LIVER.
SORROW TEARS THE LARGE INTESTINE.
EXPECTATION, THE SPLEEN.
SURPRISE, ALSO THE LARGE INTESTINE ...
KATSURA! AND THE REST IS?
U... MM...
FEAR, THE KIDNEYS... AND...
GREED...
SUNDERS THE SOUL.
CRASH

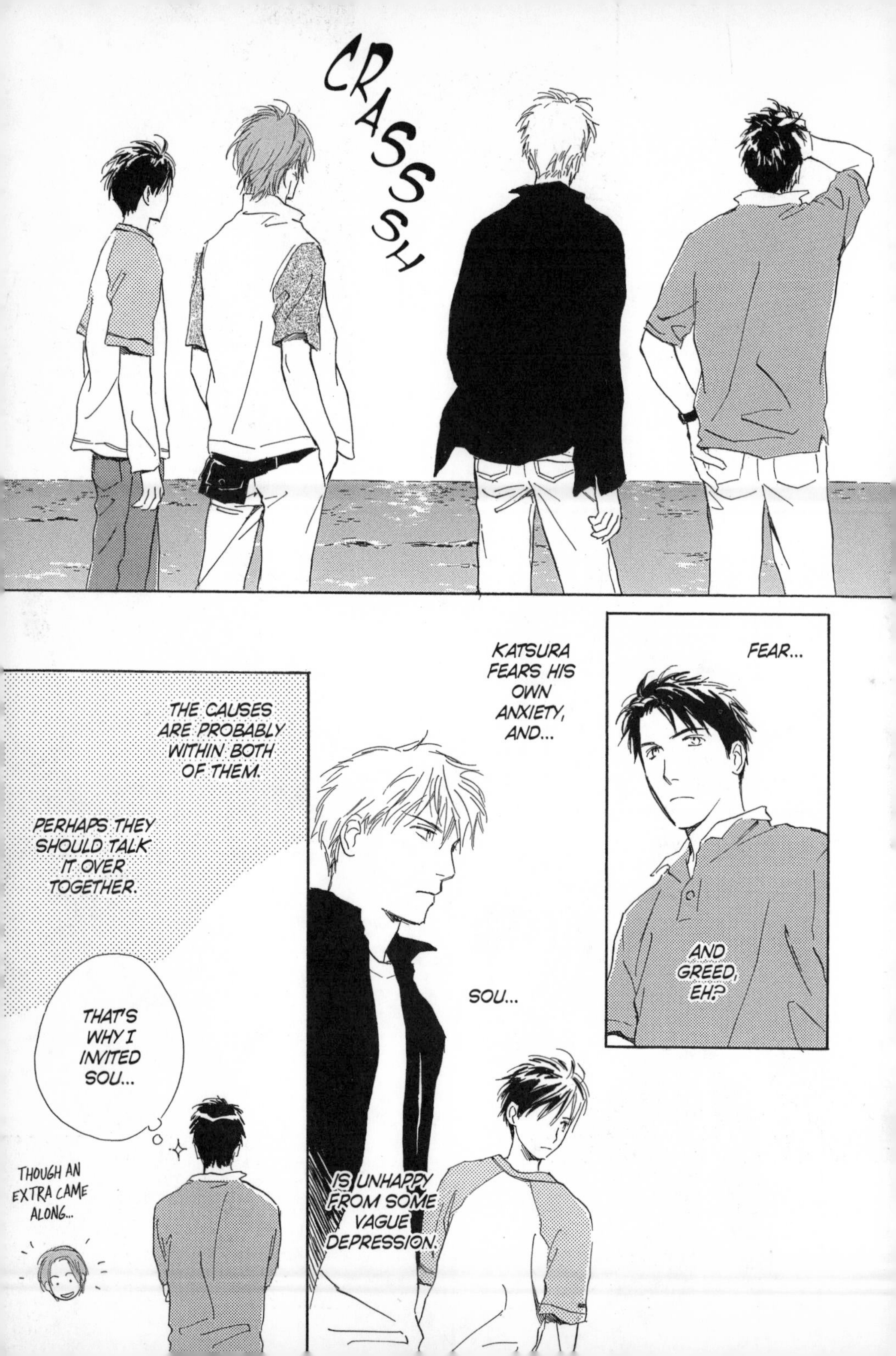
CRASSSH
FEAR...
AND GREED, EH?
KATSURA FEARS HIS OWN ANXIETY, AND...
SOU...
IS UNHAPPY FROM SOME VAGUE DEPRESSION.
THE CAUSES ARE PROBABLY WITHIN BOTH OF THEM.
PERHAPS THEY SHOULD TALK IT OVER TOGETHER.
THAT'S WHY I INVITED SOU...
THOUGH AN EXTRA CAME ALONG...

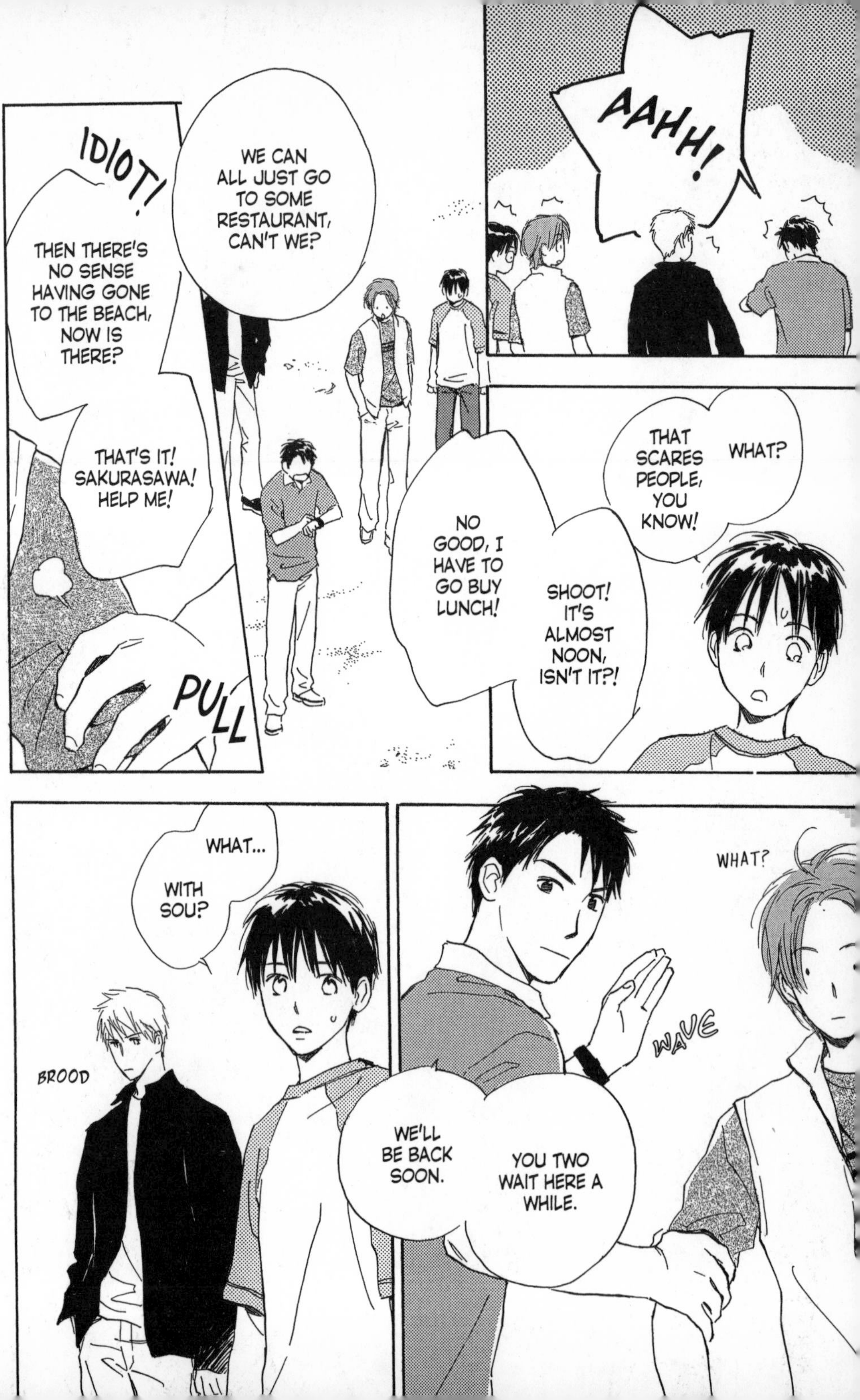
AAHH!
WHAT?
THAT SCARES PEOPLE, YOU KNOW!
SHOOT! IT'S ALMOST NOON, ISN'T IT?!
NO GOOD, I HAVE TO GO BUY LUNCH!
WE CAN ALL JUST GO TO SOME RESTAURANT, CAN'T WE?
IDIOT!
THEN THERE'S NO SENSE HAVING GONE TO THE BEACH, NOW IS THERE?
THAT'S IT! SAKURASAWA! HELP ME!
PULL
WHAT?
WAVE
YOU TWO WAIT HERE A WHILE.
WE'LL BE BACK SOON.
WHAT...
WITH SOU?
BROOD

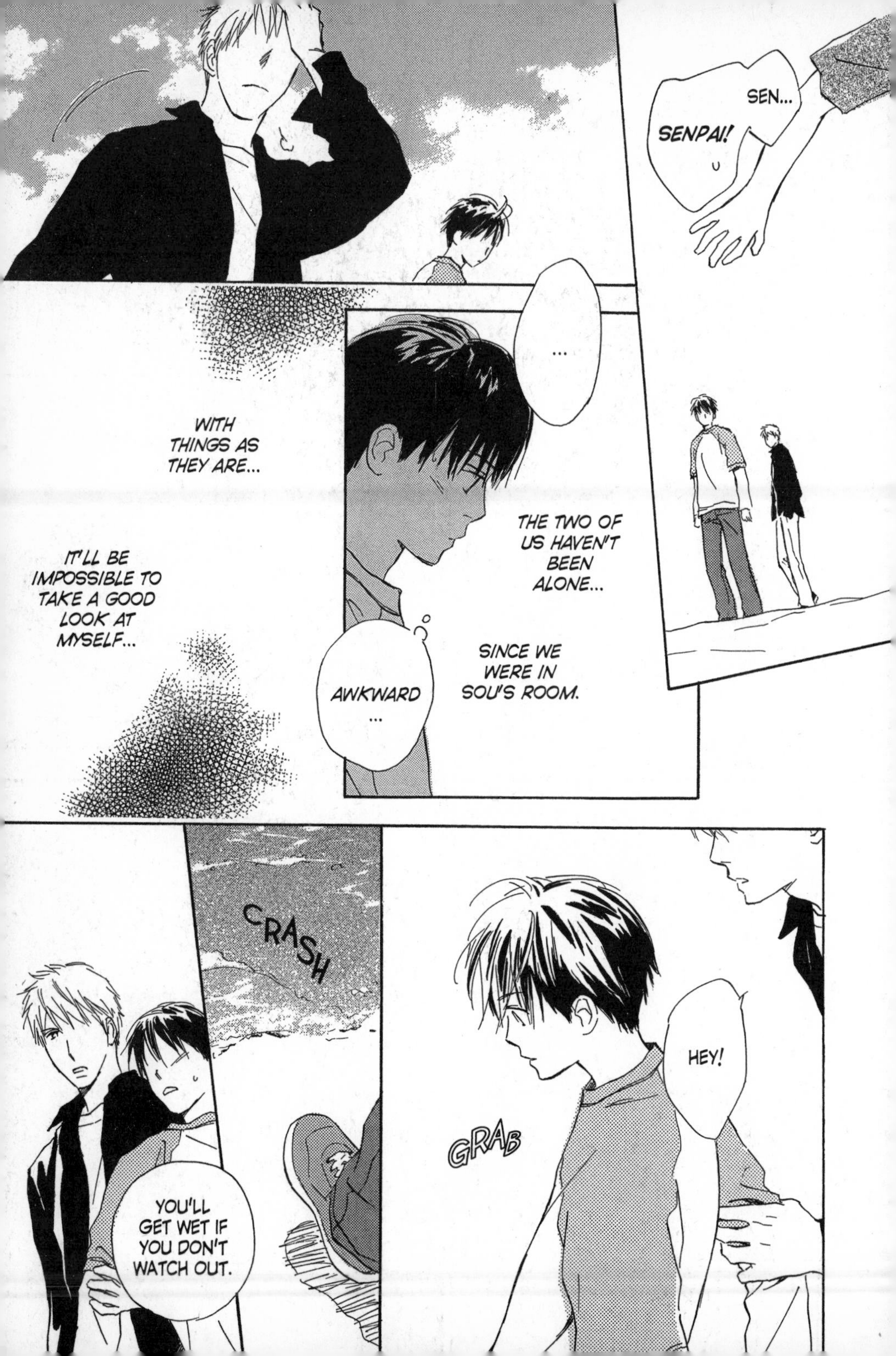
SEN... SENPAI!
...
THE TWO OF US HAVEN'T BEEN ALONE...
SINCE WE WERE IN SOU'S ROOM.
AWKWARD ...
WITH THINGS AS THEY ARE...
IT'LL BE IMPOSSIBLE TO TAKE A GOOD LOOK AT MYSELF...
HEY!
GRAB
CRASH
YOU'LL GET WET IF YOU DON'T WATCH OUT.

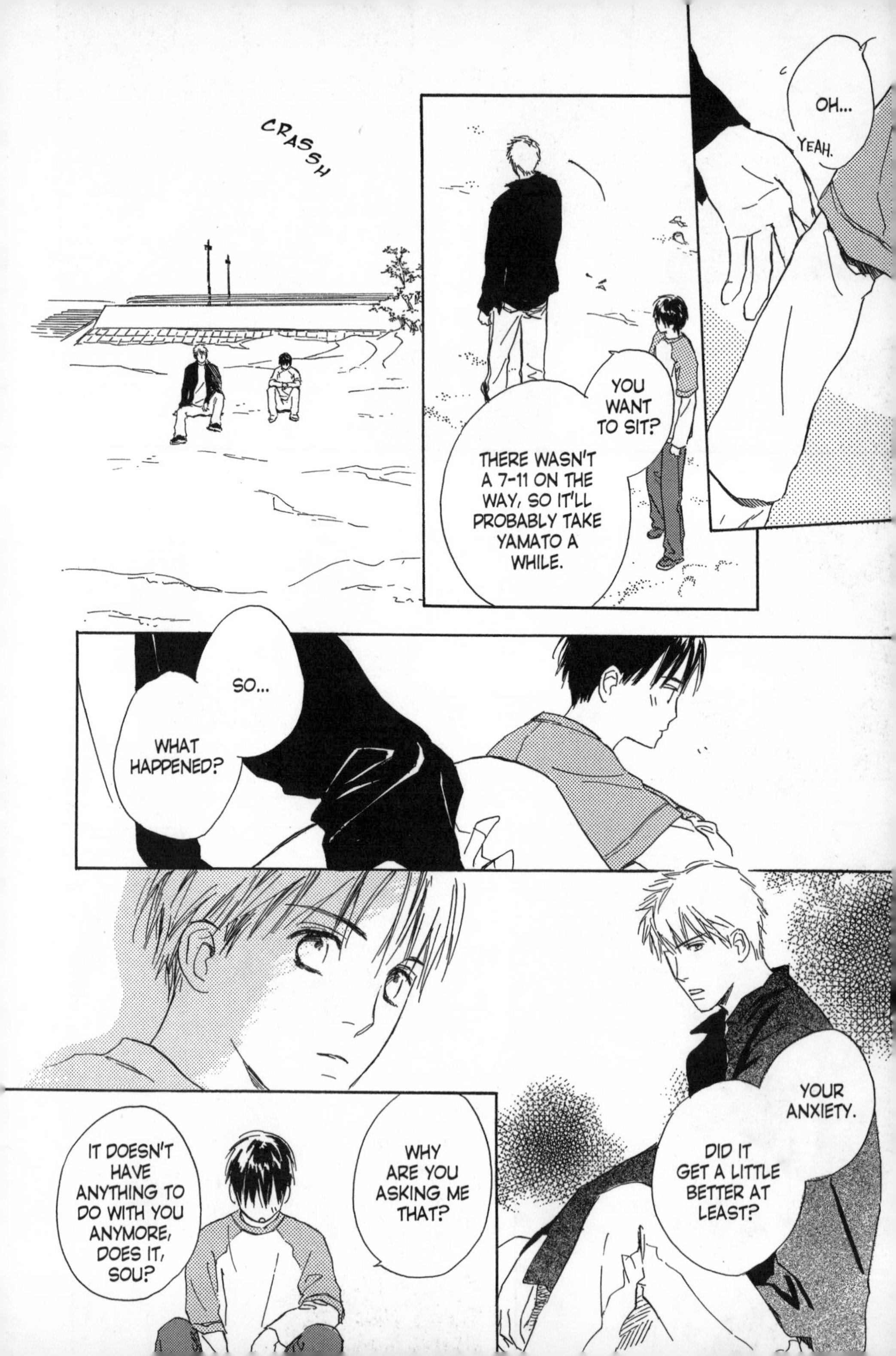
OH...
YEAH.
YOU WANT TO SIT?
THERE WASN'T A 7-11 ON THE WAY, SO IT'LL PROBABLY TAKE YAMATO A WHILE.
CRASSH
SO...
WHAT HAPPENED?
YOUR ANXIETY.
DID IT GET A LITTLE BETTER AT LEAST?
WHY ARE YOU ASKING ME THAT?
IT DOESN'T HAVE ANYTHING TO DO WITH YOU ANYMORE, DOES IT, SOU?

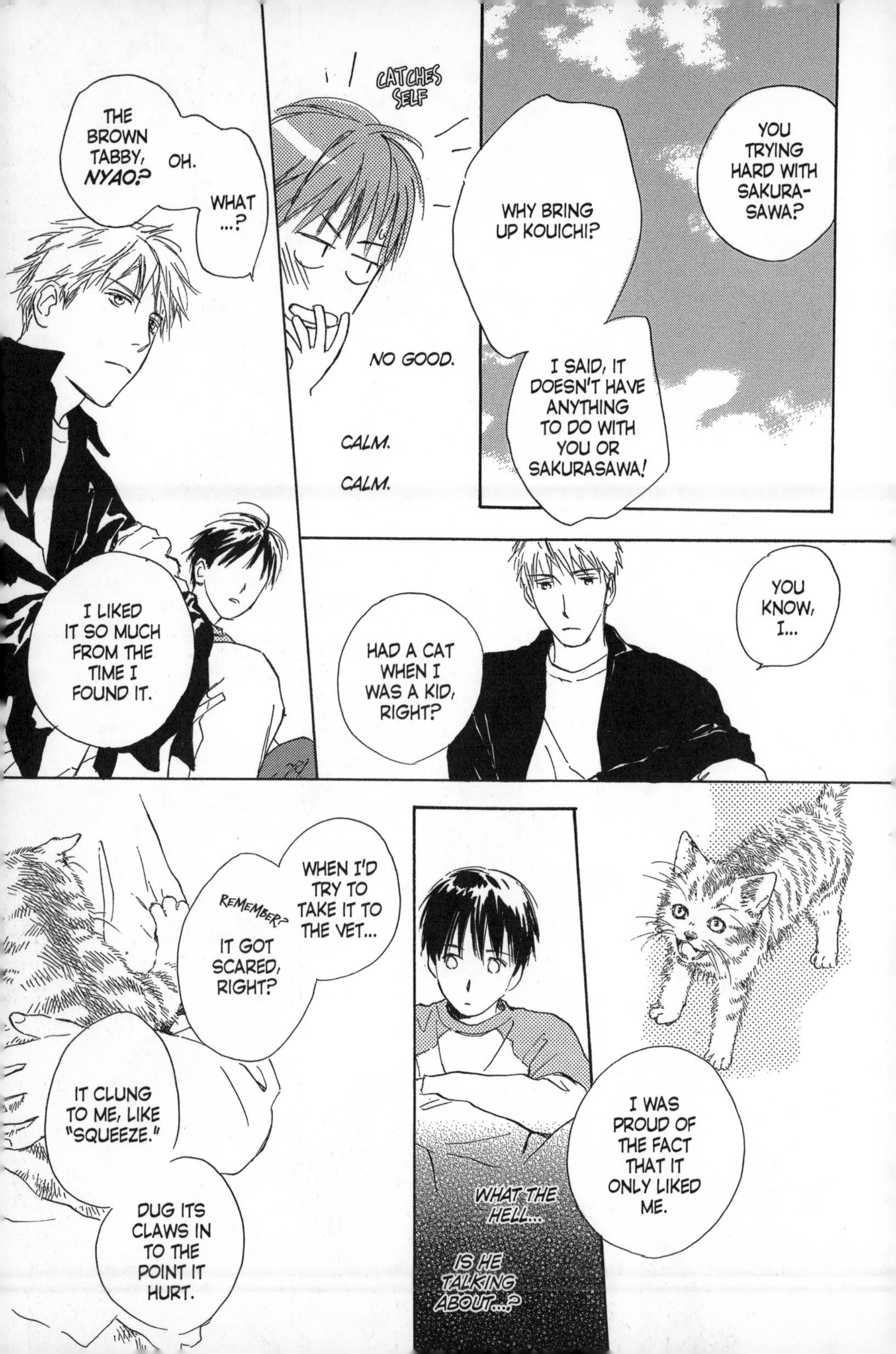
YOU TRYING HARD WITH SAKURA-SAWA?
WHY BRING UP KOUICHI?
I SAID, IT DOESN'T HAVE ANYTHING TO DO WITH YOU OR SAKURASAWA!
CATCHES SELF
NO GOOD.
CALM.
CALM.
YOU KNOW, I...
HAD A CAT WHEN I WAS A KID, RIGHT?
THE BROWN TABBY, NYAO?
OH.
WHAT ...?
I LIKED IT SO MUCH FROM THE TIME I FOUND IT.
I WAS PROUD OF THE FACT THAT IT ONLY LIKED ME.
WHAT THE HELL...
IS HE TALKING ABOUT...?
WHEN I'D TRY TO TAKE IT TO THE VET...
REMEMBER?
IT GOT SCARED, RIGHT?
IT CLUNG TO ME, LIKE "SQUEEZE."
DUG ITS CLAWS IN TO THE POINT IT HURT.

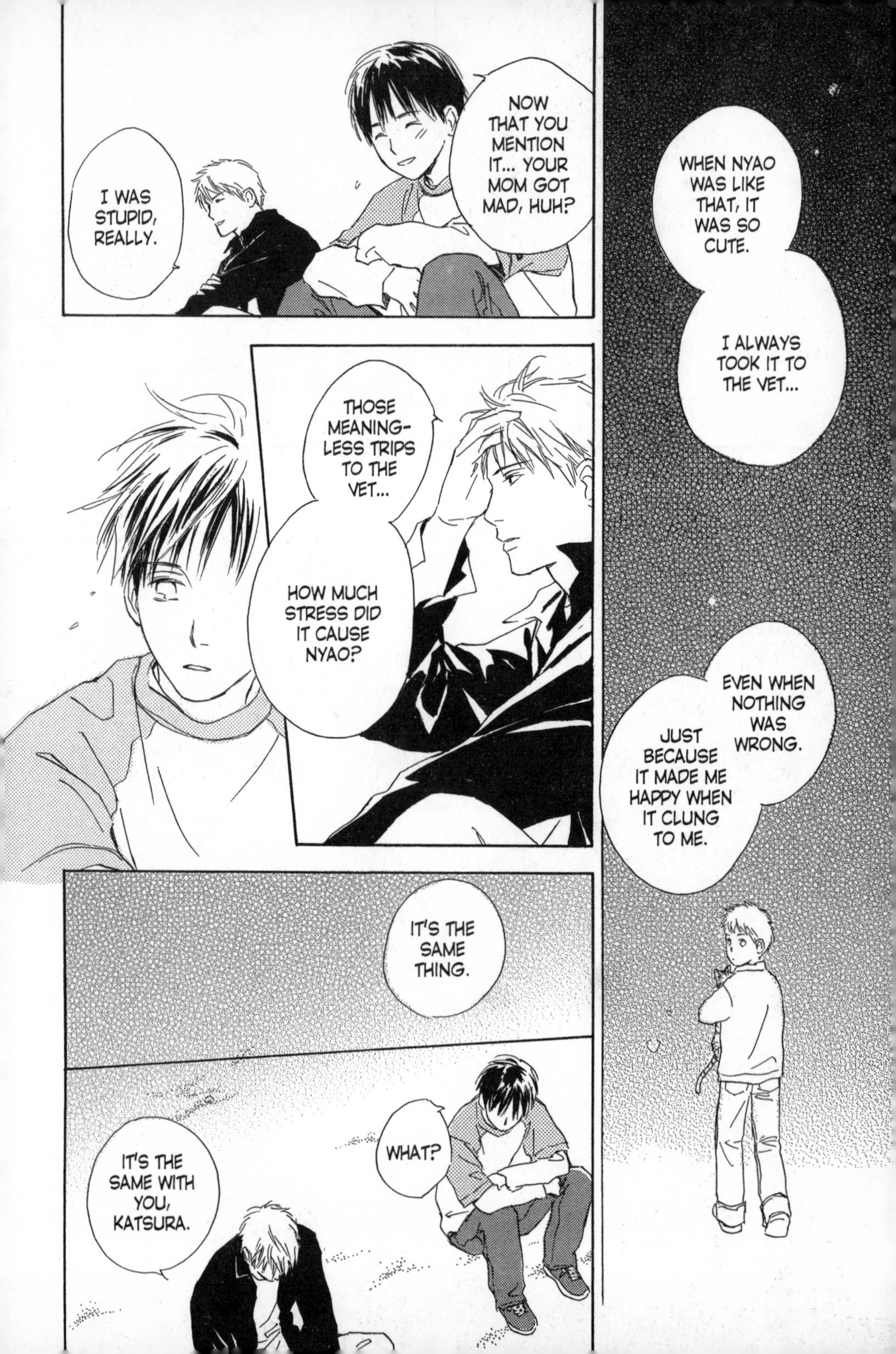
WHEN NYAO WAS LIKE THAT, IT WAS SO CUTE.
I ALWAYS TOOK IT TO THE VET...
EVEN WHEN NOTHING WAS WRONG.
JUST BECAUSE IT MADE ME HAPPY WHEN IT CLUNG TO ME.
NOW THAT YOU MENTION IT... YOUR MOM GOT MAD, HUH?
I WAS STUPID, REALLY.
THOSE MEANING-LESS TRIPS TO THE VET...
HOW MUCH STRESS DID IT CAUSE NYAO?
IT'S THE SAME THING.
WHAT?
IT'S THE SAME WITH YOU, KATSURA.

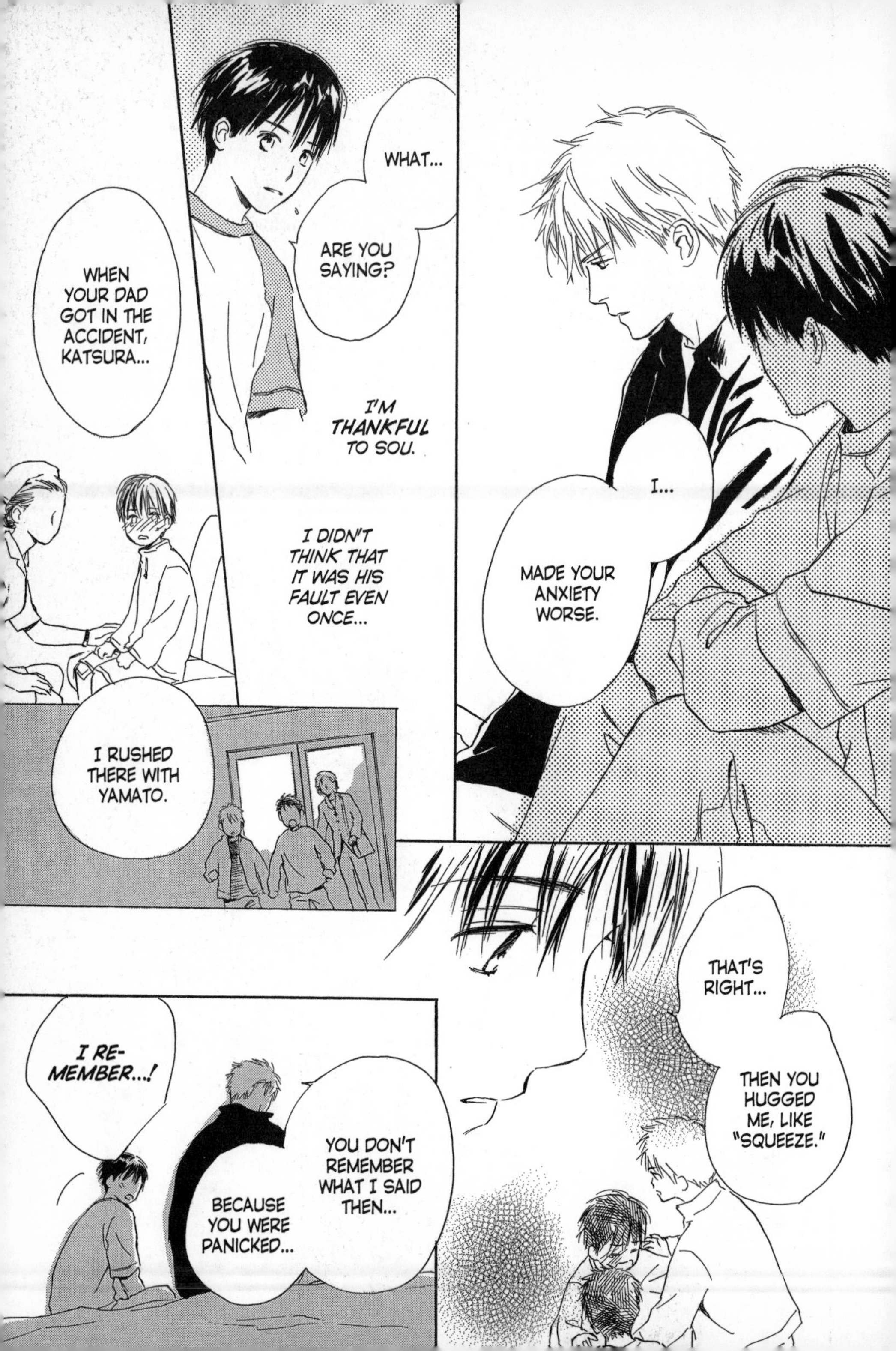
I...
MADE YOUR ANXIETY WORSE.
WHAT...
ARE YOU SAYING?
I'M *THANKFUL* TO SOU.
I DIDN'T THINK THAT IT WAS HIS FAULT EVEN ONCE...
WHEN YOUR DAD GOT IN THE ACCIDENT, KATSURA...
I RUSHED THERE WITH YAMATO.
THAT'S RIGHT...
THEN YOU HUGGED ME, LIKE "SQUEEZE."
YOU DON'T REMEMBER WHAT I SAID THEN...
BECAUSE YOU WERE PANICKED...
I RE-MEMBER...!

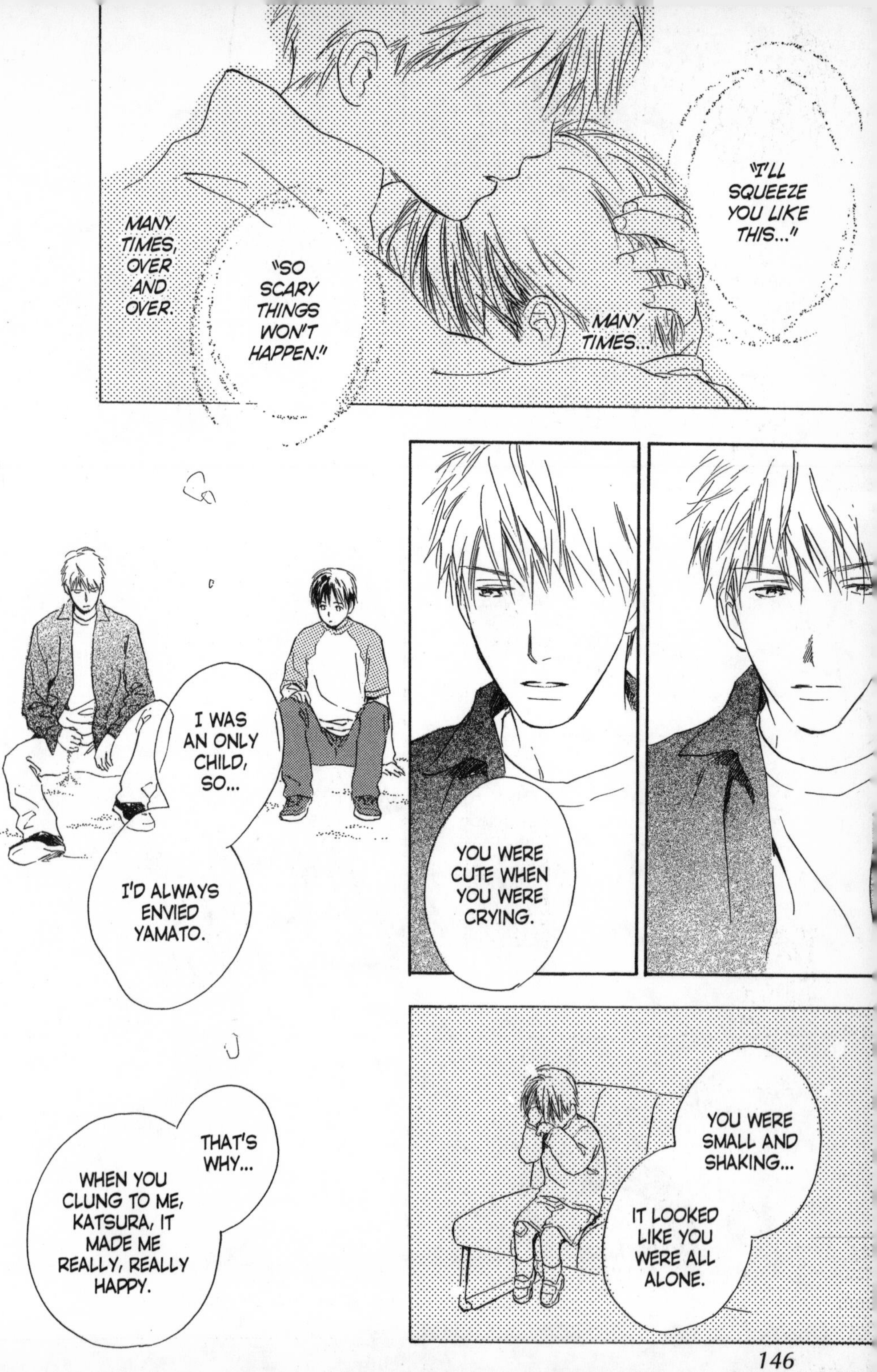
"I'LL SQUEEZE YOU LIKE THIS..."
MANY TIMES...
"SO SCARY THINGS WON'T HAPPEN."
MANY TIMES, OVER AND OVER.
YOU WERE CUTE WHEN YOU WERE CRYING.
YOU WERE SMALL AND SHAKING...
IT LOOKED LIKE YOU WERE ALL ALONE.
I WAS AN ONLY CHILD, SO...
I'D ALWAYS ENVIED YAMATO.
THAT'S WHY...
WHEN YOU CLUNG TO ME, KATSURA, IT MADE ME REALLY, REALLY HAPPY.

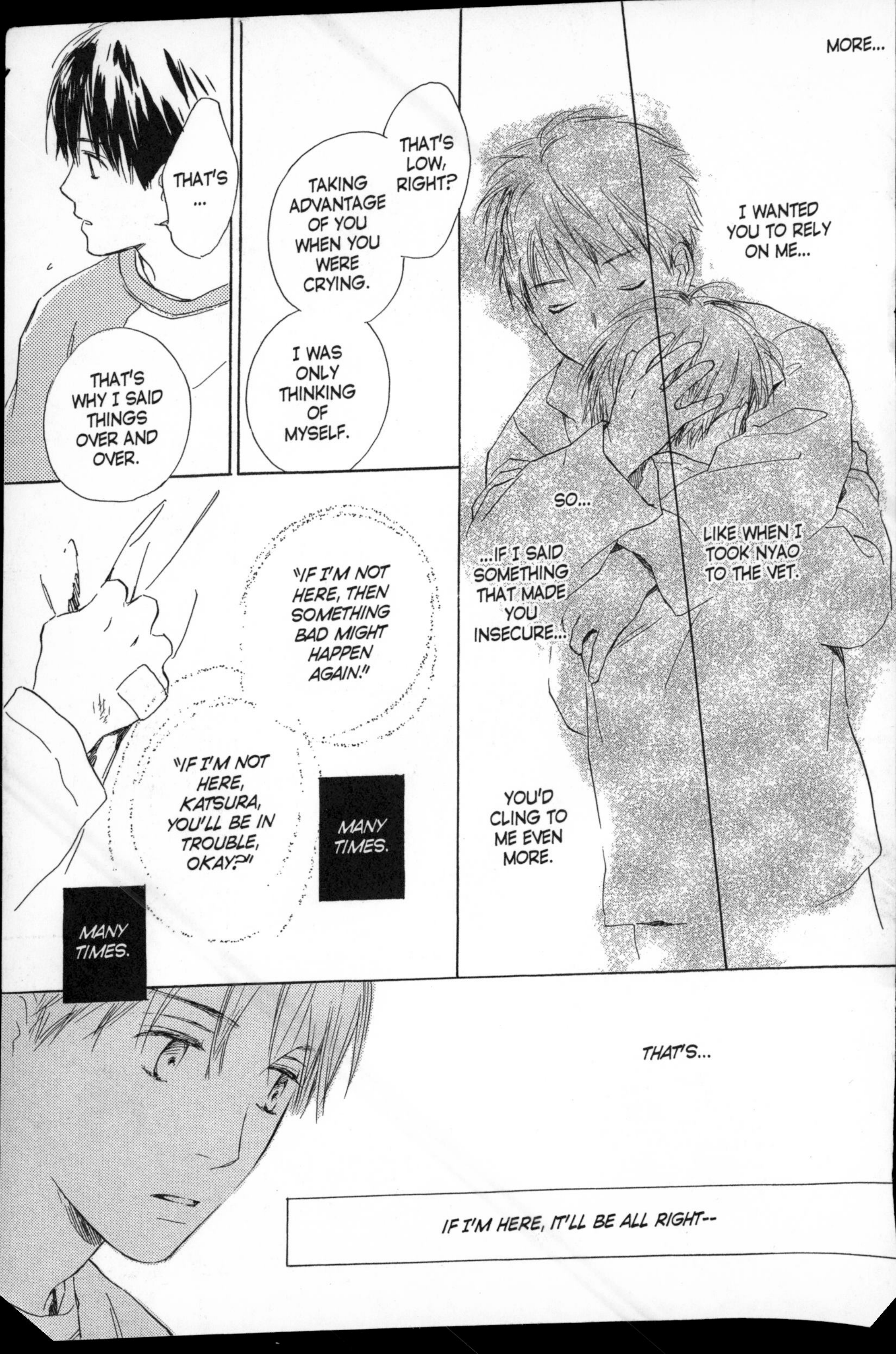
MORE...
I WANTED YOU TO RELY ON ME...
LIKE WHEN I TOOK NYAO TO THE VET.
SO...
...IF I SAID SOMETHING THAT MADE YOU INSECURE...
YOU'D CLING TO ME EVEN MORE.
THAT'S LOW, RIGHT?
TAKING ADVANTAGE OF YOU WHEN YOU WERE CRYING.
I WAS ONLY THINKING OF MYSELF.
THAT'S...
THAT'S WHY I SAID THINGS OVER AND OVER.
"IF I'M NOT HERE, THEN SOMETHING BAD MIGHT HAPPEN AGAIN."
MANY TIMES.
"IF I'M NOT HERE, KATSURA, YOU'LL BE IN TROUBLE, OKAY?"
MANY TIMES.
THAT'S...
IF I'M HERE, IT'LL BE ALL RIGHT--

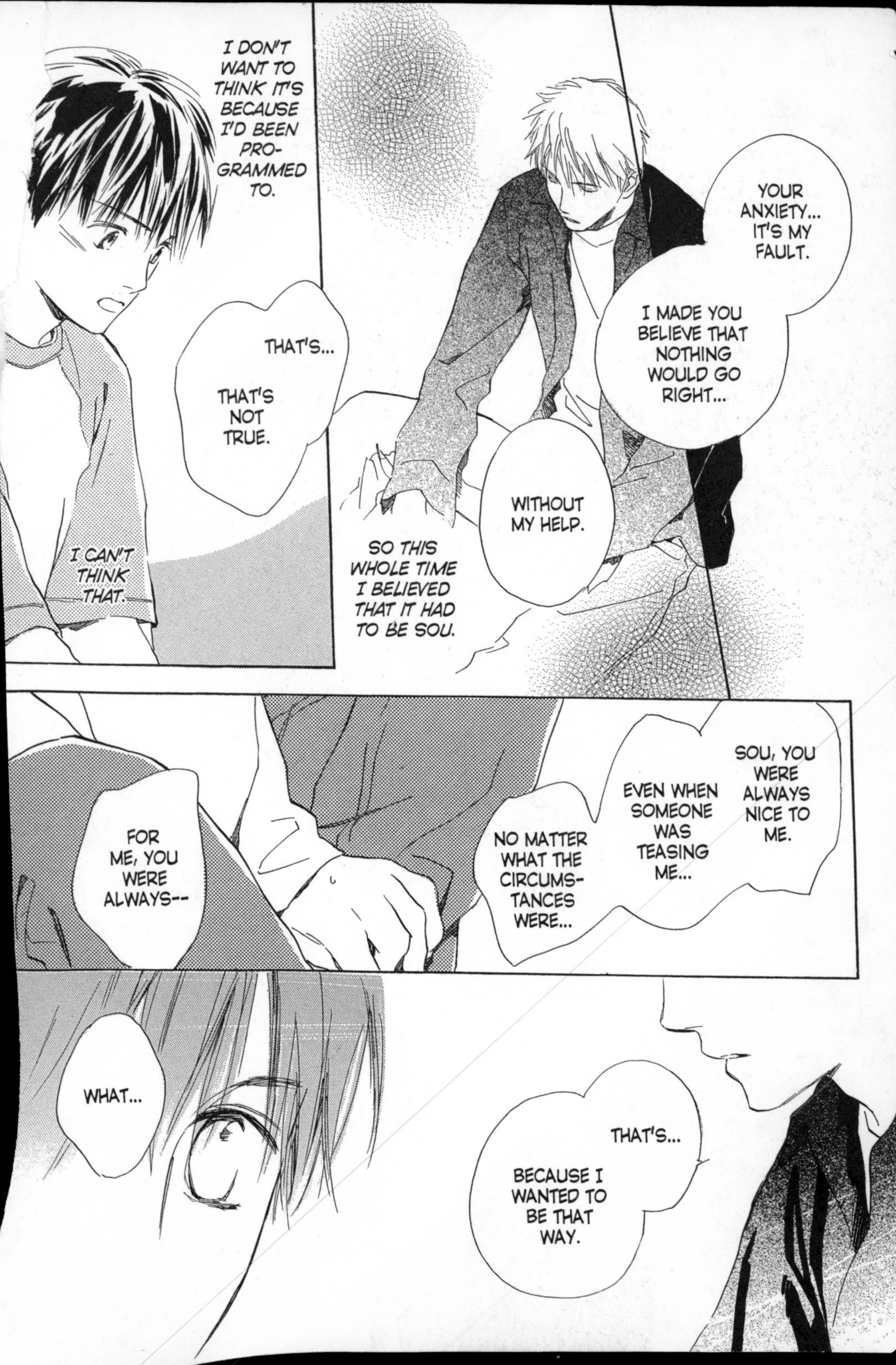
YOUR ANXIETY... IT'S MY FAULT.
I MADE YOU BELIEVE THAT NOTHING WOULD GO RIGHT...
WITHOUT MY HELP.
SO THIS WHOLE TIME I BELIEVED THAT IT HAD TO BE SOU.
I DON'T WANT TO THINK IT'S BECAUSE I'D BEEN PRO-GRAMMED TO.
THAT'S...
THAT'S NOT TRUE.
I CAN'T THINK THAT.
SOU, YOU WERE ALWAYS NICE TO ME.
EVEN WHEN SOMEONE WAS TEASING ME...
NO MATTER WHAT THE CIRCUMS-TANCES WERE...
FOR ME, YOU WERE ALWAYS--
THAT'S...
BECAUSE I WANTED TO BE THAT WAY.
WHAT...

MORE...

THAT'S ...

TAKING ADVANTAGE OF YOU WHEN YOU WERE CRYING.

THAT'S LOW, RIGHT?

I WANTED YOU TO RELY ON ME...

THAT'S WHY I SAID THINGS OVER AND OVER.

I WAS ONLY THINKING OF MYSELF.

SO...

...IF I SAID SOMETHING THAT MADE YOU INSECURE...

LIKE WHEN I TOOK NYAO TO THE VET.

"IF I'M NOT HERE, THEN SOMETHING BAD MIGHT HAPPEN AGAIN!"

"IF I'M NOT HERE, KATSURA, YOU'LL BE IN TROUBLE, OKAY?"

MANY TIMES.

MANY TIMES.

YOU'D CLING TO ME EVEN MORE.

THAT'S...

IF I'M HERE, IT'LL BE ALL RIGHT--

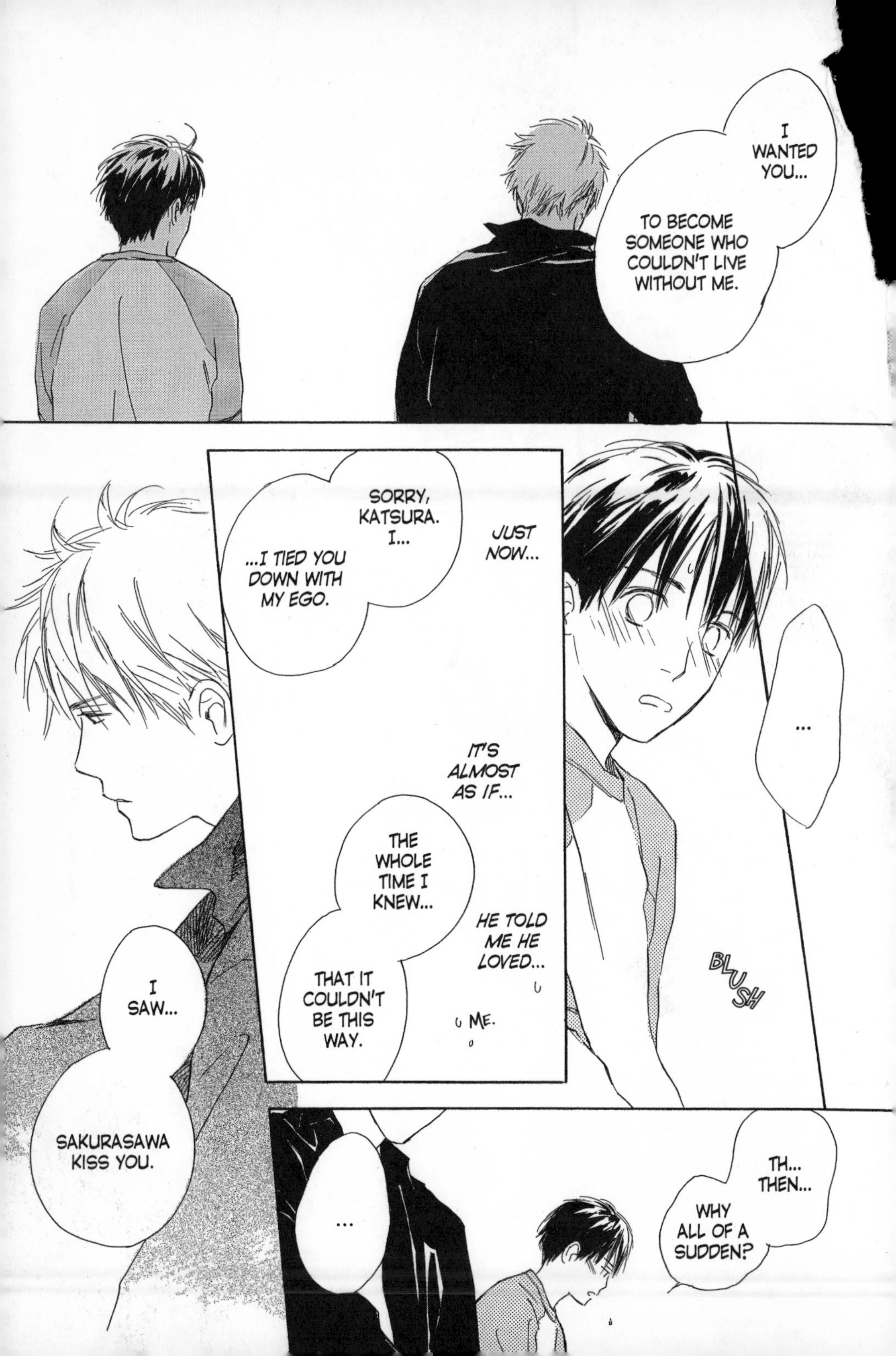
I WANTED YOU...
TO BECOME SOMEONE WHO COULDN'T LIVE WITHOUT ME.
...
I SAW...
SAKURASAWA KISS YOU.
SORRY, KATSURA. I...
...I TIED YOU DOWN WITH MY EGO.
JUST NOW...
IT'S ALMOST AS IF...
HE TOLD ME HE LOVED...
ME.
THE WHOLE TIME I KNEW...
THAT IT COULDN'T BE THIS WAY.
BLUSH
TH... THEN...
WHY ALL OF A SUDDEN?
...

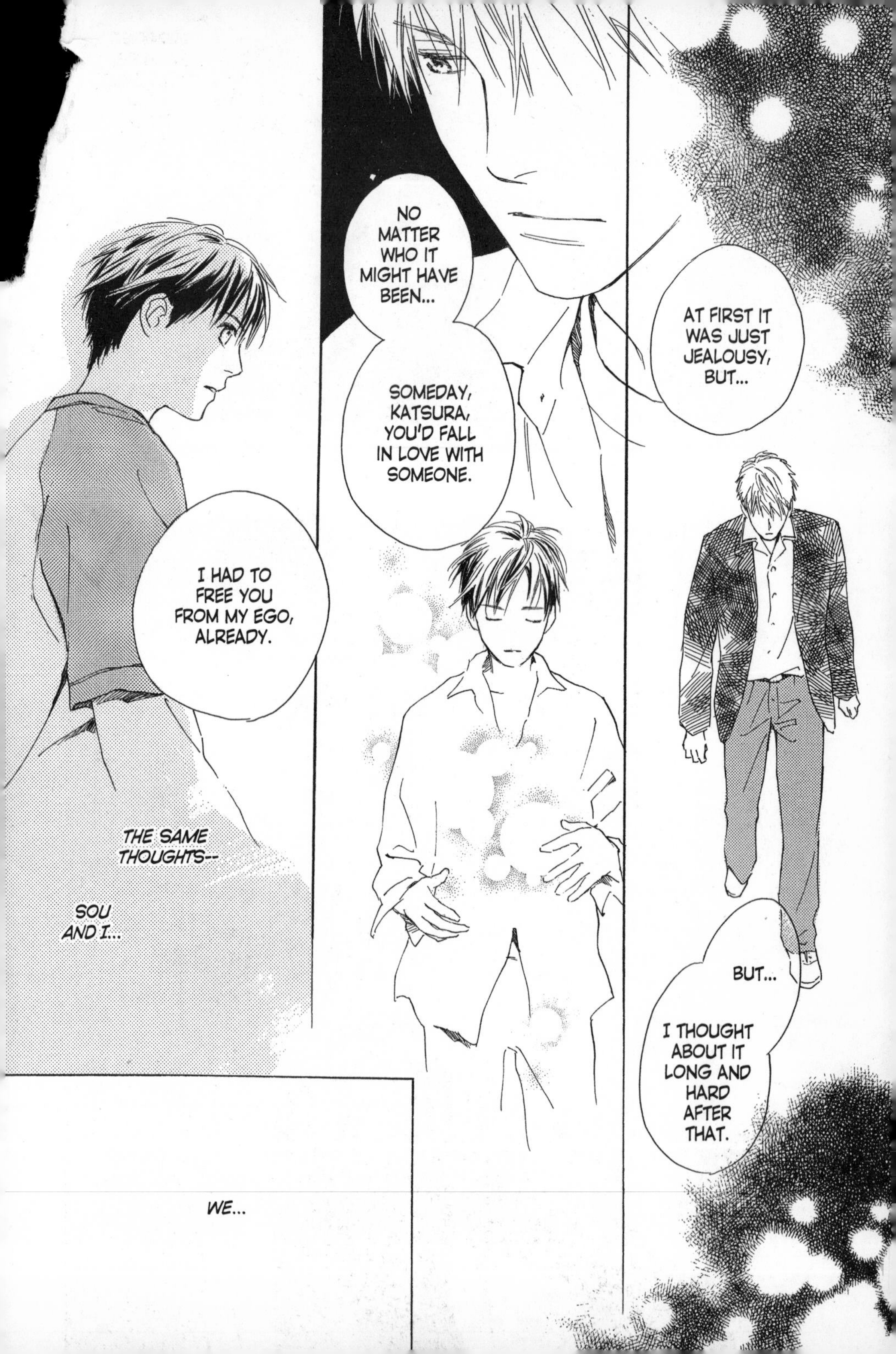
AT FIRST IT WAS JUST JEALOUSY, BUT...
BUT...
I THOUGHT ABOUT IT LONG AND HARD AFTER THAT.
NO MATTER WHO IT MIGHT HAVE BEEN...
SOMEDAY, KATSURA, YOU'D FALL IN LOVE WITH SOMEONE.
I HAD TO FREE YOU FROM MY EGO, ALREADY.
THE SAME THOUGHTS--
SOU AND I...
WE...

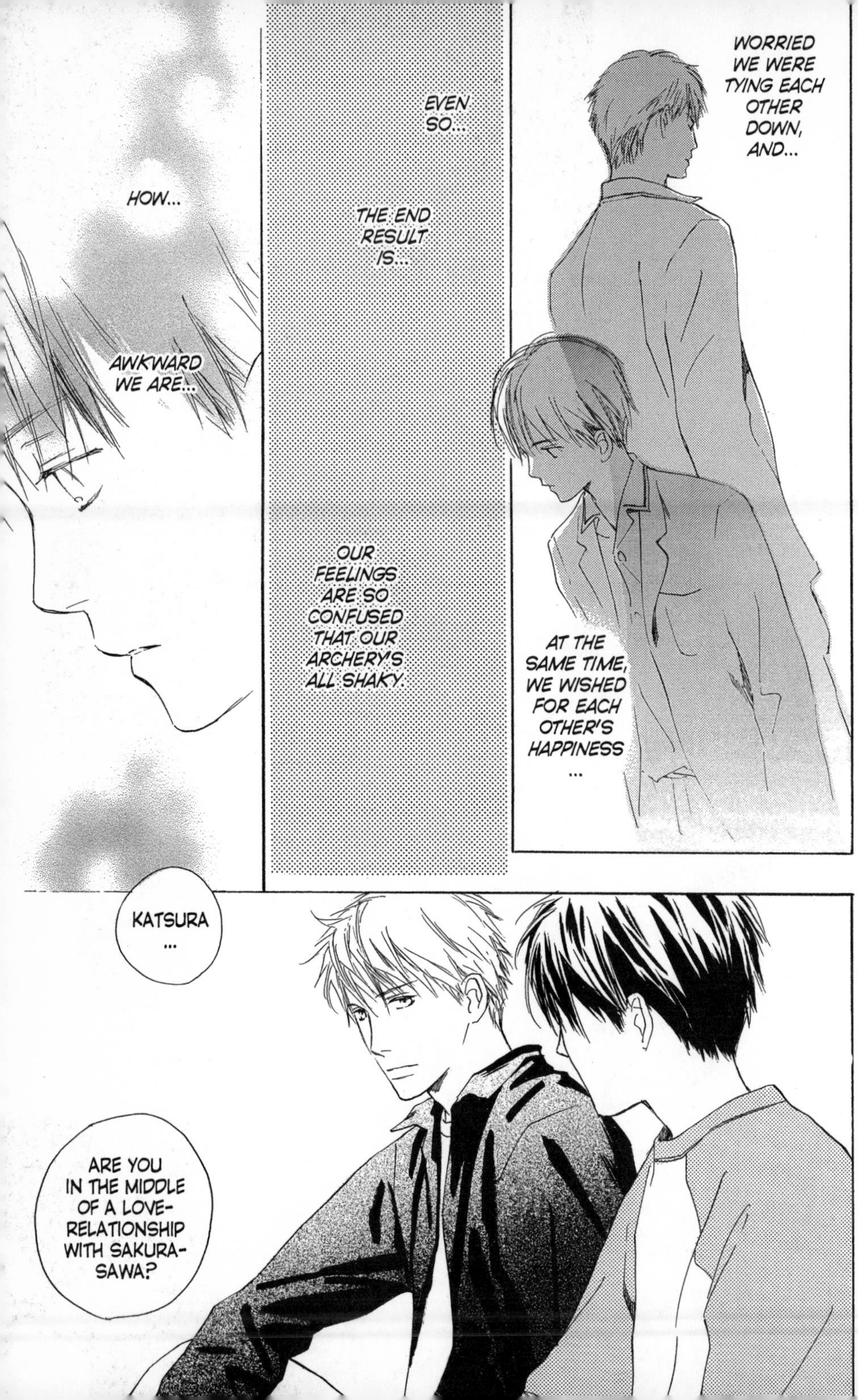
WORRIED WE WERE TYING EACH OTHER DOWN, AND...
AT THE SAME TIME, WE WISHED FOR EACH OTHER'S HAPPINESS...
EVEN SO...
THE END RESULT IS...
OUR FEELINGS ARE SO CONFUSED THAT OUR ARCHERY'S ALL SHAKY.
HOW...
AWKWARD WE ARE...
KATSURA...
ARE YOU IN THE MIDDLE OF A LOVE-RELATIONSHIP WITH SAKURA-SAWA?

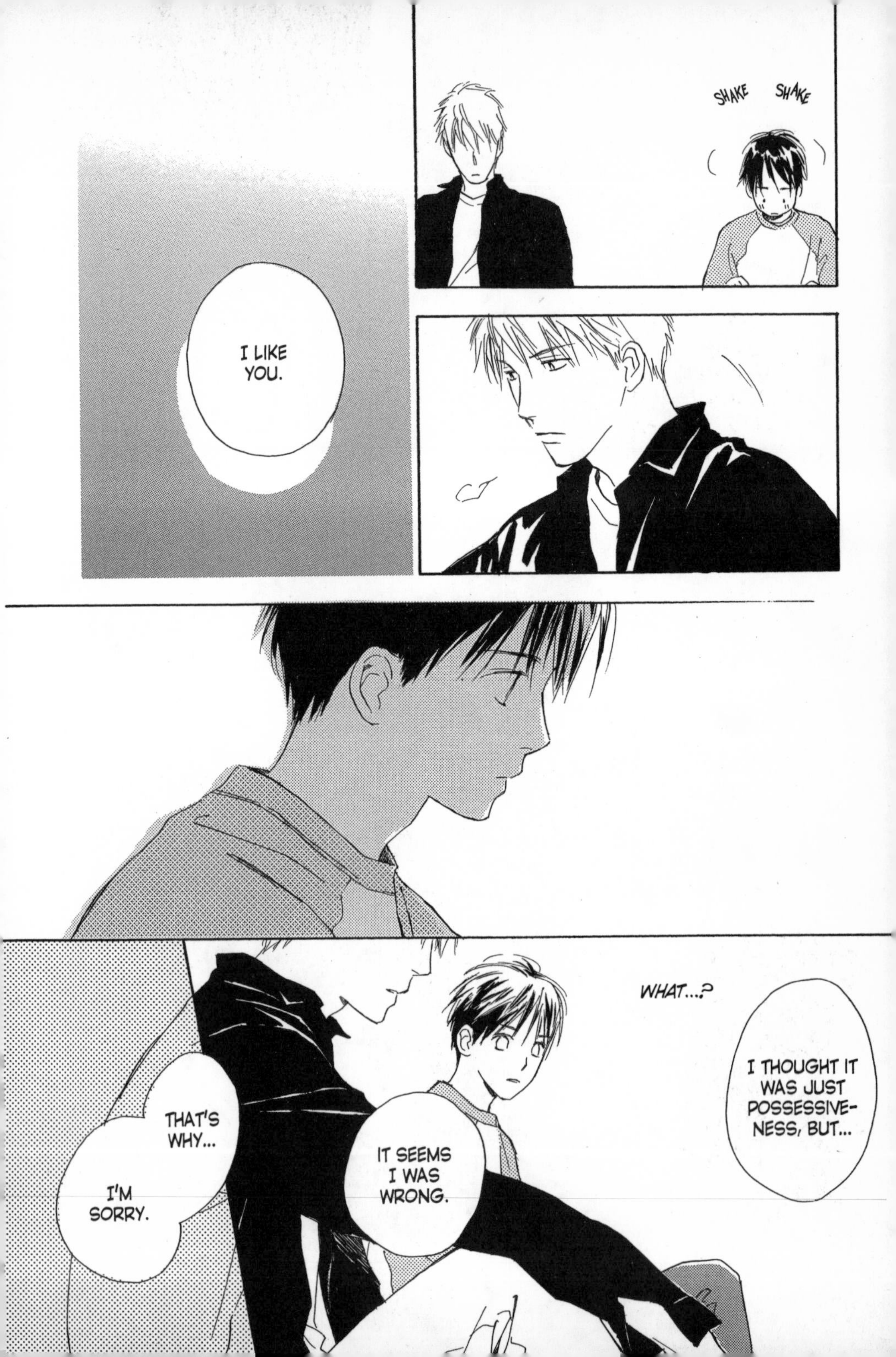
SHAKE SHAKE
I LIKE YOU.
WHAT...?
I THOUGHT IT WAS JUST POSSESSIVE-NESS, BUT...
IT SEEMS I WAS WRONG.
THAT'S WHY...
I'M SORRY.

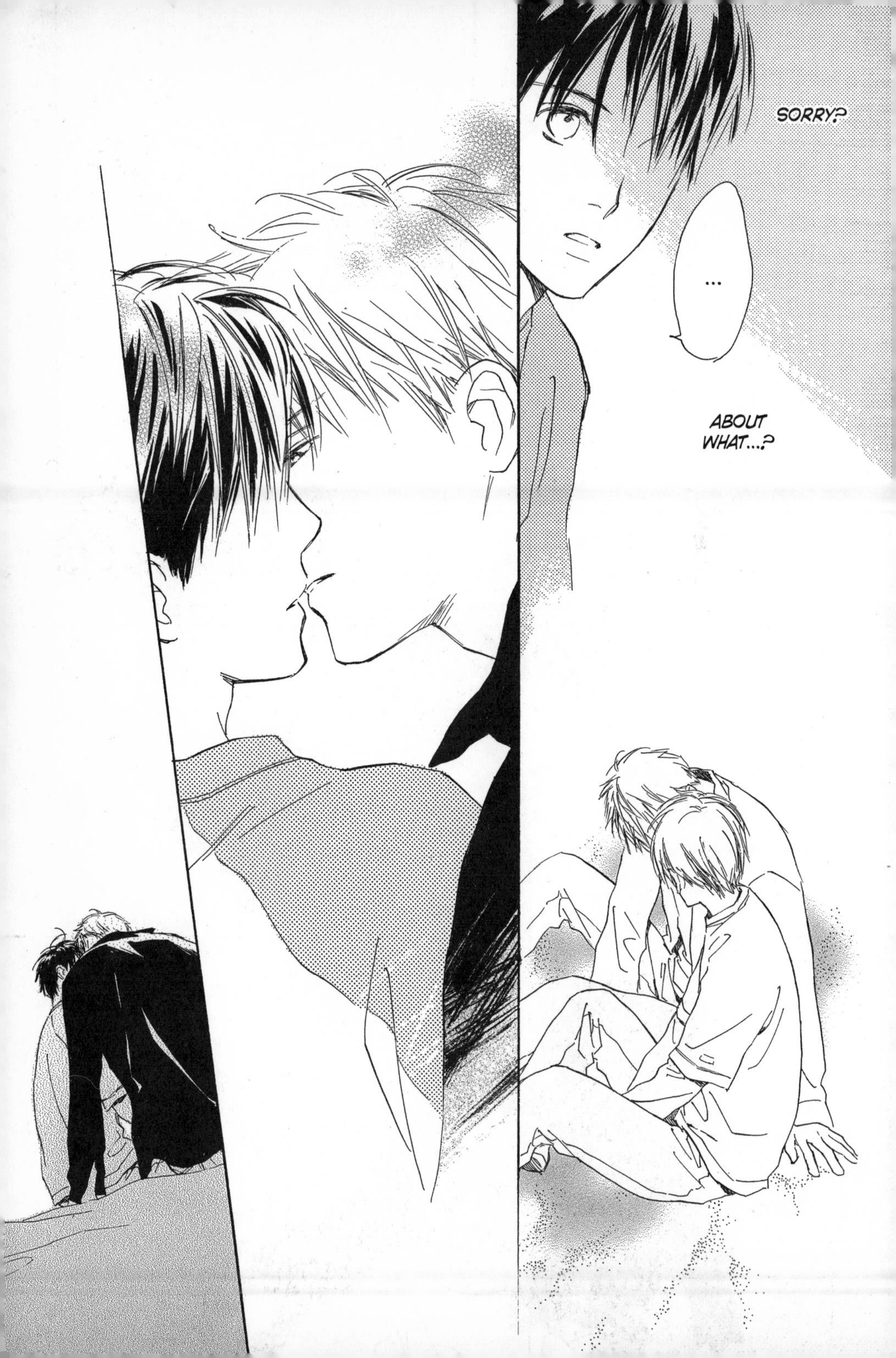
SORRY?
...
ABOUT WHAT...?

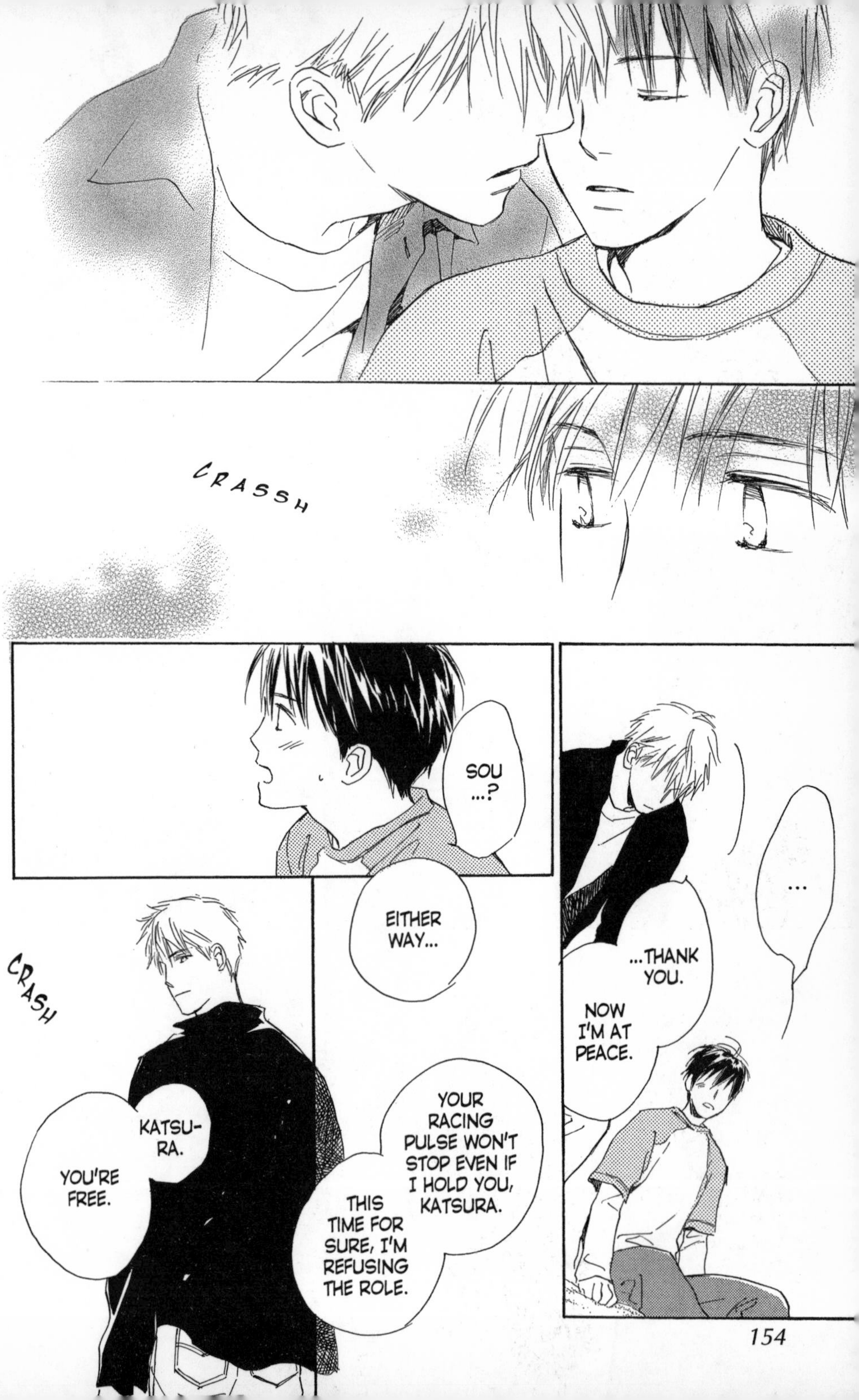
CRASSH
...
...THANK YOU.
NOW I'M AT PEACE.
SOU ...?
EITHER WAY...
YOUR RACING PULSE WON'T STOP EVEN IF I HOLD YOU, KATSURA.
THIS TIME FOR SURE, I'M REFUSING THE ROLE.
CRASH
KATSU-RA.
YOU'RE FREE.

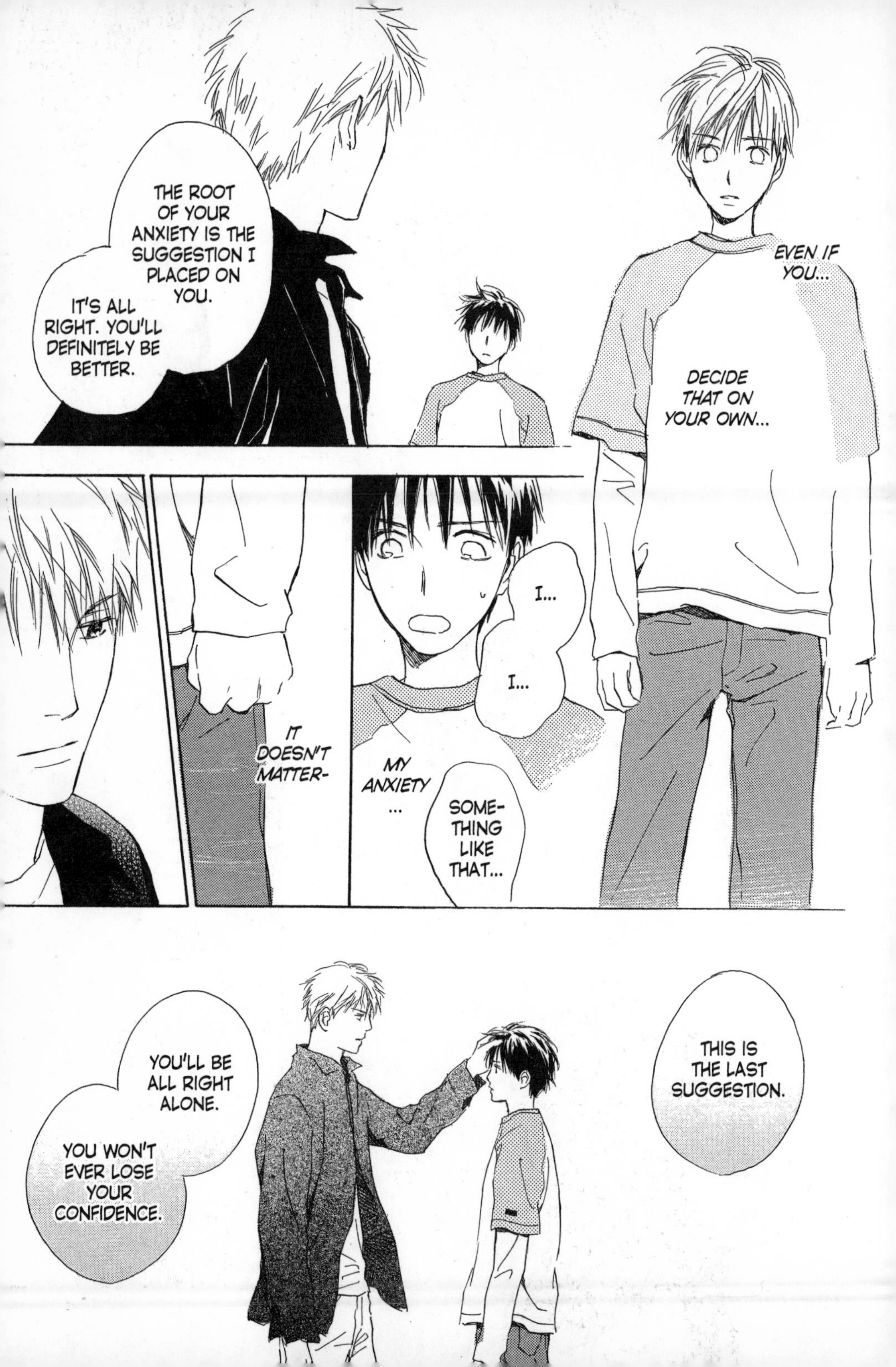
EVEN IF YOU...
DECIDE THAT ON YOUR OWN...
THE ROOT OF YOUR ANXIETY IS THE SUGGESTION I PLACED ON YOU.
IT'S ALL RIGHT. YOU'LL DEFINITELY BE BETTER.
I...
I...
MY ANXIETY...
SOMETHING LIKE THAT...
IT DOESN'T MATTER-
THIS IS THE LAST SUGGESTION.
YOU'LL BE ALL RIGHT ALONE.
YOU WON'T EVER LOSE YOUR CONFIDENCE.

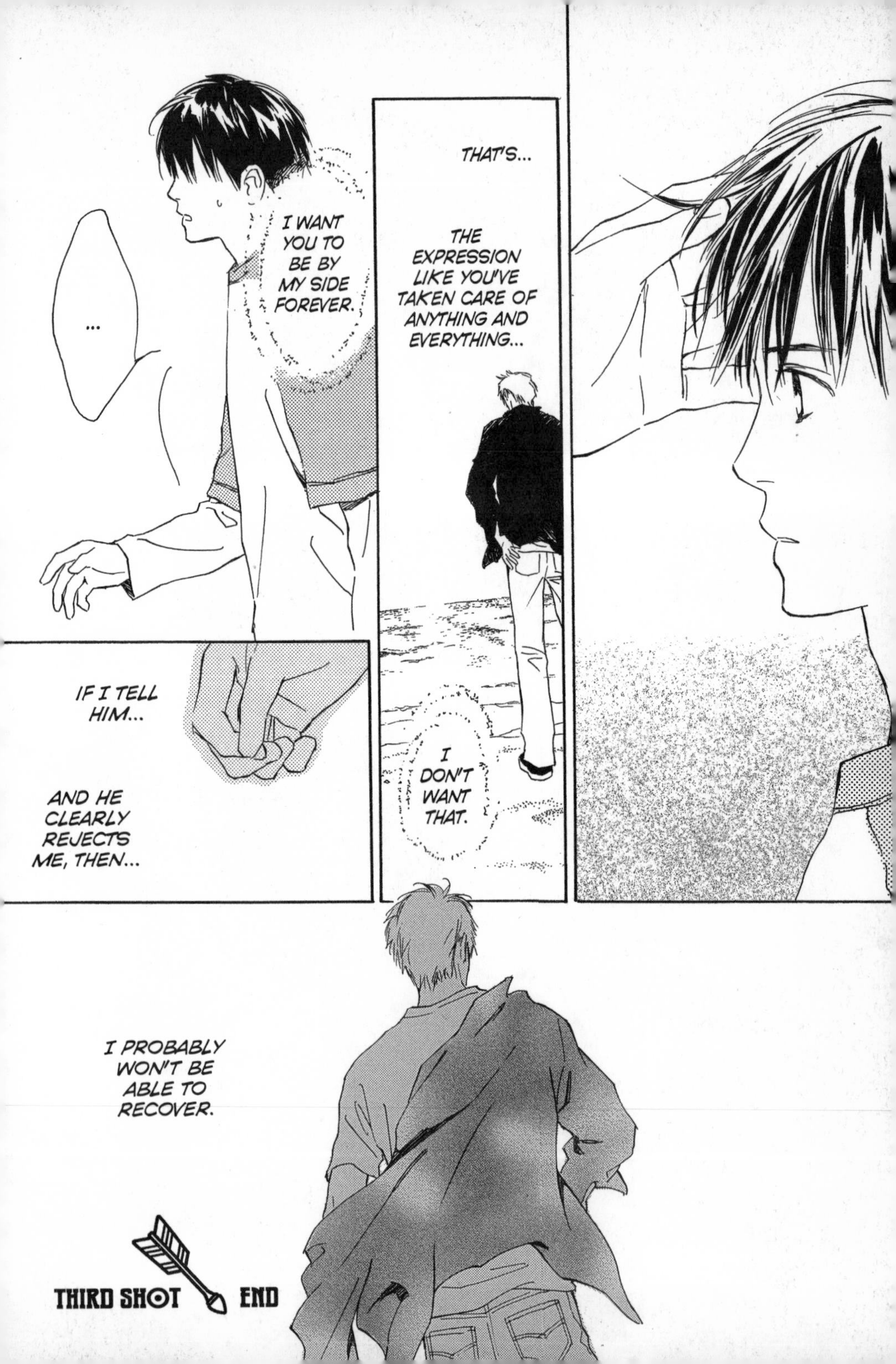
THAT'S...
THE EXPRESSION LIKE YOU'VE TAKEN CARE OF ANYTHING AND EVERYTHING...
I DON'T WANT THAT.
I WANT YOU TO BE BY MY SIDE FOREVER.
...
IF I TELL HIM...
AND HE CLEARLY REJECTS ME, THEN...
I PROBABLY WON'T BE ABLE TO RECOVER.
THIRD SHOT END

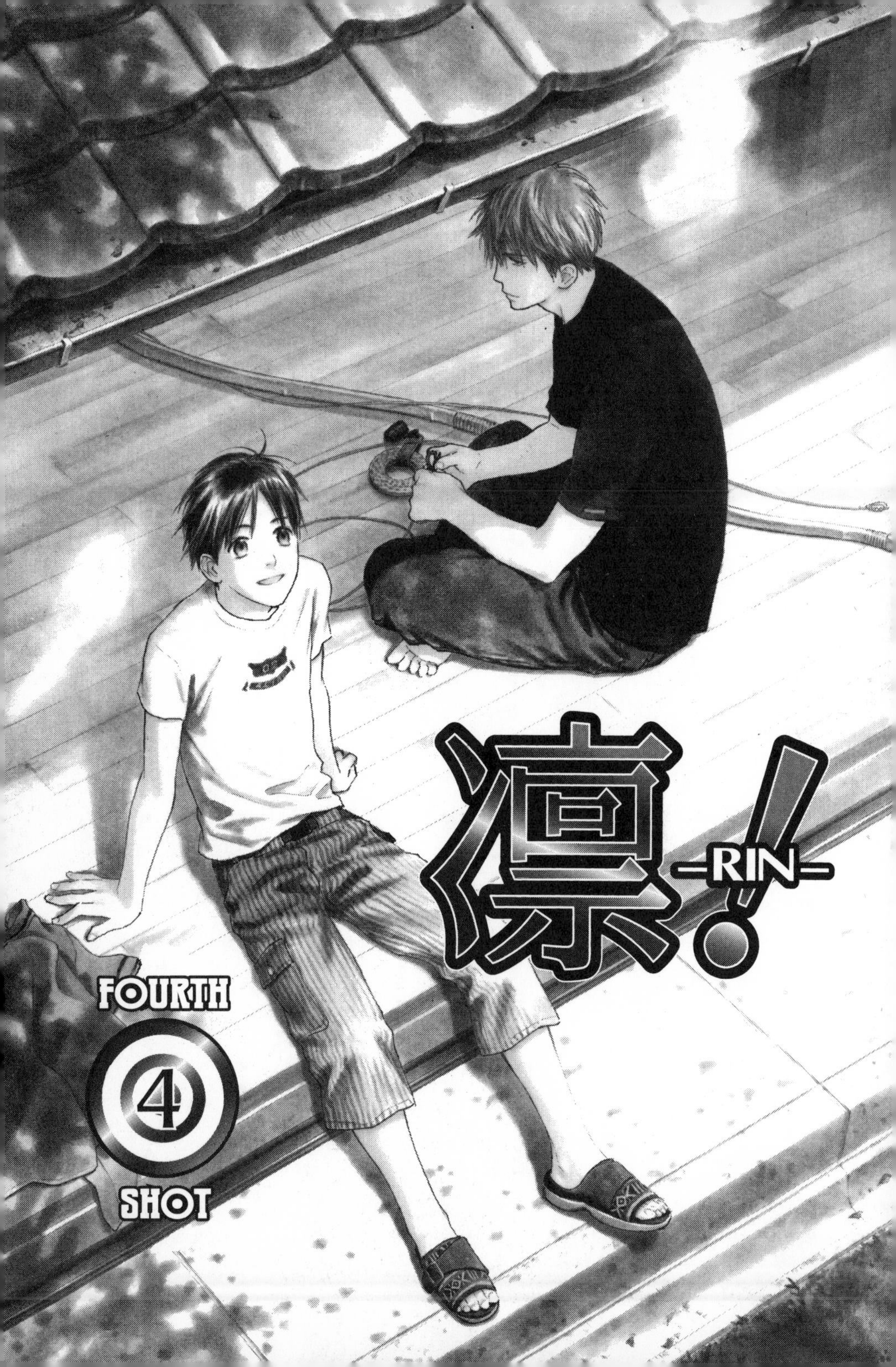
凛!
—RIN—
FOURTH
4
SHOT

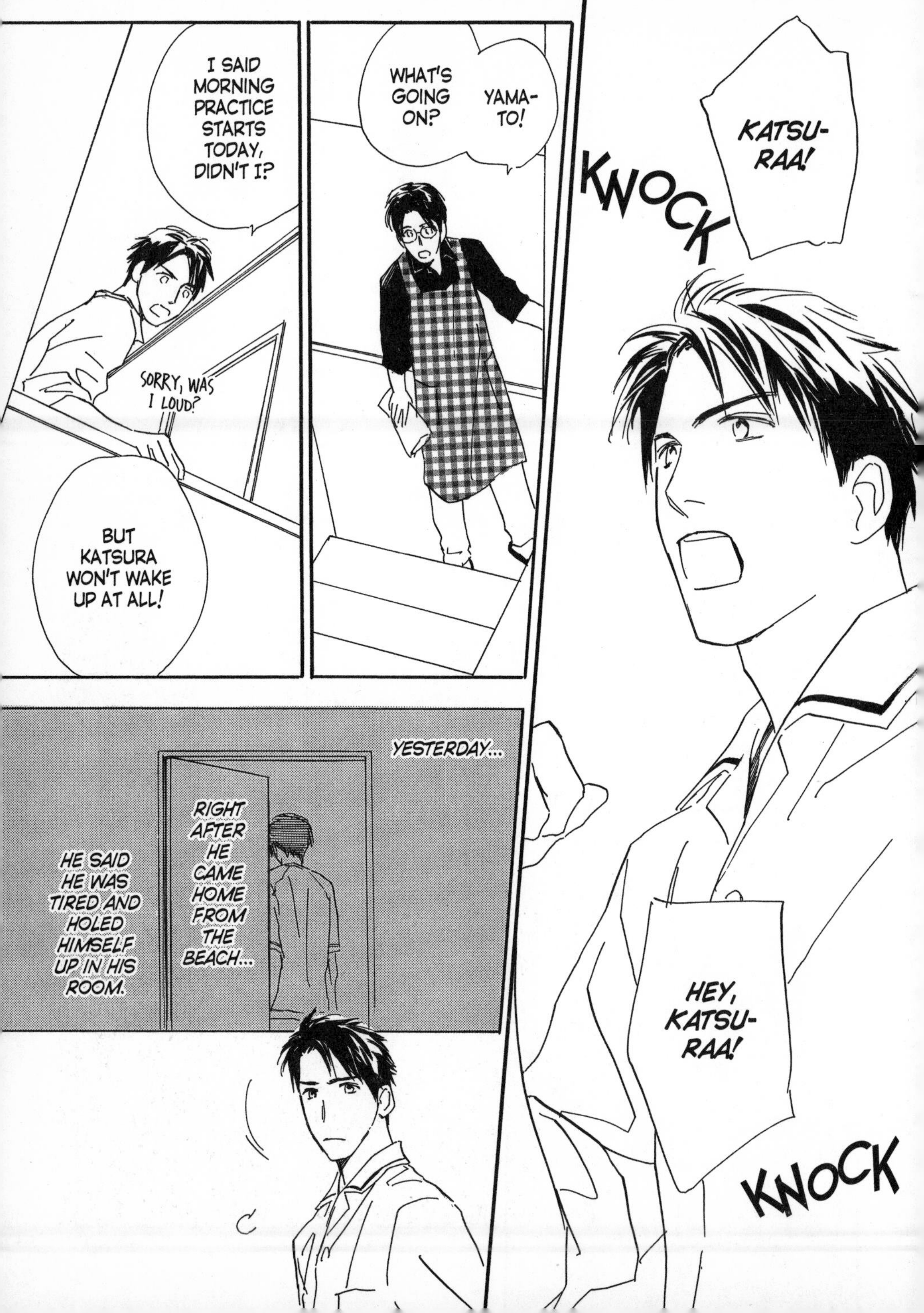

KATSURAA!
KNOCK
HEY, KATSURAA!
KNOCK
YAMATO!
WHAT'S GOING ON?
I SAID MORNING PRACTICE STARTS TODAY, DIDN'T I?
SORRY, WAS I LOUD?
BUT KATSURA WON'T WAKE UP AT ALL!
YESTERDAY...
RIGHT AFTER HE CAME HOME FROM THE BEACH...
HE SAID HE WAS TIRED AND HOLED HIMSELF UP IN HIS ROOM.

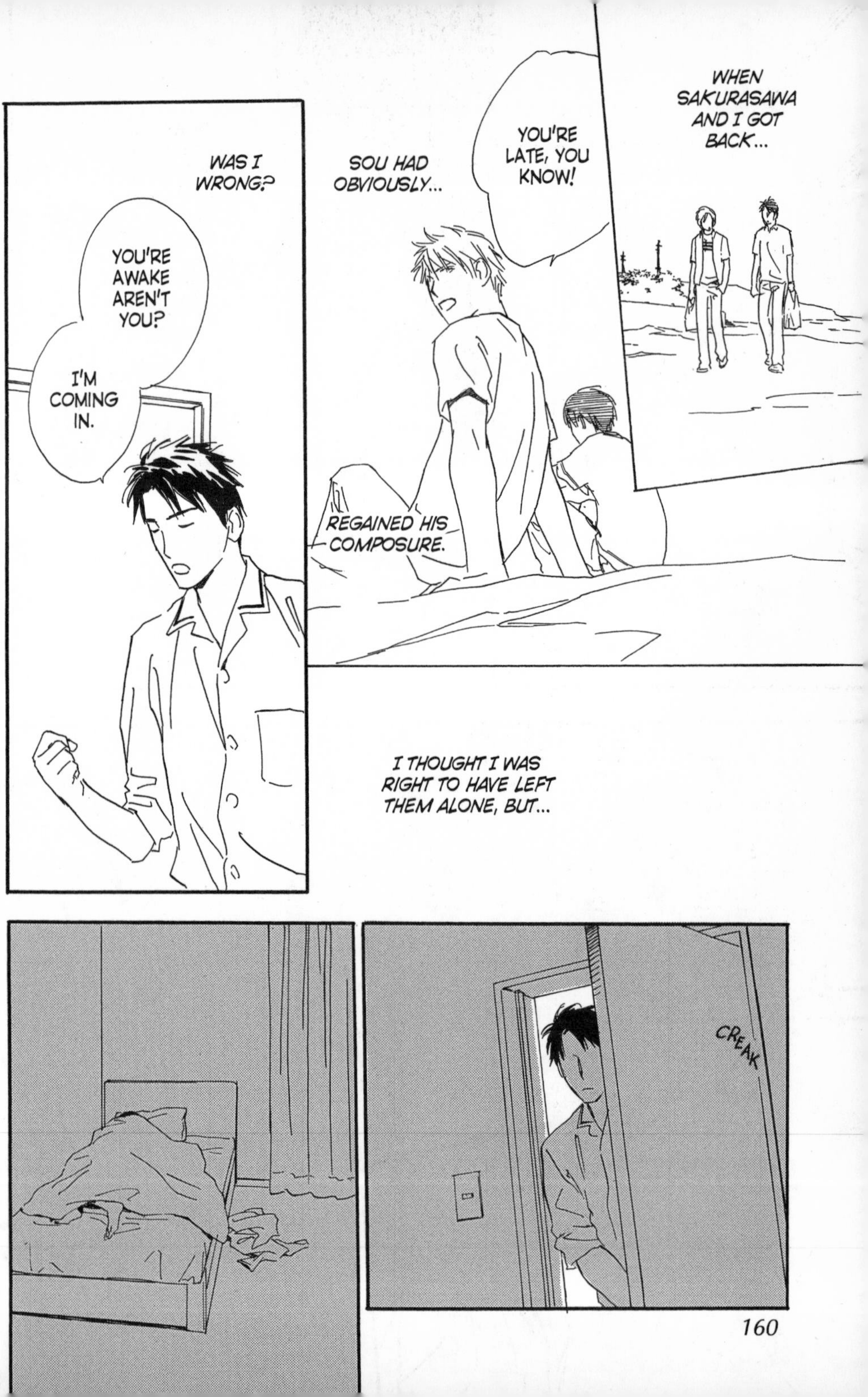
WHEN SAKURASAWA AND I GOT BACK...
YOU'RE LATE, YOU KNOW!
SOU HAD OBVIOUSLY...
REGAINED HIS COMPOSURE.
I THOUGHT I WAS RIGHT TO HAVE LEFT THEM ALONE, BUT...
WAS I WRONG?
YOU'RE AWAKE AREN'T YOU?
I'M COMING IN.
CREAK

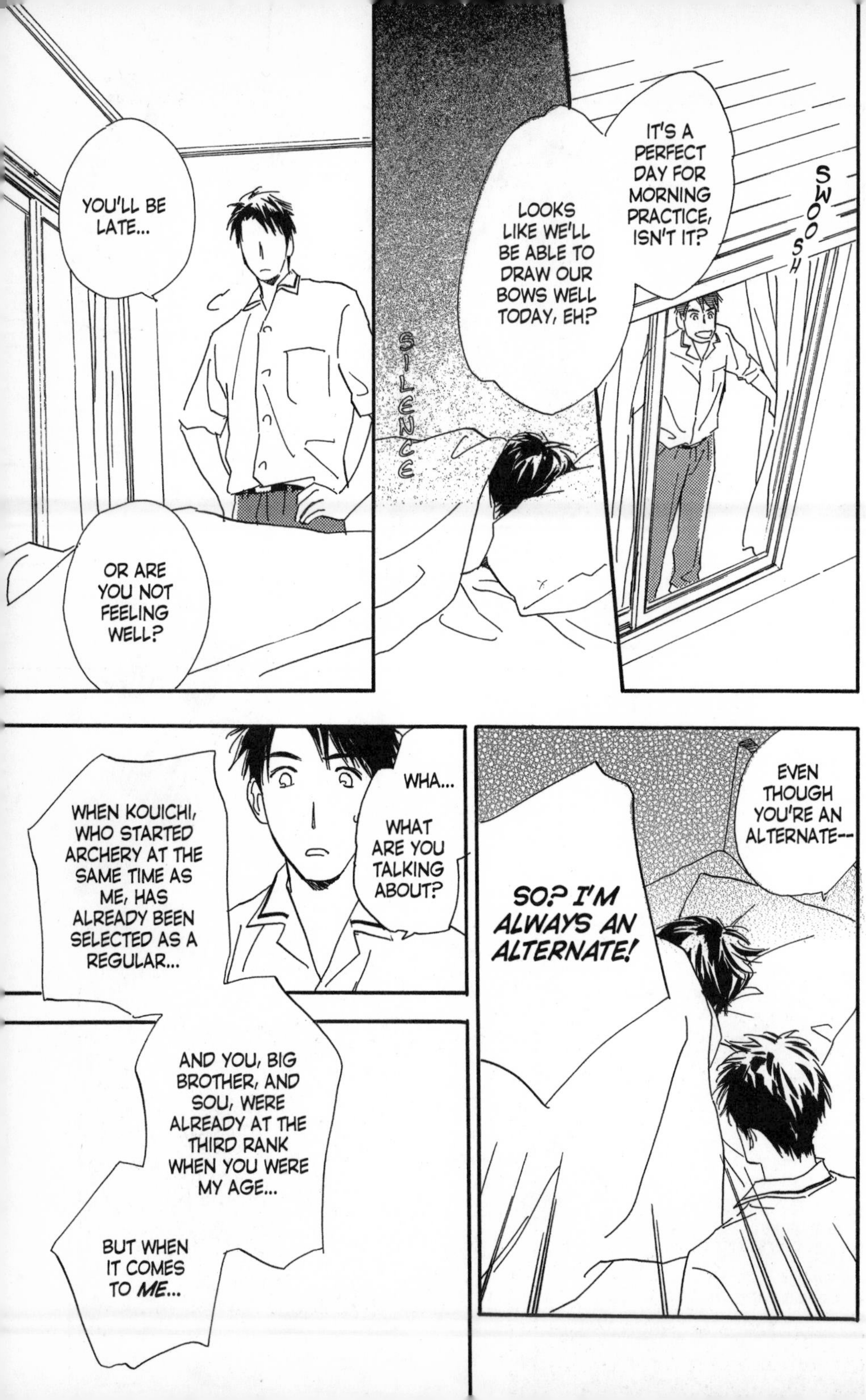
SWOOSH
IT'S A PERFECT DAY FOR MORNING PRACTICE, ISN'T IT?
LOOKS LIKE WE'LL BE ABLE TO DRAW OUR BOWS WELL TODAY, EH?
SILENCE
YOU'LL BE LATE...
OR ARE YOU NOT FEELING WELL?
EVEN THOUGH YOU'RE AN ALTERNATE--
SO? I'M ALWAYS AN ALTERNATE!
WHA...
WHAT ARE YOU TALKING ABOUT?
WHEN KOUICHI, WHO STARTED ARCHERY AT THE SAME TIME AS ME, HAS ALREADY BEEN SELECTED AS A REGULAR...
AND YOU, BIG BROTHER, AND SOU, WERE ALREADY AT THE THIRD RANK WHEN YOU WERE MY AGE...
BUT WHEN IT COMES TO *ME*...

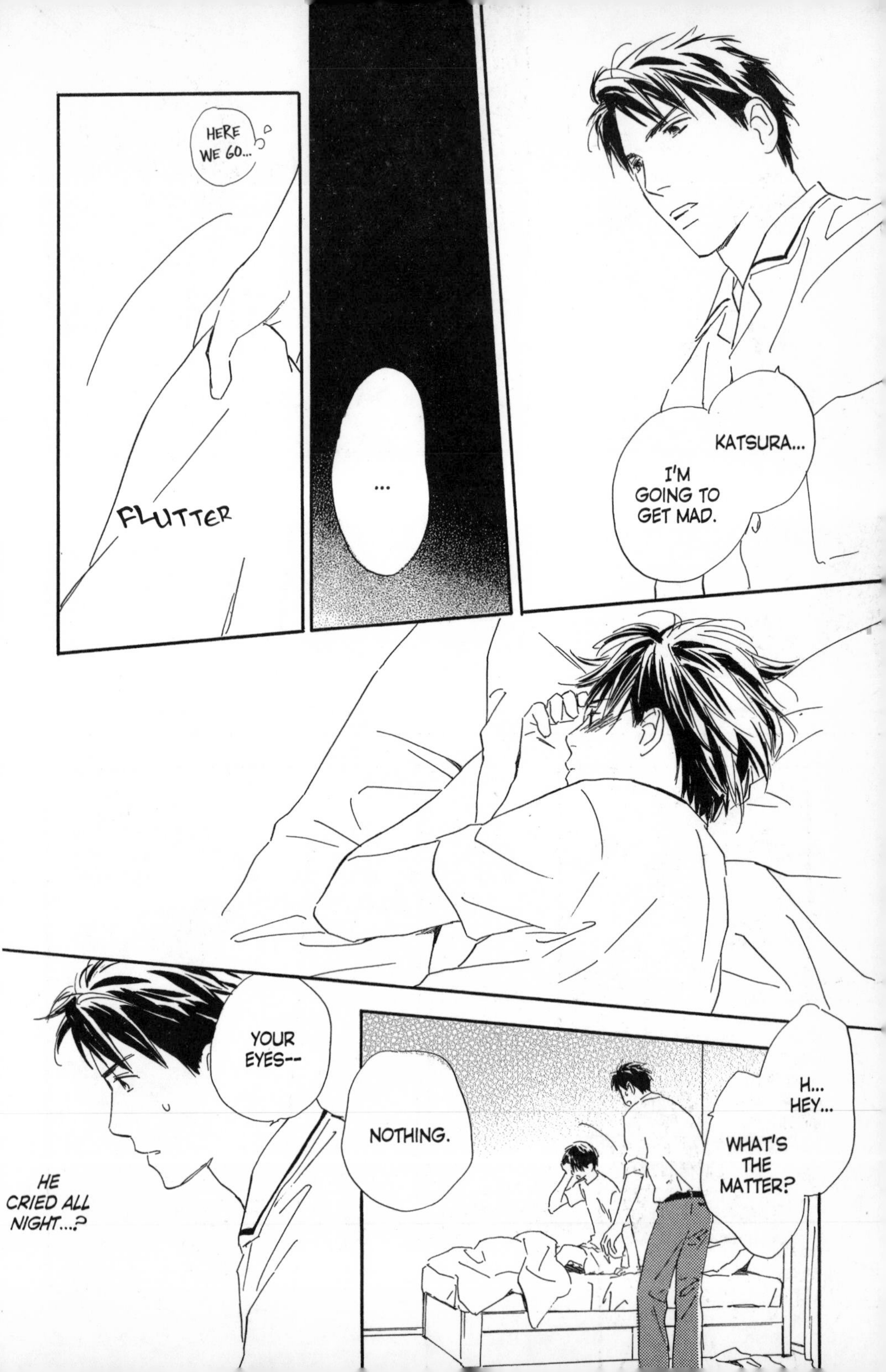
KATSURA...
I'M GOING TO GET MAD.
...
HERE WE GO...
FLUTTER
H... HEY...
WHAT'S THE MATTER?
NOTHING.
YOUR EYES--
HE CRIED ALL NIGHT...?

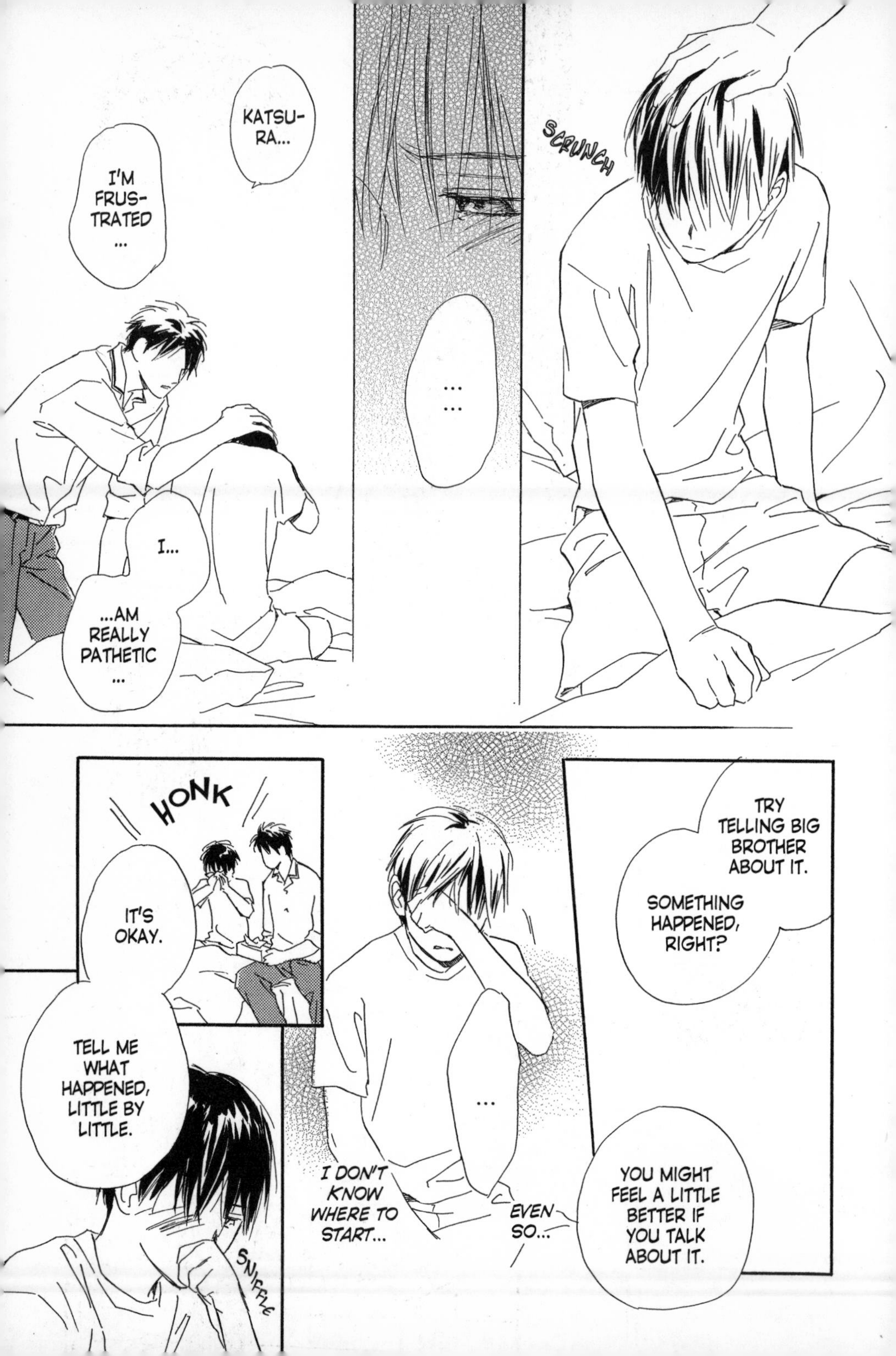
SCRUNCH
......
KATSU-RA...
I'M FRUS-TRATED...
I...
...AM REALLY PATHETIC...
TRY TELLING BIG BROTHER ABOUT IT.
SOMETHING HAPPENED, RIGHT?
...
I DON'T KNOW WHERE TO START...
EVEN SO...
YOU MIGHT FEEL A LITTLE BETTER IF YOU TALK ABOUT IT.
HONK
IT'S OKAY.
TELL ME WHAT HAPPENED, LITTLE BY LITTLE.
SNIFFLE

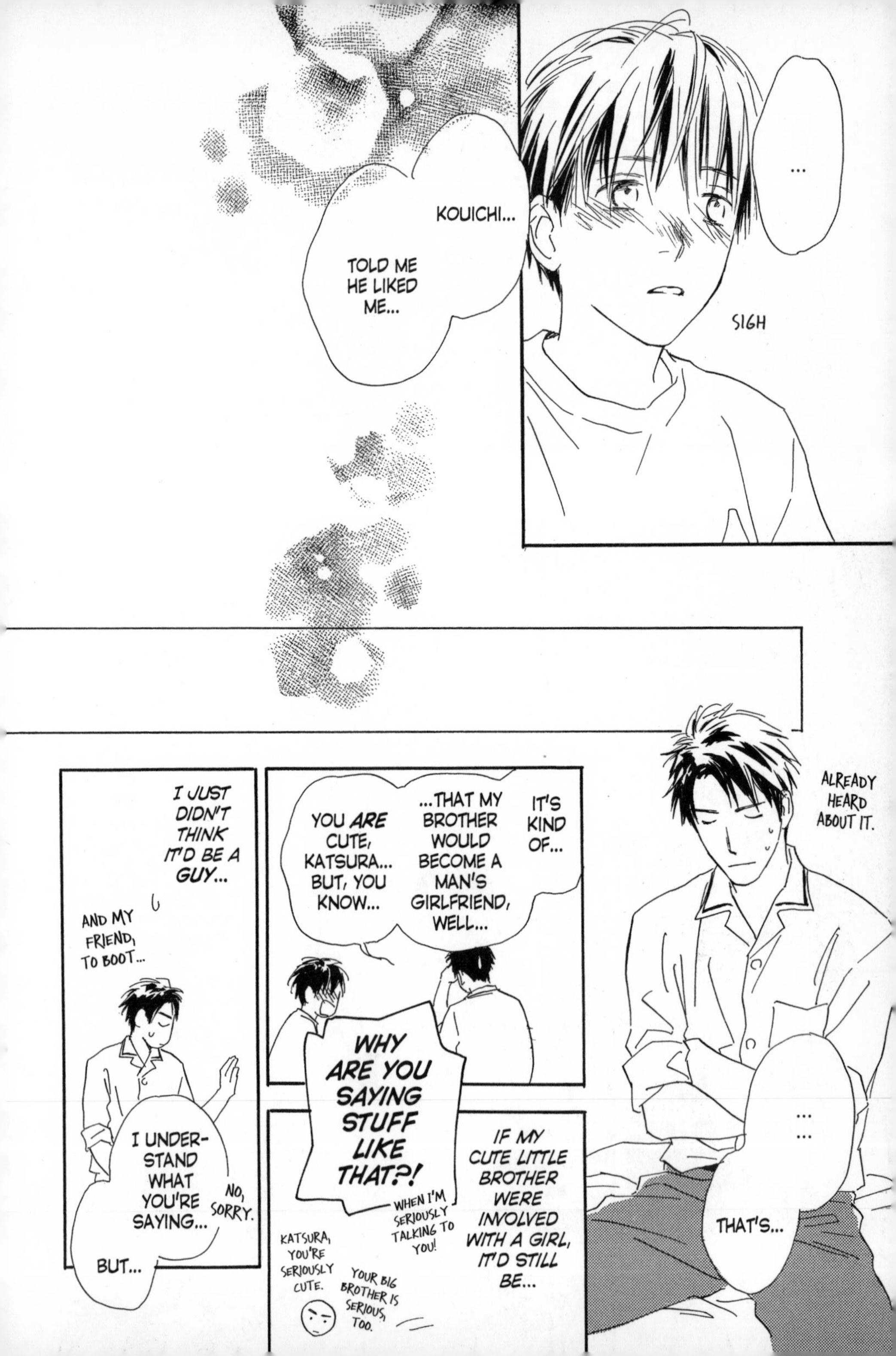
...
KOUICHI...
TOLD ME HE LIKED ME...
SIGH
ALREADY HEARD ABOUT IT.
......
THAT'S...
IT'S KIND OF...
...THAT MY BROTHER WOULD BECOME A MAN'S GIRLFRIEND, WELL...
YOU *ARE* CUTE, KATSURA... BUT, YOU KNOW...
WHY ARE YOU SAYING STUFF LIKE THAT?!
IF MY CUTE LITTLE BROTHER WERE INVOLVED WITH A GIRL, IT'D STILL BE...
WHEN I'M SERIOUSLY TALKING TO YOU!
YOUR BIG BROTHER IS SERIOUS, TOO.
KATSURA, YOU'RE SERIOUSLY CUTE.
I JUST DIDN'T THINK IT'D BE A *GUY*...
AND MY FRIEND, TO BOOT...
NO, SORRY.
I UNDER-STAND WHAT YOU'RE SAYING...
BUT...

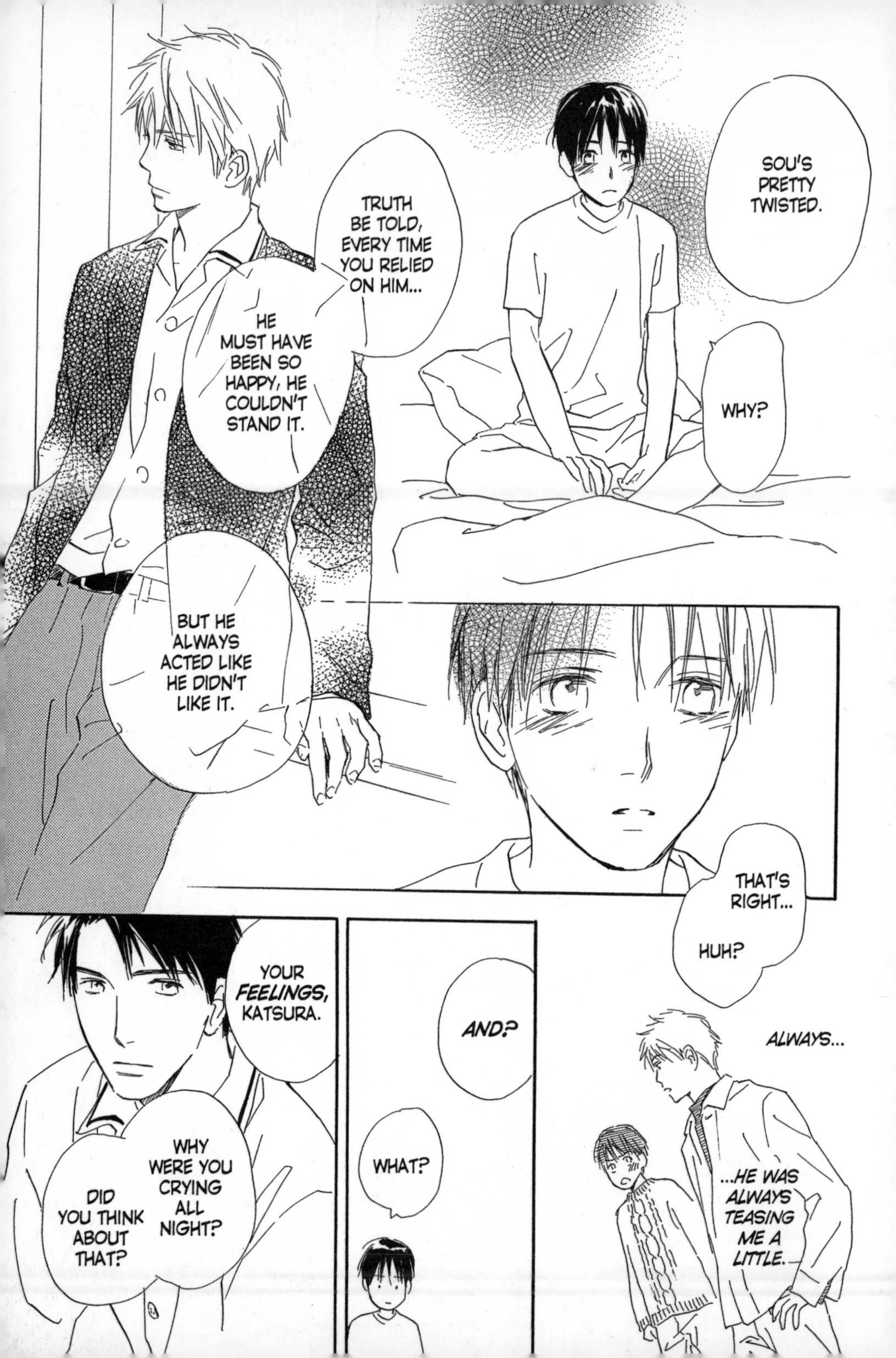
SOU'S PRETTY TWISTED.
WHY?
TRUTH BE TOLD, EVERY TIME YOU RELIED ON HIM...
HE MUST HAVE BEEN SO HAPPY, HE COULDN'T STAND IT.
BUT HE ALWAYS ACTED LIKE HE DIDN'T LIKE IT.
THAT'S RIGHT...
HUH?
ALWAYS...
...HE WAS ALWAYS TEASING ME A LITTLE.
AND?
WHAT?
YOUR FEELINGS, KATSURA.
WHY WERE YOU CRYING ALL NIGHT?
DID YOU THINK ABOUT THAT?

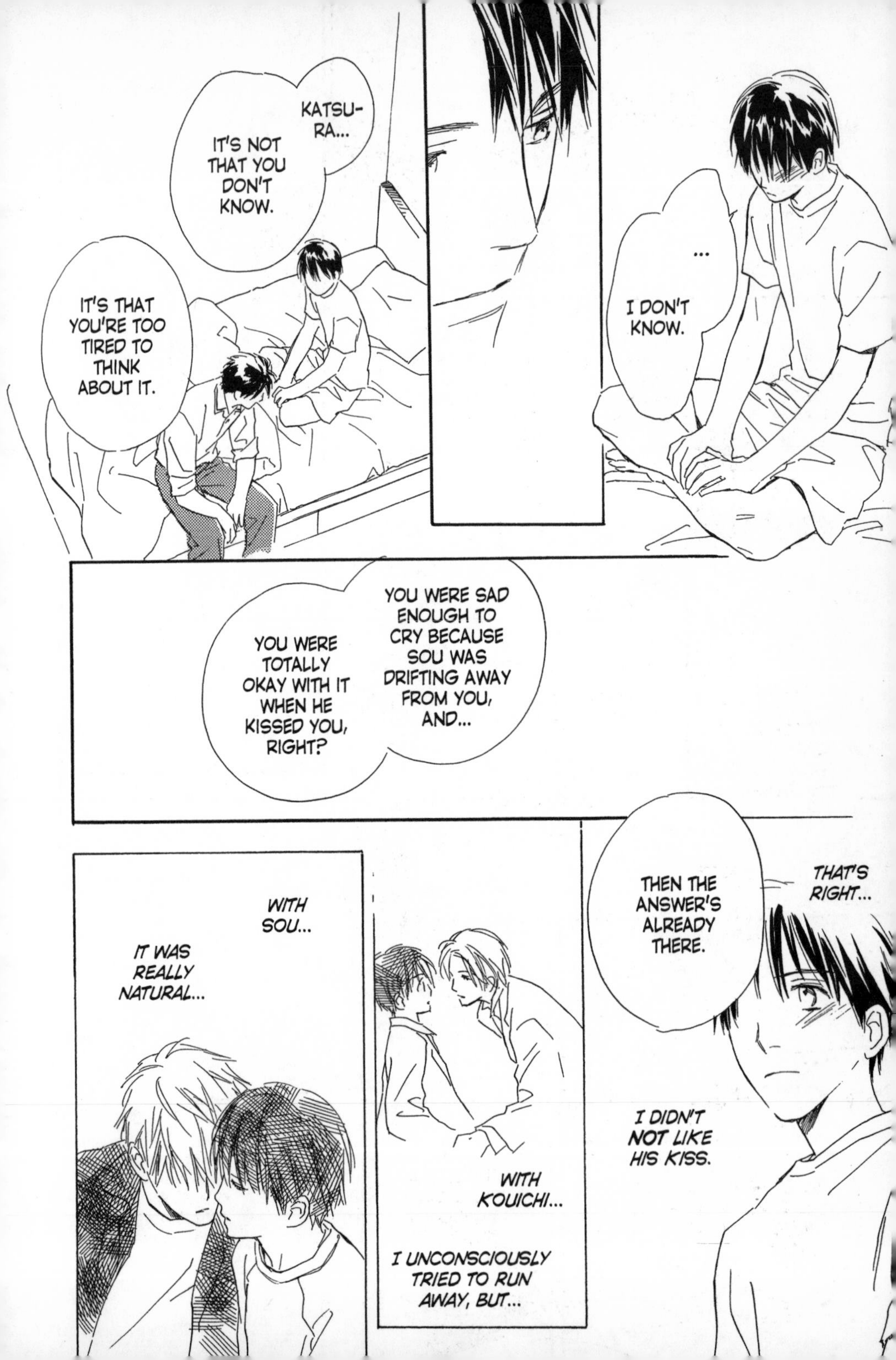
...
I DON'T KNOW.
KATSURA...
IT'S NOT THAT YOU DON'T KNOW.
IT'S THAT YOU'RE TOO TIRED TO THINK ABOUT IT.
YOU WERE SAD ENOUGH TO CRY BECAUSE SOU WAS DRIFTING AWAY FROM YOU, AND...
YOU WERE TOTALLY OKAY WITH IT WHEN HE KISSED YOU, RIGHT?
THEN THE ANSWER'S ALREADY THERE.
THAT'S RIGHT...
I DIDN'T NOT LIKE HIS KISS.
WITH KOUICHI...
I UNCONSCIOUSLY TRIED TO RUN AWAY, BUT...
WITH SOU...
IT WAS REALLY NATURAL...

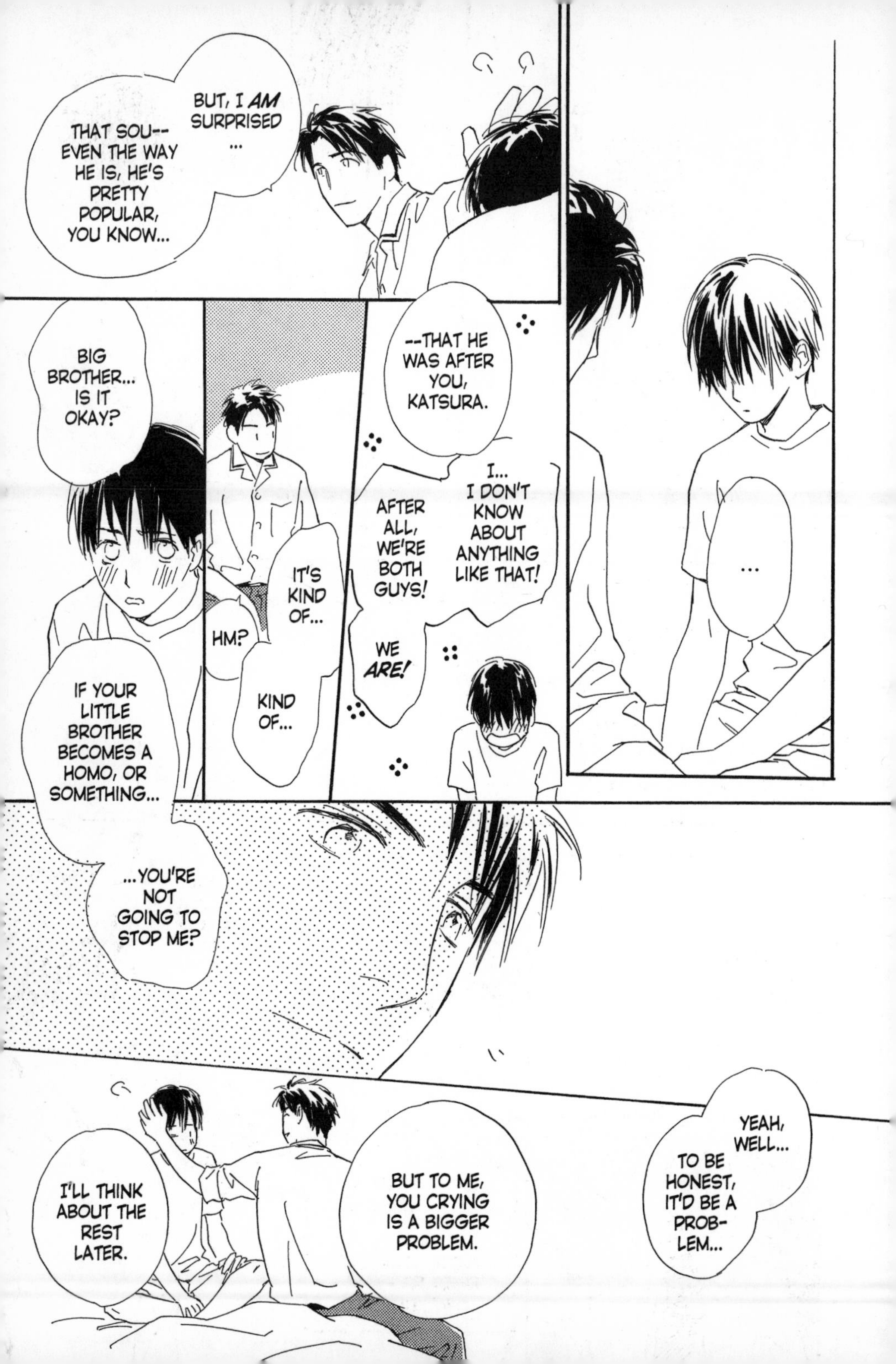
...
BUT, I *AM* SURPRISED ...
THAT SOU-- EVEN THE WAY HE IS, HE'S PRETTY POPULAR, YOU KNOW...
--THAT HE WAS AFTER YOU, KATSURA.
I... I DON'T KNOW ABOUT ANYTHING LIKE THAT!
AFTER ALL, WE'RE BOTH GUYS!
WE *ARE!*
IT'S KIND OF...
HM?
KIND OF...
BIG BROTHER... IS IT OKAY?
IF YOUR LITTLE BROTHER BECOMES A HOMO, OR SOMETHING...
...YOU'RE NOT GOING TO STOP ME?
YEAH, WELL...
TO BE HONEST, IT'D BE A PROB-LEM...
BUT TO ME, YOU CRYING IS A BIGGER PROBLEM.
I'LL THINK ABOUT THE REST LATER.

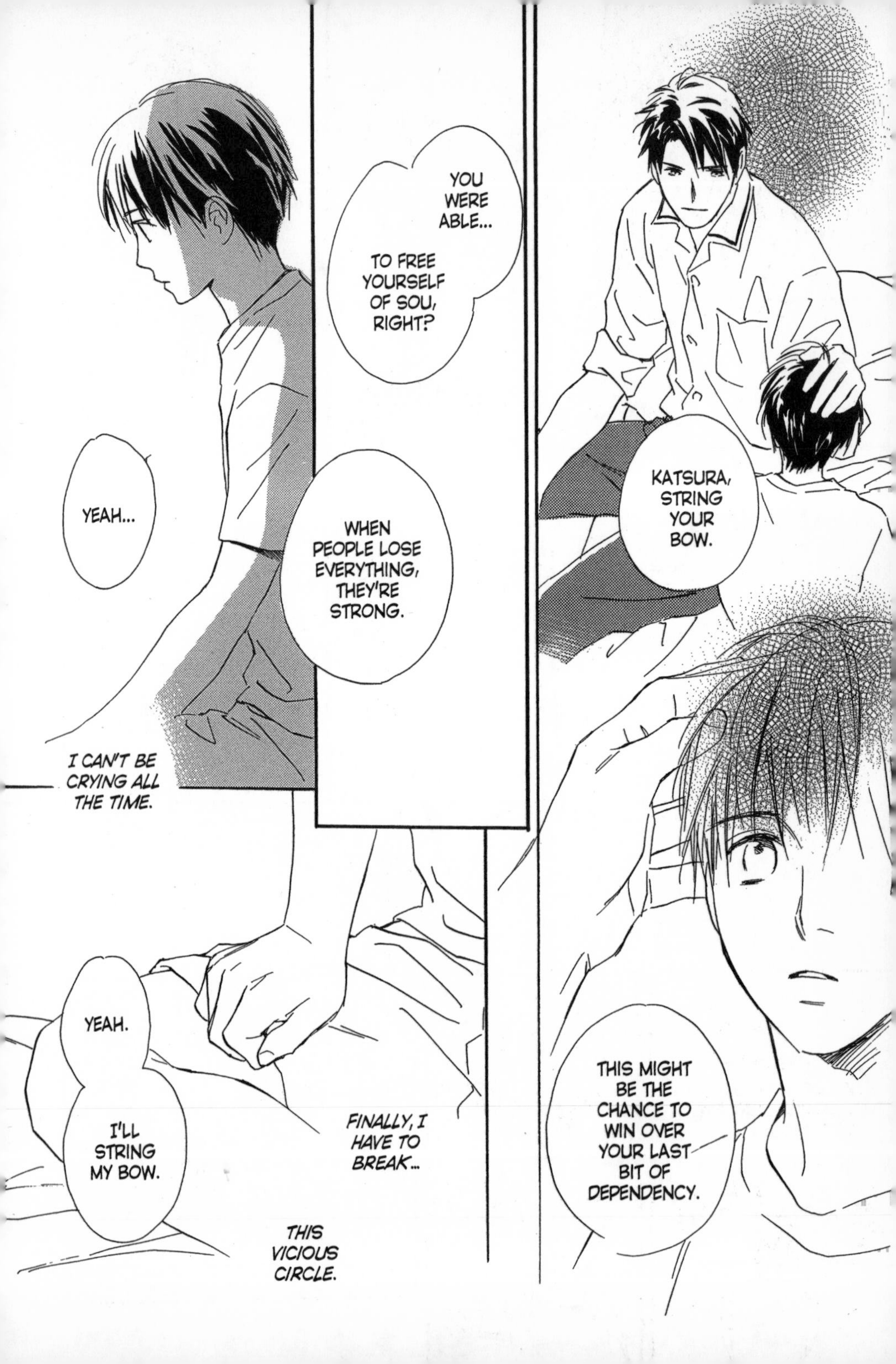
KATSURA, STRING YOUR BOW.
THIS MIGHT BE THE CHANCE TO WIN OVER YOUR LAST BIT OF DEPENDENCY.
YOU WERE ABLE...
TO FREE YOURSELF OF SOU, RIGHT?
WHEN PEOPLE LOSE EVERYTHING, THEY'RE STRONG.
YEAH...
I CAN'T BE CRYING ALL THE TIME.
YEAH.
I'LL STRING MY BOW.
FINALLY, I HAVE TO BREAK...
THIS VICIOUS CIRCLE.

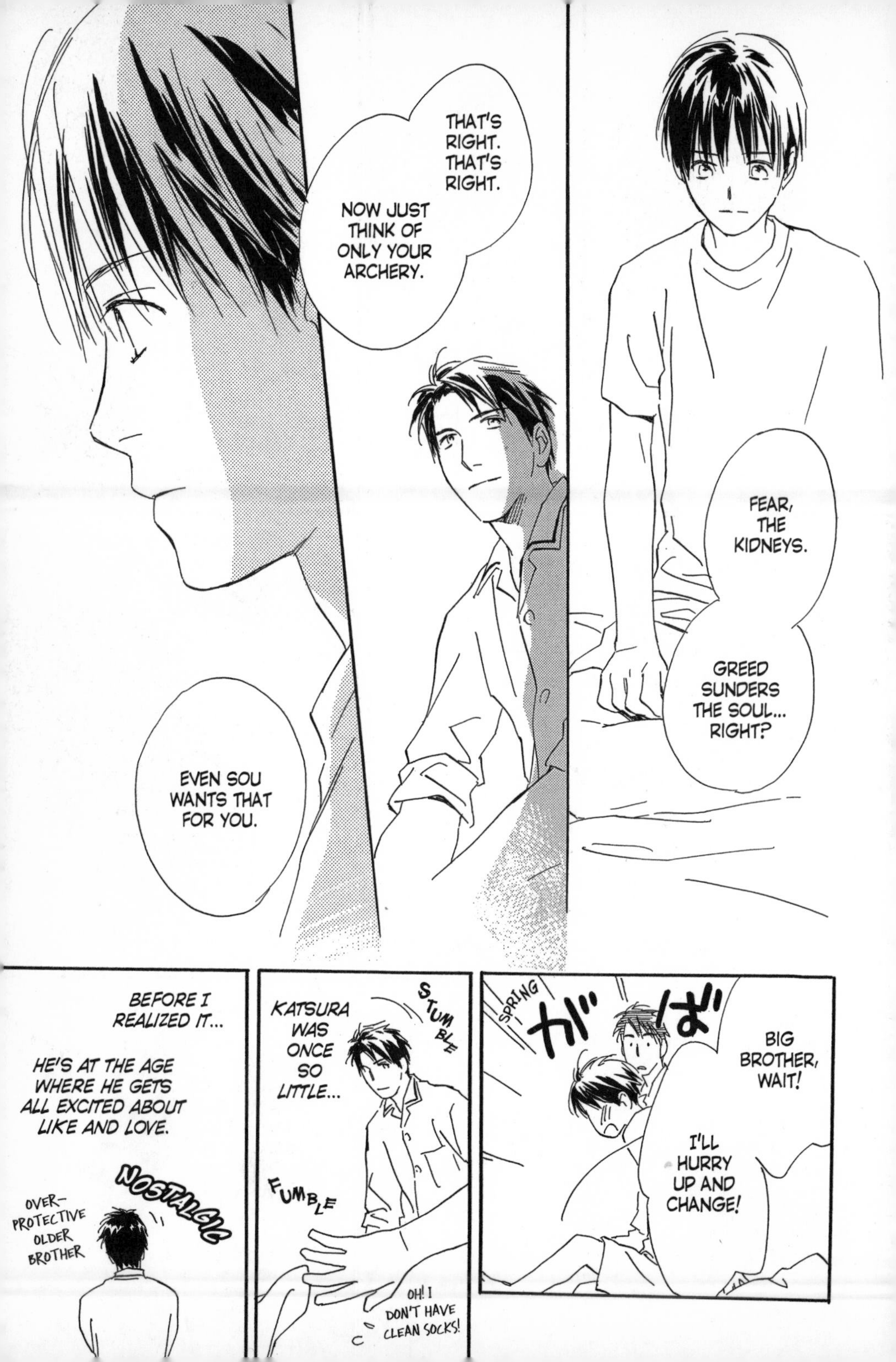
FEAR, THE KIDNEYS.
GREED SUNDERS THE SOUL... RIGHT?
THAT'S RIGHT. THAT'S RIGHT.
NOW JUST THINK OF ONLY YOUR ARCHERY.
EVEN SOU WANTS THAT FOR YOU.
SPRING
がば
BIG BROTHER, WAIT!
I'LL HURRY UP AND CHANGE!
STUMBLE
KATSURA WAS ONCE SO LITTLE...
FUMBLE
OH! I DON'T HAVE CLEAN SOCKS!
BEFORE I REALIZED IT...
HE'S AT THE AGE WHERE HE GETS ALL EXCITED ABOUT LIKE AND LOVE.
NOSTALGIC
OVER-PROTECTIVE OLDER BROTHER

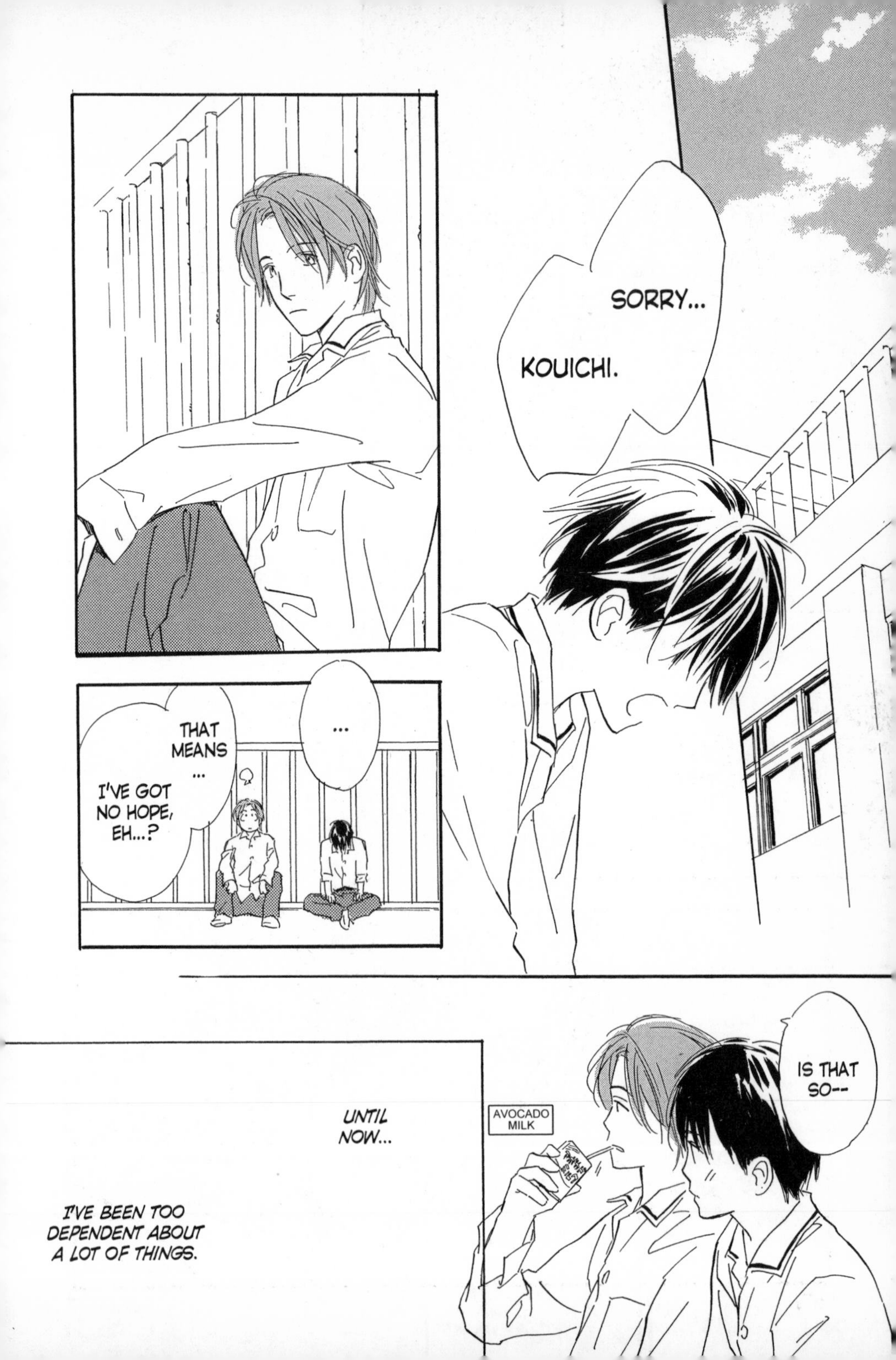
SORRY... KOUICHI.
...
THAT MEANS ... I'VE GOT NO HOPE, EH...?
IS THAT SO--
AVOCADO MILK
UNTIL NOW...
I'VE BEEN TOO DEPENDENT ABOUT A LOT OF THINGS.

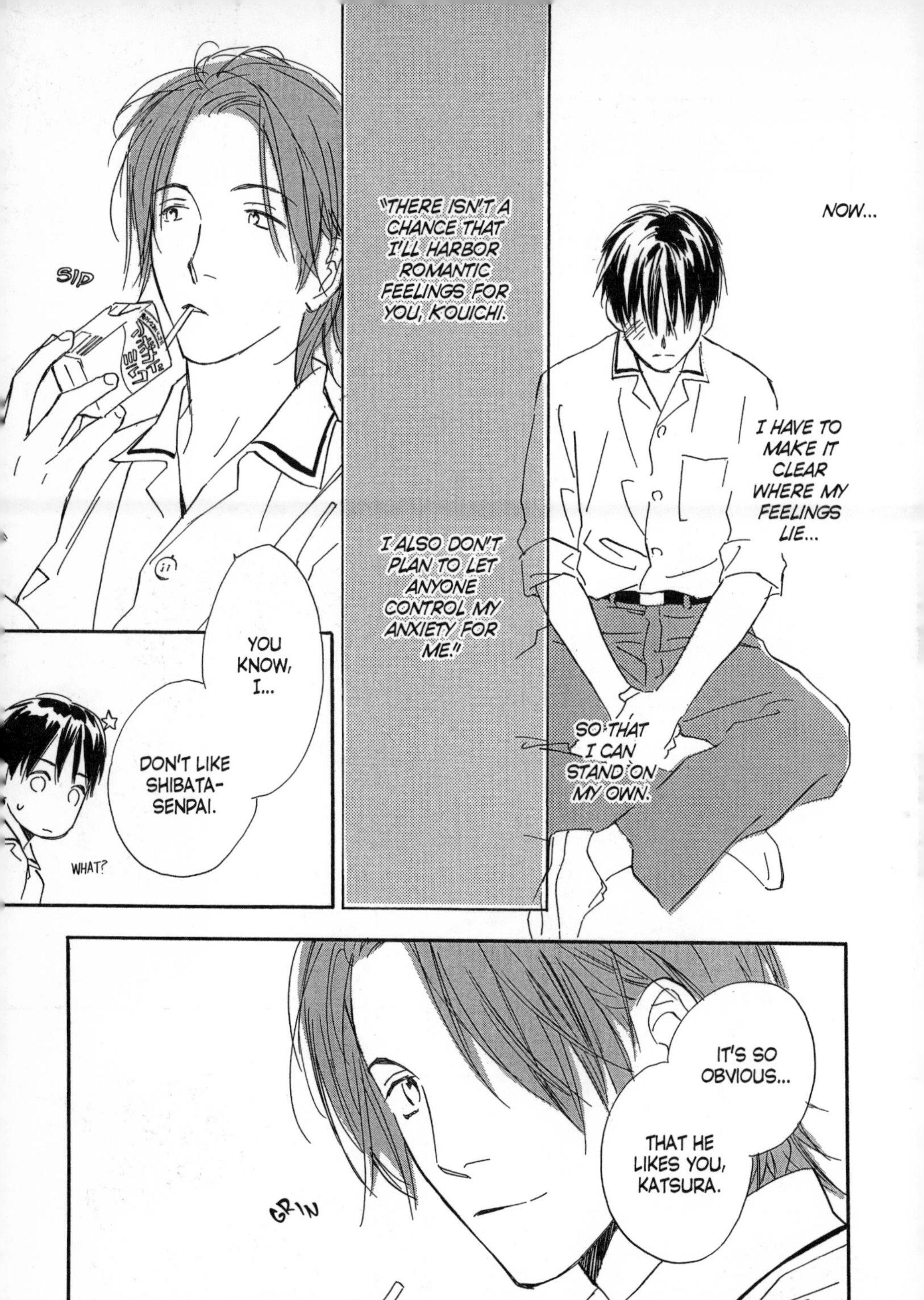
NOW...
I HAVE TO MAKE IT CLEAR WHERE MY FEELINGS LIE...
SO THAT I CAN STAND ON MY OWN.
"THERE ISN'T A CHANCE THAT I'LL HARBOR ROMANTIC FEELINGS FOR YOU, KOUICHI.
I ALSO DON'T PLAN TO LET ANYONE CONTROL MY ANXIETY FOR ME."
SID
YOU KNOW, I...
DON'T LIKE SHIBATA-SENPAI.
WHAT?
IT'S SO OBVIOUS...
THAT HE LIKES YOU, KATSURA.
GRIN

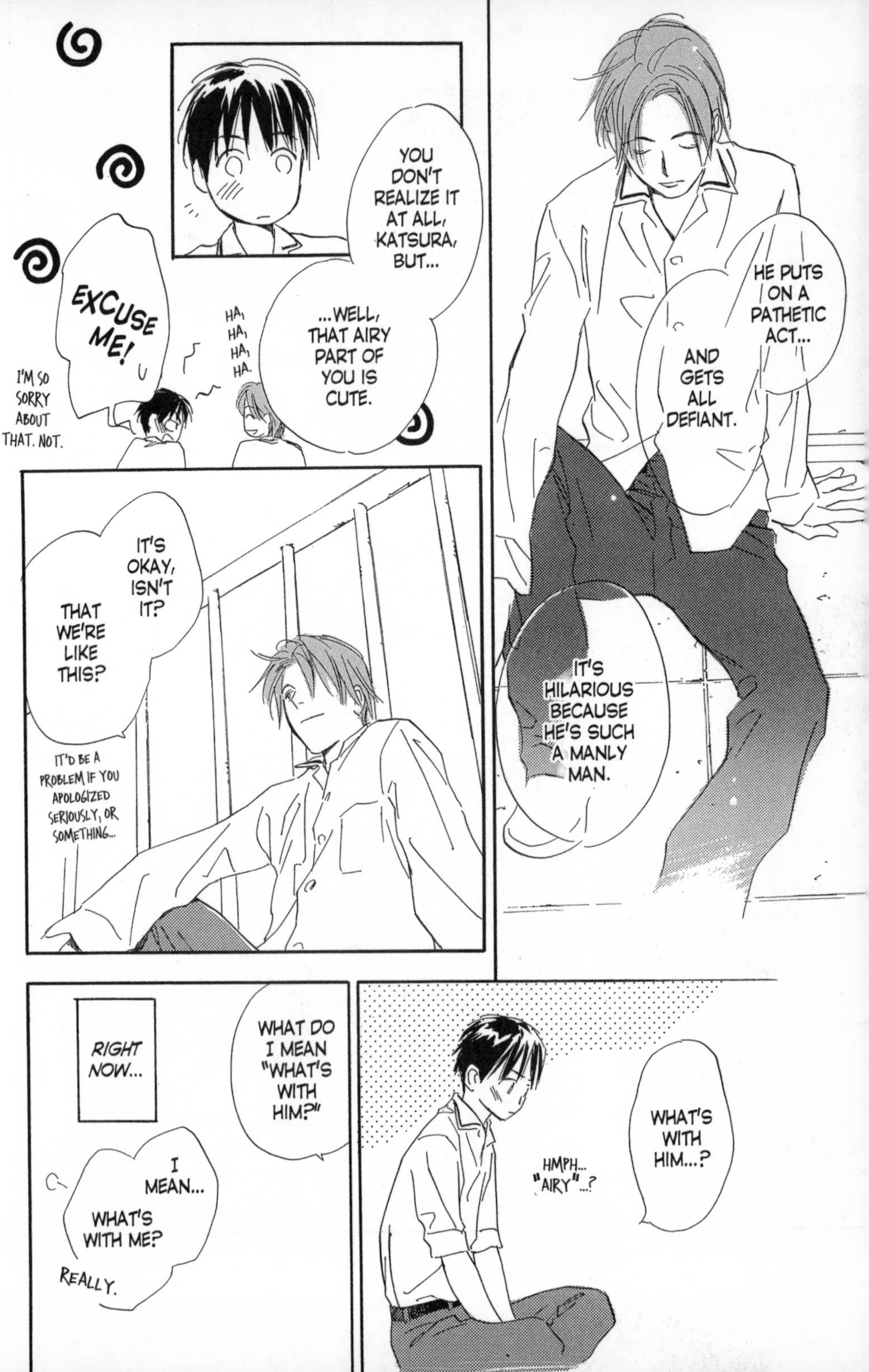
HE PUTS ON A PATHETIC ACT...
AND GETS ALL DEFIANT.
IT'S HILARIOUS BECAUSE HE'S SUCH A MANLY MAN.
YOU DON'T REALIZE IT AT ALL, KATSURA, BUT...
...WELL, THAT AIRY PART OF YOU IS CUTE.
HA, HA, HA, HA.
EXCUSE ME!
I'M SO SORRY ABOUT THAT. NOT.
IT'S OKAY, ISN'T IT?
THAT WE'RE LIKE THIS?
IT'D BE A PROBLEM IF YOU APOLOGIZED SERIOUSLY, OR SOMETHING...
WHAT'S WITH HIM...?
HMPH... "AIRY"...?
RIGHT NOW...
WHAT DO I MEAN "WHAT'S WITH HIM?"
I MEAN...
WHAT'S WITH ME?
REALLY.

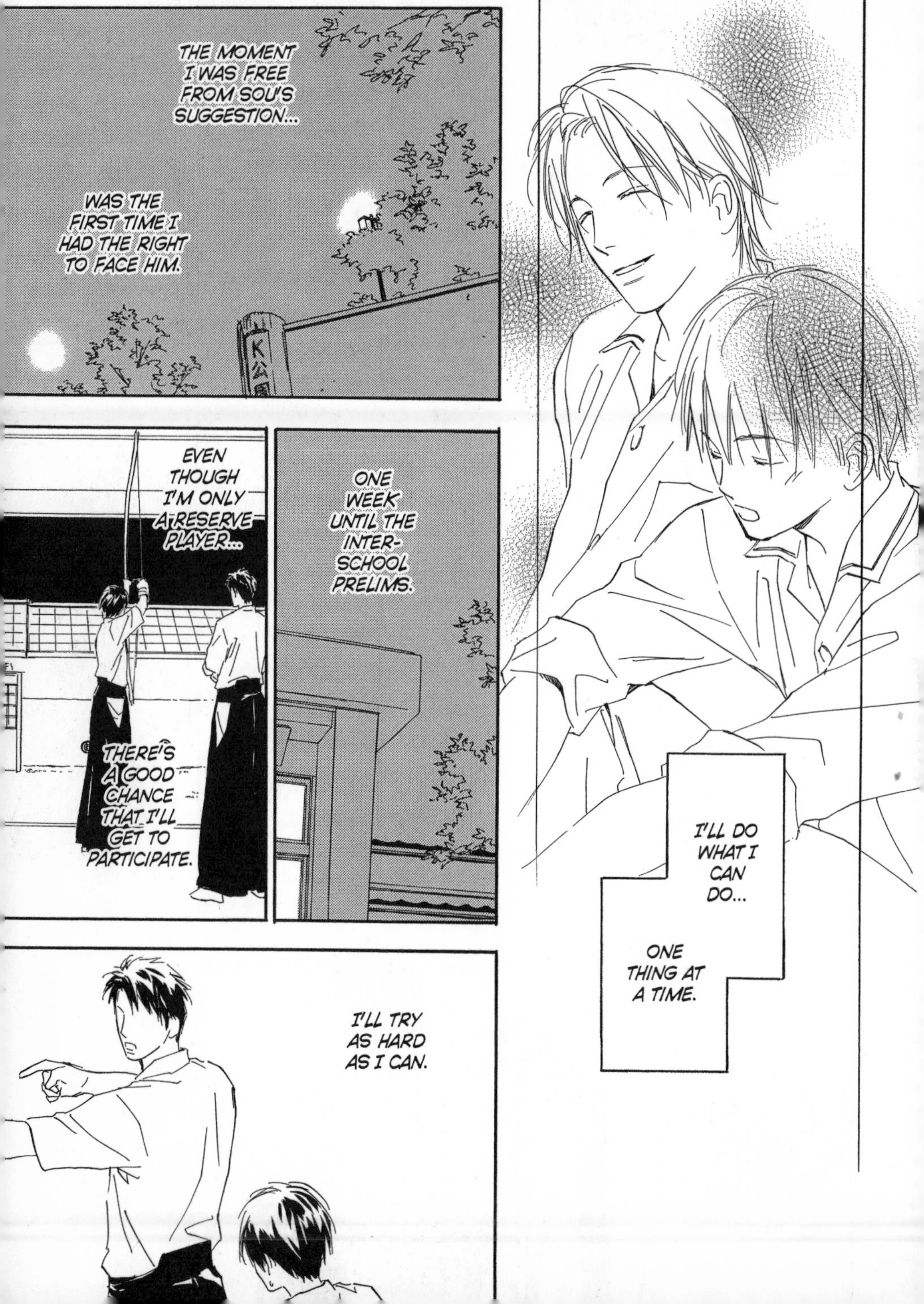
I'LL DO WHAT I CAN DO...
ONE THING AT A TIME.
THE MOMENT I WAS FREE FROM SOU'S SUGGESTION...
WAS THE FIRST TIME I HAD THE RIGHT TO FACE HIM.
ONE WEEK UNTIL THE INTER-SCHOOL PRELIMS.
EVEN THOUGH I'M ONLY A RESERVE PLAYER...
THERE'S A GOOD CHANCE THAT I'LL GET TO PARTICIPATE.
I'LL TRY AS HARD AS I CAN.

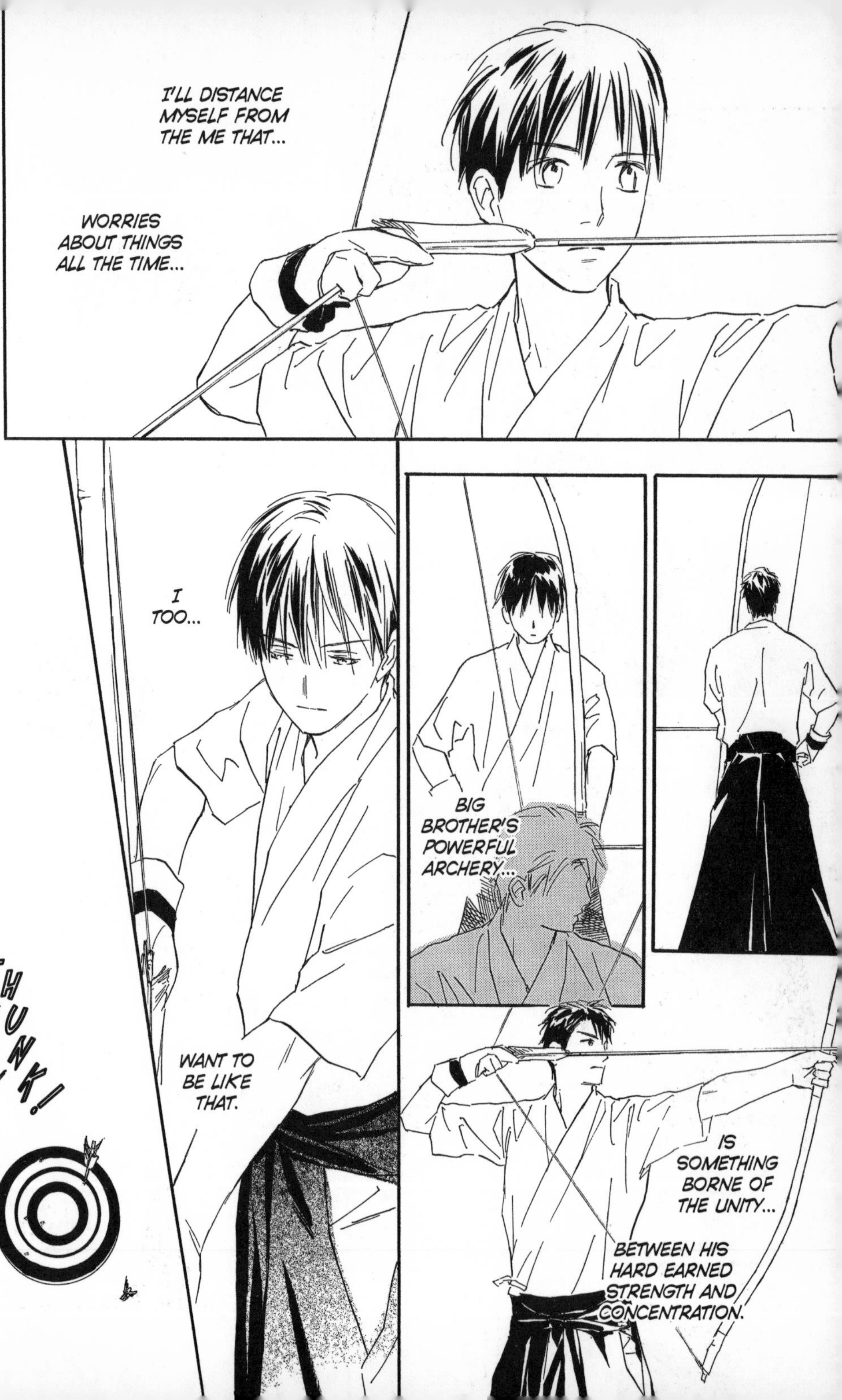
I'LL DISTANCE MYSELF FROM THE ME THAT...
WORRIES ABOUT THINGS ALL THE TIME...
BIG BROTHER'S POWERFUL ARCHERY...
IS SOMETHING BORNE OF THE UNITY...
BETWEEN HIS HARD EARNED STRENGTH AND CONCENTRATION.
I TOO...
WANT TO BE LIKE THAT.
THUNK!
—!!

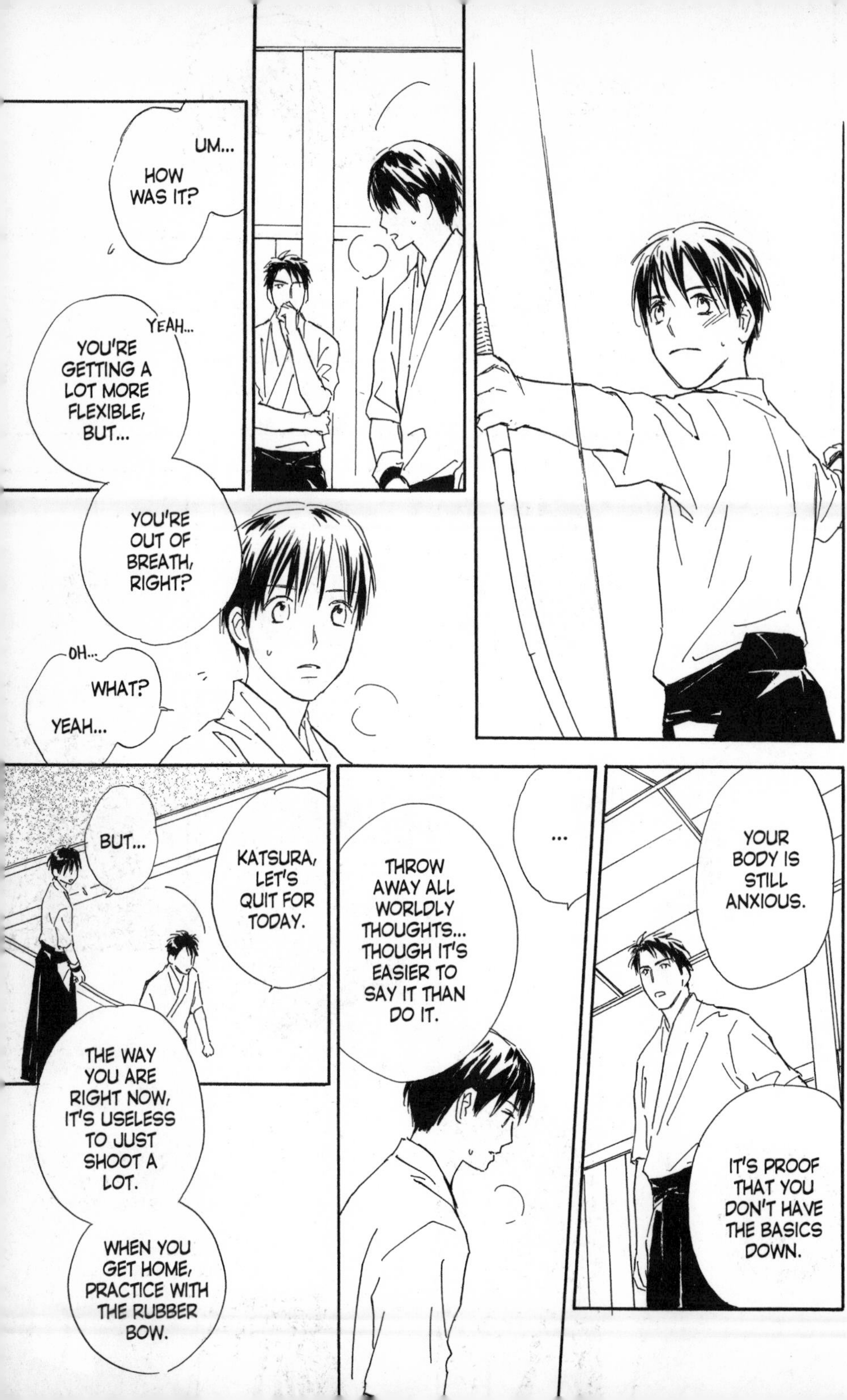
UM... HOW WAS IT?
YEAH... YOU'RE GETTING A LOT MORE FLEXIBLE, BUT...
YOU'RE OUT OF BREATH, RIGHT?
OH... WHAT? YEAH...
YOUR BODY IS STILL ANXIOUS.
IT'S PROOF THAT YOU DON'T HAVE THE BASICS DOWN.
...
THROW AWAY ALL WORLDLY THOUGHTS... THOUGH IT'S EASIER TO SAY IT THAN DO IT.
KATSURA, LET'S QUIT FOR TODAY.
BUT...
THE WAY YOU ARE RIGHT NOW, IT'S USELESS TO JUST SHOOT A LOT.
WHEN YOU GET HOME, PRACTICE WITH THE RUBBER BOW.

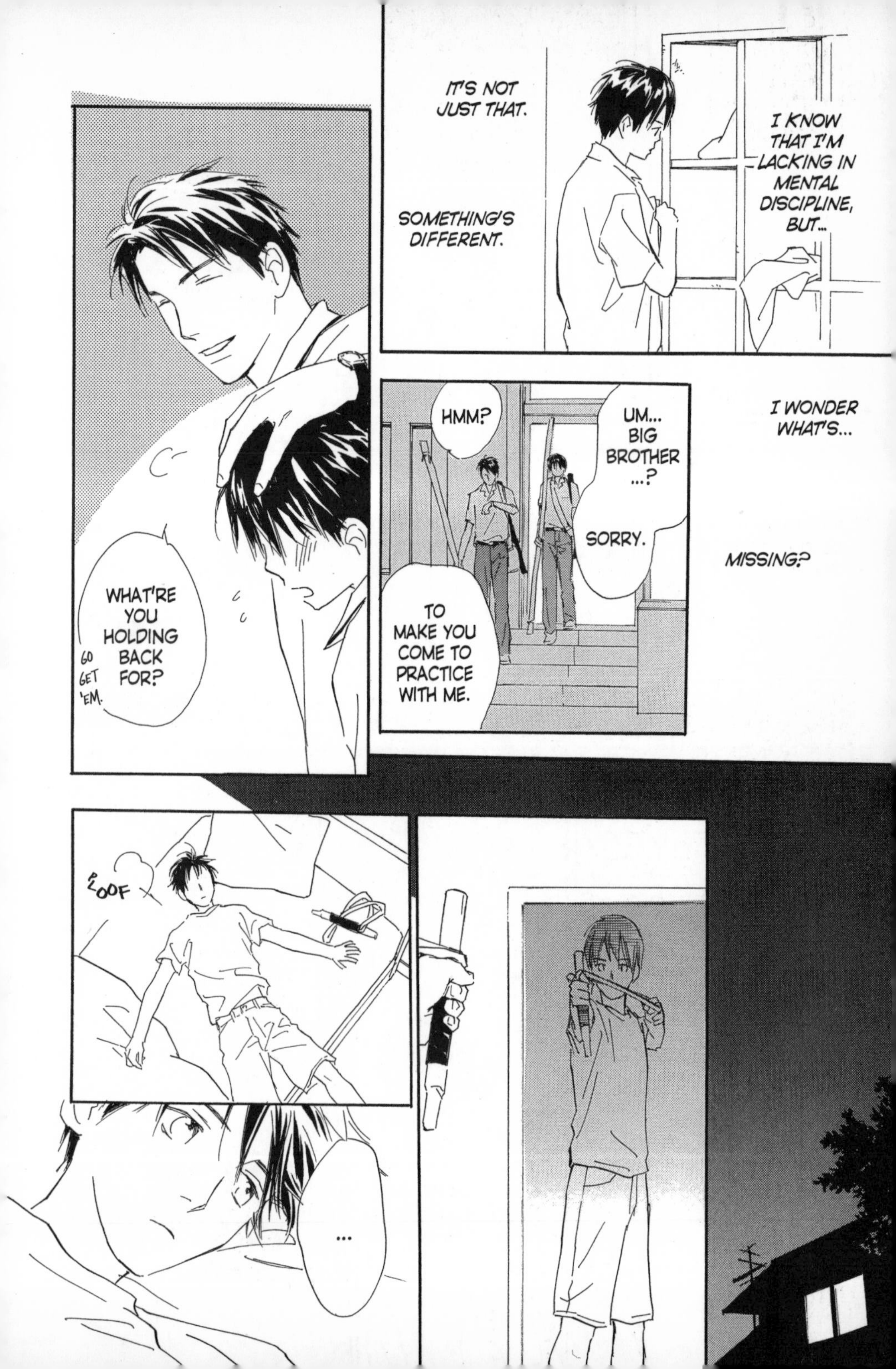
I KNOW THAT I'M LACKING IN MENTAL DISCIPLINE, BUT...
IT'S NOT JUST THAT.
SOMETHING'S DIFFERENT.
I WONDER WHAT'S...
MISSING?
UM... BIG BROTHER ...?
HMM?
SORRY.
TO MAKE YOU COME TO PRACTICE WITH ME.
WHAT'RE YOU HOLDING BACK FOR?
GO GET 'EM.
PLOOF
...

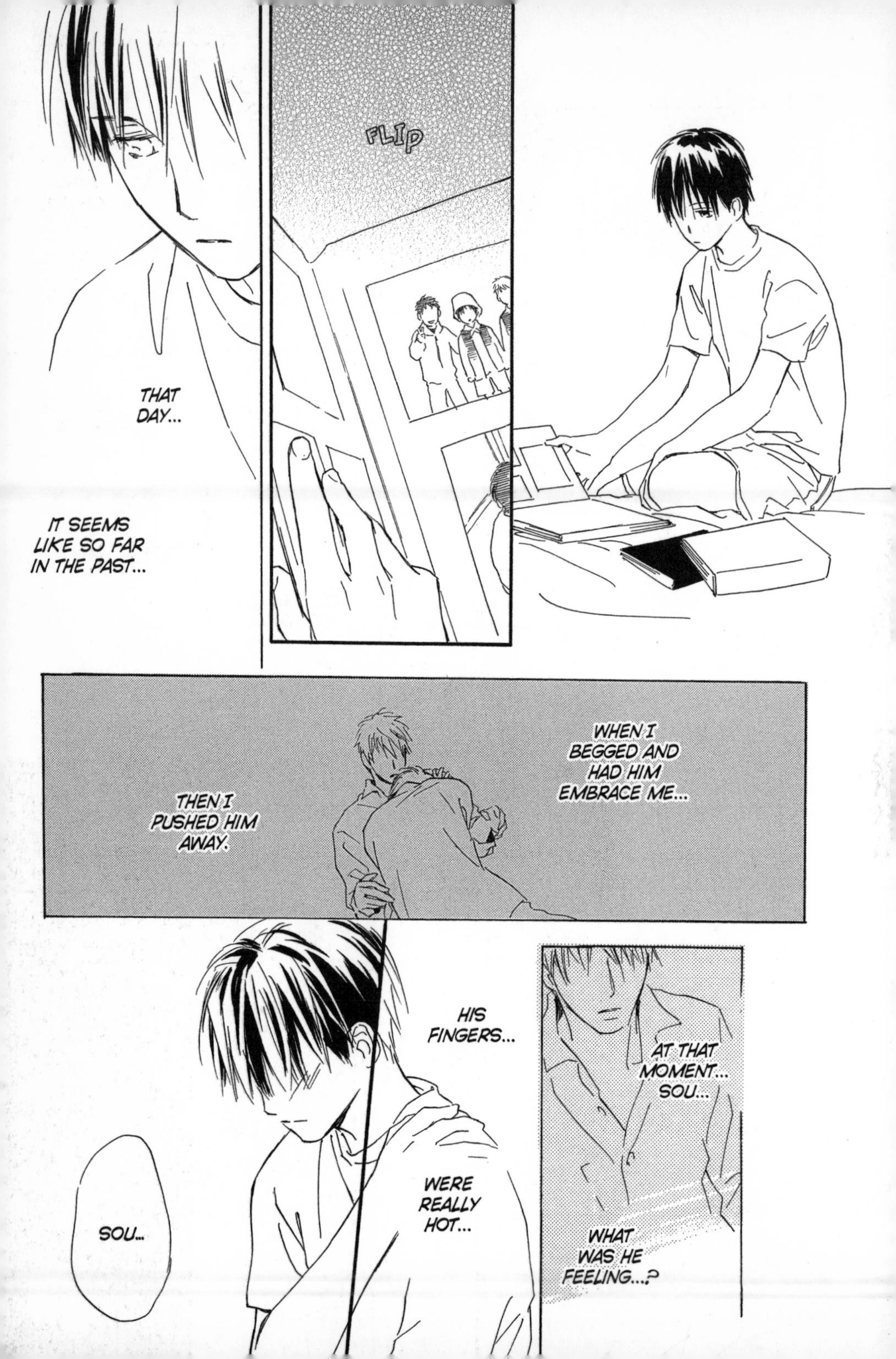
FLIP
THAT DAY...
IT SEEMS LIKE SO FAR IN THE PAST...
WHEN I BEGGED AND HAD HIM EMBRACE ME...
THEN I PUSHED HIM AWAY.
AT THAT MOMENT... SOU...
WHAT WAS HE FEELING...?
HIS FINGERS...
WERE REALLY HOT...
SOU...

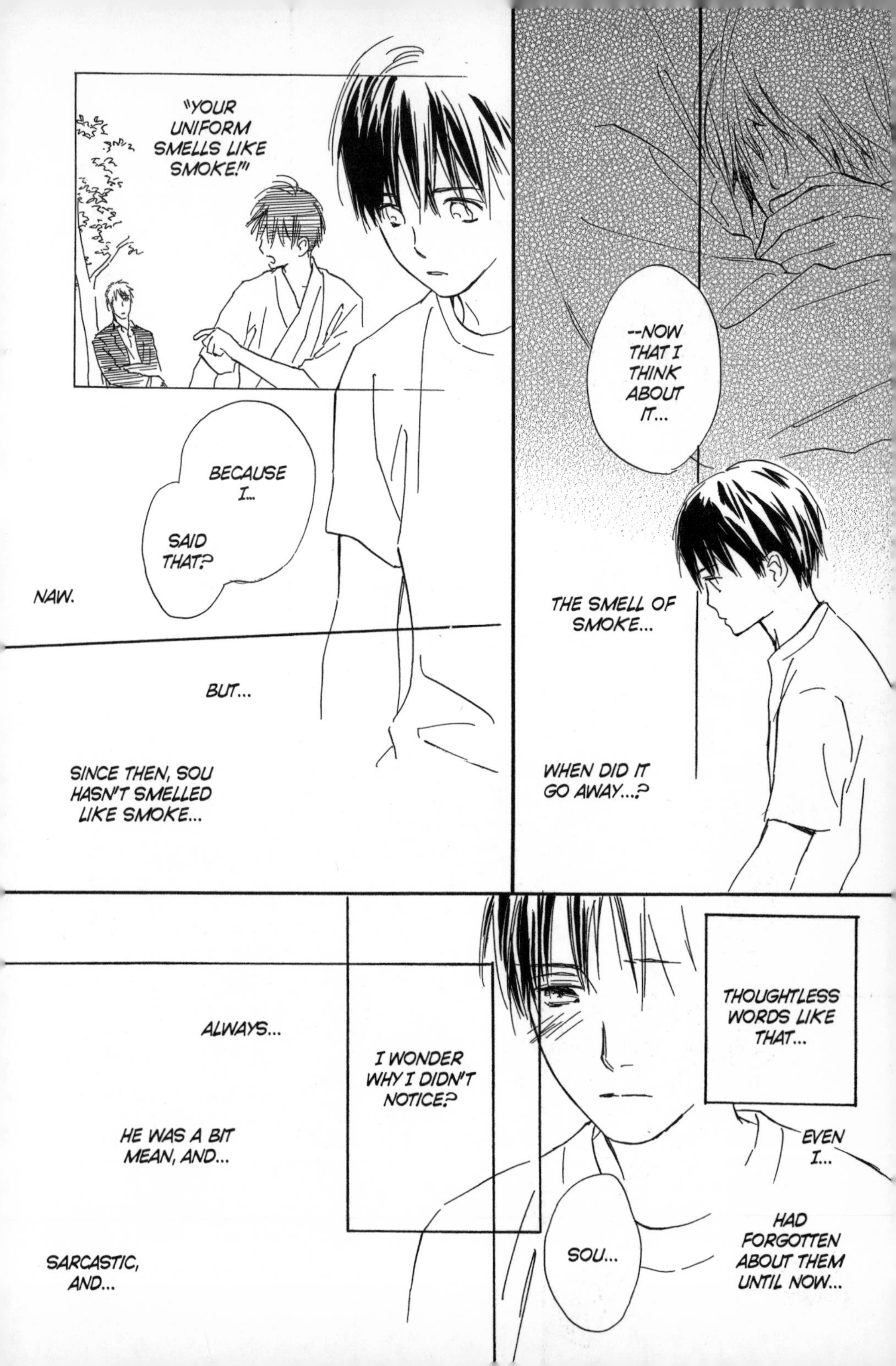
--NOW THAT I THINK ABOUT IT...
THE SMELL OF SMOKE...
WHEN DID IT GO AWAY...?
"YOUR UNIFORM SMELLS LIKE SMOKE!"
BECAUSE I... SAID THAT?
NAW.
BUT...
SINCE THEN, SOU HASN'T SMELLED LIKE SMOKE...
THOUGHTLESS WORDS LIKE THAT...
EVEN I...
HAD FORGOTTEN ABOUT THEM UNTIL NOW...
SOU...
I WONDER WHY I DIDN'T NOTICE?
ALWAYS...
HE WAS A BIT MEAN, AND...
SARCASTIC, AND...

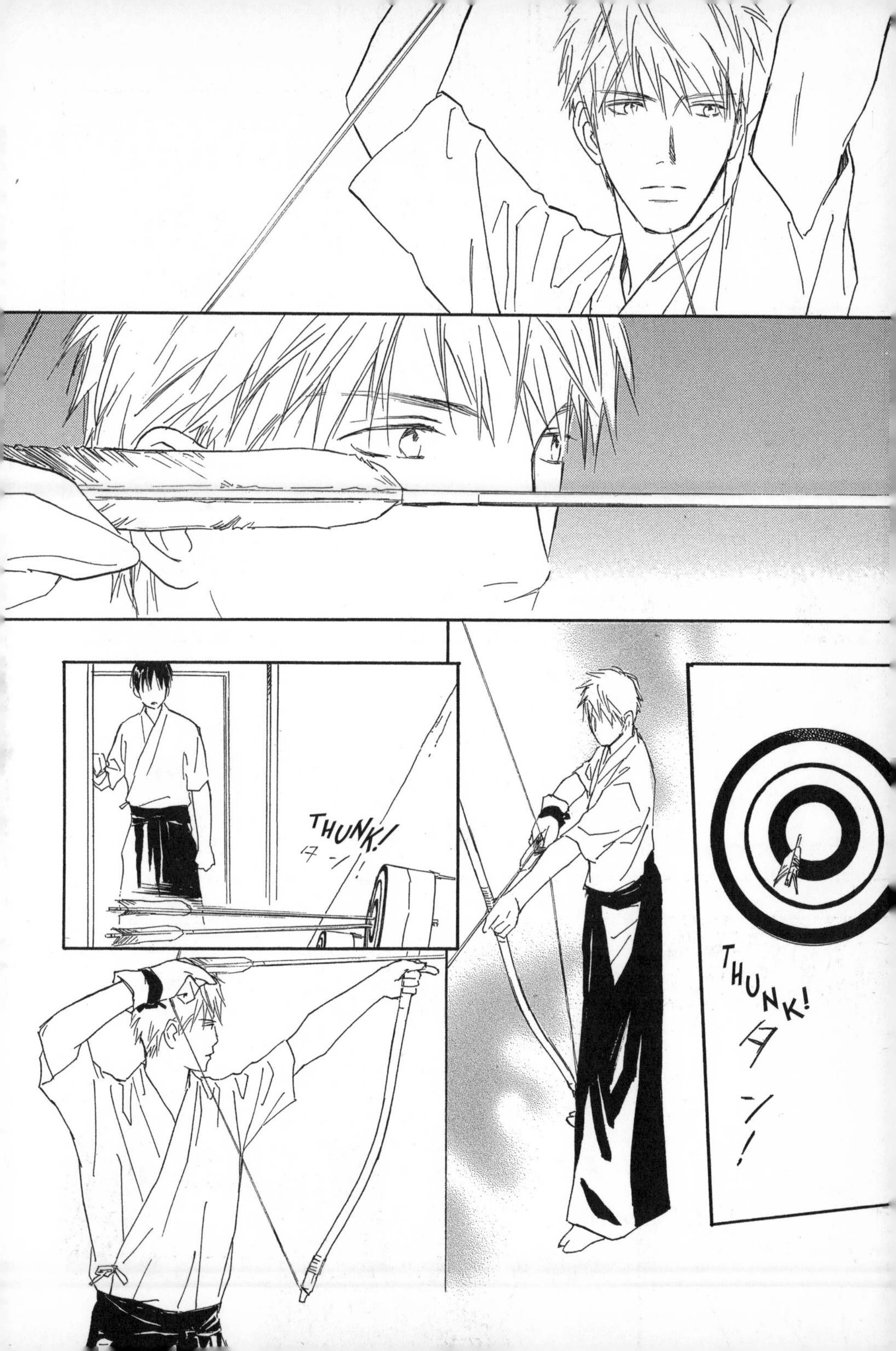
THUNK!
タン!
THUNK!
ターン!

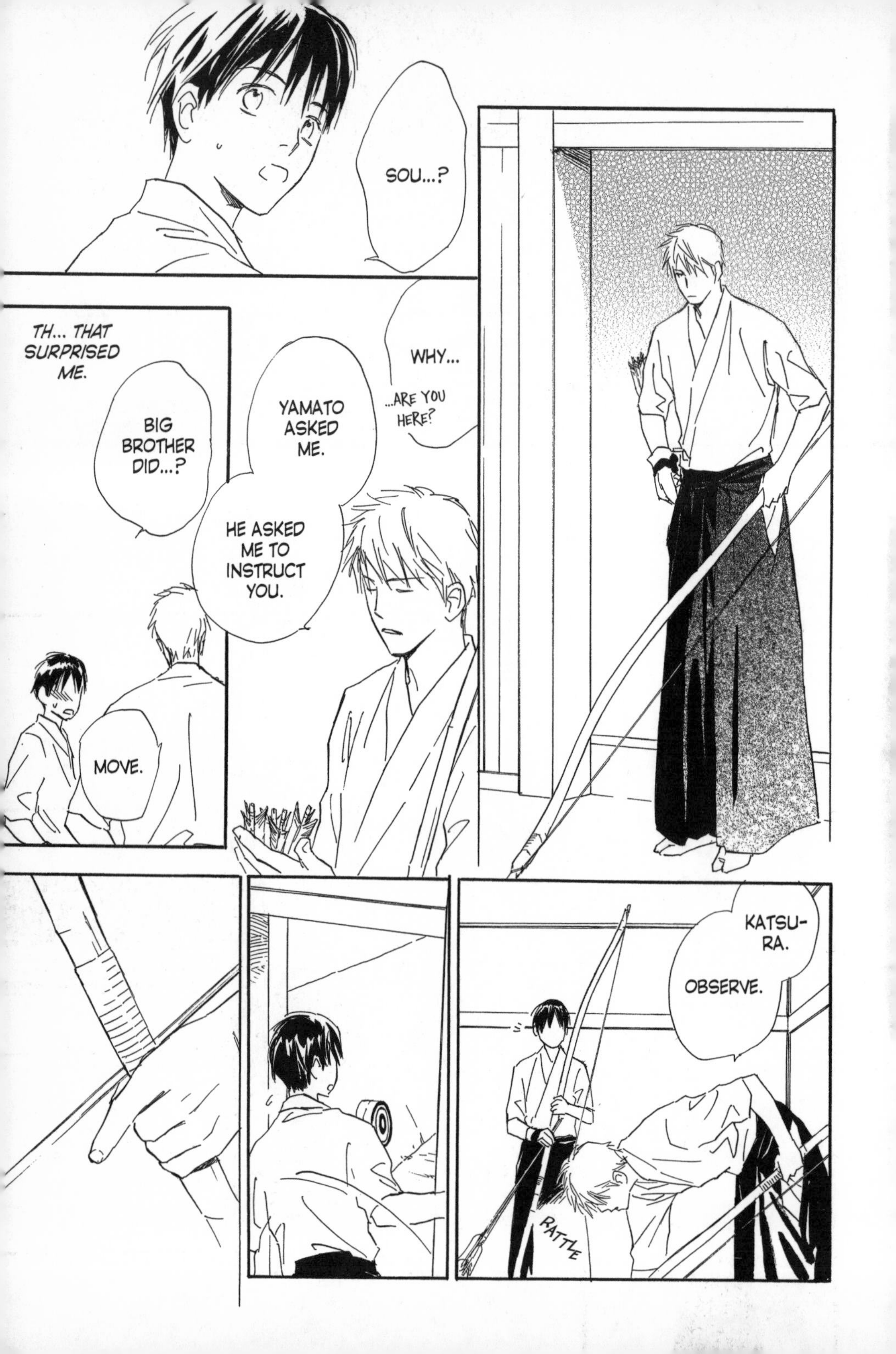
SOU...?
WHY...
...ARE YOU HERE?
YAMATO ASKED ME.
BIG BROTHER DID...?
HE ASKED ME TO INSTRUCT YOU.
TH... THAT SURPRISED ME.
MOVE.
KATSU-RA.
OBSERVE.
RATTLE

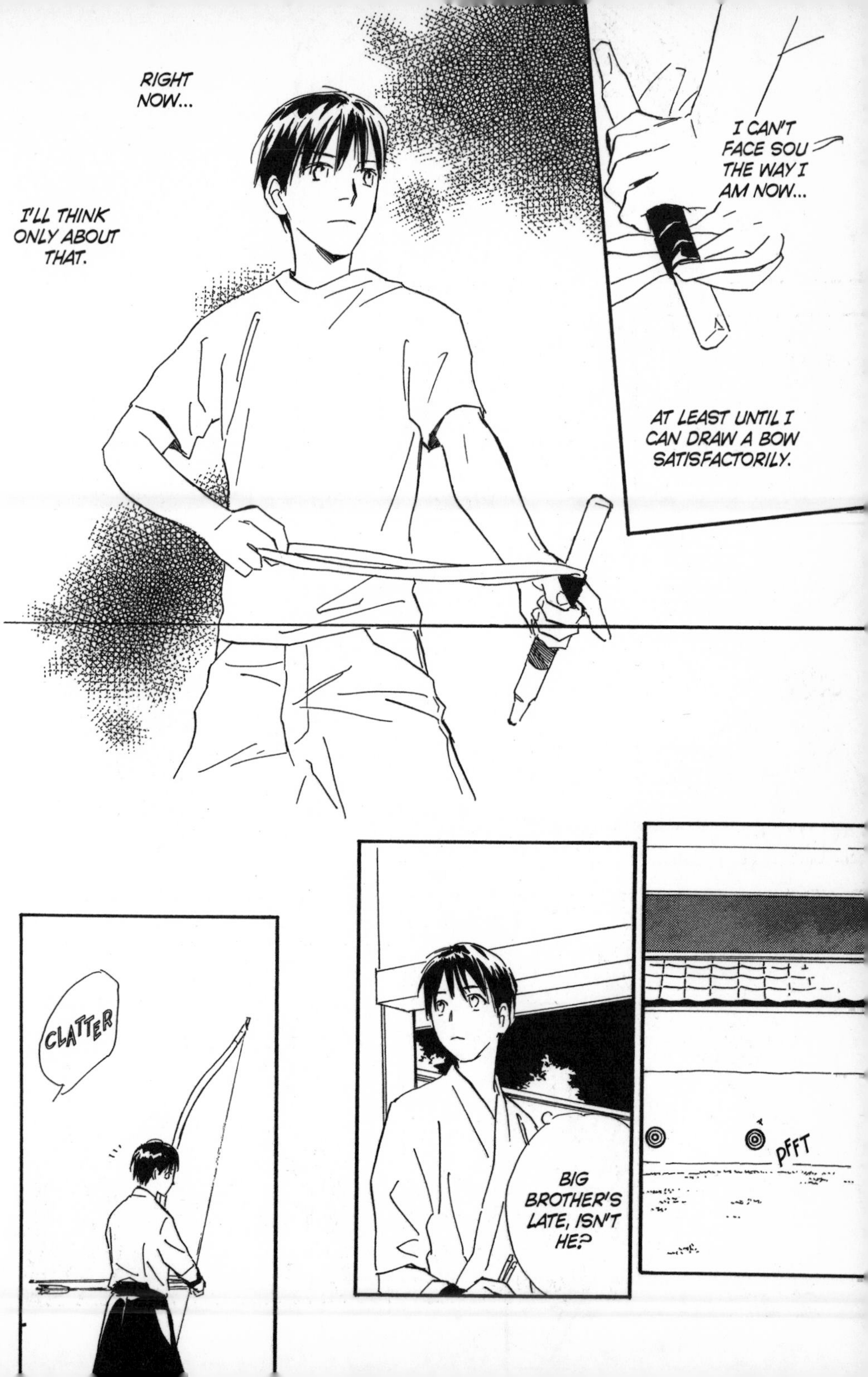
I CAN'T FACE SOU THE WAY I AM NOW...
AT LEAST UNTIL I CAN DRAW A BOW SATISFACTORILY.
RIGHT NOW...
I'LL THINK ONLY ABOUT THAT.
PFFT
BIG BROTHER'S LATE, ISN'T HE?
CLATTER

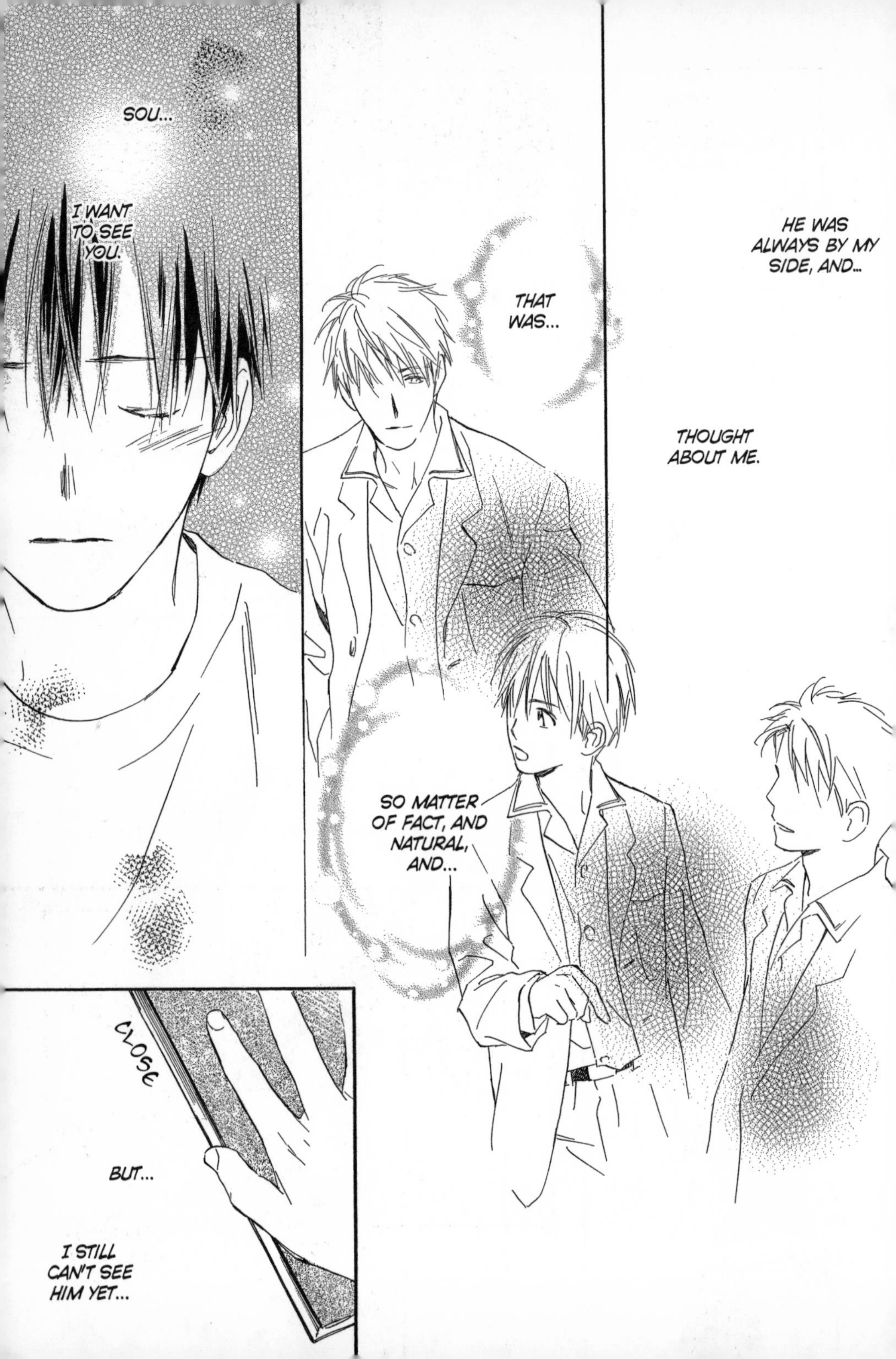
HE WAS ALWAYS BY MY SIDE, AND...
THOUGHT ABOUT ME.
THAT WAS...
SO MATTER OF FACT, AND NATURAL, AND...
SOU...
I WANT TO SEE YOU.
CLOSE
BUT...
I STILL CAN'T SEE HIM YET...

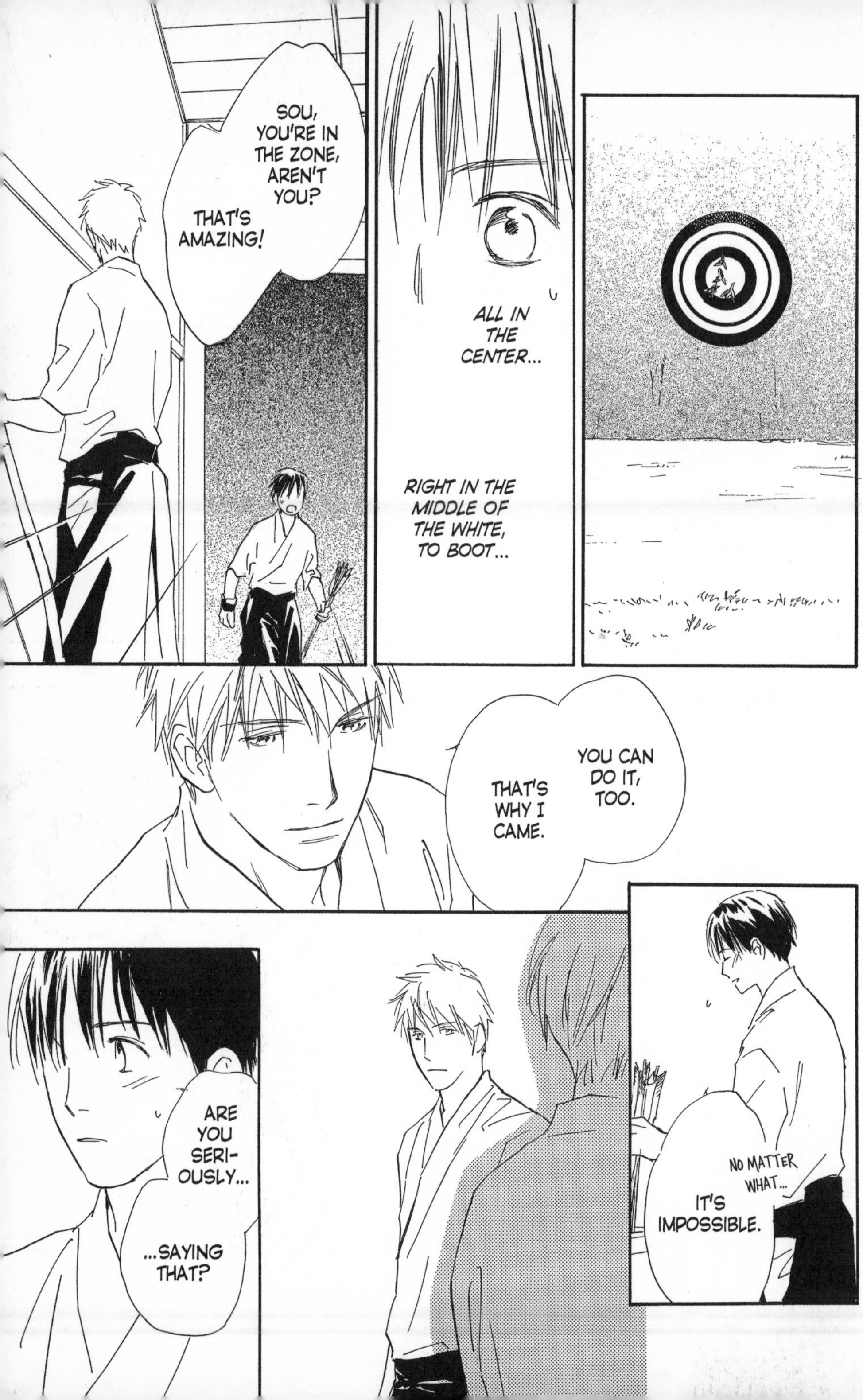
ALL IN THE CENTER...
RIGHT IN THE MIDDLE OF THE WHITE, TO BOOT...
SOU, YOU'RE IN THE ZONE, AREN'T YOU?
THAT'S AMAZING!
YOU CAN DO IT, TOO.
THAT'S WHY I CAME.
NO MATTER WHAT...
IT'S IMPOSSIBLE.
ARE YOU SERIOUSLY...
...SAYING THAT?

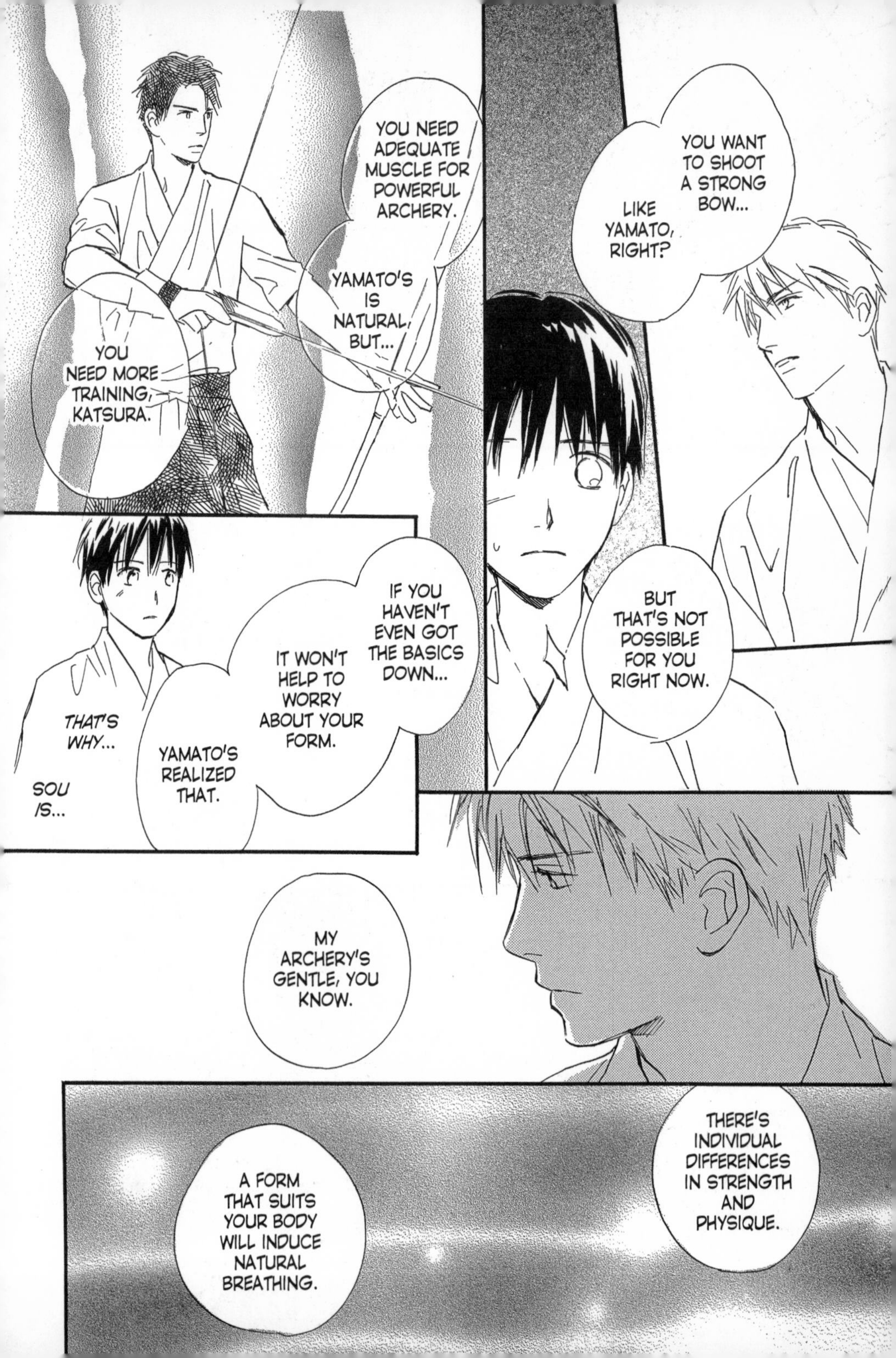
YOU WANT TO SHOOT A STRONG BOW...
LIKE YAMATO, RIGHT?
BUT THAT'S NOT POSSIBLE FOR YOU RIGHT NOW.
YOU NEED ADEQUATE MUSCLE FOR POWERFUL ARCHERY.
YAMATO'S IS NATURAL, BUT...
YOU NEED MORE TRAINING, KATSURA.
IF YOU HAVEN'T EVEN GOT THE BASICS DOWN...
IT WON'T HELP TO WORRY ABOUT YOUR FORM.
YAMATO'S REALIZED THAT.
THAT'S WHY...
SOU IS...
MY ARCHERY'S GENTLE, YOU KNOW.
THERE'S INDIVIDUAL DIFFERENCES IN STRENGTH AND PHYSIQUE.
A FORM THAT SUITS YOUR BODY WILL INDUCE NATURAL BREATHING.

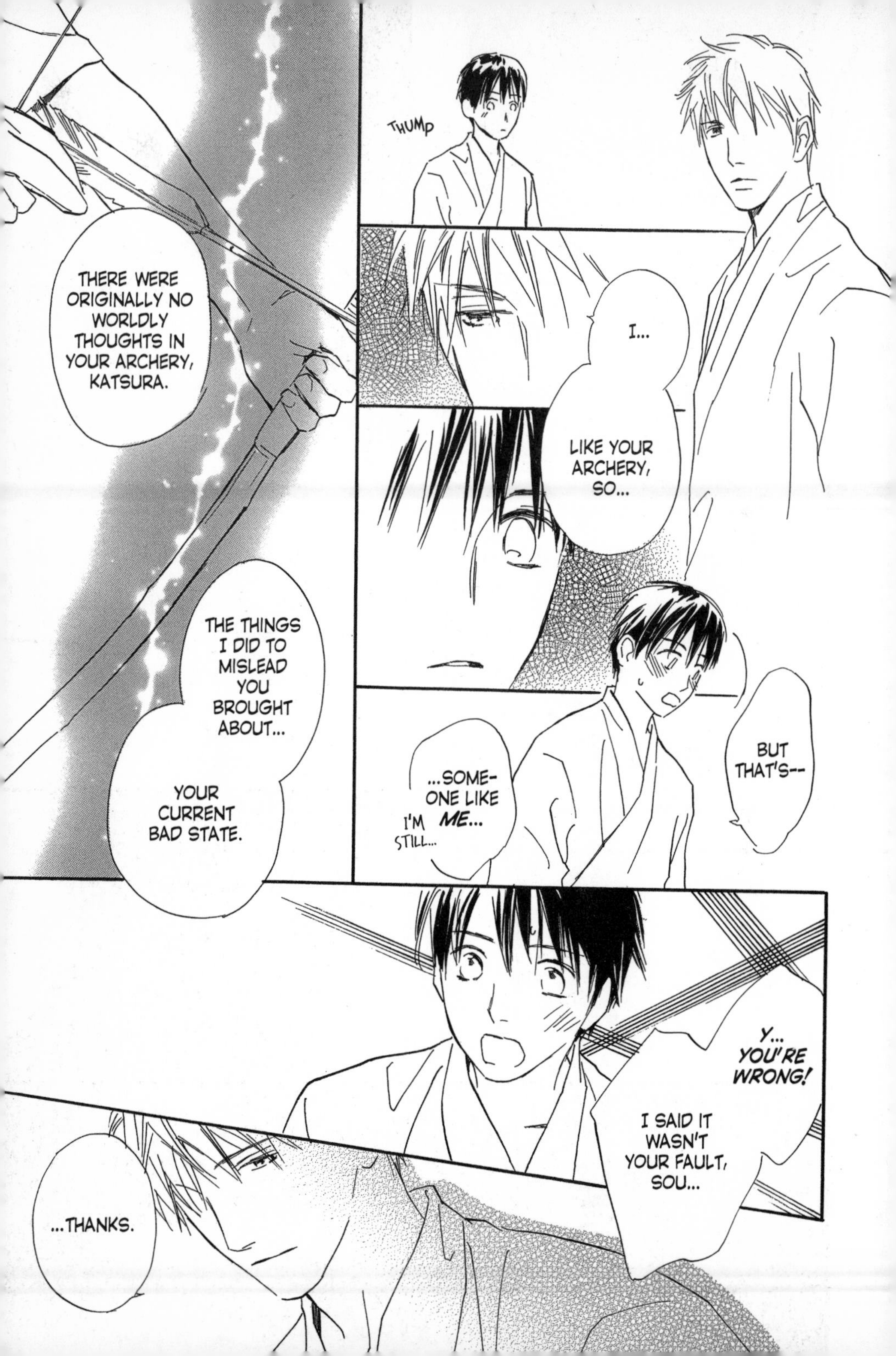
THUMP
I...
LIKE YOUR ARCHERY, SO...
BUT THAT'S--
...SOME-ONE LIKE ME...
I'M STILL...
THERE WERE ORIGINALLY NO WORLDLY THOUGHTS IN YOUR ARCHERY, KATSURA.
THE THINGS I DID TO MISLEAD YOU BROUGHT ABOUT...
YOUR CURRENT BAD STATE.
Y... YOU'RE WRONG!
I SAID IT WASN'T YOUR FAULT, SOU...
...THANKS.

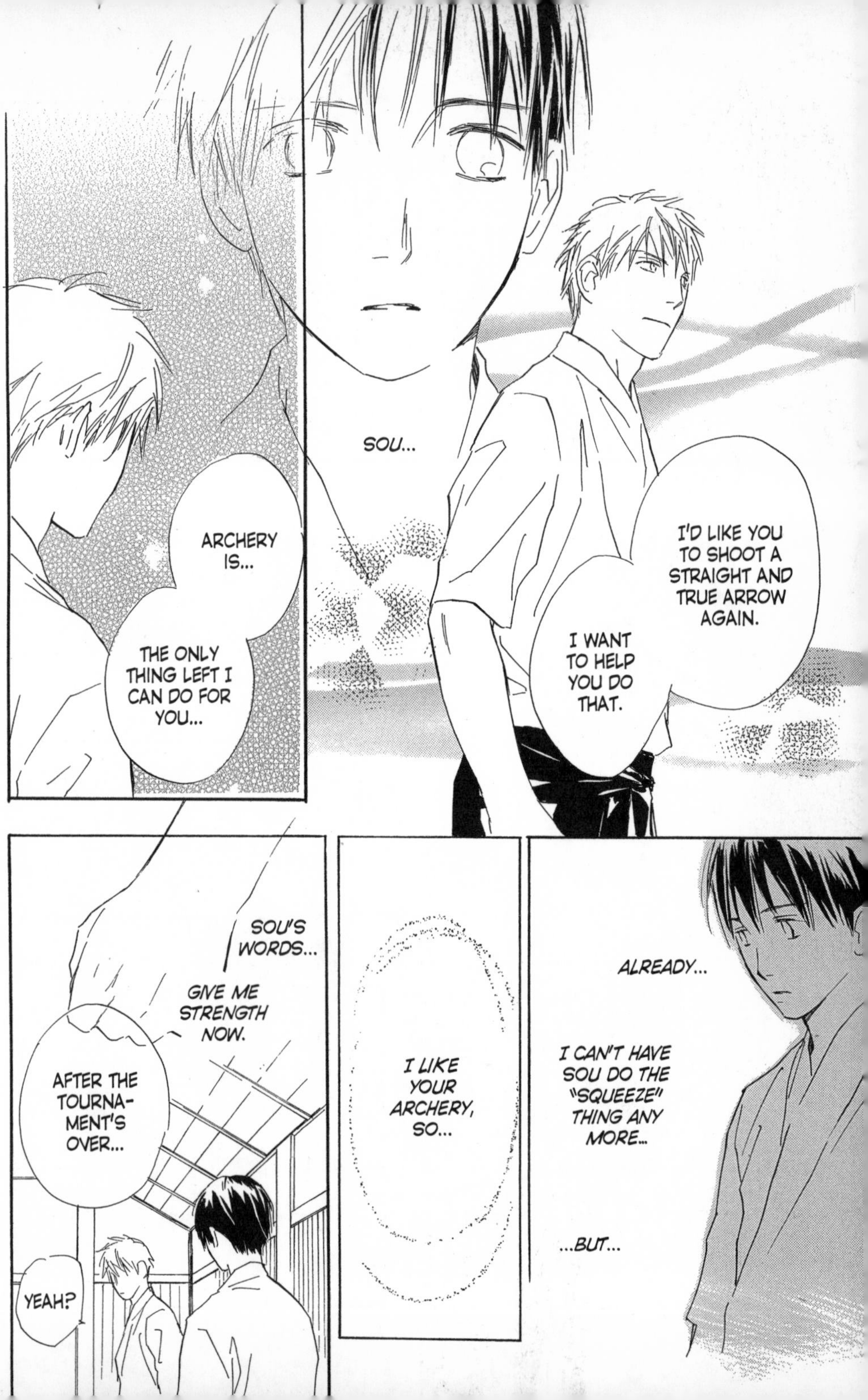
SOU...
I'D LIKE YOU TO SHOOT A STRAIGHT AND TRUE ARROW AGAIN.
I WANT TO HELP YOU DO THAT.
ARCHERY IS...
THE ONLY THING LEFT I CAN DO FOR YOU...
ALREADY...
I CAN'T HAVE SOU DO THE "SQUEEZE" THING ANY MORE...
...BUT...
I LIKE YOUR ARCHERY, SO...
SOU'S WORDS...
GIVE ME STRENGTH NOW.
AFTER THE TOURNA-MENT'S OVER...
YEAH?

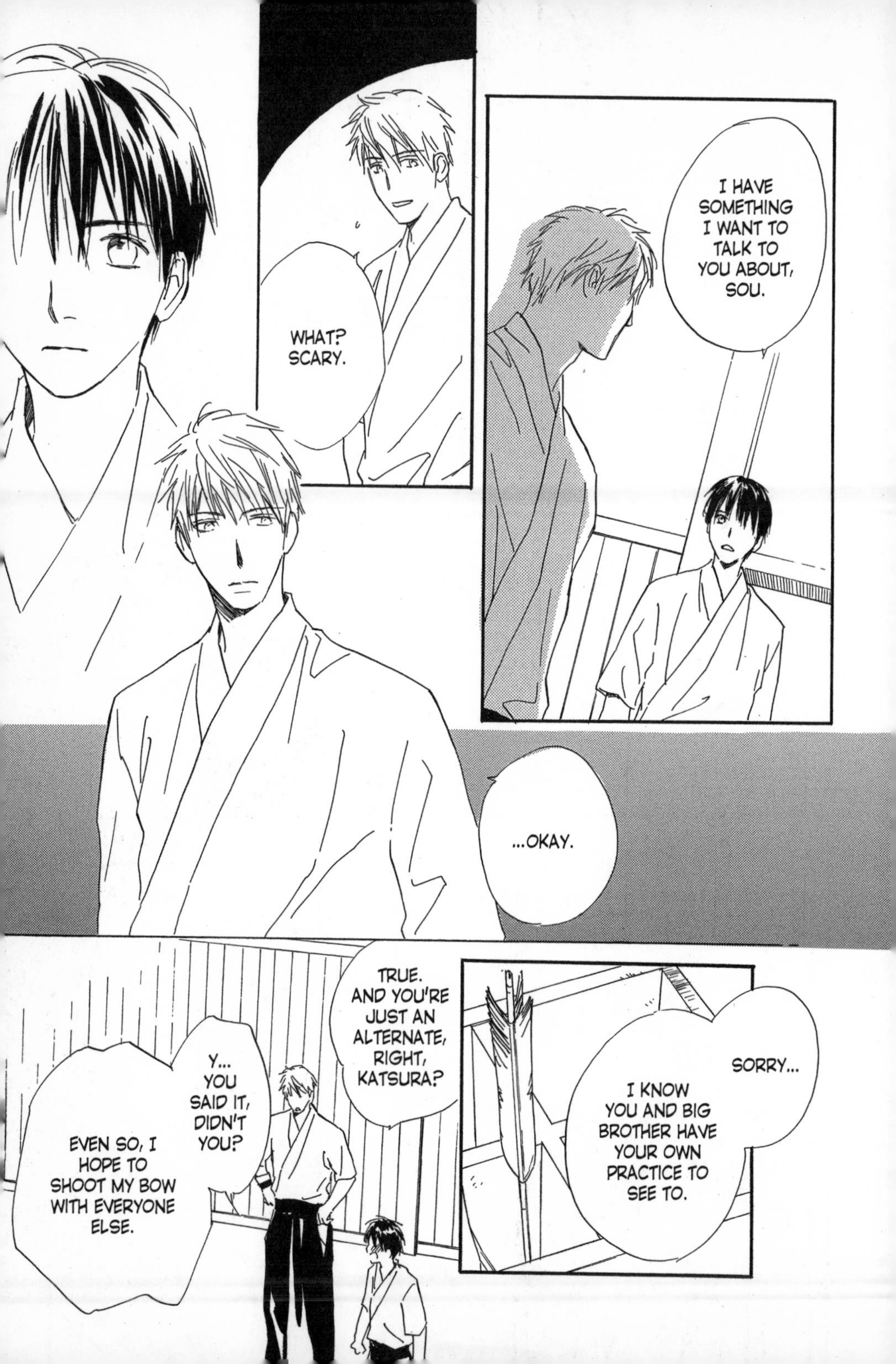
I HAVE SOMETHING I WANT TO TALK TO YOU ABOUT, SOU.
WHAT? SCARY.
...OKAY.
SORRY...
I KNOW YOU AND BIG BROTHER HAVE YOUR OWN PRACTICE TO SEE TO.
TRUE. AND YOU'RE JUST AN ALTERNATE, RIGHT, KATSURA?
Y... YOU SAID IT, DIDN'T YOU?
EVEN SO, I HOPE TO SHOOT MY BOW WITH EVERYONE ELSE.

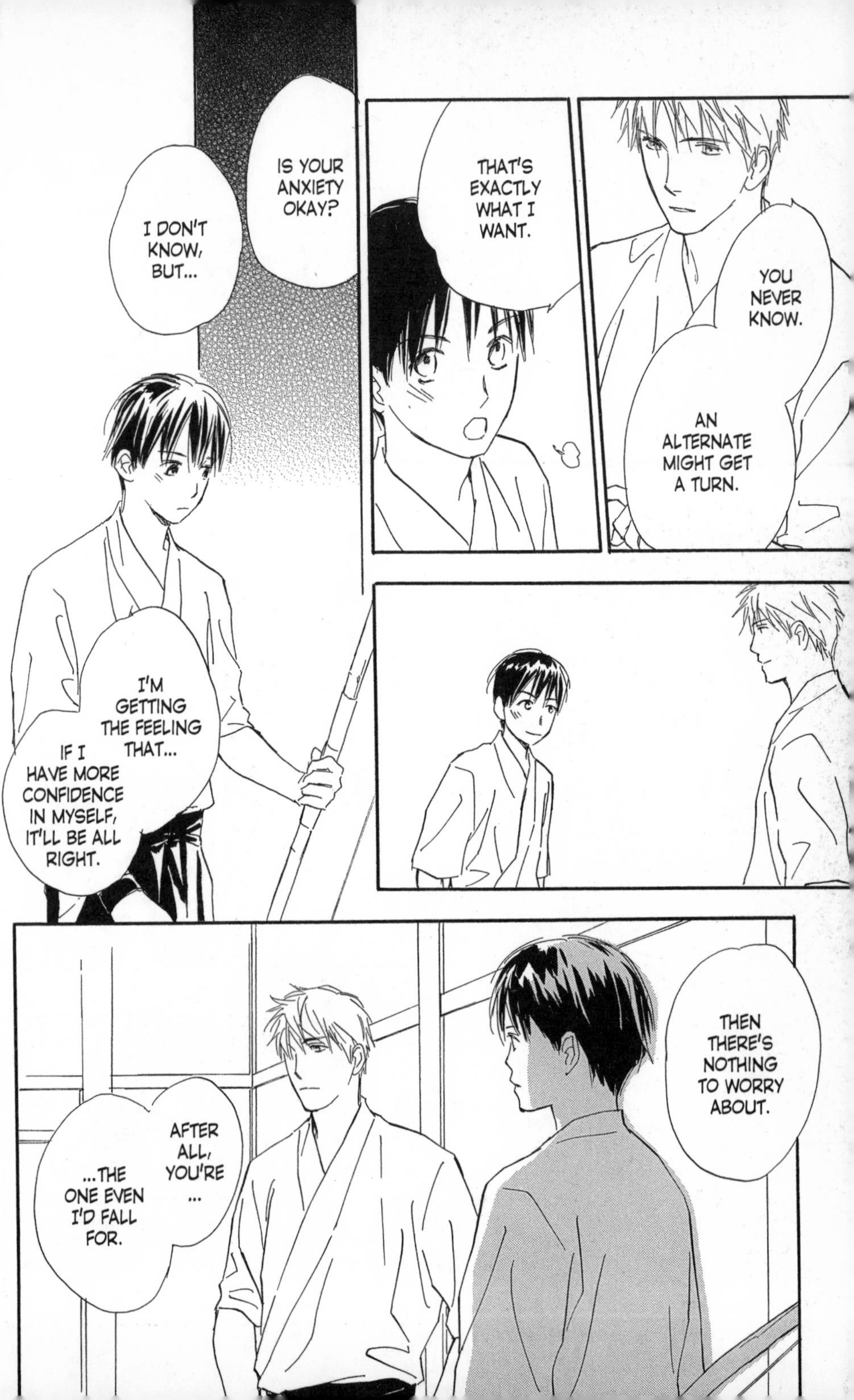
YOU NEVER KNOW.
AN ALTERNATE MIGHT GET A TURN.
THAT'S EXACTLY WHAT I WANT.
IS YOUR ANXIETY OKAY?
I DON'T KNOW, BUT...
I'M GETTING THE FEELING THAT...
IF I HAVE MORE CONFIDENCE IN MYSELF, IT'LL BE ALL RIGHT.
THEN THERE'S NOTHING TO WORRY ABOUT.
AFTER ALL, YOU'RE ...
...THE ONE EVEN I'D FALL FOR.

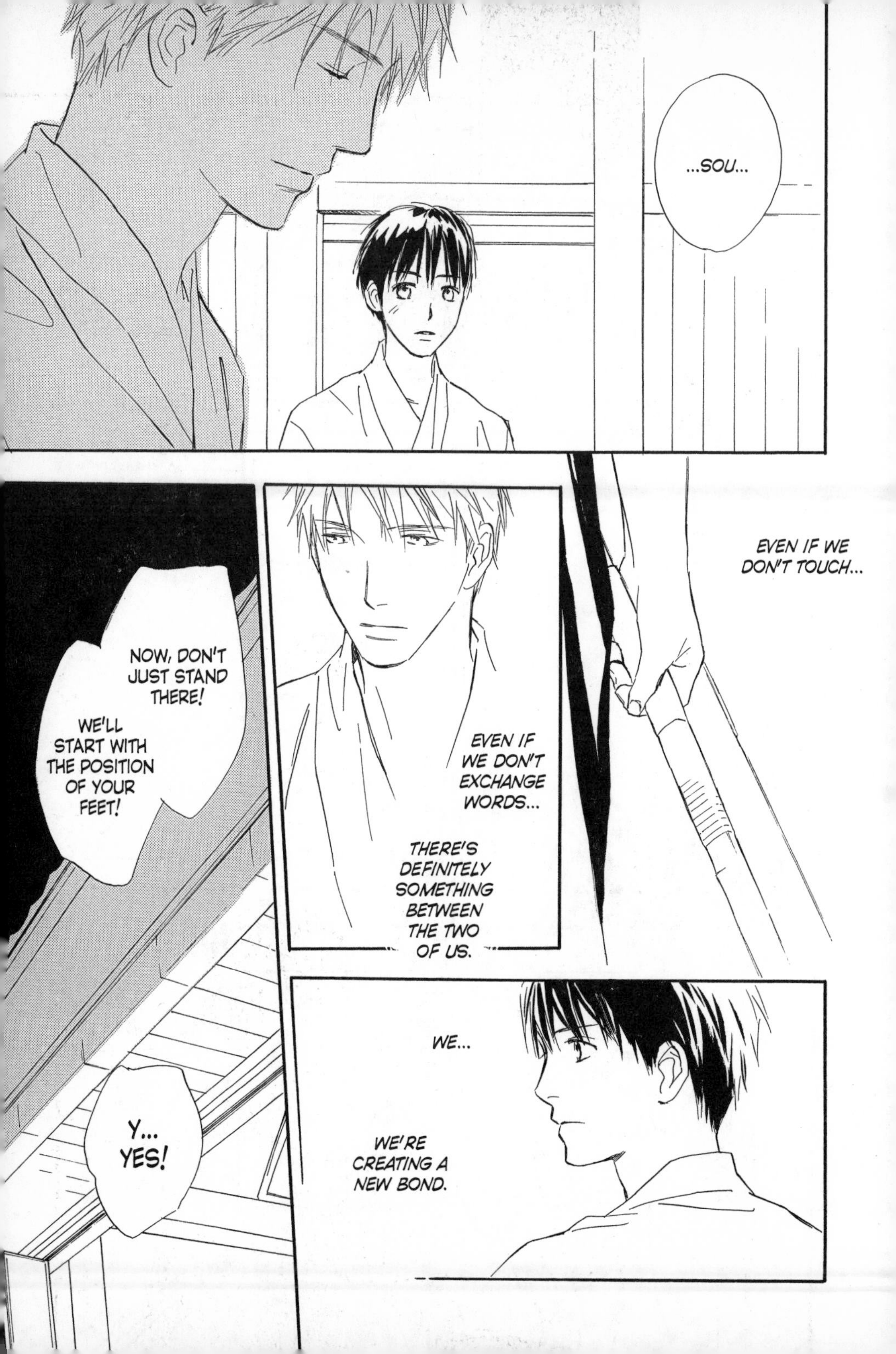
...SOU...
EVEN IF WE DON'T TOUCH...
EVEN IF WE DON'T EXCHANGE WORDS...
THERE'S DEFINITELY SOMETHING BETWEEN THE TWO OF US.
WE...
WE'RE CREATING A NEW BOND.
NOW, DON'T JUST STAND THERE!
WE'LL START WITH THE POSITION OF YOUR FEET!
Y... YES!

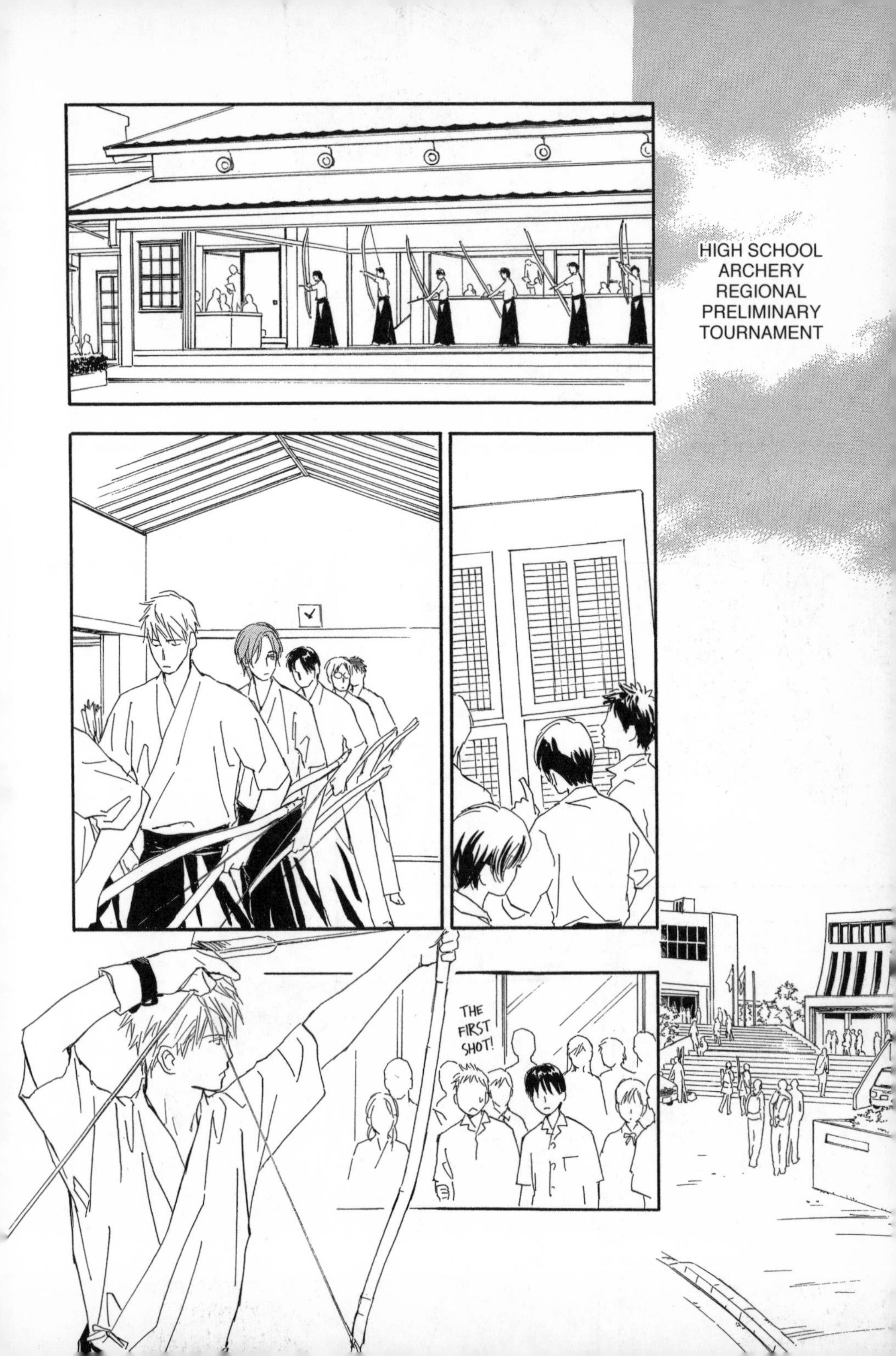
HIGH SCHOOL
ARCHERY
REGIONAL
PRELIMINARY
TOURNAMENT
THE FIRST SHOT!

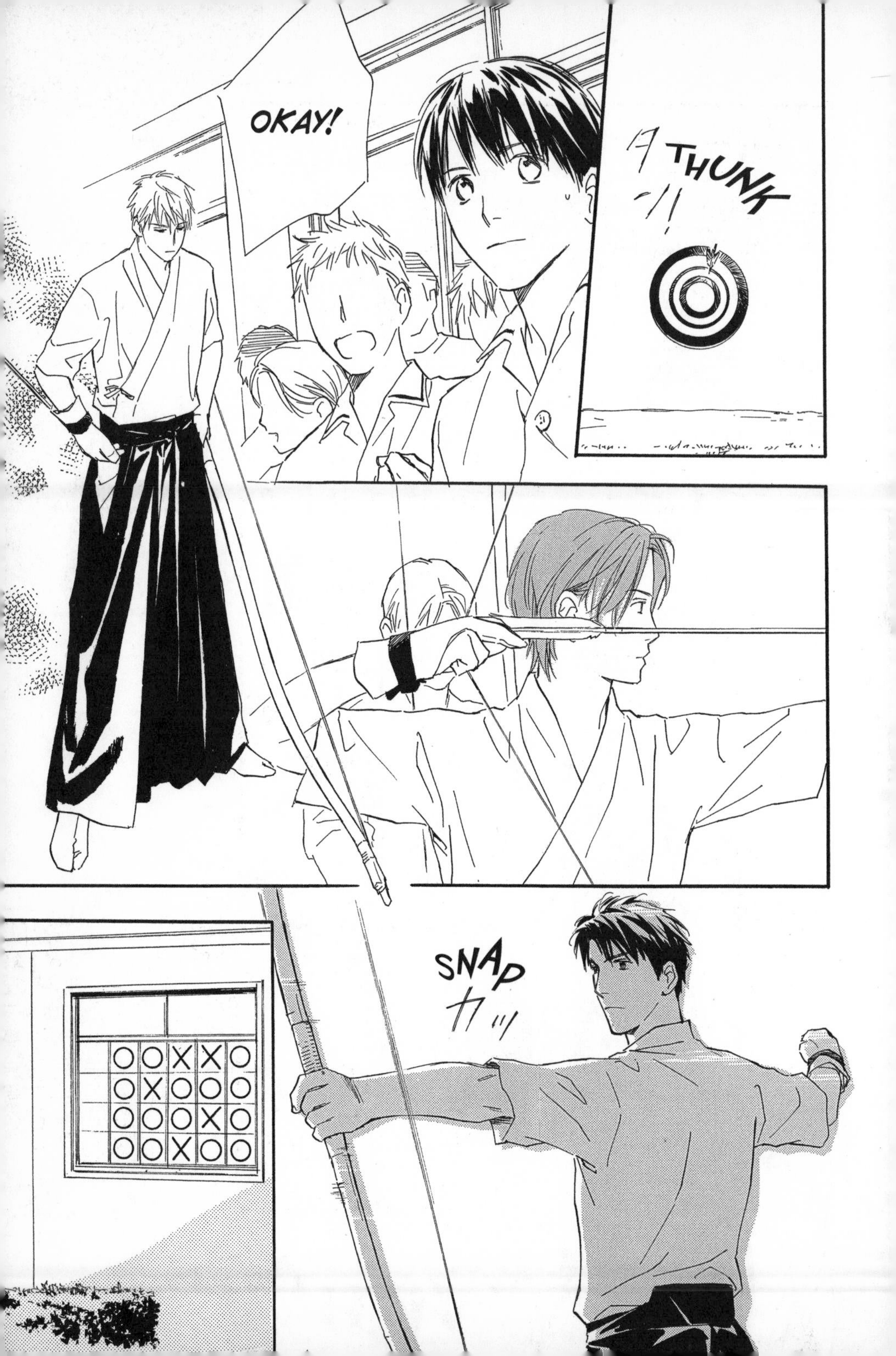
タ
THUNK
ッ!
OKAY!
SNAP
カッ

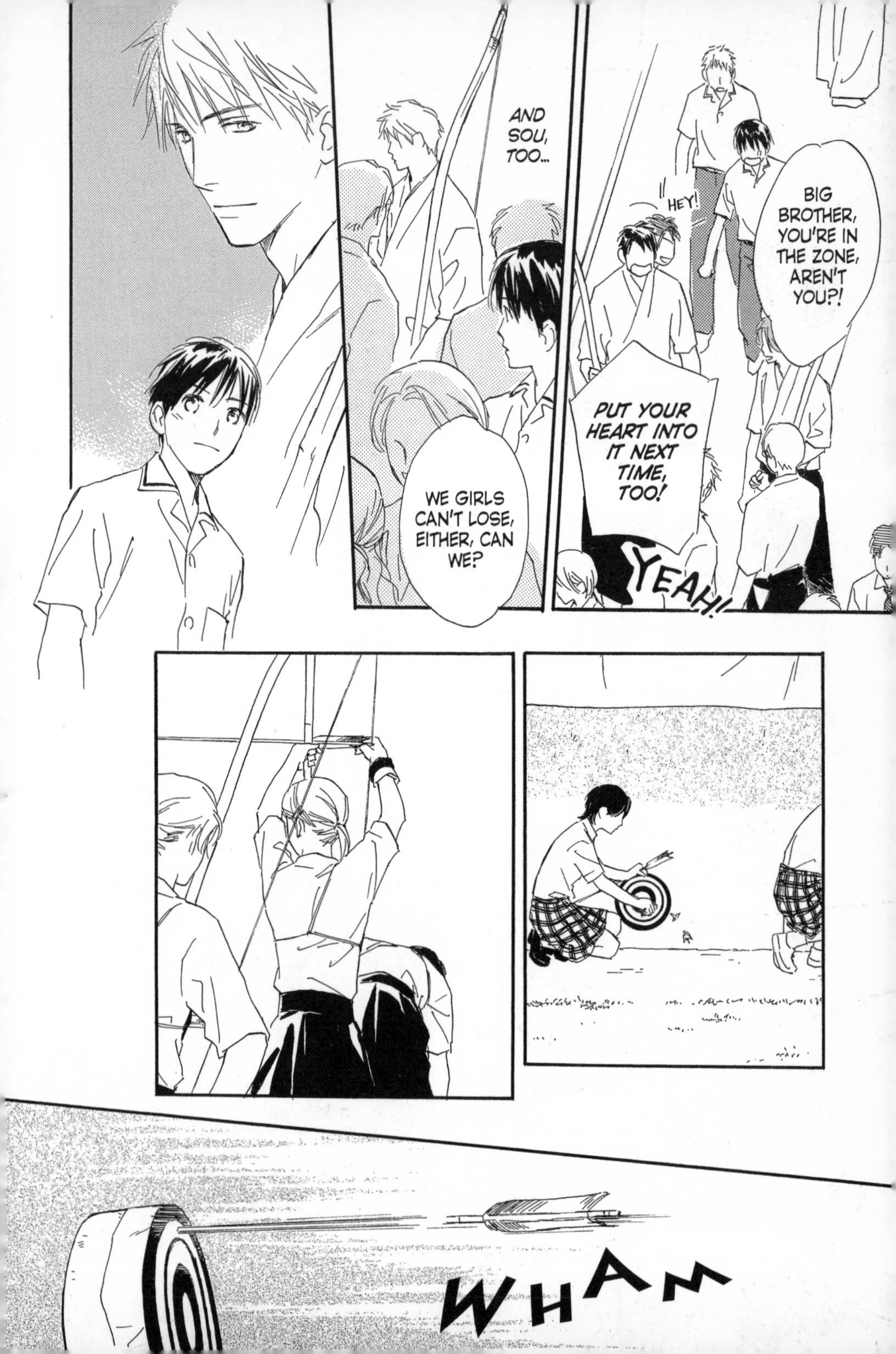
BIG BROTHER, YOU'RE IN THE ZONE, AREN'T YOU?!
HEY!
PUT YOUR HEART INTO IT NEXT TIME, TOO!
YEAH!
AND SOU, TOO...
WE GIRLS CAN'T LOSE, EITHER, CAN WE?
WHAM

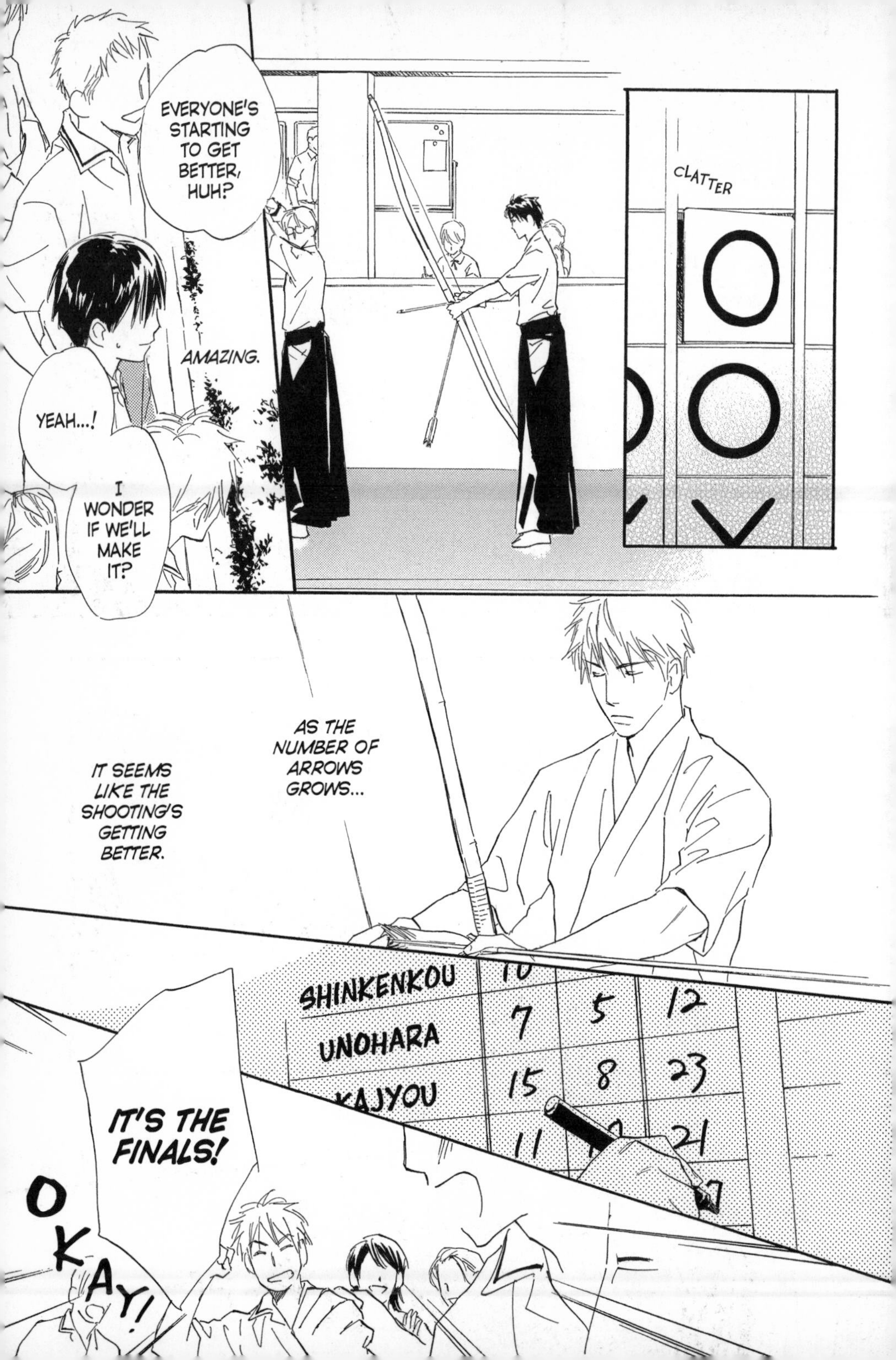
CLATTER
EVERYONE'S STARTING TO GET BETTER, HUH?
AMAZING.
YEAH...!
I WONDER IF WE'LL MAKE IT?
AS THE NUMBER OF ARROWS GROWS...
IT SEEMS LIKE THE SHOOTING'S GETTING BETTER.
SHINKENKOU
7 5 12
UNOHARA
15 8 23
KAJYOU
IT'S THE FINALS!
OKAY!

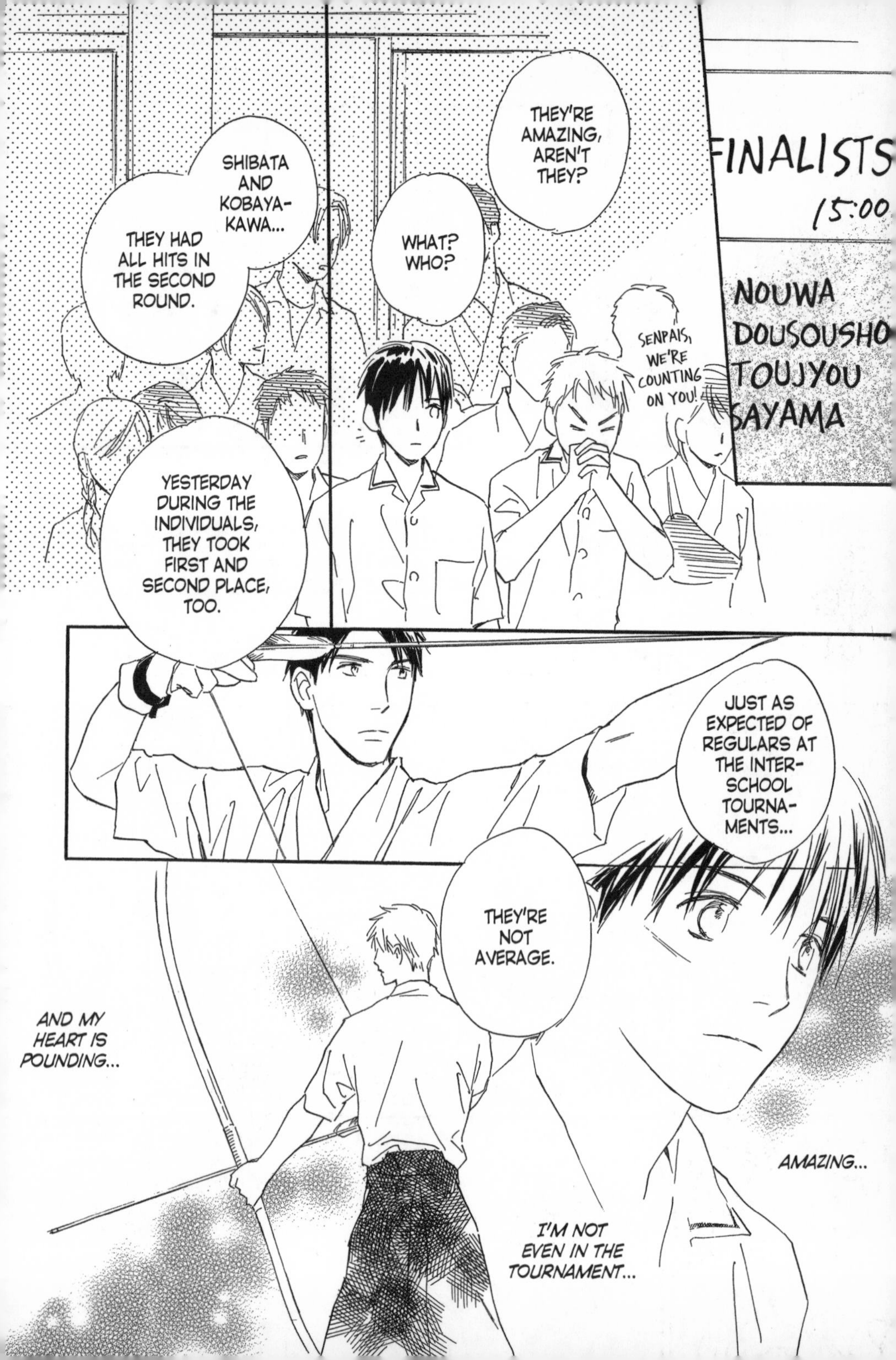
FINALISTS
15:00
NOUWA
DOUSOUSHO
TOUJYOU
SAYAMA
THEY'RE AMAZING, AREN'T THEY?
WHAT? WHO?
SENPAIS, WE'RE COUNTING ON YOU!
SHIBATA AND KOBAYA-KAWA...
THEY HAD ALL HITS IN THE SECOND ROUND.
YESTERDAY DURING THE INDIVIDUALS, THEY TOOK FIRST AND SECOND PLACE, TOO.
JUST AS EXPECTED OF REGULARS AT THE INTER-SCHOOL TOURNA-MENTS...
THEY'RE NOT AVERAGE.
AMAZING...
I'M NOT EVEN IN THE TOURNAMENT...
AND MY HEART IS POUNDING...

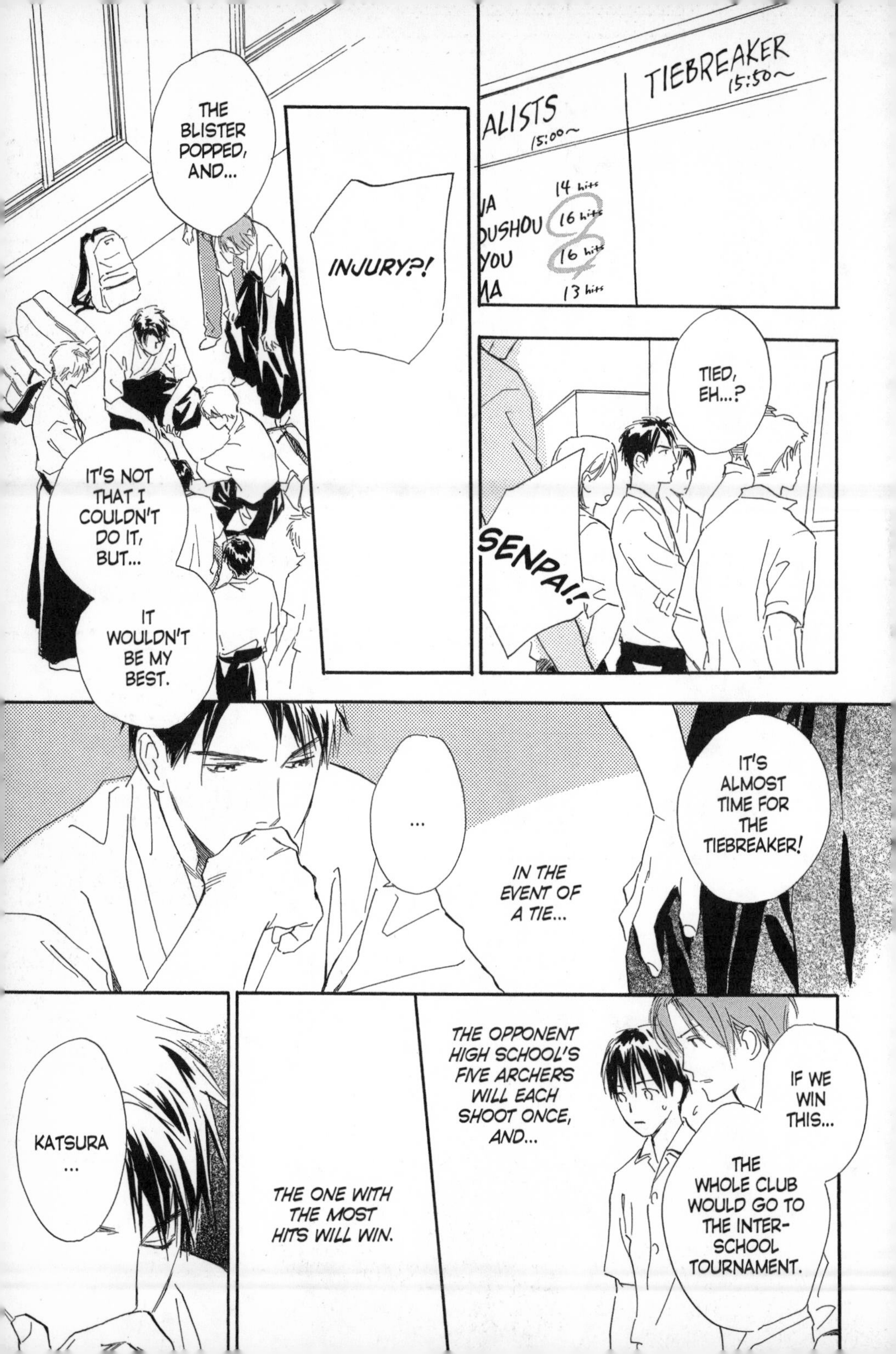
TIEBREAKER 15:50~
ALISTS 15:00~
JA 14 hits
OUSHOU 16 hits
YOU 16 hits
MA 13 hits
TIED, EH...?
SENPAI!!
INJURY?!
THE BLISTER POPPED, AND...
IT'S NOT THAT I COULDN'T DO IT, BUT...
IT WOULDN'T BE MY BEST.
IT'S ALMOST TIME FOR THE TIEBREAKER!
IN THE EVENT OF A TIE...
...
IF WE WIN THIS...
THE WHOLE CLUB WOULD GO TO THE INTER-SCHOOL TOURNAMENT.
THE OPPONENT HIGH SCHOOL'S FIVE ARCHERS WILL EACH SHOOT ONCE, AND...
THE ONE WITH THE MOST HITS WILL WIN.
KATSURA ...

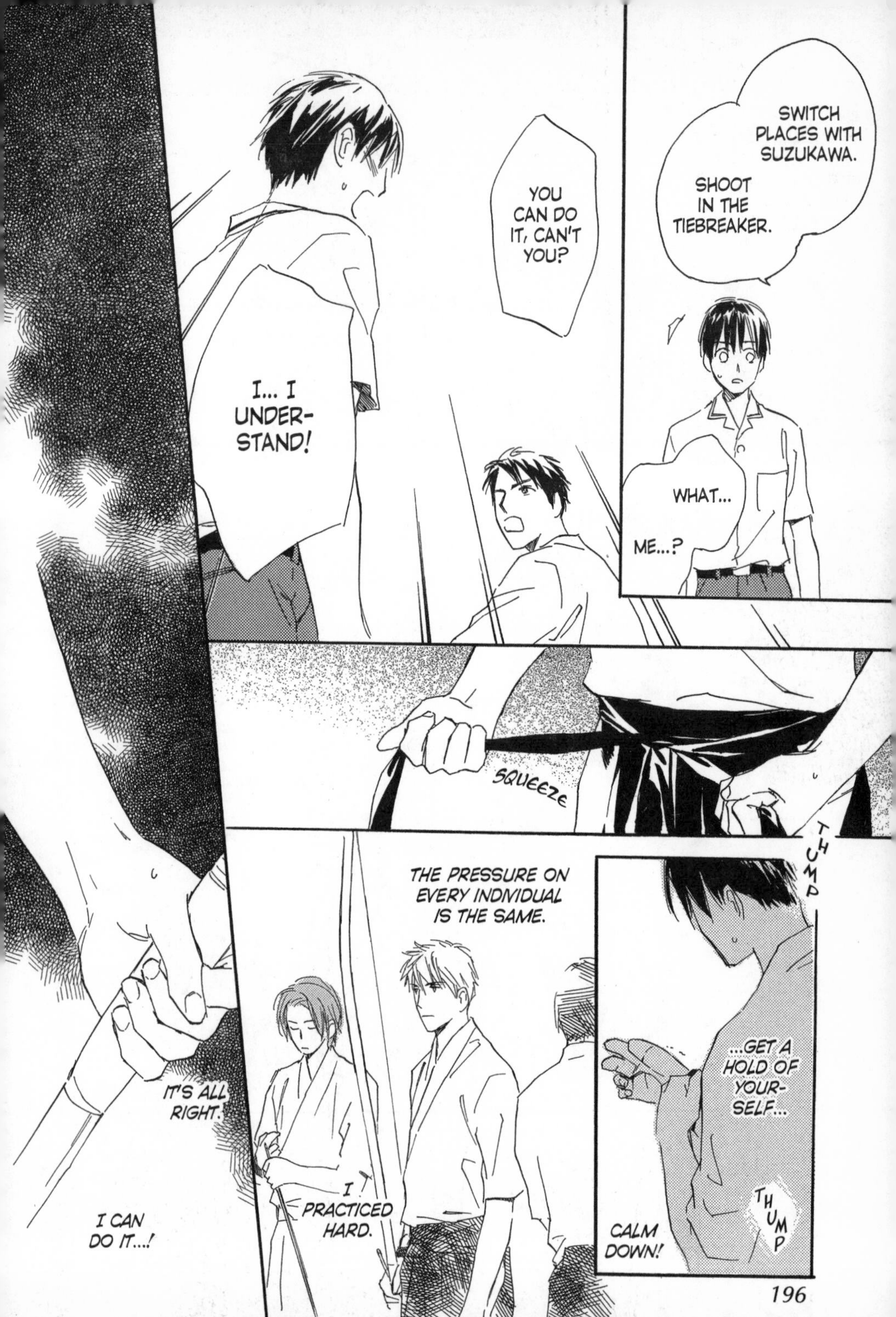
SWITCH PLACES WITH SUZUKAWA.
SHOOT IN THE TIEBREAKER.
WHAT...
ME...?
YOU CAN DO IT, CAN'T YOU?
I... I UNDER-STAND!
SQUEEZE
THUMP
...GET A HOLD OF YOUR-SELF...
THUMP
CALM DOWN!
THE PRESSURE ON EVERY INDIVIDUAL IS THE SAME.
I PRACTICED HARD.
IT'S ALL RIGHT.
I CAN DO IT...!

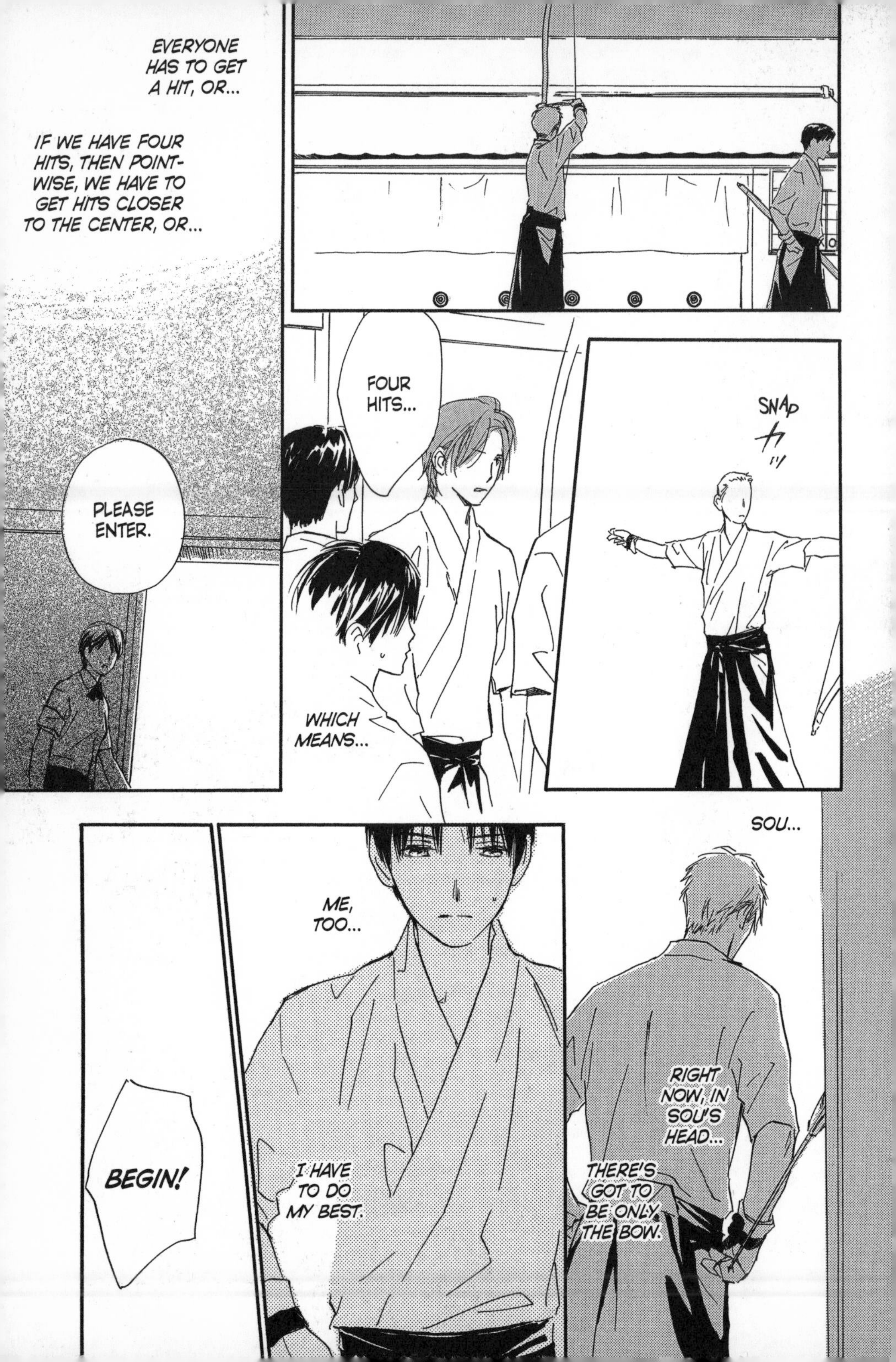
SNAP
FOUR HITS...
WHICH MEANS...
EVERYONE HAS TO GET A HIT, OR...
IF WE HAVE FOUR HITS, THEN POINT-WISE, WE HAVE TO GET HITS CLOSER TO THE CENTER, OR...
PLEASE ENTER.
SOU...
RIGHT NOW, IN SOU'S HEAD...
THERE'S GOT TO BE ONLY THE BOW.
ME, TOO...
I HAVE TO DO MY BEST.
BEGIN!

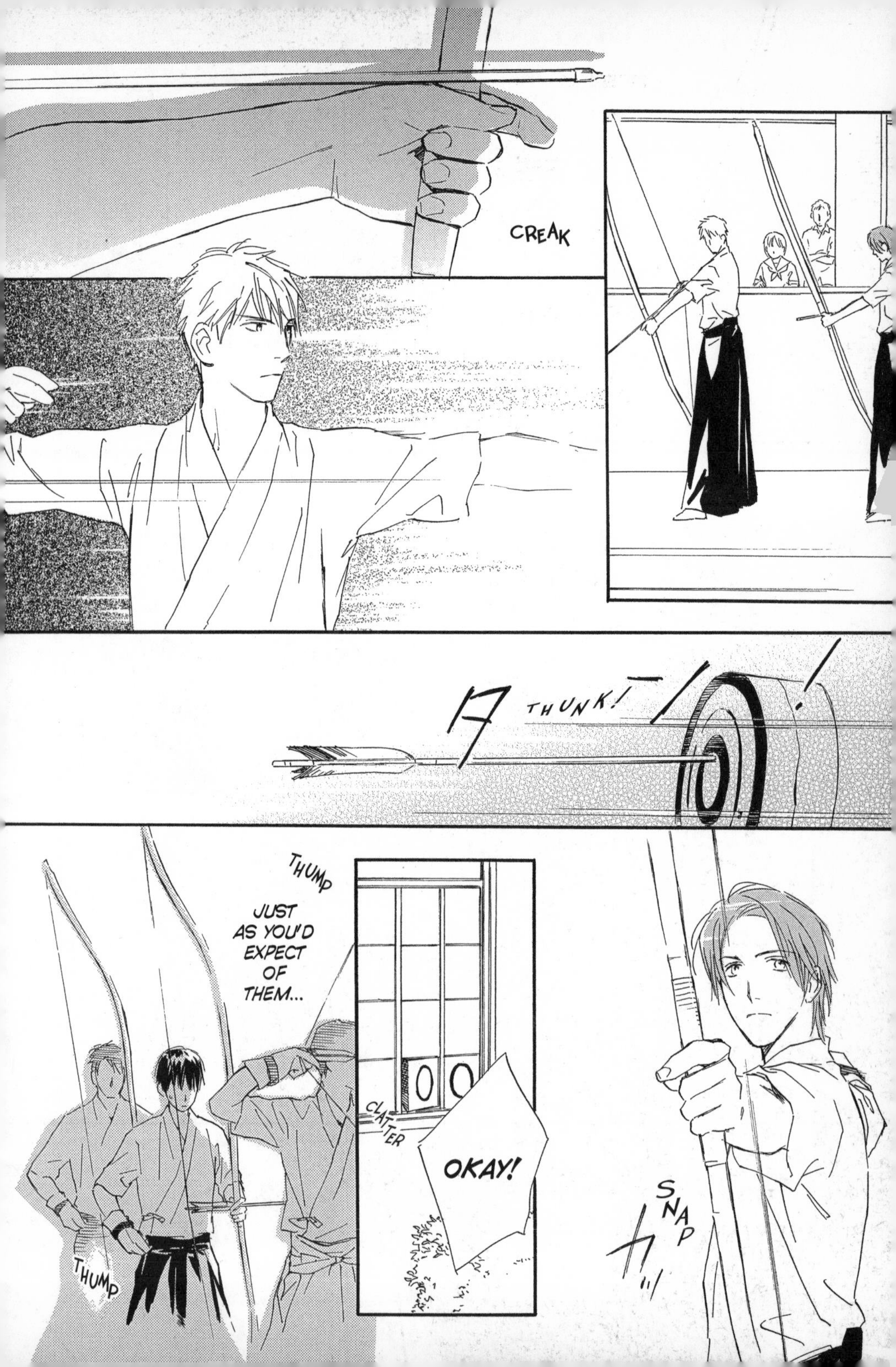
CREAK
THUNK!
SNAP
CLATTER
OKAY!
THUMP
JUST AS YOU'D EXPECT OF THEM...
THUMP

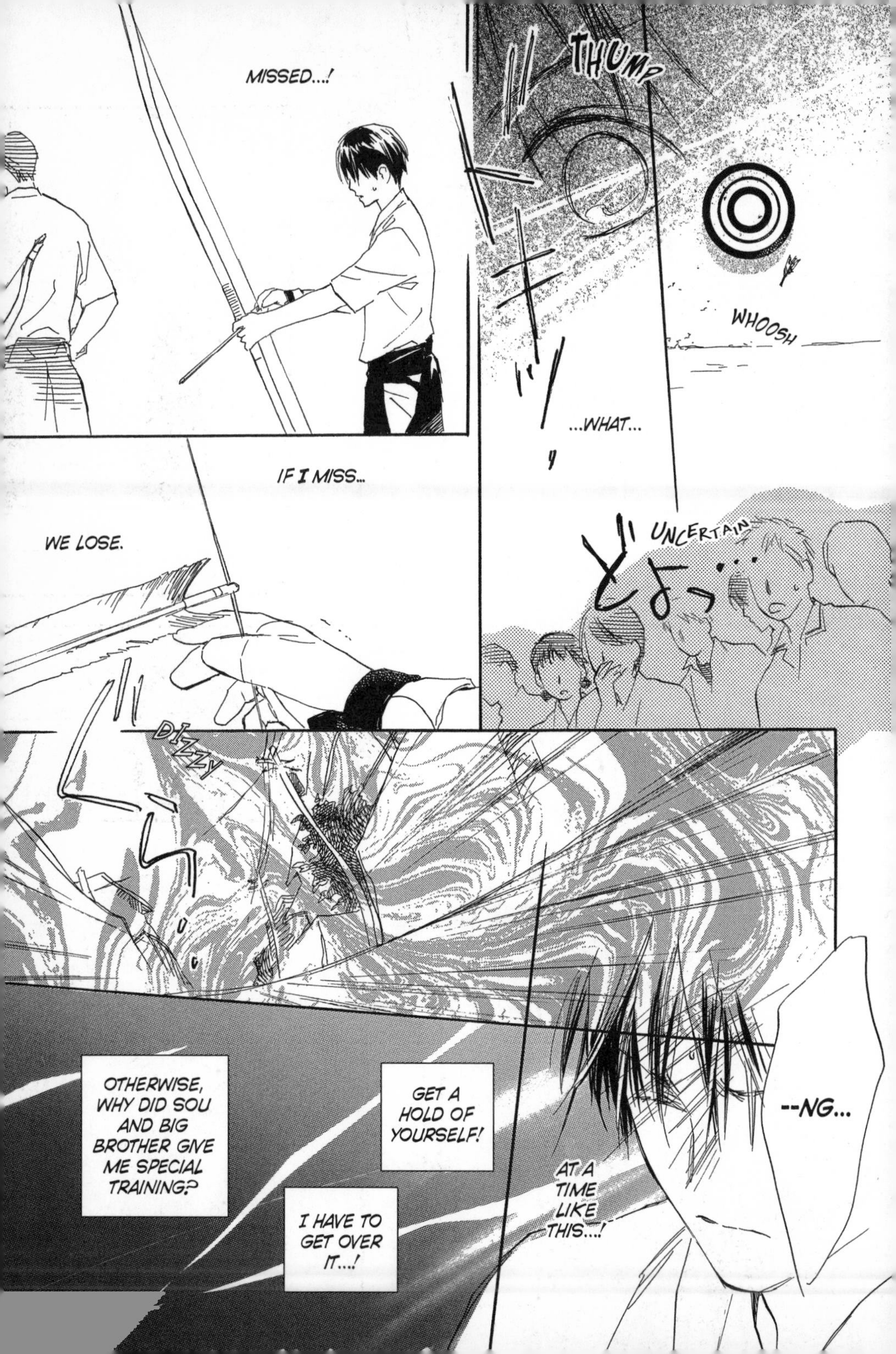

THUMP
WHOOSH
...WHAT...
MISSED...!
UNCERTAIN
IF I MISS...
WE LOSE.
DIZZY
--NG...
AT A TIME LIKE THIS...!
GET A HOLD OF YOURSELF!
I HAVE TO GET OVER IT...!
OTHERWISE, WHY DID SOU AND BIG BROTHER GIVE ME SPECIAL TRAINING?

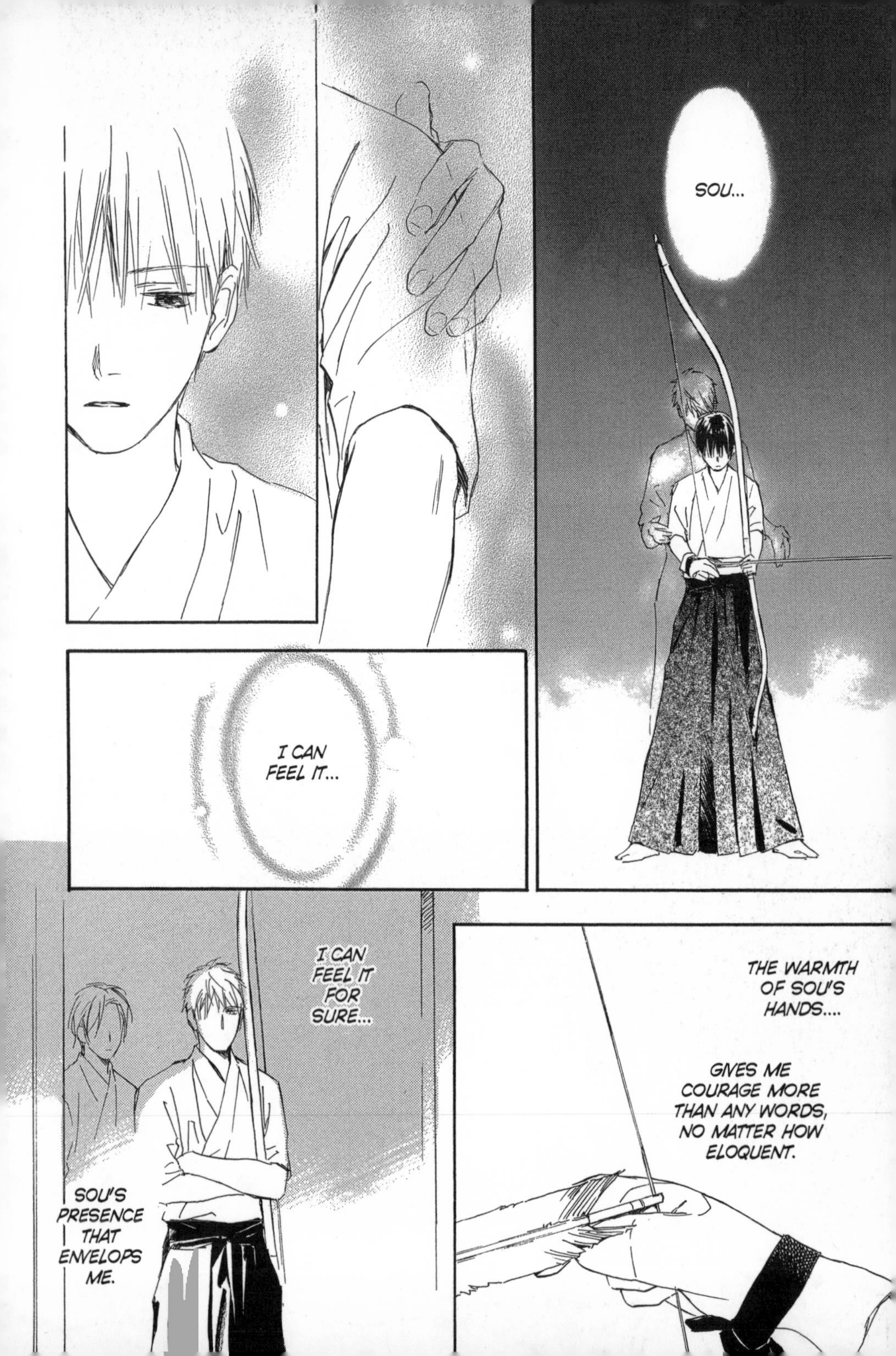
SOU...
I CAN FEEL IT...
THE WARMTH OF SOU'S HANDS....
GIVES ME COURAGE MORE THAN ANY WORDS, NO MATTER HOW ELOQUENT.
I CAN FEEL IT FOR SURE...
SOU'S PRESENCE THAT ENVELOPS ME.

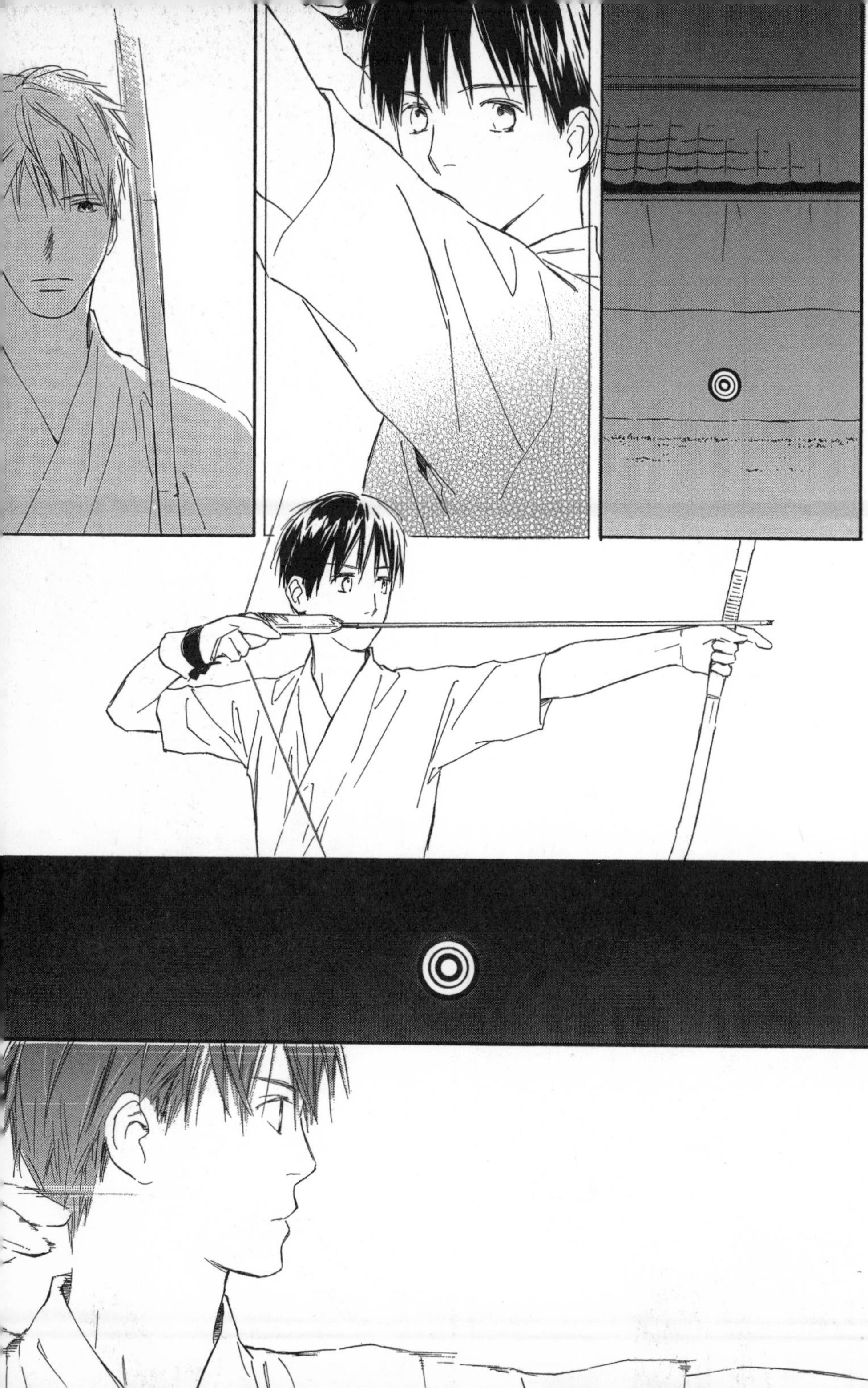

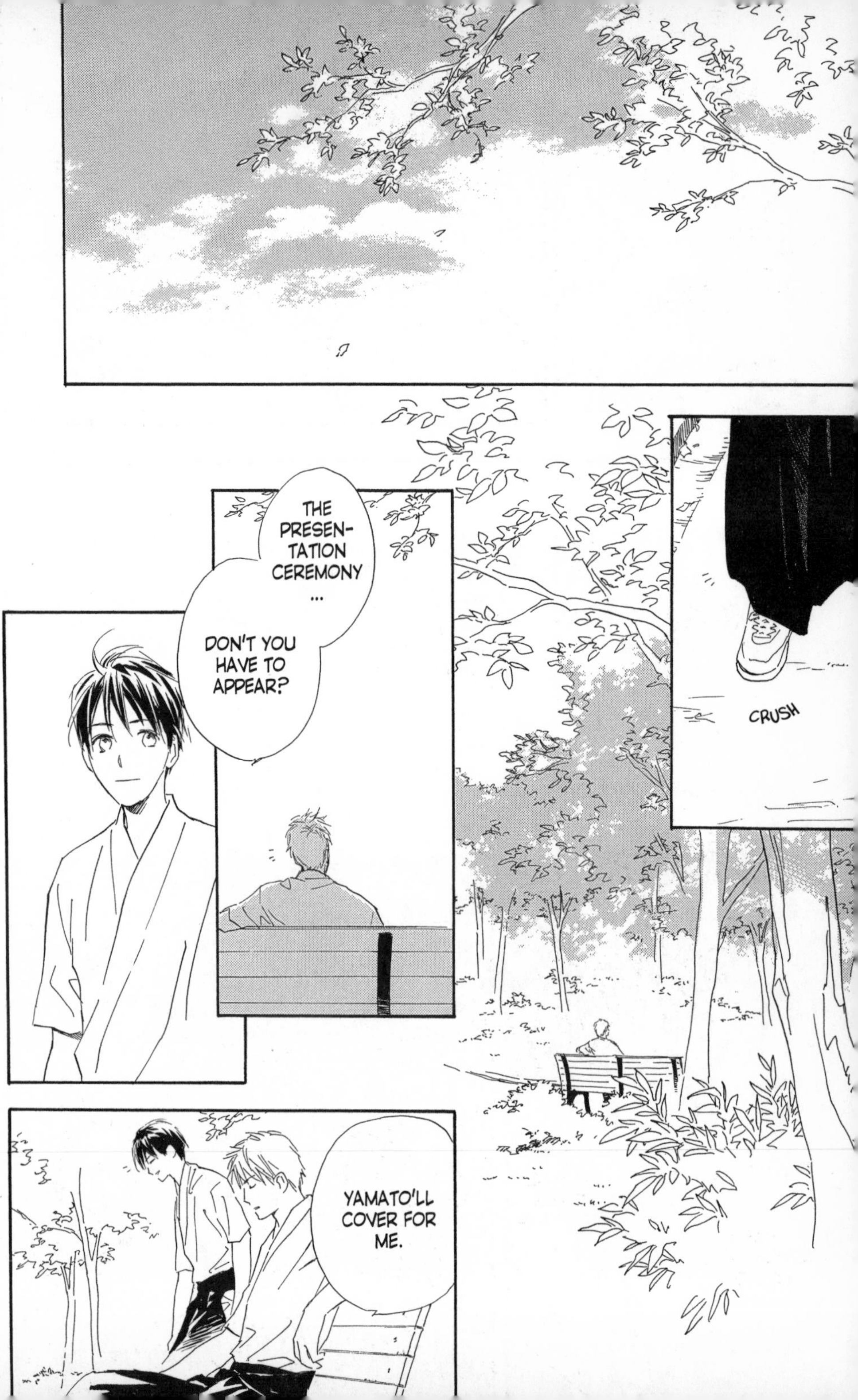
CRUSH
THE PRESEN-TATION CEREMONY ...
DON'T YOU HAVE TO APPEAR?
YAMATO'LL COVER FOR ME.

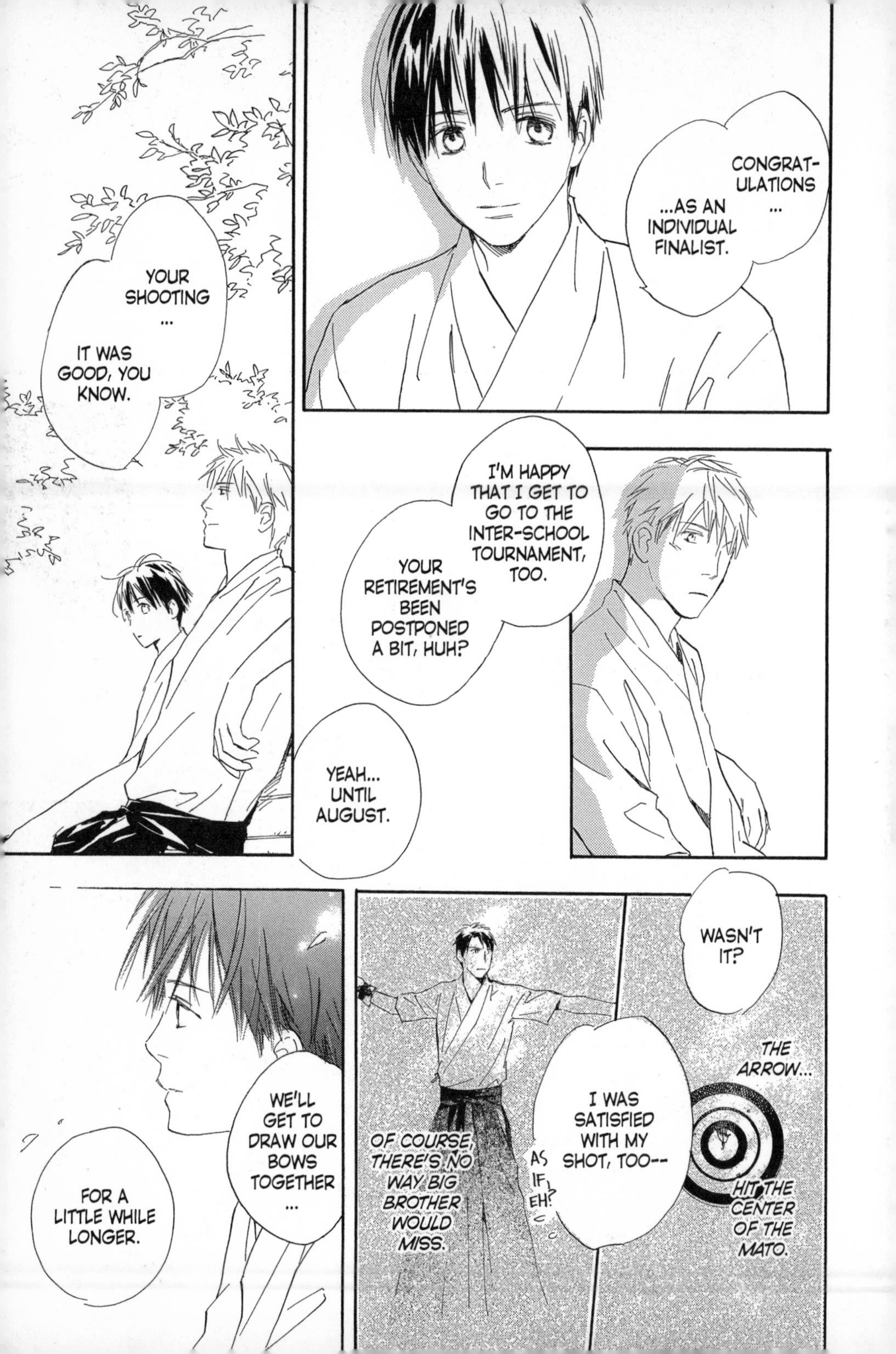
CONGRAT-ULATIONS ...
...AS AN INDIVIDUAL FINALIST.
I'M HAPPY THAT I GET TO GO TO THE INTER-SCHOOL TOURNAMENT, TOO.
YOUR RETIREMENT'S BEEN POSTPONED A BIT, HUH?
YEAH... UNTIL AUGUST.
YOUR SHOOTING ...
IT WAS GOOD, YOU KNOW.
WASN'T IT?
THE ARROW...
HIT THE CENTER OF THE MATO.
I WAS SATISFIED WITH MY SHOT, TOO--
AS IF, EH?
OF COURSE, THERE'S NO WAY BIG BROTHER WOULD MISS.
WE'LL GET TO DRAW OUR BOWS TOGETHER ...
FOR A LITTLE WHILE LONGER.

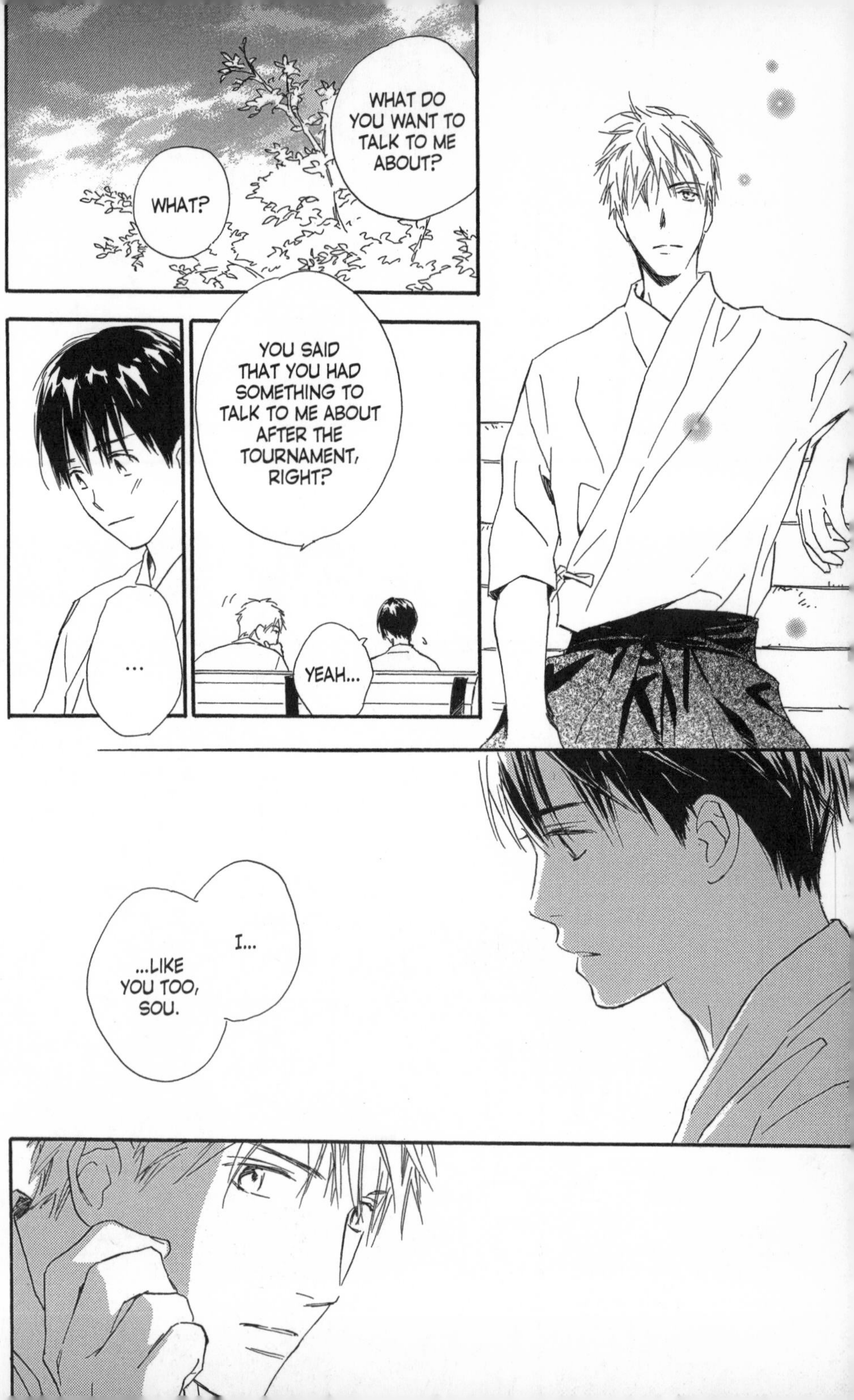
WHAT DO YOU WANT TO TALK TO ME ABOUT?
WHAT?
YOU SAID THAT YOU HAD SOMETHING TO TALK TO ME ABOUT AFTER THE TOURNAMENT, RIGHT?
YEAH...
...
I...
...LIKE YOU TOO, SOU.

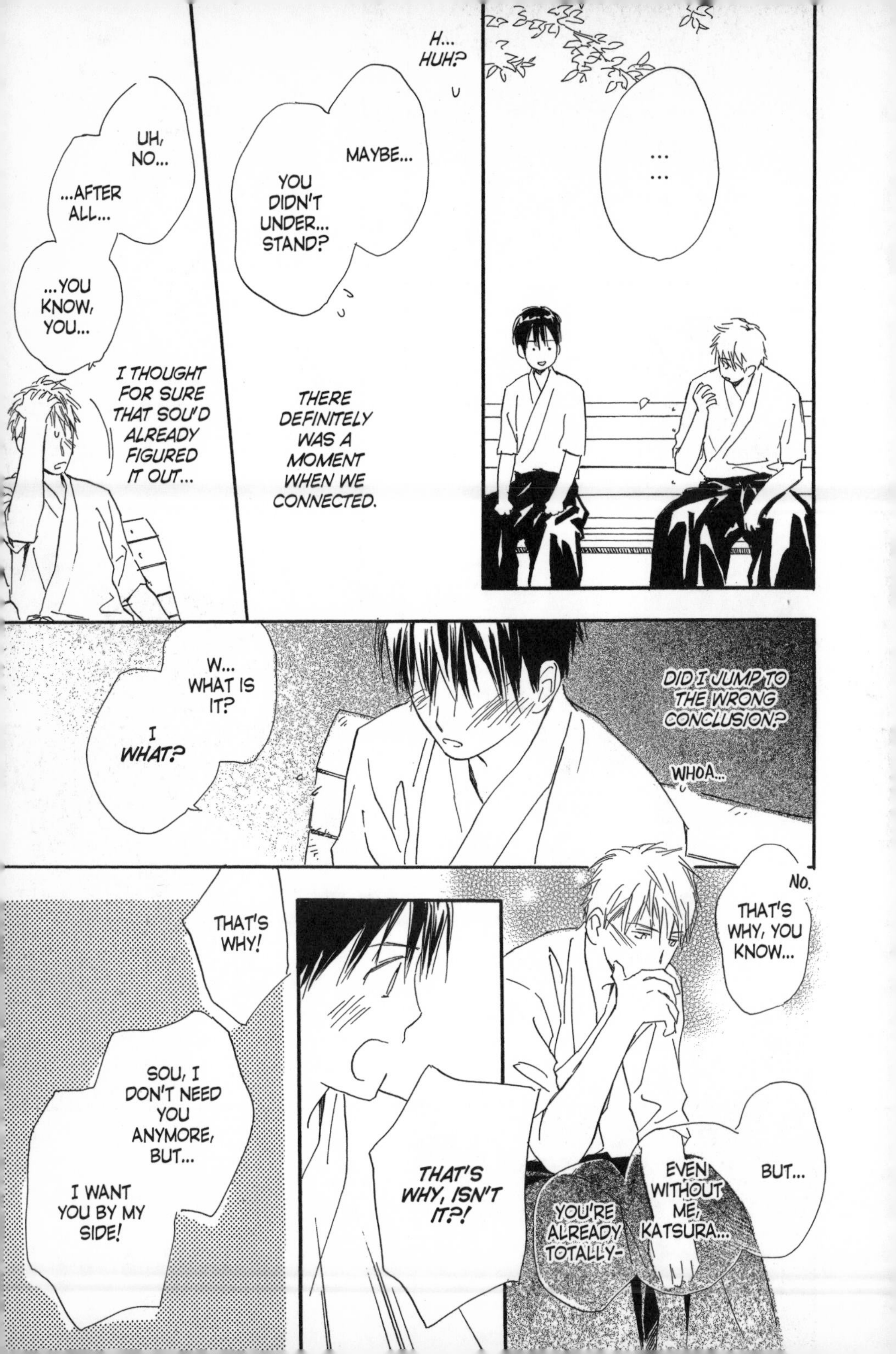
... ...
H... HUH?
MAYBE...
YOU DIDN'T UNDER... STAND?
THERE DEFINITELY WAS A MOMENT WHEN WE CONNECTED.
UH, NO...
...AFTER ALL...
...YOU KNOW, YOU...
I THOUGHT FOR SURE THAT SOU'D ALREADY FIGURED IT OUT...
DID I JUMP TO THE WRONG CONCLUSION?
WHOA...
W... WHAT IS IT?
I WHAT?
NO.
THAT'S WHY, YOU KNOW...
BUT...
EVEN WITHOUT ME, KATSURA...
YOU'RE ALREADY TOTALLY-
THAT'S WHY!
THAT'S WHY, ISN'T IT?!
SOU, I DON'T NEED YOU ANYMORE, BUT...
I WANT YOU BY MY SIDE!

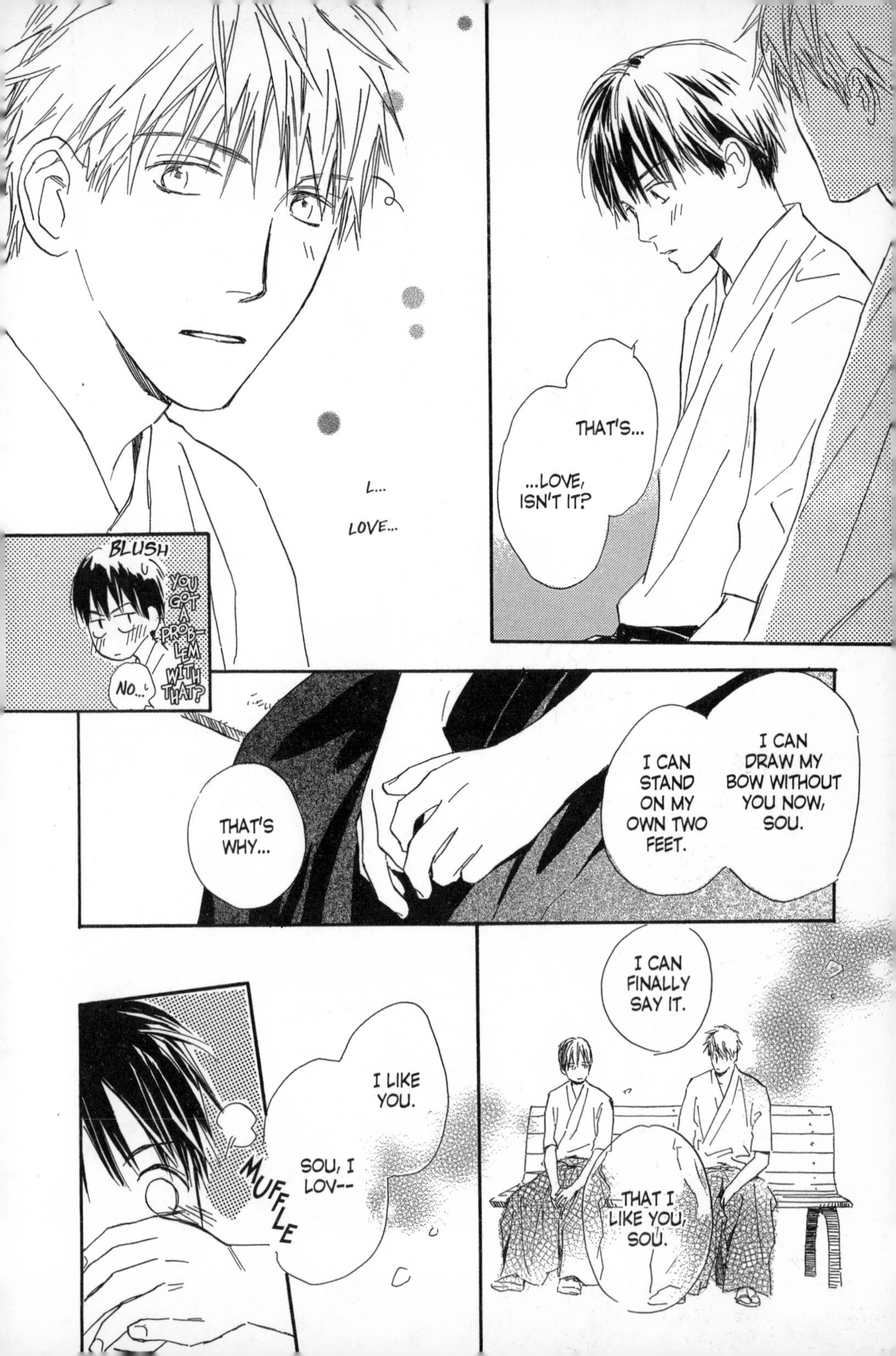
THAT'S...
...LOVE, ISN'T IT?
L...
LOVE...
BLUSH
YOU GOT A PROB-LEM WITH THAT?
NO...
I CAN DRAW MY BOW WITHOUT YOU NOW, SOU.
I CAN STAND ON MY OWN TWO FEET.
THAT'S WHY...
I CAN FINALLY SAY IT.
THAT I LIKE YOU, SOU.
I LIKE YOU.
SOU, I LOV--
MUFFLE

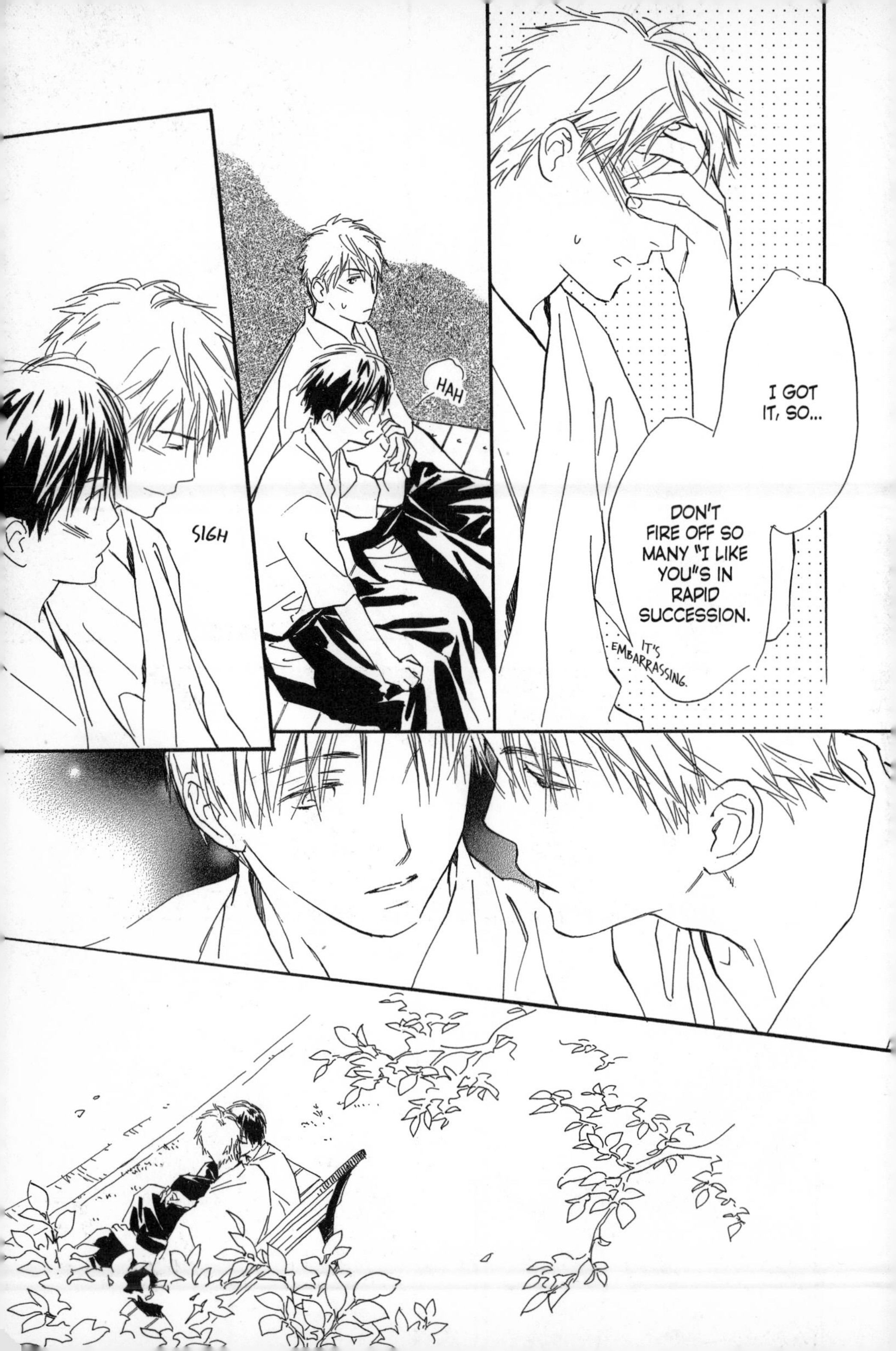
I GOT IT, SO...
DON'T FIRE OFF SO MANY "I LIKE YOU"S IN RAPID SUCCESSION.
IT'S EMBARRASSING.
HAH
SIGH

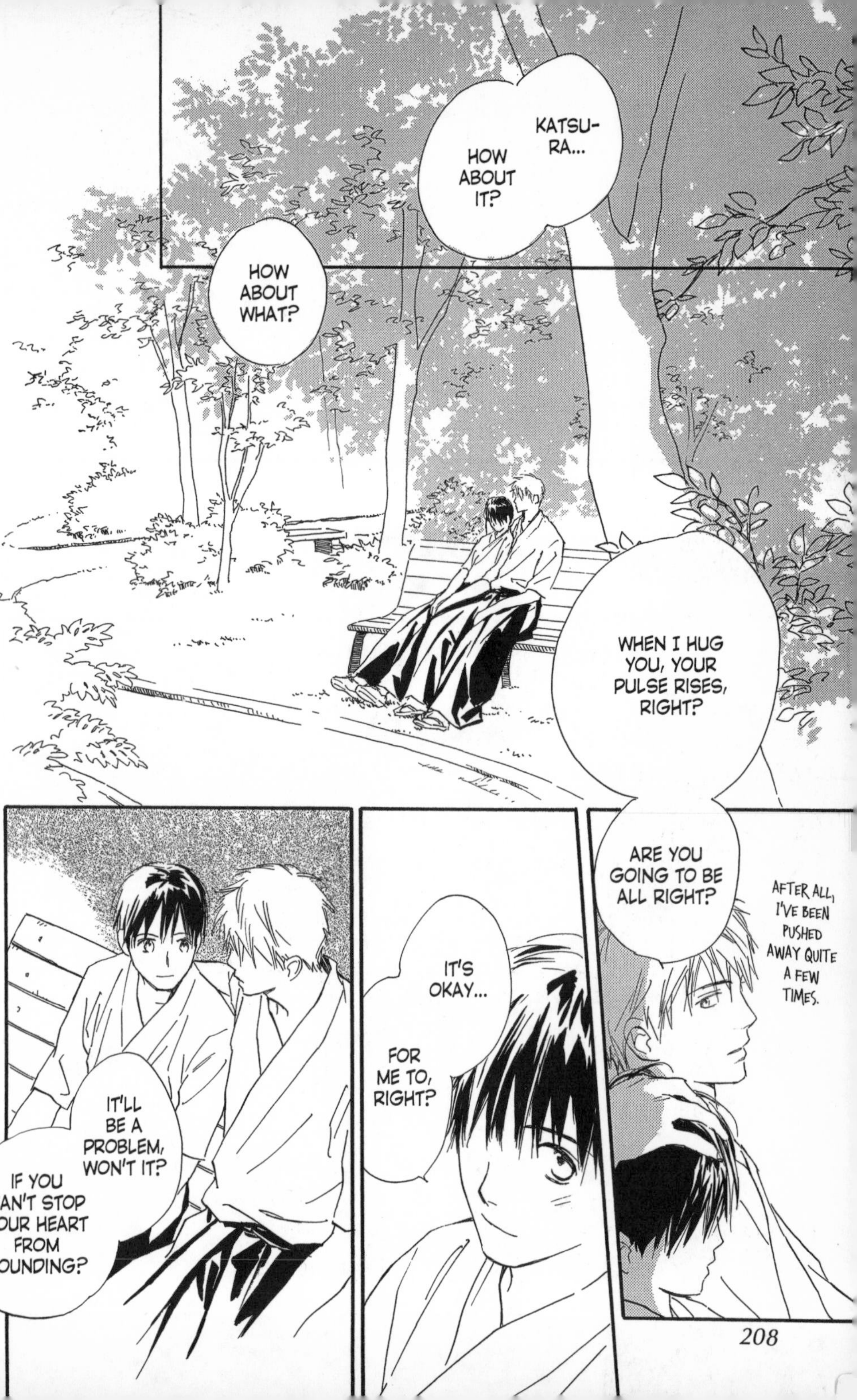
KATSU-RA... HOW ABOUT IT?
HOW ABOUT WHAT?
WHEN I HUG YOU, YOUR PULSE RISES, RIGHT?
ARE YOU GOING TO BE ALL RIGHT?
AFTER ALL, I'VE BEEN PUSHED AWAY QUITE A FEW TIMES.
IT'S OKAY...
FOR ME TO, RIGHT?
IT'LL BE A PROBLEM, WON'T IT?
IF YOU CAN'T STOP YOUR HEART FROM POUNDING?

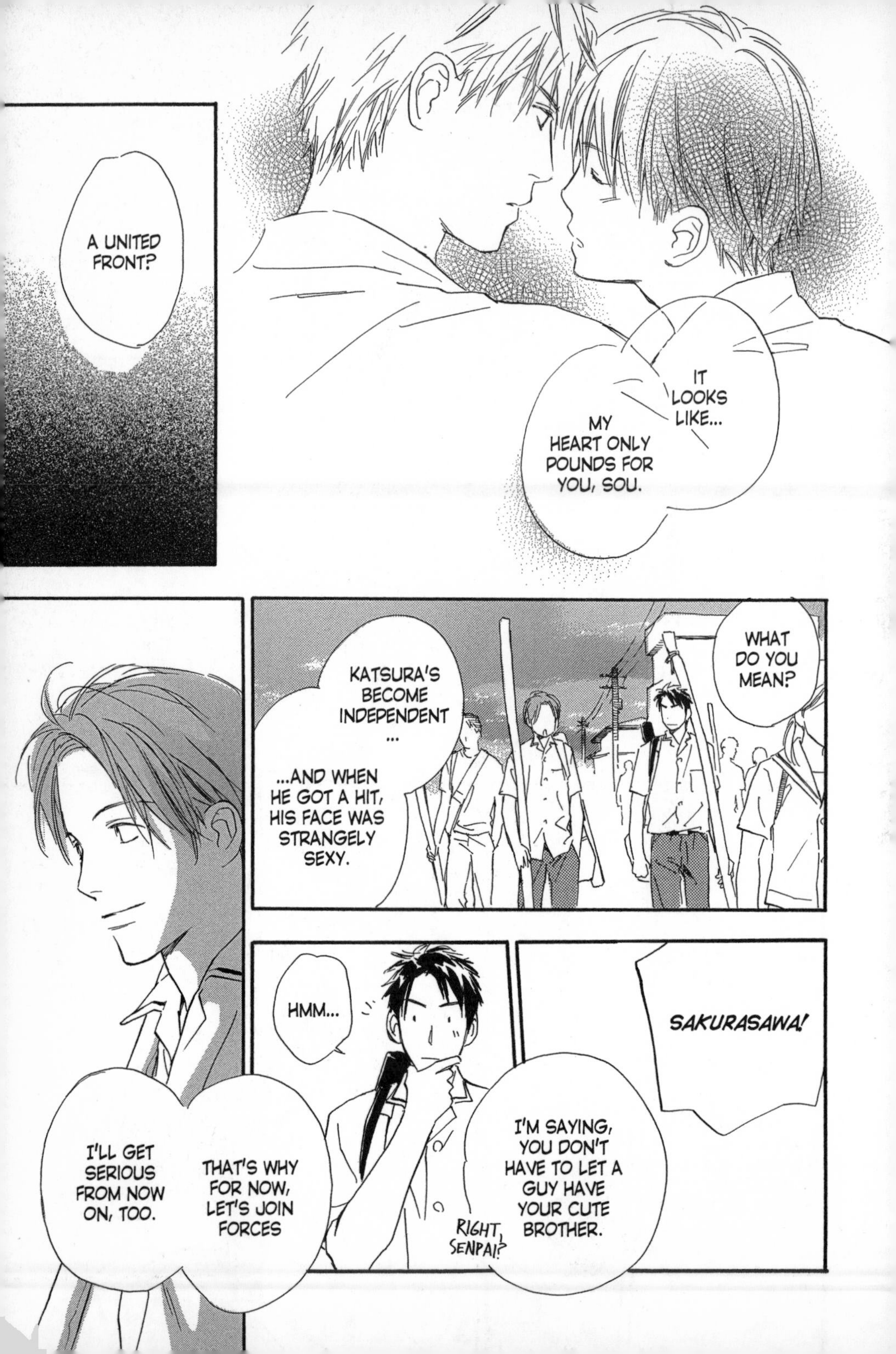
IT LOOKS LIKE...
MY HEART ONLY POUNDS FOR YOU, SOU.
A UNITED FRONT?
WHAT DO YOU MEAN?
KATSURA'S BECOME INDEPENDENT ...
...AND WHEN HE GOT A HIT, HIS FACE WAS STRANGELY SEXY.
SAKURASAWA!
HMM...
I'M SAYING, YOU DON'T HAVE TO LET A GUY HAVE YOUR CUTE BROTHER.
RIGHT, SENPAI?
THAT'S WHY FOR NOW, LET'S JOIN FORCES
I'LL GET SERIOUS FROM NOW ON, TOO.

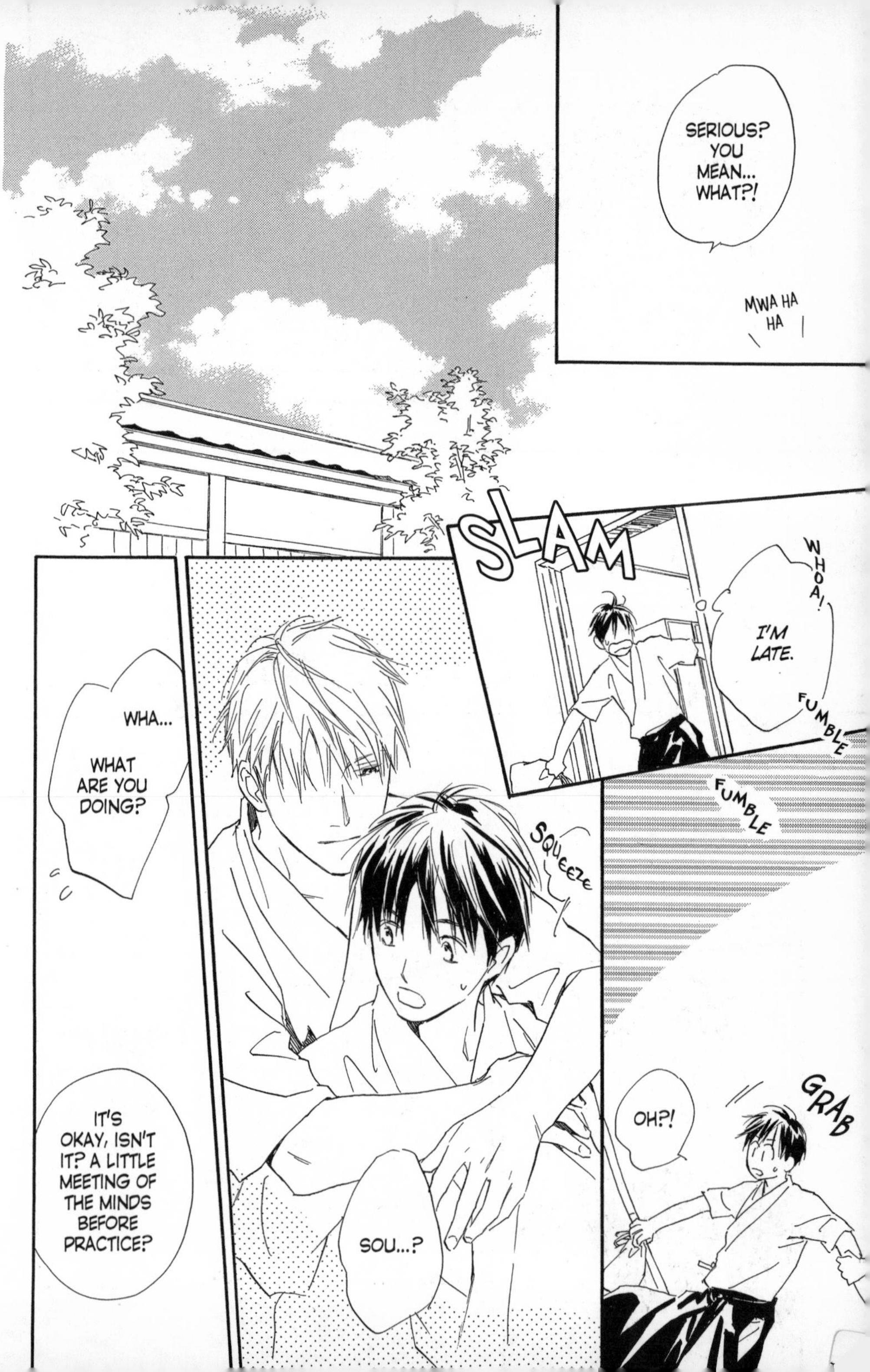
SERIOUS? YOU MEAN... WHAT?!
MWA HA HA
SLAM
WHOA!
I'M LATE.
FUMBLE
FUMBLE
GRAB
OH?!
SQUEEZE
SOU...?
WHA...
WHAT ARE YOU DOING?
IT'S OKAY, ISN'T IT? A LITTLE MEETING OF THE MINDS BEFORE PRACTICE?

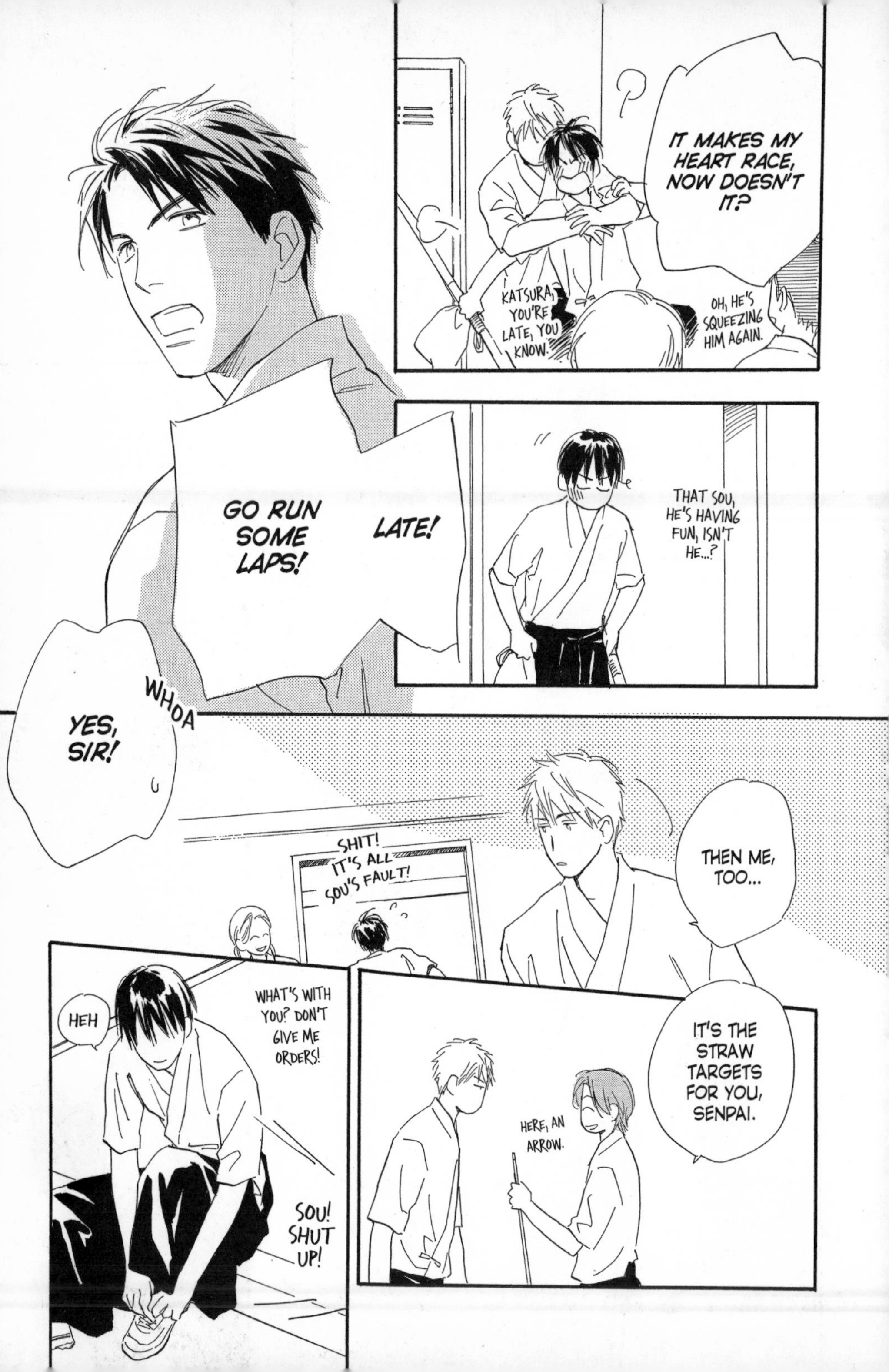
IT MAKES MY HEART RACE, NOW DOESN'T IT?
OH, HE'S SQUEEZING HIM AGAIN.
KATSURA, YOU'RE LATE, YOU KNOW.
THAT SOU, HE'S HAVING FUN, ISN'T HE...?
LATE!
GO RUN SOME LAPS!
WHOA
YES, SIR!
THEN ME, TOO...
SHIT! IT'S ALL SOU'S FAULT!
IT'S THE STRAW TARGETS FOR YOU, SENPAI.
HERE, AN ARROW.
WHAT'S WITH YOU? DON'T GIVE ME ORDERS!
HEH
SOU! SHUT UP!

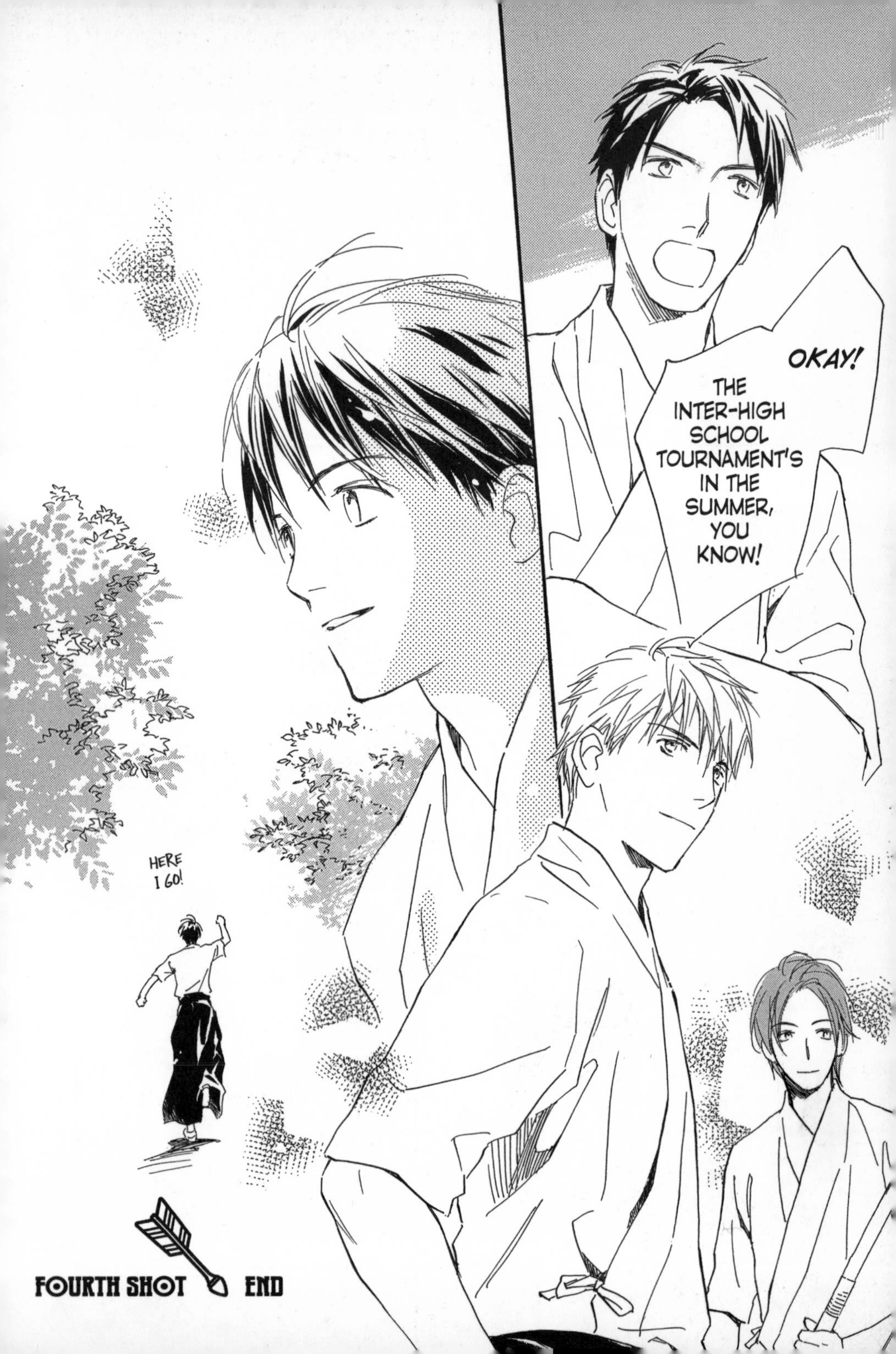
OKAY!
THE INTER-HIGH SCHOOL TOURNAMENT'S IN THE SUMMER, YOU KNOW!
HERE I GO!
FOURTH SHOT END

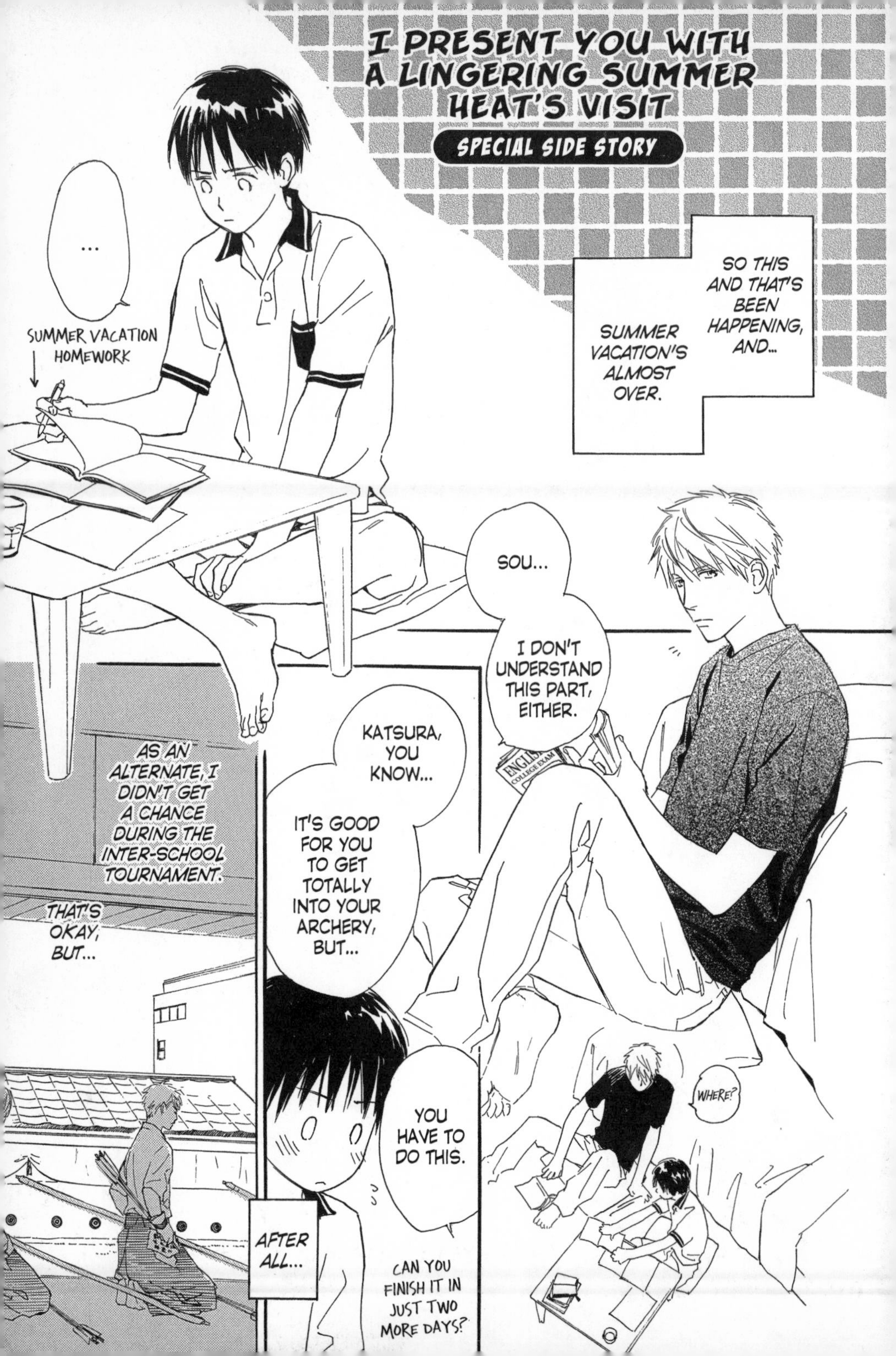
I PRESENT YOU WITH A LINGERING SUMMER HEAT'S VISIT
SPECIAL SIDE STORY
SO THIS AND THAT'S BEEN HAPPENING, AND...
SUMMER VACATION'S ALMOST OVER.
...
SUMMER VACATION HOMEWORK
SOU...
I DON'T UNDERSTAND THIS PART, EITHER.
KATSURA, YOU KNOW...
IT'S GOOD FOR YOU TO GET TOTALLY INTO YOUR ARCHERY, BUT...
ENGLISH COLLEGE EXAM
WHERE?
YOU HAVE TO DO THIS.
CAN YOU FINISH IT IN JUST TWO MORE DAYS?
AS AN ALTERNATE, I DIDN'T GET A CHANCE DURING THE INTER-SCHOOL TOURNAMENT.
THAT'S OKAY, BUT...
AFTER ALL...

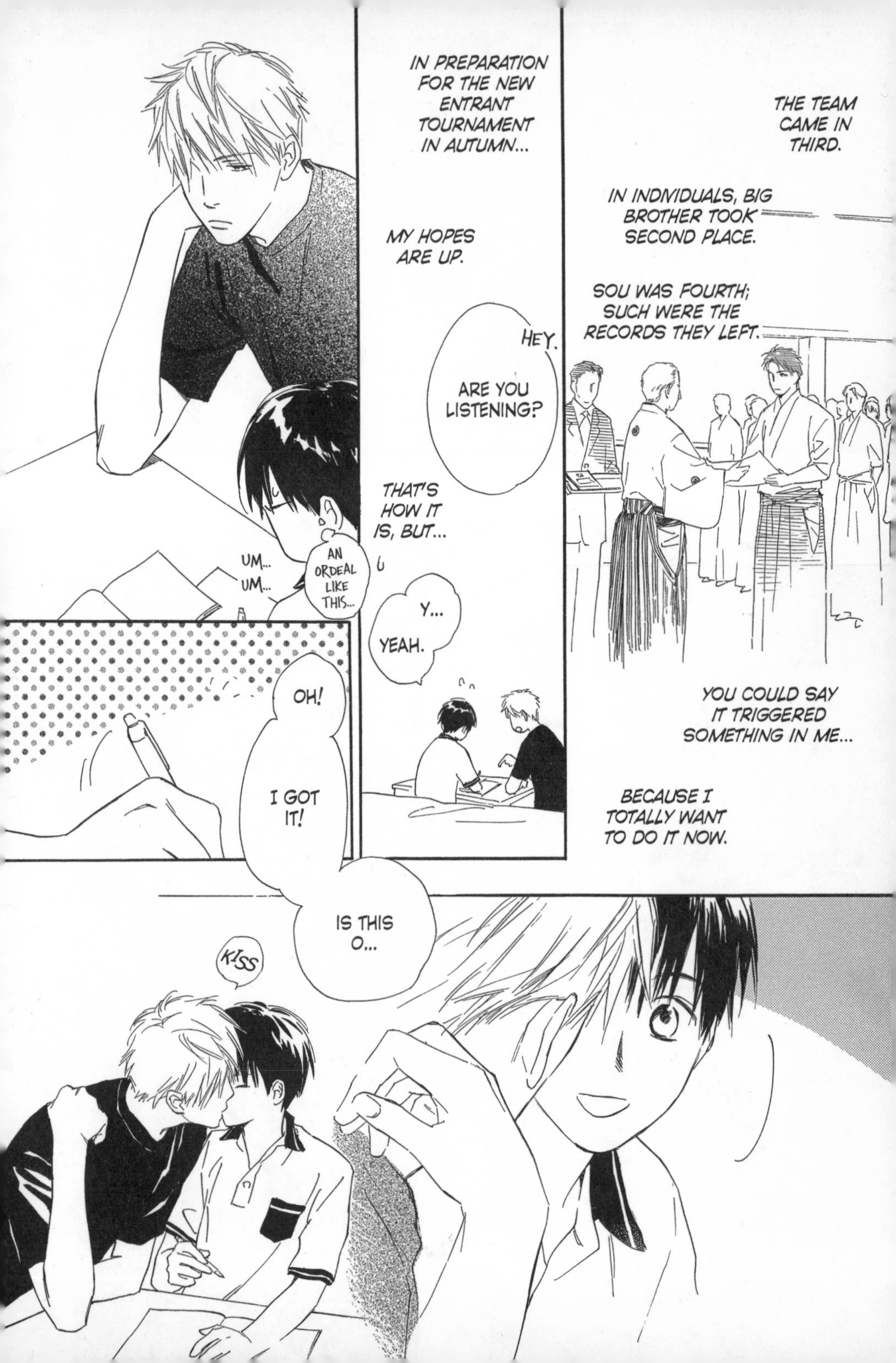
THE TEAM CAME IN THIRD.
IN INDIVIDUALS, BIG BROTHER TOOK SECOND PLACE.
SOU WAS FOURTH; SUCH WERE THE RECORDS THEY LEFT.
YOU COULD SAY IT TRIGGERED SOMETHING IN ME...
BECAUSE I TOTALLY WANT TO DO IT NOW.
IN PREPARATION FOR THE NEW ENTRANT TOURNAMENT IN AUTUMN...
MY HOPES ARE UP.
HEY.
ARE YOU LISTENING?
THAT'S HOW IT IS, BUT...
Y...
YEAH.
AN ORDEAL LIKE THIS...
UM... UM...
OH!
I GOT IT!
IS THIS O...
KISS

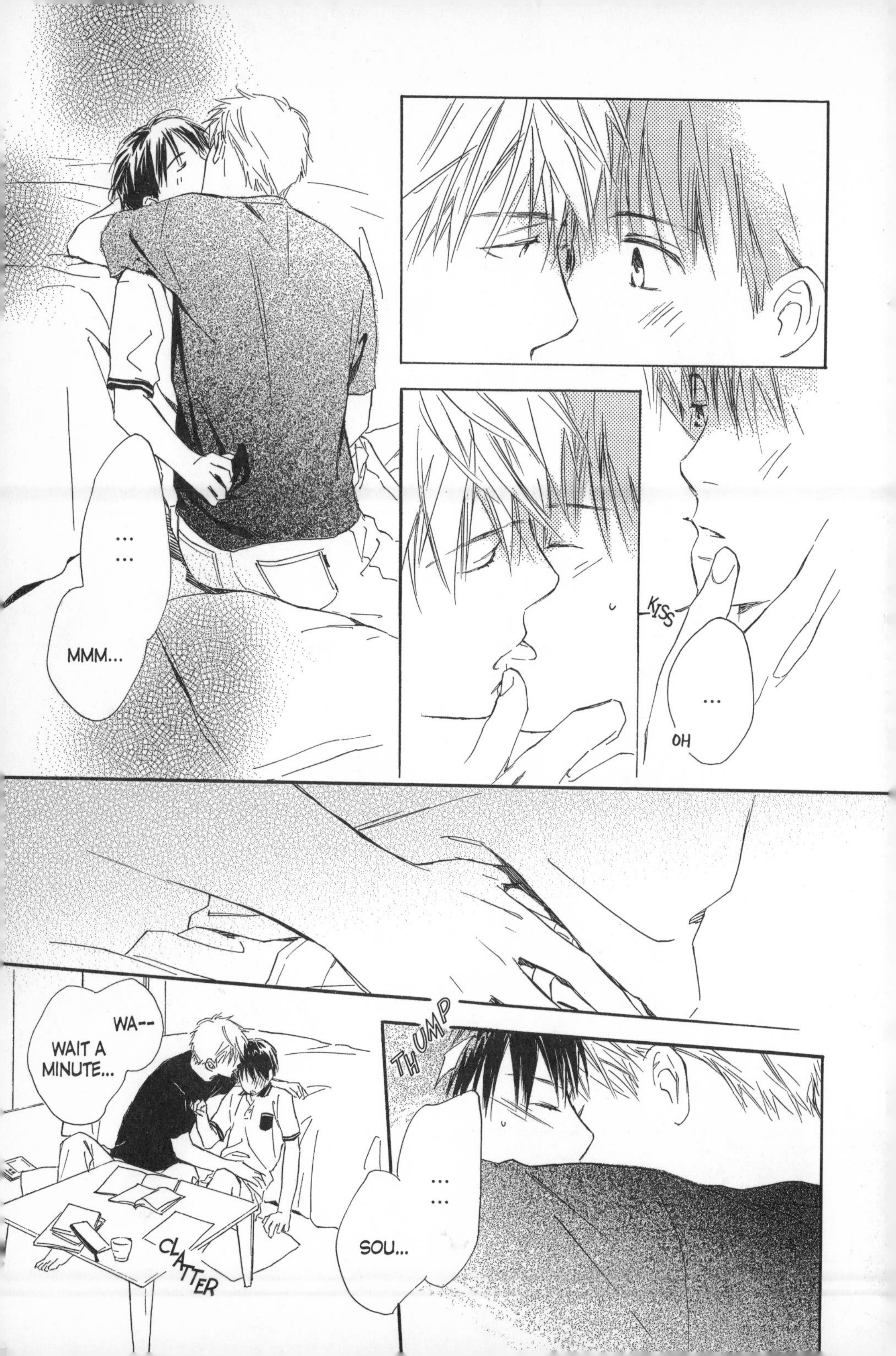
KISS
... OH
... ... MMM...
THUMP
... ... SOU...
WA-- WAIT A MINUTE...
CLATTER

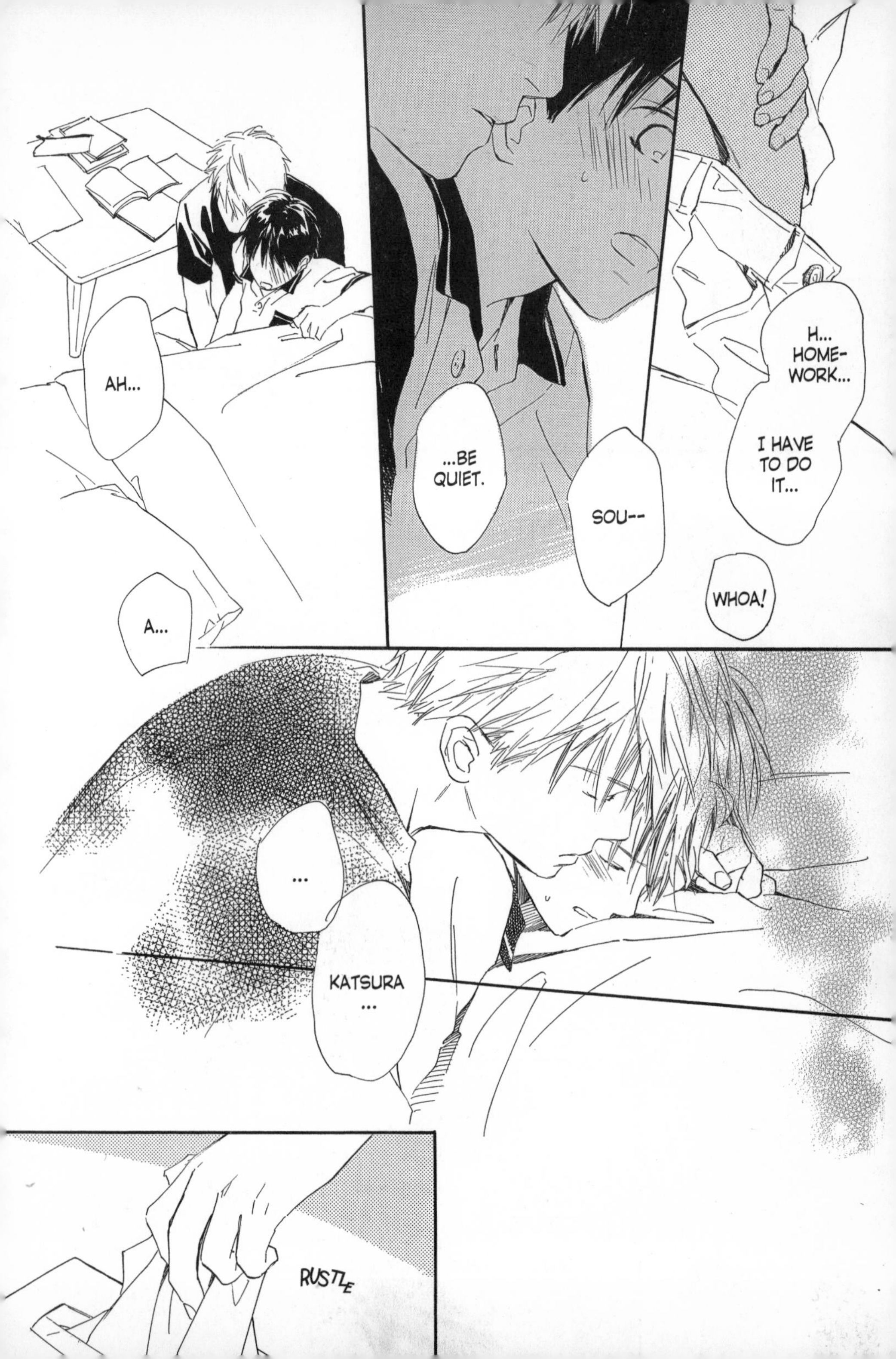
H... HOME-WORK...
I HAVE TO DO IT...
WHOA!
SOU--
...BE QUIET.
AH...
A...
...
KATSURA ...
RUSTLE

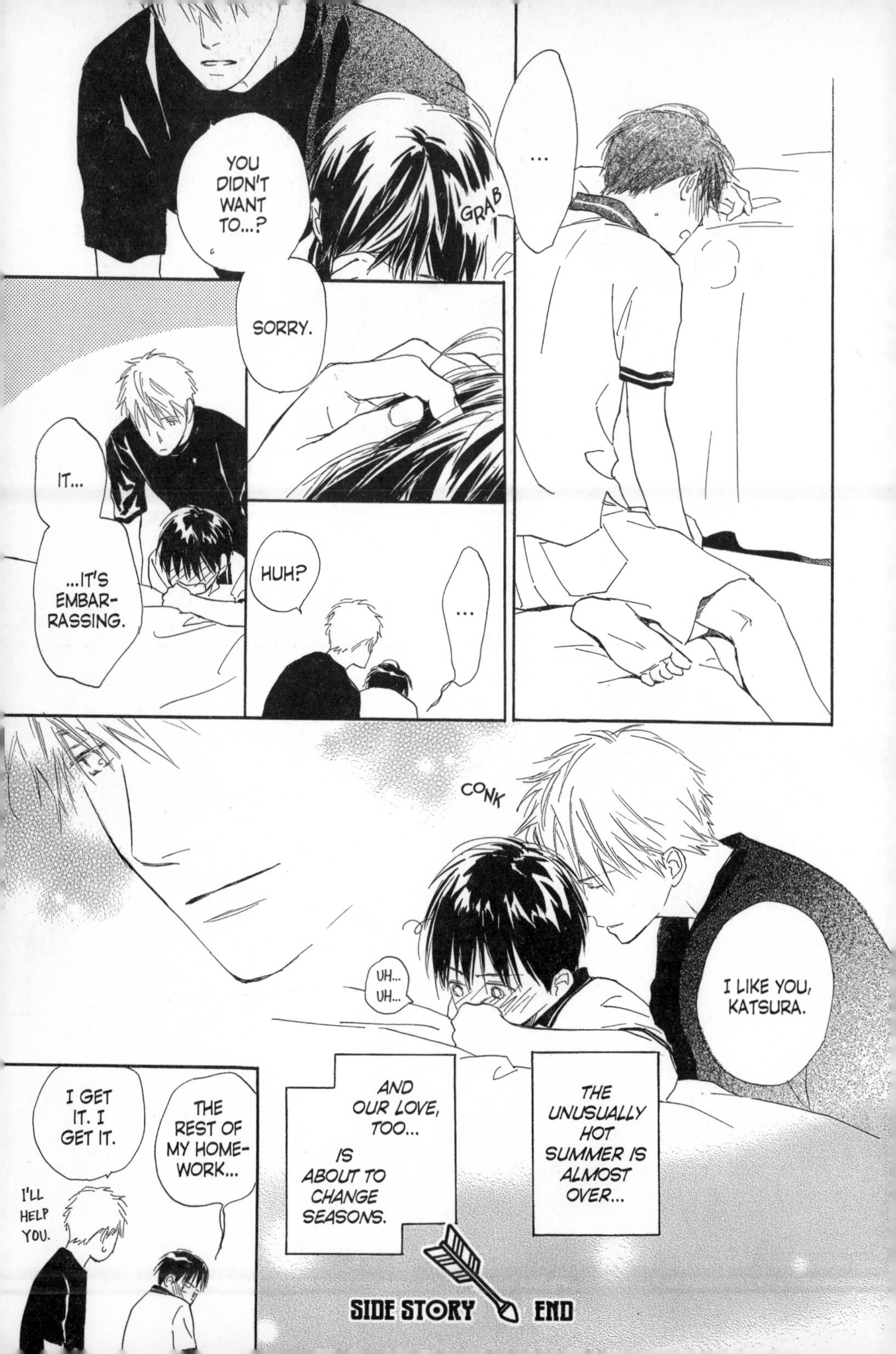
...
YOU DIDN'T WANT TO...?
GRAB
SORRY.
IT...
...IT'S EMBARRASSING.
HUH?
...
CONK
I LIKE YOU, KATSURA.
UH... UH...
THE UNUSUALLY HOT SUMMER IS ALMOST OVER...
AND OUR LOVE, TOO... IS ABOUT TO CHANGE SEASONS.
THE REST OF MY HOMEWORK...
I GET IT. I GET IT.
I'LL HELP YOU.
SIDE STORY END

Satoru Kannagi
Afterwords

NO MATTER WHAT ANYONE SAYS, THE BEST PART ABOUT WRITING RESIDES WHERE ONE GETS TO SEE HIS OR HER WILD IDEAS VISUALIZED. AT THE POINT IN TIME WHEN I RECEIVED THE JOB OF WRITING THE MANGA, AND HEARD THAT HONAMI-SAN WOULD ILLUSTRATE IT, THE SITUATION IN MY HEAD WAS IMMEDIATELY PRETTY DANGEROUS (HA HA). THE CHARACTERS I CREATED WOULD BEGIN TO MOVE WITH HONAMI-SAN'S ILLUSTRATIONS... CAN THERE BE SUCH HAPPINESS AS THIS?

SUCH IS THE SITUATION, AND THUS THIS IS "RIN!" IT IS MY FAVORITE KANJI. WHILE WRITING A WORK, THIS WORD ALWAYS INSCRIBES ITSELF IN MY SOUL. TO BE HONEST, I HAD A HARD TIME WITH THIS TITLE, BUT WHEN I PUT A NUMBER OF THE FINAL CANDIDATES WITH HONAMI-SAN'S PREVIEW CUT, I GOT THE FEELING, "THIS IS IT!" THERE IS ALSO THE FACT THAT THE STAGE IS SET IN A JAPANESE ARCHERY CLUB, BUT IT'S A FITTING RESONANCE FOR SOU, KATSURA AND COMPANY'S COOL DEMEANOR. THE CHARACTERS HONAMI-SAN ILLUSTRATES EXUDE MYRIAD ATTRACTIONS THAT ENCOMPASS CUTE, BEAUTI-FUL, AND COOL. FEW PEOPLE COULD ILLUSTRATE THEIR APPEARANCE IN ARCHERY UNIFORMS SO STOICALLY AND CHARMINGLY.

FROM THE IMPRESSIONS THAT REACHED ME DURING THE SERIALIZATION, IT WAS INTERESTING TO SEE HOW THE FAVORITES DIFFER. KOUICHI-KUN, WHO WAS POPULAR FOR A STALKING-HORSE; YAMATO WON AS "THE CHARACTER YOU WANT TO MARRY" IN THE SURVEY IN THE "CHARA" MAGAZINE. KANNAGI'S SOFT SPOT IS FOR... DAD, THE HOUSEHUSBAND. I WOULD LIKE TO SCREAM, "MARRY ME" TO THE CHARACTER THAT HONAMI-SAN DREW!

AND THEN THE EXTRA MANGA AT THE END OF THE VOLUME. THANK YOU, HONAMI-SAN! KANNAGI'S WILD IDEAS HAVE EXPLODED ONCE MORE. WHILE I WROTE THE ORIGINAL STORY, BECAUSE I AM REALLY STUPID, I UNTHINKINGLY SHOT THE SHARP QUESTION WITH REGARD TO THE LAST EPISODE, "IT ENDS WITH ONLY A KISS?!" MY WISH, WITH HONAMI-SAN'S TALENT AND THE SUPPORT OF THE READERS, HAS BLOSSOMED INTO A SECOND VOLUME!

THAT'S RIGHT! SOU AND KATSURA ARE RETURNING! PLEASE LOOK FORWARD TO THE START OF A NEW STORY WITH THE TWO OF THEM!

SATORU KANNAGI

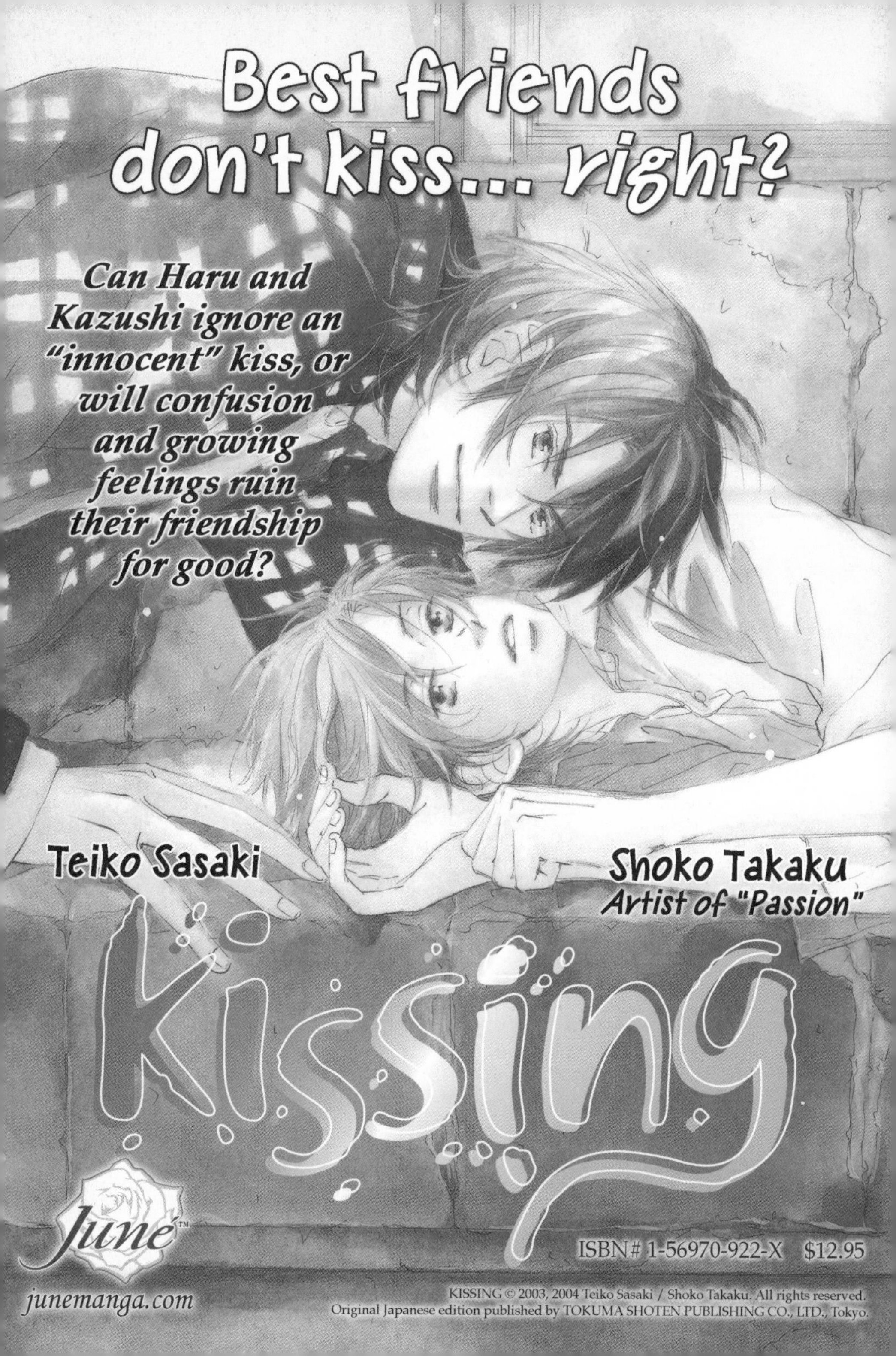
Best friends don't kiss... right?
Can Haru and Kazushi ignore an "innocent" kiss, or will confusion and growing feelings ruin their friendship for good?
Teiko Sasaki
Shoko Takaku
Artist of "Passion"
Kissing
June™
ISBN# 1-56970-922-X $12.95
junemanga.com
KISSING © 2003, 2004 Teiko Sasaki / Shoko Takaku. All rights reserved.
Original Japanese edition published by TOKUMA SHOTEN PUBLISHING CO., LTD., Tokyo.

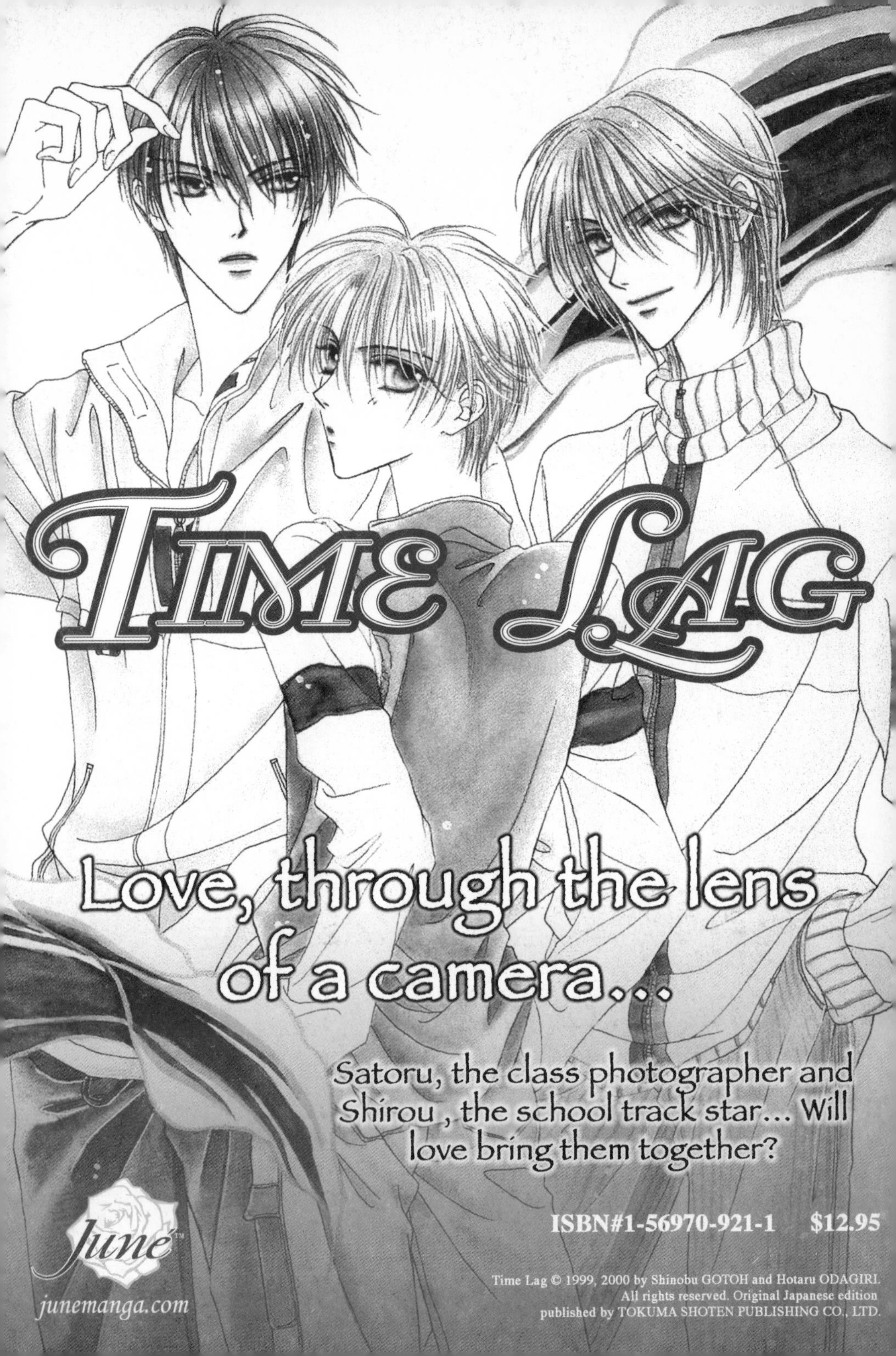
TIME LAG
Love, through the lens of a camera...
Satoru, the class photographer and Shirou , the school track star... Will love bring them together?
June™
junemanga.com
ISBN#1-56970-921-1
$12.95
Time Lag © 1999, 2000 by Shinobu GOTOH and Hotaru ODAGIRI. All rights reserved. Original Japanese edition published by TOKUMA SHOTEN PUBLISHING CO., LTD.

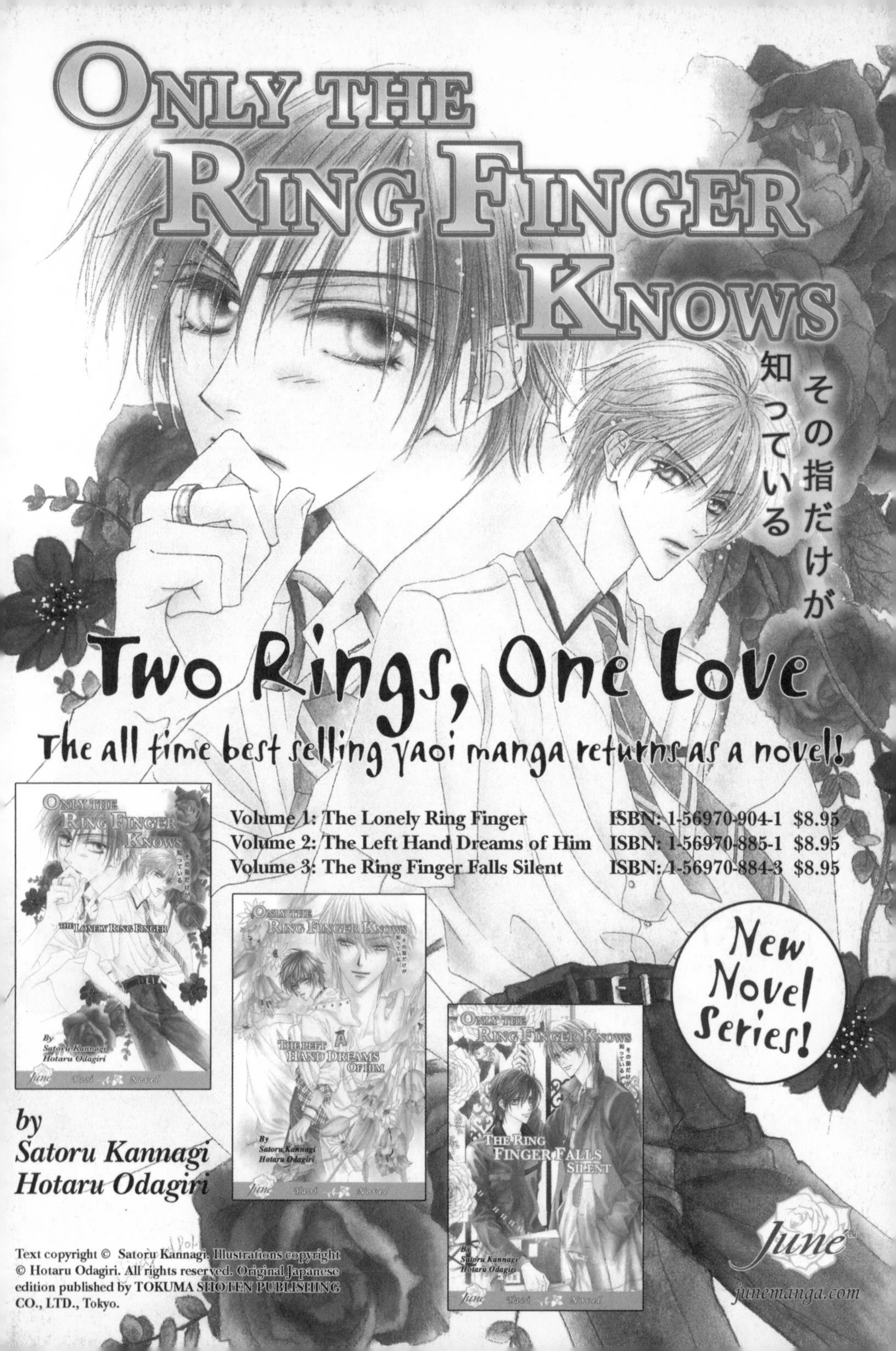
ONLY THE RING FINGER KNOWS
その指だけが知っている
Two Rings, One Love
The all time best selling yaoi manga returns as a novel!
Volume 1: The Lonely Ring Finger ISBN: 1-56970-904-1 $8.95
Volume 2: The Left Hand Dreams of Him ISBN: 1-56970-885-1 $8.95
Volume 3: The Ring Finger Falls Silent ISBN: 1-56970-884-3 $8.95
New Novel Series!
by
Satoru Kannagi
Hotaru Odagiri
Text copyright © Satoru Kannagi. Illustrations copyright © Hotaru Odagiri. All rights reserved. Original Japanese edition published by TOKUMA SHOTEN PUBLISHING CO., LTD., Tokyo.
June
junemanga.com

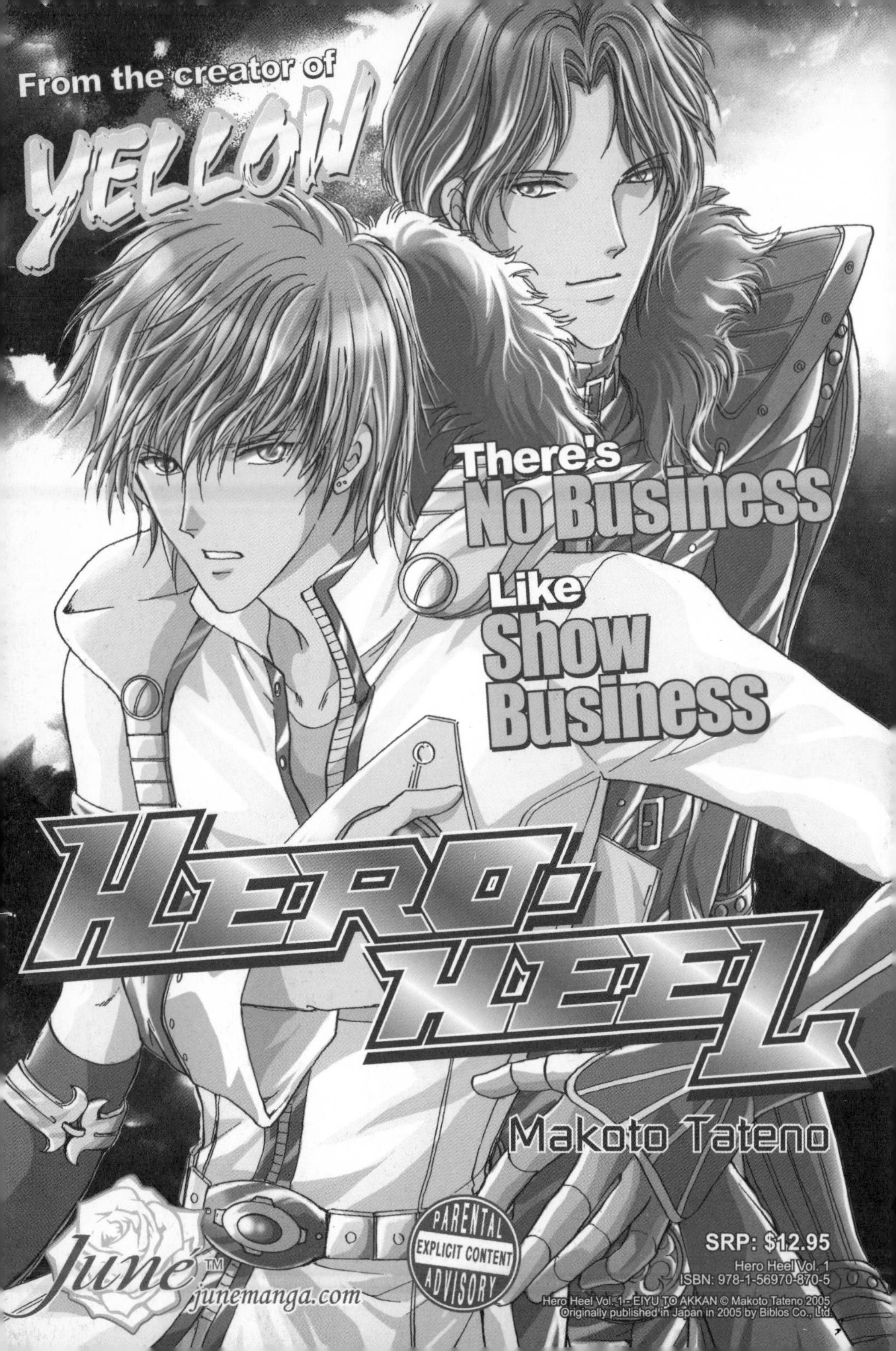
From the creator of
YELLOW
There's
No Business
Like
Show
Business
HERO HEEL
Makoto Tateno
PARENTAL
EXPLICIT CONTENT
ADVISORY
June™
junemanga.com
SRP: $12.95
Hero Heel Vol. 1
ISBN: 978-1-56970-870-5
Hero Heel Vol. 1 - EIYU TO AKKAN © Makoto Tateno 2005
Originally published in Japan in 2005 by Biblos Co., Ltd.

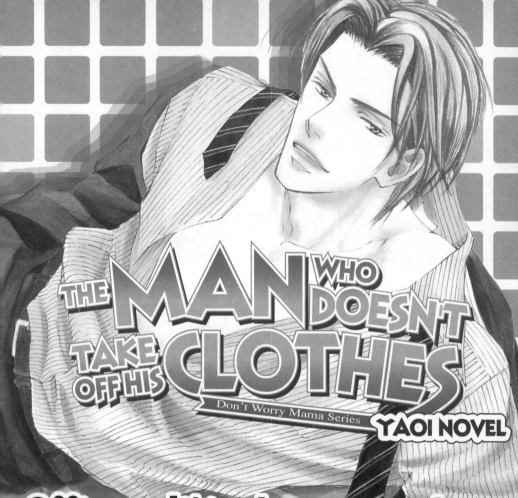

THE MAN WHO DOESN'T TAKE OFF HIS CLOTHES

Don't Worry Mama Series

YAOI NOVEL

Office politics have never been *THIS* stimulating...

Written by Narise Konohara *(Cold Sleep, Don't Worry Mama)*
Illustrations by Yuki Shimizu *(Love Mode)*

Volume 1   ISBN# 1-56970-877-0 $8.95
Volume 2   ISBN# 1-56970-876-2 $8.95

June™

junemanga.com

Princess·Princess

By **MIKIYO TSUDA**

Peer pressure...
has never been this intense!

When students need a boost, the Princesses arrive in gothic lolita outfits to show their school spirit! Join Kouno and friends in this crazy, cross-dressing comedy.

VOLUME 1 - ISBN# 978-1-56970-856-9 $12.95
VOLUME 2 - ISBN# 978-1-56970-855-2 $12.95
VOLUME 3 - ISBN# 978-1-56970-852-1 $12.95
VOLUME 4 - ISBN# 978-1-56970-851-4 $12.95
VOLUME 5 - ISBN# 978-1-56970-850-7 $12.95

DIGITAL MANGA PUBLISHING
www.dmpbooks.com